"The World is all the richer for having the devil in it, so long as we keep our foot upon his neck."

William James

P.S. Check out
Chapter 14, you'll enjoy it!

M.F.

Jihad the Jerk at Work

Get Rid of That Idiot Who's Making Your Life Miserable

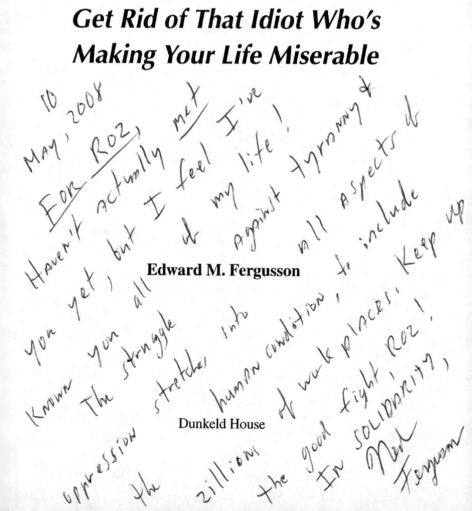

Edward M. Fergusson

Dunkeld House

10 MAY, 2008

FOR ROZ,

Haven't actually met you yet, but I feel I've known you all my life! The struggle against tyranny & oppression stretches into all aspects of human condition, to include the zillions of work places. Keep up the good fight, ROZ! In SOLIDARITY,

Ned Ferguson

Jihad the Jerk at Work: Get Rid of That Idiot Who's Making Your Life Miserable

Copyright © 2005 by Edward M. Fergusson.

Published by Dunkeld House, P.O. Box 438, Lake Hiawatha, NJ 07034-0438
(877) 386-5353   First Edition, Third Printing   2006

ISBN 0-9747137-0-8

Library of Congress Control Number: 2003098829

Cover Photo (Reuters): Enron VP Sherron Watkins, who courageously tried to halt massive fraud and corruption in her Company, watches skeptically as former Enron CEO Jeffrey Skilling attempts to absolve himself before a Senate Commerce subcommittee on February 26, 2002. The Senators were not fooled, nor would the courts be. Skilling was later indicted on conspiracy, securities fraud, and insider trading charges.

"Jihad"

Some may feel apprehension at the use of the term "Jihad" in this book's title. Actually, Jihad is a benign, honorable concept among decent, moderate Muslims everywhere, who define it as a "just struggle", an effort every honest person wages internally to overcome character faults, the effort to create a just society, a "person's inner struggle to do good", "the effort (jihad) to live in the way that God had intended for human beings."[2]

Extreme, violent radicals hijacked the term on 9/11, in a murderous action that is condemned by the Quran, and certainly would have been condemned by the Prophet Muhammad himself. The Quran clearly states that jihad through war is a defensive act to be invoked only when Muslims are attacked.

It's worthy of note that Muslims in Rwanda who saved thousands of innocents from genocide in 1994, used the concept of "jihad" to characterize their courageous, selfless actions. Sadly, too many so-called "Christians" in that tortured nation, to include some Catholic priests and nuns, succumbed to the madness and enthusiastically joined in the slaughter of 800,000 minority Tutsi's and moderate Hutus. After witnessing this stark contrast in behavior, "huge numbers of Rwandans converted to Islam".[3] Perhaps, then, we in the West can all learn and benefit from the positive side of the Islamic concept of Jihad, which very rarely gets a fair shake in our sensational, fear-mongering media.

Therefore, the use of the term "Jihad" in the noble and just cause of creating a decent workplace free from pervasive fear and intimidation and bullying is appropriate and useful.

for All those Indomitable Souls
who resolve to rid their workplace
and their society of the truly intolerable —

and thus create a much better world …

*"Without courage there cannot be truth,
and without truth there can be no other virtue."*[4]

Sir Walter Scott

Contents

Bonus Section!!

PART IV – Reforming "Hopelessly Dead-End" Monopolies: Government Agencies, Academia, and the Military

Super-Bonus Section!!

PART V – Moving Beyond the Workplace: Emboldened to Do More

WEBSITE FORMS: at http://www.upublishing.com/forms.htm

Author's Preface to the Third Printing (1st Edition)

Here's a concise summary of the Jerk-Elimination Method of this book:

STEP ONE: Confirm you actually have a serious "Jerk at Work" problem (see Chapters Two and Four)

STEP TWO: Thoroughly read and study this entire book. Carefully prepare your plan of action. Clarify your objective. Form & consult with an anonymous committee of like minds. Decide on your recommendation to the Jerk's boss. Set a 30-day deadline. See Chapter Four for invaluable advice to avoid major mistakes.

NOTE: If you're in a terrible hurry, *at least* thoroughly read Chapters 2, 4, and 6

STEP THREE: Go to www.upublishing.com/forms.htm
user id: "reformer"   password: "progress"
Fill in the blanks on *Character Faults* form and *Generic Letter to the Jerk's Boss* form (or, if you don't like PC's, just use the same forms found in Chapter 6)

STEP FOUR: "PRINT" out the two forms

STEP FIVE: PAPER CLIP the two completed forms to the front of this book, *Jihad the Jerk at Work.*

STEP SIX: Send entire Complaint Package, anonymously, to the Jerk's boss.

STEP SEVEN: Wait 30 calendar days, carefully monitoring management's actions – escalate to higher levels immediately
if any foolishness is detected. See Chapter Four.

STEP EIGHT: If the Jerk at Work problem is resolved per your stated Objective (usually by the transfer of the Jerk far
away), celebrate . . . quietly. If not, then escalate the
Complaint Package to the next higher level.

STEP NINE: Don't give up until the Jerk is gone. Keep escalating, if
need be.

READ THIS!! SOME SINCERE ADVICE

This is a big, long book – intentionally so, because the task of remov-
ing a "jerk at work" can be a difficult and dangerous one for the unprepared.
So get yourself prepared! Included herein is a lot of important advice, tips
that make it much more likely you'll succeed.

It's also a big plus that this book, attached to the two sizzling Complaint
Forms that land on the Jerk's boss's desk, is a large, imposing one. He just
can't ignore it, and it's just too huge to get "lost" in the shuffle. In the real
world, this rather mundane factor is an important one acting in your favor.

I also wish to impress upon you that you must develop a solid understanding of the nature of evil in this world, and the tyrants, bullies, predators,
incompetents, and arrogant jerks that it routinely spawns. *Jihad the Jerk at
Work* will get you up to speed in this department. Only then will you possess
the true motivation to see this thing through, to actually get rid of that jerk
who's ruining your workplace and your life. **Motivation is everything** when
you embark on an eject-a-jerk campaign.

**I strongly recommend that you set aside enough time to carefully
go through all sixteen chapters of *Jihad the Jerk at Work*.** Think about
what's on every page – resist the urge to rush through the book like it's the
100 yard dash. Take notes. Come up with a workable plan that makes sense
to you. This is a **textbook**, folks, not a novel. It's time to plant your feet
firmly on Planet Earth. And once learned well, this is a skill which will
serve you well for the rest of your working years.

You'll reap **major rewards** by following this steady, careful approach.

Conversely, skimming and racing through the book, or even worse, skipping the text entirely and just submitting the Complaint Forms, is a big mistake. "Haste makes waste." This is a serious task, a momentous step. Prepare for it with care. If you decline to exercise the proper self-discipline, the proper preparation time, forget about getting rid of the jerk at work – that dog won't hunt.

Edward M. Fergusson
April, 2006

Part I . . .

Understanding the Problem

*"When we told our friends and family that we were entertaining the idea of writing a book on personality disorder in the workplace, we had a very intriguing reaction. A **smile of recognition** would come to their faces, and they would say something like, 'Oh, why don't you come to where I work? There's enough there to give you material for three books! I'm working for this guy who . . . ' They would then go on to tell their stories about some individual at work who was continually making them crazy . . . often the stories that people told us were quite amazing, describing behavior that was next to unbelievable. What struck us even more was that, with rare exception, **everyone seemed to have a horror story, no matter who we talked to**: our family, our students, and our patients (even our co-workers and book editors we submitted this manuscript to!). It seemed like everybody had somebody who was driving them crazy at work . . . the reader must understand that we're not talking about the normal types of spats or the occasional head-butting that arises from time to time at work. **The type of stories we heard were far more destructive and damaging** . . . "* [1] (author's emphasis)

Alan A. Cavaiola, PhD and
Neil J. Lavender, PhD
. . . from their book, *Toxic Coworkers*

Introduction . . .
A Primer for Actually, Really Getting Rid of That Jerk at Work

"The right to happiness is fundamental. Men live so little time and die alone." [1]

> Bertolt Brecht
> 1898–1956
> German playwright, poet

"Knowledge of what is possible is the beginning of happiness." [1]

> George Santayana
> 1863–1952
> Spanish born American philosopher

AT LONG LAST – THE PERFECT SOLUTION FOR A MAJOR PROBLEM

Let's face it: one of the most vexing problems in any workplace is our inability to get rid of shameless, arrogant, selfish, incompetent, dangerous, annoying, hopeless jerks – either a terrible boss or a flaky fellow employee – in a swift, easy, *safe*, surefire manner.

UNTIL NOW!!

This book presents the *only* foolproof, **easy to use** method of solving this age-old dilemma – it really works well, because it has

3

evolved and been refined to perfection during the 1980's and 90's in
real workplaces like yours, in *real* situations, with *real* jerks being
ousted with consistent, decisive success – not in some ivory tower,
theoretical vacuum. The "fill in the blanks" and "check where
appropriate" format on pre-printed forms allows you to assemble an
amazingly powerful Complaint Package in a short time. You're a busy
person, you don't have a lot of time to spend reinventing the wheel.

THIRTY YEARS OF DARWINIAN EVOLUTION

During the past 30 years, I've enjoyed working in many
challenging positions in several large U.S. corporations, as well as
some mid-sized businesses, as well as other types of organizations
(government, military). Despite many of the great people I've
worked with, and some excellent managers I've had the good fortune
to work for, and exciting jobs, I could not help but too often notice
major, consistent, and extremely high levels of very justified dissatisfaction felt by large numbers of co-workers towards a handful of
others in the organization – either one or a few peer employees, or,
more commonly, a weak low-level or mid-level manager whose
character, behavior, and job performance was distinctly poor and
damaging to the business and work environment.

I was a reluctant witness to this same scenario over and over and
over again – almost like being locked in a purgatory and being
forced to watch the same grainy, B-grade movie repeatedly, as some
kind of sadistic punishment. I saw the same tale of woe in some of
the groups I was in, as well as in other nearby organizations. It
became so predictable I could actually mouth the words, in advance
before they spoke, of the different players as they moved through
the various episodes of the typical cycle of battling Jerks in the
workplace – Bill Murray in "Groundhog Day."

These obvious managerial disaster areas, which should have been
quickly resolved and good order restored by wise, decisive intervention by higher levels of competent management, were usually *not* –
in fact, too often the obvious abuses seemed to get progressively

worse, as outstanding and valuable employees desperately bailed out to go work in other departments, or even left the company, in droves.

And, invariably, there were no solid reasons *not* to get rid of these clowns who caused these disasters. There was always plenty of good, decent replacement managerial talent available, who could have done a much better job.

ANGER IN THE WORKPLACE

In this thirty year timeframe, I've all too often witnessed a disturbing amount and intensity of pent-up anger generated by the conditions described – usually about 70% directed towards lower management levels, 20% towards Director / VP levels, and 10% toward peers. These observations are consistent with the experience of American and European newspapers and magazines, who are often surprised at the overwhelming, intense, even angry, reader response when topics discussing "How's Your Boss Doing?" and other work-place issues are broached, even humorously.

For example, *Maxim*, a rather moderate-circulation monthly magazine targeted towards younger men, recently "asked readers to reveal their tender feelings toward the people they work for. In other words . . . what is it about your boss that drives you stark raving postal?? " *Maxim* was stunned at the avalanche of respondent mail, " . . . more than 2,000 replied, many angrily relating stories of managerial abuse of power and gross misbehaviors . . . the question obviously struck a nerve."[2]

BLOWBACK ON THE INTERNET

"Striking a nerve" is an accurate characterization of almost *any* inquiry or discussion of the suppressed-workplace-anger phenome-non. The advent of the Internet also provides some startling insights. According to *New York Times* reporter Reed Abelson, in the past several years, thousands of companies have set up Internet message boards – no surprise, no big deal – but when the protocol allows employees to post their thoughts *anonymously* on a 3rd party website, all hell breaks loose. " . . . employees are . . . expressing thoughts they would not dare say out loud." Managers at all levels, as well as fellow employees, are being vehemently blasted, the pent-up anger and frustration exploding onto the Internet. Reed reports that "it can be useful to managers to find out what their employees really think of them, but also devastating when hurtful and hateful gossip is laid out for all to see."[3]

Reed continues: " 'This is a problem that has exploded recently, in the last six months,' says Parry Aftab, a lawyer at Darby & Darby in New York, who specializes in Internet-related issues."[4] Some messages posted are petty, malicious, and perhaps even blatant exaggeration – on the other hand, an exposure of one grievance can unleash a torrent of supporting statements, akin to the lancing of a putrid, festering wound with a scalpel.

Reed cites an example of a Home Depot employee who complained on the Internet that managers were having coercive sex with employees. What followed was a barrage of confirming Internet statements from other Home Depot employees, who also took things a step further and named names! Pretty strong stuff, to all come spilling out within a 24-hour period. Must have given the poor company HR (Human Resources) Vice President a stroke.

"Home Depot said it investigated any claims brought to its attention," says Reed.[5] Of course, the major question is, without the *anonymity* of this Internet message board, would the facts of this travesty *ever* have surfaced at all?? *Hold the thought, we'll revisit it soon.*

UNHAPPY CAMPERS

Another telling bellwether comes from one of my favorite sources, "Harpers Index", a one-page list of fascinating statistics and numbers appearing in every monthly issue of *Harpers Magazine*. In the November 2000 issue, right below the entry "Average number of male clients served in America in 1999 by each female prostitute"

(OK, OK, 694, if you *must* know) lies another seminal (pardon the pun) gauge of 20th Century American culture:[6]

> "Rank of dissatisfaction with the 'level of support from supervisors or colleagues' : **1** "

A conclusion that could be ventured is that in the workplace, Americans are very unhappy campers, and much of that dissatisfaction is centered on the behavior of a very few people in that workplace. It's not pay, not medical care, not pensions, not perks that *really* sticks in their craw – it's the jerky behavior of one or two people! And that there appears to be no relief in sight.

Granted, there can be many sources of unhappiness in the workplace: low pay, recession, high pressure working environments, unreasonable customers, impatient shareholders, business declines, etc, etc – but it's been my experience that good, honest, hard-working, competent managers can fix most ills. However, poor managers, and those with bizarre personality traits – in the vernacular, often referred to as "Jerks" (see Chapter Two for more extensive definitions) – only make things much, much worse. *Jihad the Jerk at Work* can be used effectively to "fix", and fix well, this persistent personnel problem, be it lousy management at any level, or dysfunctional fellow employees.

DEADLY OFFICE POLITICS

Another important factor to address up front: often "office politics" or, the "workplace jungle" is stereotypically characterized as unpleasant, but really rather trivial, the butt of many media and pundit jokes. *Au contraire* – upon any serious study of the subject, it becomes readily apparent that dysfunctional, unhappy workplaces plagued by absurd politics and bizarre managerial or employee behavior unnecessarily create huge problems for large numbers of good people, to include hypertension, sickness, chronic paranoia, and even workplace violence and too many suicides. (see Chapter 1, "How Bad Is It?" and Chapter 3, "Consequences of Jerkism").

Reasonable, constructive office politics – diplomacy, performing well for the boss and co-workers, consideration for others, getting and giving credit where it is due – is perfectly acceptable and even desirable.

But beware when you hear runaway, rampant, destructive types of "office politics" accepted as an amusing, normal part of a work environment. Excessive office politics and gamesmanship is always bad news for any organization – wherever it's rife, you can be sure there are one or more "Jerks" busily at work – prime targets for discretely sending *this book*, with the appropriate tear-out forms attached, to proactive, no-nonsense higher-level (we'll generically refer to this person as "the Director", as in a Department Director) managers who will not hesitate to clean house (unless you work for a dysfunctional Enron or Catholic Archdiocese of Boston or FBI type organization, in which case I'd invoke the "Bombshell" approach of Chapter 8).

Office Politics is not only far from trivial, it can literally be quite deadly. In the wake of September 11, whilst the smoke was still billowing from the ruins in lower Manhattan, *Time* magazine (Sept 24, 2001) reported that one reason the FBI was caught flat-footed was that it "tolerated office politics that has driven out many of its savviest counterterrorism agents"![7] Eight months later we learn more chilling details behind this assertion. *The New York Times* reports,

> *By early 2000, Mr. Williams had received a tip that would ultimately lead to his memo to Washington. He began to investigate Middle Eastern students at a Flight school in Prescott, about two hours from Phoenix, and became suspicious that they might be terrorists. But by the account of a former agent, Mr. Williams soon requested a transfer from the international terrorism squad to a related team, foreign counterintelligence.*
>
> ***He had apparently become worn out by internal politics. 'He was going home with knots in his stomach,' Mr.***

*Hauswirth said. 'It shouldn't have been that way. Here's
a guy who was one of the best terrorism agents in the FBI,
and he's got to fight city hall.'*[8] (author's emphasis added)

One of the idiotic problems he had to deal with was the FBI's
sudden penny pinching that made it impossible to pay off informers
who'd penetrated suspected terrorist cells in Arizona. Even after it
was well known Al Qaeda was blowing up US Embassies and troops
worldwide! This kind of gross incompetence and negligence just
boggles the mind.

The article proceeds to detail that Agent Williams did return to
the international terrorism squad, just about the time the terrorist who
would pilot the Boeing 757 into the Pentagon, Hani Hanjour, was
enrolling in a Phoenix flight school. However his squad was diverted
to a politically sensitive local arson case (!), so Mr. Williams was once
again pulled off the scent by "office politics", and the rest is nightmarish history.

Also eight months later, we discover just how pervasive "office
politics" is at the FBI, with Agent Coleen Rowley's bombshell letter
that revealed FBI Headquarter's gross incompetence in refusing to
support Minneapolis Field Agents' investigation of the "20th Hi-
jacker", Zacarias Moussaoui.

Of course, the more that's published on the NYPD, FBI, and CIA
screwups in the decade leading up to 9/11, the more incredible the
dominant role of stupid office politics, blithering incompetence, and
gross criminal negligence becomes. It's no wonder the Bush Administration has tried to stifle any coherent blue-ribbon investigation into
the fiasco – as all the facts are revealed, the picture is painted of a
Government at Federal and Local levels that make the Keystone Cops
look like Scotland Yard in comparison. Time after time, intelligent,
competent detectives or agents on the crime scenes were stopped
cold, overruled by moronic, politically driven supervisors and directors who should now be charged and brought to trial for major
negligence.

Any doubts you may reserve towards this conclusion will be
swept away when you read John Miller and Michael Stone's *The Cell*,

which relates so many gross blunders by the FBI and CIA, "it takes nine pages of epilogue just to sum them up". From firing the only informer in deep penetration of Al Qaeda in the US, to forcing out the few high-level chiefs who "took Al Qaeda seriously", many Federal Agencies were paralyzed and made impotent by rampant office politics by the end of the 1990's.[9]

In the same vein, experienced CIA field operative Robert Baer's recent book, *See No Evil*, documents the incredible incompetence and startling negligence of the CIA during the 1980's and 1990's, as it shredded off most of its human operatives in the Middle East and western Asia in favor of expensive, ineffective high-tech gadgetry that gave not a whiff of warning of 9/11. The stories he relates are truly chilling, with Jerks hard at Work, in abundance, and with *nothing* to put the break on them.[10] This book would have been helpful to him, had it existed back then. Sorry, Bob.

Humorous references to excessive "office politics" fade rapidly in the cold light of day. 3,000 innocents died needlessly on 9/11, in large part due to inexcusable "office politics" run amok.

NEEDLESS TRAGEDY – USE THIS BOOK NOW

The tragedy is that many of these outrageous conditions could be vastly improved, and more likely *eliminated*, if employees could safely, *i.e.*, anonymously, make known their unhappiness to higher levels in the corporation, or organization, in a swift and effective way, and get rid of the source of the problem, usually an inept "jerky" lower or middle level manager. This book provides that alternative.

Why the big emphasis on anonymity?? For those who have worked in almost *any* Corporate or organizational environment, the question is a no-brainer. Anyone who has ever openly complained to a Director about a manager can recall the cold denial, the fear, the pressure to recant or "just drop it", the icy disapproval, the distinct feeling one was treading onto forbidden territory, the "I really don't need this *now*, I'm quite busy, you see, thanks", the "you're digging your own hole", the "so why don't I just fire *you* right now?" attitude.

Remember the Internet-fueled revelations we just discussed didn't take off until the "revealers" felt safe, *i.e.*, *completely anonymous*. While most reasonable people would agree the mass-distribution via Internet of complaints of this sort is very inappropriate, and can cause needless turmoil and disruption, the power and *need* for the protection of anonymity is understandable. In fact, it is expected that the more focused use of this book's surgical method, instead of indiscriminate Internet mud-slinging, can bring reason and order to employees' need to correct disasters in the workplace. Much more on anonymity in Chapters 4 – 6, the execution process.

20TH / 21ST CENTURY SLAVERY

What's the root cause of this sorry state of affairs in most workplaces?? If, as I estimate in Chapter Two, 80% of those in the workplace are decent, great people, and only 5% are hard-core "jerks", why do too many workplaces come under the domination of jerks and their fellow travelers??

The answer is simple, actually, and I'll bet nine out of ten of you readers already can guess. I've seen hundreds of examples during the last few decades. The typical workplace is dominated by a "slavery" mindset, a fear of authority and of losing one's job. Jerks play on and thrive on this fear to advance their careers whilst stepping all over decent people with impunity. Workers are often sheep-like, afraid to speak out, putting up with outrages day after day, month after month, year after year, often for their *entire adult lives*, even as it eats away their insides (*e.g.*, "knots in his stomach", in the FBI Phoenix 9/11 blunder), and turns all too many into hopeless, bitter, Dilbert-like cynics.

With this book, this kind of hellish suffering can be immediately cured

Up to now, honest, decent people have felt totally isolated and completely powerless – we discuss this in detail in Chapter Three.

Now the tables can be turned, and good people finally have a huge, avenging club in their hands.

Steven Biko, the courageous anti-apartheid activist who was murdered by South African authorities while in police custody in 1977, was the founder and leader of the Black Consciousness Movement. His take on the nature of this oppression was:

> *"The most potent weapon in the hands of the oppressor is the mind of the oppressed."*[11]

Zora Neale Hurston, African American writer, novelist, and anthropologist, 1903–1960, stated it similarly:

> *"People can be slave-ships in shoes."*[12]

In other words, we're really just doing it to ourselves. The two quotes above were written by blacks, who historically have a keen understanding of slavery and the nature of crushing oppression – all of humanity can benefit from their direct experience, because all of us are or have been or will be subjected to various forms of oppression. If we listen carefully, we can learn volumes.

But let's not be *too* hard on ourselves. Face it, it's human nature, and a very justifiable fear of bosses, arbitrary authority, and jerky unpredictable bizarre personalities have been a part of the human condition since the days of Attila the Hun, and long before that!! This is not just a 20th / 21st Century, or American, phenomenon. Once we can objectively see what the problem is, we can fairly easily resolve it. It's exciting to realize that a little reason and wisdom can obliterate seemingly insurmountable problems, cleanly and efficiently.

Now, with **Jihad the Jerk at Work,** *there's no need to put up with this oppression. Any worker, or manager or anyone at any level can safely expose the abominations of lousy managers and others, quickly and with little to no risk to himself.*

UNDERSTANDING THE ENEMY – EVIL RAMPANT WORLDWIDE

In order to come to grips with, and wipe out jerks populating the workplace, we must face the unpleasant fact that evil is rampant in the world – unrestrained, growing wildly, fierce, spreading uncontrollably. If you understand and truly accept this basic concept, you'll be properly conditioned and motivated to do what needs to be done to effectively use this book.

Many workplaces are Enron-like untended gardens, clogged with weeds that choke out decency and integrity. But to put a positive spin on it, we "jerk-busters" are now going to have a field day, because we finally have the awesome arsenal on hand with *Jihad the Jerk at Work*, and we just can't miss. If we play our cards right, it's like shooting fish in a barrel – enjoy it.

Rampant evil, unchecked, has spread like a cancer everywhere. We're not just talking business corporations – the rot has permeated into academia, churches, all levels of government, the judiciary, the military, police, and medical establishments. It's not just limited to the U.S., it's a worldwide plague. Of course it's at its worst in societies with absolutely no checks and balances. It is no coincidence that societies with *no* brakes on human foolishness . . . cowed media, co-opted judiciary, totally corrupted political systems, such as absolute monarchies, Fascist Germany, the Soviet Union, and the Taliban self-destruct, or are themselves destroyed, rather quickly.

IMPLODING CORPORATIONS

Business corporations that are fear-ridden and rigidly/autocratically controlled also have short life spans. Today there are many corporate cultures – large, medium, small – that are rapidly imploding. One of my favorite analogies from MBA case studies was a company where "management was so clueless it was still smiling when it hit the wall at 80 mph" – sounds like Enron, or Worldcom, or Arthur Anderson.

These are sclerotic entities that tolerate an atmosphere of shrinking integrity, a fear-ridden workforce, needless waste and inefficiencies, atrophying backbone. *Jihad the Jerk at Work*, used in large numbers by concerned employees, can help these companies clean house and halt this headlong rush to self-destruction, *before* their workplace Enrots out!!

Of course our work is clearly cut out for us. There are numerous deeply-rooted corporate cultures where 20% of the population "never grows up" (*e.g.*, Jeffrey Skilling's "Mighty Men"[13]), where imbecilic behavior is tolerated and even admired, where too many managers simply don't do their jobs because they're so busy trying to cover their political behinds.

In too many organizations, Jerks often get promoted at higher rates mainly because they lack scruples and will not hesitate to aggressively bulldoze over decent people. This, however, is all about to change when this book gets into the hands of principled, angry, disgusted workers who are fed up with all the shenanigans. This book will be like Stinger missiles in the hands of Afghan resistance fighters (the *dukhi* – Russian for "ghost"[14]) downing Soviet Mi-8 helicopters and jet fighters in the 1980's.

THE TWO BEST KEPT SECRETS OF CORPORATIONS

This is possible because there are powerful, decent people in most corporations (excepting totally rotten Enron-type entities that call for different, more draconian tactics, discussed in Chapter 8) *that if accurately informed of managerial or other misbehavior, and confirming the same in their own follow-up investigation, will act quickly and ruthlessly to rectify the situation.* This is the first best-kept secret of corporations, and other organizations. I've seen it happen, and it's a satisfying scenario to precipitate and then observe unfold. Chapter 4–6 covers this sequence in more detail, but it's important to know at the outset that when your filled-out forms and complaints attached to an annotated copy of this book get to the right person, good things will happen fast. This is specially true if you give him a *30-day deadline to produce* . . . or see the whole ball of wax bounced up to VP levels! Directors can perform miracles, given the proper facts and motivation. **Just never let'em up for air**.

Although "the Director" may not be ecstatic when he sees your anonymous committee's bombshell sitting on his desk, in the long run, you're doing him a huge favor. Mid and High level executives are often perplexed at low employee morale and high turnover. Behind the smokescreens generated by Jerks at work, they often really can't get at the truth of the situation. Hard core jerks are masters at erecting elaborate Potemkin Villages* that can confound even experienced Directors. Laziness does play a role here – often the higher Manager likes the comfortable illusion, so it's up to competent employees to shed light on reality, *á la* Sherron Watkins, the ***only*** hero to emerge from the Enron debacle.

With your Complaint Package in hand, Director's and VP's will finally get a clear understanding of what the real problems are, who the likely culprit is, know the right questions to ask, and where & who to go to to get the right information. Best of all, they'll have a **deadline** to meet, to wrap up the problem (usually it means getting rid of a jerk) to preempt this bombshell being elevated to a higher level. Good Managers and Directors desire to quickly clean up their own dirty laundry, so as not to have to endure the embarrassment of their VP or CEO having to step in to wash it for them. *Deadlines* have the *magical effect of spurring decisive action*, precluding the favorite managerial ploy of stonewalling and endless delay, hoping the problem will just go away – "a problem slow-rolled is a problem solved".

But, even better, because you're doing all this anonymously, your chances of being retaliated against are small, **assuming you follow**

---

*And you never thought you'd use your History 302 course after college! A Potemkin Village is an elaborate facade erected to cover up gritty reality and impress gullible VIP's. Named for Prince Grigori Potemkin who built gilded facades to hide impoverished towns along the Volga River in 1787 to impress Empress Catherine the Great & her European visitors, as they sailed by, with Russia's newfound "prosperity". Used extensively by authoritarian regimes, enronesque corporations, and jerks with a lot to hide.

all the security guidelines detailed in this book. For 95% of the situations I've seen, it's far more prudent to launch the campaign anonymously – more on this in Chapter Four.

It's also been my experience that you may unknowingly have a *lot* of allies in lower and middle and upper management, folks who've been locking horns, over other issues, with the very Jerk you're trying to get rid of. Sometimes your Complaint Package will be the proverbial "straw that breaks the camel's back", the final evidence senior management needs to get rid of a marginal lower- or middle-level manager. I've seen this phenomenon in play, and it's a powerful, glorious endgame.

There is often serious infighting among corporate executives – it's the norm, not the exception!!! Take advantage of this little-known reality – your Committee can directly weigh in, and often cast the decisive blow to evil and Jerkism.

And this is truly the second best-kept secret of business corporations, and all other types of organizations. Finally, we now have an effective methodology for all the good folks, at all levels, to gang up on total idiots to get rid of them forever.

CONNECTING THE DOTS

Because by filling out the forms in Chapter 6, and sending them attached to a copy of this book (with your Post-It Note tabs and highlighting of passages relevant to the jerk in question) to higher management, you're taking the step that the typical Jerk at Work *dreads above all else . . .* you're *exposing his racket to the light of day.* This precipitates his slide downhill. From then on, like Dracula at high noon, it's just a matter of time before he melts down. The more he struggles and lashes out, the sooner he'll be fired, or at least transferred and gotten rid of.

MAKING A LIST, CHECKING IT TWICE

Chapter 2, and the "Forms" section of Chapter 6 have a much more detailed "fault list", but when you and your committee laundry-list the faults of the typical jerk (and the hard core ones usually rack up 15 – 25 without breaking a sweat), such as "having no sense of shame", "selfishness", "ingratitude", "excessive micromanagement", "arrogance", "intemperate", *etc., etc. ad nauseam*, and can directly tie this performance to damage caused to the business (*e.g.*, good people abandoning ship, plummeting employee morale, loss of business, financial waste, loss of investor confidence, damage to customer relationships, *etc.*), senior management will want to get rid of him posthaste.

You and your committee will discover how much fun it is to "award" these well-deserved traits by marking the appropriate ones on the pre-printed checklist, filling in some short and pithy backup comments by selected traits where the spirit moves you, and even, best of all, adding on additional bizarre faults I didn't think of. The capacity of Jerks to astound us with surreal and novel misbehaviors is a never ending wonder to behold.

H.R. FOLLIES

I mentioned that powerful people in your organization will welcome your reform efforts, even though (or, should I say *especially if*) your identity remains anonymous. One of the big beneficiaries is the Human Resources (HR) Department, which has tried in vain for fifty years and more to root out substandard, terrible managers. In effect, you're doing their job for them, and *much* more effectively.

HR Departments, in general, have been colossal failures in most organizations, although in the past I have to confess I personally did · meet two HR managers, and know of three more, who were really superb and courageous, and even instituted some effective reforms. In fact, if it weren't for this handful of heroic people giving us some hope for the future of the HR profession, I would have written off the whole institution as hopeless, and would not have bothered to include Chapter 9 on "HR Reform" in this book. I'm still skeptical that HR Departments will *ever* pull their weight and do their jobs, but miracles do happen, and perhaps sharp CEO's can shake them out of their indolent, deadly lethargy.

For the most part, HR Departments' ludicrous attempts at improving management's effectiveness and clearing organizations' atmosphere of inappropriate behaviors would be considered downright comical if they weren't so devastating to corporate well-being. We cover the root causes in Chapter 9, to include essential but botched "upward feedback" programs, and non-existent or ineffective or desperate stopgap "management training" geared up when HR and the CEO wake up to fact that 40% of their top talent has fled into the parking lot, and to competitors, never to return.

HR Departments and CEO's are right to worry about the plague of stupidity and foolishness and chicanery that causes mass migrations of talent away from Corporations. After decades in various corporations and organizations, I can testify that the deadly linkage between the level of jerkism and a host of organization-killing ills is beyond question. Jerky managers and flaky employees cast a pall over companies, killing off innovation, jacking up inefficiencies and costs, and driving off good people.

A SLIPPERY SLOPE

But it gets much worse than that. Once that downward spiral begins, it trajects into a bottomless pit of disaster. **Jerks tend to hire and collect other jerks around them** – and when a lower management jerk is promoted to mid-level by clueless, blind senior managers, *the damage expands exponentially.* Overt corruption and even more serious criminal activity can become ingrained into the corporate fabric, and it's a short journey from there to Corporate destruction.

Observation #1 : *Show me a corrupt business organization, Enron or anybody else, and I'll show you a corporation riddled with jerky, corrupt personalities. Jerkism and corruption go hand in glove. If "Kenny Boy" Lay, Jeffrey Skilling, Andrew Fastow, and Cardinal Bernard Law weren't first-class Jerks at*

*Work, then Pigs can fly, IRS audits are designed
to help taxpayers, and the Pope's a closet Uni-
tarian.*

IT'S OFFICIAL: JERK-INDUCED STRESS *DESTROYS* EMPLOYEE HEALTH

In Chapter 3 we'll delve more into the "Consequences of Jerkism Unrestrained", but it's important to note in this introduction that as of December 2002, Medical Science has finally confirmed what many have suspected for years: the *direct* cause & effect linkage between "chronic (jerk caused) stress" in employees and managers at work and a whole host of serious **physical** as well as psychological medical problems to include:

* heart disease   *premature aging   *diabetes
*increased vulnerability to infectious diseases, strokes, and illness
*inhibiting the functioning of the immune system (!)
*damaging brain nerves, causing atrophy of memory
*high blood pressure   *damage to blood vessels in heart and brain
*hardening of arteries   *depression   *mental disorders
*rheumatoid arthritis   *fibromyalgia   *shutting down reproductive
function

(Source: New York Times, 2002) [15]

Holy Mackerel.

Note again that the above list is not conjecture or hypothesis – major medical studies at leading US and Canadian Medical institutes have confirmed these effects of chronic stress in numerous laboratory tests with animals and humans during the 1990's.

There is also evidence, but not as solid yet as the medical studies above, that high rates of violence and suicides in the workplace can be directly linked to the activities of hard core Jerks.

These tragic prices to pay for retaining Jerks in your work-place are UNACCEPTABLY HIGH! *Start your planning* **to anonymously get these morons run out TODAY. Just do it, if it needs to be done.**

SEE'N IS BELIEV'N

Had I not been a front row witness, over a two year period, of just such a mind-boggling corruption scenario in a major US corporation, the initial burning driving motivation that inspired this book may not have materialized. To *really* despise jerks, and to resolve to roll back and obliterate their insidious influence worldwide, it's helpful to see with one's own eyes the boundless evil they'll engage in, and observe firsthand the indelible damage they will inflict upon their own Corporations. Like so many tawdry scandals, the sordid end-game begged a searching analysis of root cause. Stephen Speilberg, in his wildest flights of Dreamworks imagination, could not have conjured up the script I watched unfold. It could have taken up four episodes of *The Sopranos*, only the producers would have rejected the story line as being too unreal to be taken seriously by an HBO audience. Truth is certainly stranger than fiction, much more bizarre.

Given a critical density of hard core jerks, linked in a cancerous cabal, in a lax moral atmosphere, with the right amount of fear and silence among employees, with no mitigating counterforce, a cesspool of corruption and stupidity was brewed that basically shut down a major part of the company's business when it got caught and exposed. Any trust between the corporation and its customer base evaporated overnight. *Jerks kill off business, it's that simple.*

I firmly believe that this book, had it been in print back then, in the right hands over a period of time, could have prevented this sad corporate debacle. **Get rid of Jerks, and 75% of problems will resolve themselves.**

As Carolyn Heilbrun (author, educator, detective story novelist pseudonym Amanda Cross) aptly states,

"Ideas move fast when their time comes." [16]

As the Enron debacle unfolds relentlessly, with each day's revelations outdoing the previous in astonishing scandal and jerky malfeasance, it's clear that *the time has come*. This book and the Crusade it inflames will move very fast, a cleansing, righteous torch of *Jihad* through the rotting decay of select corporations and other organizations.

THE BIG PICTURE

With the techniques in this book which I've developed over the years, success is highly probable – notice I didn't say guaranteed (what *guarantee* really exists in a modern workplace?), but highly probable. There's just no reason to continue to suffer from irresponsible jerks. Getting rid of them is surprisingly easy, **if** you adhere to the simple, basic strategies and tactics detailed in Chapters 4, 5 and 6. And all this can be done without the "messenger being shot" (*i.e.,* *you!*). Before this book, real reform and positive change rarely could occur in corporations unless it flowed "top down". Therefore, it rarely occurred! Now, it can flow "bottom up – then top down". *Now, any employee, without risk or fear, can have a major role in shaping his work environment for the better*.

Pause a moment, and think about what this means. This is truly unprecedented and revolutionary . . . when I overlay this impact on the typical corporate and organizational worlds I've known, I firmly believe the positive influence on human society will be equal to and probably greater than the printing press, the transistor, the personal computer, and the Internet combined!! And it won't happen just because this book was written – **it will happen because principled, courageous people like yourself, using this book as a guide, will run with the ball and clean up their work environment. It will happen one campaign at a time, and the most important campaign is the one** *you'll* **orchestrate.**

IT'S NOT ABOUT "REVENGE"

One skeptical "Middle of the Roader" (a borderline "Clueless One" actually) once asked an EAJ Committee of mine, "Isn't what you're doing just exacting a petty revenge??" Well, considering the colossal Jerk we successfully got rid of, I'd hardly call it "petty."

And more importantly, classifying it "revenge" is totally missing the point of the EAJ Campaign. What we're really doing is creating a "Jerk-Free Zone" in our workplace. That means, even if we oust the major Jerk irritant in the group, we must be continually vigilant and be prepared to tackle *any* Jerk who gets too close to our space.

"Revenge" is a shallow concept we have not the luxury of indulging in. Creating and maintaining the Jerk Free Zone is a lifetime skill that will become even more powerful as we gain experience. Also, if enough of these blissful, productive "Zones" are established in the corporate fabric, you eventually end up with Jerk-Free Departments, and even Jerk-Free Companies / Organizations. Imagine the possibilities. Kind of exciting, actually.

CAUTION ADVISED

A caution here – *don't launch a campaign unless there's clear justification to do so*. This is not a recreational activity, it's only to be engaged when you're convinced that the weight of evidence meets the standard of proof detailed in Chapter 2. This is serious business, this is a powerful procedure – save it for an appropriate situation. If none is looming on your horizon, consider yourself blessed and fortunate . . . you may have a friend who's in a more difficult situation, and could use this procedure – by all means, let her know about this book, so she can obtain a copy to employ posthaste.

KEEP YOUR POWDER DRY

My own view is that even if you don't have an immediate need to launch an "eliminate a jerk (EAJ)" campaign, it's wise to retain a copy of this book, and actually read it now to understand the basics . . . and annually, to keep in a prepared *mental* tone. First of all, I think you'll find it quite illuminating, and even entertaining. Secondly, it will help you ramp up to speed quickly if it ever becomes apparent that trouble is brewing . . . and that's the way Jerks sometimes pop up on your radar screen, no warning given, or even as a huge Pearl

Harbor type surprise. You'll attend a meeting, or have a conversation with a new boss, or hear an amazing story from a trusted associate about an unusual altercation in an associated group, and suddenly you'll be asking yourself, "Did I just hear what I thought I heard, or am I hallucinating??" Uh oh. Tune in *fast*! See Chapter 4 for a key discussion on how *timing* plays a vital role in the success of a EAJ mission. Sometimes a Chapter 7-style low key issue complaint, or a quick, devastating overnight counterattack can preclude the need for a major 30/60/90 day EAJ campaign.

PREVENTIVE MEDICINE: THE BEST MEDICINE, TAKE HEED

There's a *third* good reason to buy and read this book *right now*, even if you're blessed with a great working environment and great people. It's called "Preventive Medicine". I too have blissfully worked in wonderful jobs in great organizations – but I can tell you, swearing on a stack of Bibles, that I've seen at least two of these Gardens of Eden transform rapidly into Pits of Hell when basic fundamentals of good work management were neglected and a classic Jerk suddenly appears on the scene, or evolves from the primeval slime.

SQUEAKING WHEELS GET THE OIL

If you see *anything* in your Company now you really detest, go ahead and **complain** about it (anonymously, of course – don't make yourself a target for retaliation). Read Chapter 7, tear out & fill in the forms, attach to the front of this book and send it to a responsible authority. Again remember, **you're just getting highly paid executives to do their damned job** – don't feel guilty about it. You'll be amazed how quickly things improve. You can even brag about it, but only to *very trusted* pals. Now you've set a high standard for your own Company, don't ever let it slide.

This is all very important because it keeps senior management on their toes – they suddenly realize they *don't* have a free ride anymore, that their performance is being closely watched by intelligent employees that, in a moderate, reasonable way will not tolerate sloppiness and stupidity. The anonymous nature of the complaint will put them on the edge they should be – now they know they're always being observed. This is a good thing because there's nothing worse than cocky, arrogant, complacent, know-it-all middle and senior managers.

Even the *knowledge* that a bombshell book like this has penetrated the sanctity of their Corporate Bubble will probably send senior executives scurrying to revamp their management training programs (see Chapter 9) to try to save at least some of their clueless lower level managers from being savaged by irate employees.

ALARM BELLS AT HUMAN RESOURCES

Continuing with our 3rd "preventive medicine" reason for your usage of this book now, even in a relatively benign working environment: do yourself a favor. If you're in one of the 98% of U.S. Corporations or organizations that doesn't have a Human Resources (HR) Upward Feedback Program that meets the *minimum standard* (see Chapter 9 for specifics), go ahead and send a copy of this book, need I say it , anonymously, to your HR Vice President or the equivalent. Instruct him to get off his behind, read Chapter 9, and start doing his job by instituting and sustaining a decent Upward Feedback program, **now**, *pronto*. Give him 30 days, and if he doesn't produce, send the identical package anonymously to the CEO with an additional recommendation the HR VP be fired (again, I'm not trying to sell more books, relentless hardball is just all too often the *only* way to get executives to do their jobs.)

JUMP-START YOUR LAGGARD HR VP

You can tell we're both going to have a lot of fun with this. Mark this *very page* with a post-it note sticker and highlight this paragraph, and the following one, in which I inform your HR VP that I really don't give a **twit** about how upset he may be to get this advice, that I believe most HR executives are *not* doing their jobs, are basically gutless clerks, and *care not one whit* about the real welfare of their employees. The sorry, pathetic, embarrassing performance of Enron's criminal HR Vice President testifying before Congress in March 2002, in which she defended her immoral coddling of the 35 senior executives who plundered **billions** since they were allowed to dump all their Enron shares, whilst screwing 20,000 regular employees by barring them from selling *any* of their rapidly devaluing Enron shares from their 401 K, leaving them destitute, was not an HR anomaly.[17]

This is **typically standard** shameless HR behavior – kowtowing before senior management, the employees be damned. Most HR execs are just lightweight clerical toadies for senior management. As you can see, I have nothing but disdain for the abysmal failure of the HR profession in general. Thanks with your highlighting, I can have   thousands of *tête-à-têtes* with these spineless overpaid clerks nationwide, and give them the reaming they so richly deserve.

Thus endeth my suggestions for your use of this book, even without a handy target jerk to dispatch immediately. Let's plow on through this introduction and overview of the book, so we can wade into the meat of the matter in Chapters 1–6.

DISCRETION *IS* THE BETTER PART OF VALOR

Remember the Home Depot Internet example given at the beginning? The truth comes out faster and stronger *when the employee has some protection afforded by anonymity.* When Enron employee Sherron Watkins (who was a highly respected Vice President in Enron, by the way) sent her famous first scathing one-page letter outlining gross accounting irregularities to CEO Kenneth Lay on 15 August 2001, **it was an *unsigned anonymous* letter**. For good reason, she really did not know how he'd react, so she was cautious. When she *openly* met with CEO Ken Lay a week later, 22 August, with her 6 page detailed letter, her identity became known, and her boss, the notorious deal maker and crook Andrew Fastow, immediately tried to have her fired, but was dissuaded by cautious corporate lawyers. Much more on the anonymous concept in Chapter 4, but any complaint / reform system that does not have a provision for anonymity built in is *doomed* to failure from the start, as any competent HR professional will readily attest.

All we're really doing here is **just getting middle and senior managers to do their jobs**. Just do their jobs. Is this too much to ask?? We think not, and we make no apologies for launching these type of campaigns – and we'll especially have zero tolerance for any whining about anonymity. See Chapter 4 for more on anonymity, and tactics to easily overwhelm red herring objections to this vital protection – objections that are usually a sign that a jerk is busily at work trying to destroy the reform effort.

PLENTY OF GOOD REPLACEMENTS

Most of all, remember the #1 Rule:

" YOU *DON'T* HAVE TO WORK FOR A JERK."

Repeat this three times a day. Then repeat the #2 Rule three times a day also:

"LIFE IS TOO *SHORT* TO WASTE ANY TIME WORKING FOR A JERK."

Your main objective, if the problem is a boss, is to get him replaced with a decent, competent person. This is not a problem. For every jerk that's canned, ten good managers or good potential managers are available to take his place. Believe it, it's true. Out with the bad, in with the good. Companies that resolutely pursue this cleansing always come out ahead – when they stick with bad apples, the rot spreads fast. Don't ever accept the tired old excuse, "Oh, Joe Blow is irreplaceable, we can't afford to get rid of him."

"THE TROUBLE WITH DILBERT"[18]

Notice that this is not the cop-out "Dilbert" approach, glorifying the resigned acceptance of workplace idiots (see Chapter 3). What it *is* about is taking the monkey off your, and other decent employees', backs and placing it where it belongs . . . on a middle or senior manager, to straighten out the mess he probably helped create in the first place, especially if he hired, promoted, or placed the targeted jerk.

HOW THIS BOOK IS DIFFERENT

Jihad the Jerk at Work makes different assumptions and takes an entirely different approach from all the "Dealing With Difficult People" and "How To Handle Bullies At Work" books currently clogging bookstore shelves. It dispenses with naïve notions that hardcore jerks can be effectively negotiated with, and is profoundly skeptical they can be "counseled and reformed". My impression upon reading some of this drivel is that many are weak academic and theoretical attempts to deal with problems the authors learn about second or third hand.

Some of the advice dispensed is truly ineffective, if not ludicrous. Filing lawsuits and initiating complicated legal action is often totally the wrong approach, overlooking the fact that most workplace problems can be solved faster and cleaner at the *lowest level possible*, just by **forcing middle and senior level managers to do properly the job they're paid to do.**

Fast and direct action gets much better results, and also has a better chance to block deadly decay and corruption at the get-go, before it can assume a strangle-hold Enronesque death grip on the corporation. The methodology laid out in this book is the only *tried and true, field verified* process that will solve serious jerk-at-work problems quickly and safely. After years of practical, real-world experience in a variety of high-pressure settings, I can tell you **it really *works***, against some of the worst kind of clowns you could

possibly imagine, and some so bizarre and warped as to be beyond
the imagination.

Now, for the first time, thousands and hundreds of thousands of
good people can begin cleaning house at work . . . and the impact on
society, for the better, is going to be enormous. It's an exciting
Crusade, and long overdue. Best of all, once the immediate scum are
removed from the equation, we can employ this process in a maintenance mode in the near and distant future to *ensure* organizations and
society **stay** relatively jerk-free. We are now freed up to move on to
make equally important reforms in our tottering society. This is a
sea-change of enormous implication (see Chapter 14, "On to the Next
Crusade"). But we must not let initial triumph lull us, we must be
forever vigilant, for like the plagues of Biblical renown, jerks will be
forever slithering amongst us, probing for weakness. This is the
Human Condition, but we can **now** manage it intelligently.

GENERAL OUTLINE OF BOOK

Briefly, let's take a tour of this book so you understand its scope
and how it can help you in your present situation.

Parts One and Two of the book, Chapters 1-6, are the core,
detailing the fundamentals of assessing and effectively dealing with
the jerk problem. All six chapters need to be studied carefully, if you
decide to launch a serious EAJ campaign.

In Chapter One, we explore the topic of "How Bad Is It?", a survey
of the depth of the problem of damaging fools in the workplace.
Needless to say, you'll find you're not alone with your problem. It's
also revealing to discover that even in lofty professions thought to be
placid and above everyday pettiness (academia, the judiciary, and the
church, for example) "jerkism" is rampant and hugely damaging. *No
profession stands unscathed by this scourge*! Nada. Nada one. *None*.
We discover the intensity of anger against jerks is shocking, certainly
often justified. The urgent need for a book and a hardball solution of
this type becomes quite clear.

Chapter Two schools us on "knowing the enemy". It's important that the truly hard-core jerks, the 5%, be targeted, and not the lightweight peripheral 10% hangers-on, who tend to disappear into the woodwork when the Patron Jerk gets exposed and eliminated. In other words, choose your target carefully. Don't waste time on Mephistopheles, nail Lucifer directly. It's key to understand the "traits and characteristics" of the truly dangerous jerk, and how he operates in the real world.

An analysis is made of their numbers—the good news is they make up a surprisingly small percentage of the total work population (5%), whilst your pool of possible allies is comfortingly large (80%). Makes the odds of success seem better already. The nature and depth of the evil hardcore Jerks breed and thrive in is explored, a chilling glimpse through the looking glass . . . the environments that incubate their rise, their traits and facades and tactics and games they play. Then, one of my favorites, is the list of characteristics, the "Fault's List". One can have a world of fun laundry-listing well-deserved labels, as indeed you will when you check off these juicy zingers on the preprinted Forms provided, whilst adding your own laser-like commentary to add damning clarity.

Chapter 3 expands on the "Consequences of Unrestrained Jerkism" – if you need any additional motivation to rid your Company or organization of a particular hardcore jerk, this chapter will inspire you. Includes a revealing look at the severe medical calamities caused by Jerk-induced stress, as well as the exposure of "Dilbert" as an unmitigated fraud.

Part II, Chapters 4–6, are the true operational essence of the book, the core of the conception, preparation, execution, and follow-through that are mandatory for any successful campaign to get rid of that jerk at work who's making your life miserable. *Read and study these three chapters with great care, you want to make as few mistakes as possible in order to pull this operation off seamlessly.* Take advantage of the wisdom of experience, stack the deck heavily in your favor.

Chapter 4 is the book's heavy-hitter. It discusses the fundamentals and guidelines for the "assault", planning, and execution. The chapter analyzes the crucial *decision making process* to "fight or flight", the importance of decisive action, the dangers of a soft "counseling" approach, the timing of the attack, the power of accurate "keeping book", the value of a little good research into the Jerk's past history, the need for alliances, forming a trusted committee, coordination & feedback, firewall and e-mail security, the power of anonymity, shifting the burden to the Director's shoulders, proper use of the cover letter and fault's list forms of the Complaint Package, creating the proper 30-day deadline and pressure to deliver, determining the ***minimum acceptable objective*** of the Operation, priming the 2d and 3rd Wave escalation Complaint Packages, targeting additional people of influence, **launching the clip-on book attack** (where the filled in complaint forms are paper clipped to the front of this book & the entire lot is sent to the Jerk's boss), the 30-day alert period, destroying counterattacks, full-court pressure tactics, overcoming defeatism, and finally: success or 2d wave assault. This is an exciting Chapter—if you plan and organize with care, chances are you'll have a very successful campaign, and a wonderfully "cleansed" workplace.

Chapter 5 considers additional factors to address in successful EAJ operations. It covers advanced EAJ operations involving pre-emptive strikes (obliterating problems before they can gain a toe-hold), and if necessary, the knockout pursuit of a Jerk to another Department.

Chapter 6 basically lays out the tools you need to conduct a rather low-effort "Clip-on Book Attack". First, a checklist to help you cover all the essential bases in this effort, then both the Cover Letter to the Director and Fault's List sample forms filled in to let you view the possibilities – then, of course, the generic blank forms themselves, which you can fill in directly. It will be a lot easier, faster, and safer however, to use the forms at our website, www.upublishing.com/forms.htm. There's even a generic letter from me, yours truly, the Author directly to your Director, that helps him see the process in a positive light.

Chapter 6 concludes the *Core* of the book.

Part III of the book, Chapters 7–9, delve into issues related to the book's core: alternative levels of action both lesser and bolder, and Upward Feedback programs coupled with HR departments' longstanding failure to perform.

Chapter 7, "Suggestions and Complaints" is based on the premise that sometimes the best defense is an early offense. It is possible that the flowering of jerk-like behavior can be cut off at the knees, pre-empted, if jerks realize early-on that they're in an *unforgiving environment that has zero tolerance for idiocy.* The forms here can be used to quickly establish "air supremacy" to stop tyranny and foolishness from gaining a toe hold. Just remember, "Never let a jerk up for air".

Forms are provided, as in Chapter 6, to give you another potent weapon in your work-environment reform arsenal. (also on Website).

Chapter 8, "The Bombshell Scenario – Damage Reduction Early-On" is an unexpected chapter I hadn't originally thought about placing in this book, but after the astounding Enron, Archdiocese of Boston, and FBI scandals of 2001-2002, I felt this was a logical and necessary extension of the scope of this book. As you may have gathered so far, the main thrust of the book is that in *most* organizations there exist competent and basically decent people at middle and top management levels who are intelligent enough to clean out the stables when the writing is on the wall.

But in the few cases where the rot permeates the **entire** organization, more draconian measures may be needed, not only to clear up your immediate work environment, but perhaps to also immediately lessen the suffering and impact on hundreds, if not thousands, of innocents. This is truly high-stakes hardball, but some situations justify it. In the 80's and 90's, the power and brazen behavior of Jerks has skyrocketed, so a massive preemptive complaint, very probably bringing the very real threat of media and judicial attention to bear, is clearly an option worth serious consideration. Just ask the hundreds of sexually molested children (now in their 20's, 30's, & 40's with ruined lives) of Catholic dioceses of Eastern Massachusetts, and thousands of bankrupt, 401K-robbed, *Enroned* employees in Houston. Earlier decisive action by knowledgeable parties, using this book (had it existed then) literally to add weight and terror effect onto corrupt bosses, could well have prevented widespread suffering.

As Wellington murmured as he casually waved his arm forward to launch the final ground assault which broke the spine of the *Grand Armee* at Waterloo, *"In for a Penny, in for a Pound"*.

As usual, Forms are provided, to oil the skids for this heroic endeavor.

Chapter 9, "HR and Upward Feedback" analyzes the abject failure of Human Resources Departments to perform their #1 job, *i.e.*, insuring that the Company is jerk-free and operating up to the full potential its people are capable of. The misuse and general failure of Upward Feedback programs is examined. HR professionals who actually care about corporate progress rather than merely serving time until retirement may find this chapter helpful in installing long-haul upward feedback programs that actually work well. Of course, nothing will assist these glorified clerks until they acquire an actual backbone and some guts, so the whole venture is problematic. The rest of us can enjoy a few chortles at the expense of clueless, bumbling HR Departments. The farce of most companies' "management training" is also exposed.

In **Part IV** of the book, Chapters 10-12, we move to the *graduate* and *doctoral* level of workplace reform: jerk-infested career fields of special interest beyond the corporate world where the tactics of the book can be effectively used, but where rather obvious major *systemic* changes and reforms must be instituted to permanently repair the dysfunction, as well as to justify the public treasure currently being poured into these bottomless, hopeless sinkholes. The monopolistic morasses of government, academia, the military, and other career areas fit this mold. Since the abuses are scandalous, and trillions of dollars are at stake, we consider this reform mandatory, and it will be irrelevant how many Cosmic Jerks we have to fire or incarcerate in order to clean out these stinking Augean Stables, which have been putrefying far longer than the mere 30 years cited in Greek mythology.

Chapter 10 views the special challenges confronting workers at various levels of local, state, and federal agencies, law enforcement, CIA, FBI, *etc.*, *etc.* This book can be very effective in these environments, but they can be even more screwed up than private businesses / corporations due to their monopolistic, dead end nature and lack of alternative career paths for government employees fed up with poorly managed or even corrupt workplaces. Worst case, these will lead to the type of FBI and CIA blunders that allowed a lot of innocent people getting killed on 9/11. This is not blind "government-bashing", it's for real – we present some stunning eyewitness accounts of the abominations found often in government agencies – 16 agencies, all disasters-in-progress, are visited. Actual structural changes are urgently needed for these career fields, mostly revolving around eliminating the dead end nature of government jobs, providing multiple paths to alternative work, and ending the "pensionitis" time-serving mentality that so deadens the productivity of the typical government entity.

So Chapter 10 can therefore provide valuable insight for those few, unusually competent directors and managers of government organizations who *really* want to put their organizations on the cutting edge par with dynamic private businesses – and instill the excitement, fearless initiative, and entrepreneurship that can galvanize government agencies and make them desirable places to work. You don't believe it can be done?? Then read Chapter 10. As Vice President, a beardless Al Gore tried in the 1990's to "reinvent Government", but was using the wrong play-book. *If the root-cause conditions are not addressed, other efforts are a waste of time.*

Chapter 11 delves into the problems of other difficult career fields that, like government, tend to breed jerkism to an even greater extent than corporations due to the monopolistic or dead end nature of their career patterns: namely academia (universities, colleges, schools), non-profits, the judiciary, medicine, and the church. Some of the worst managed organizations in the US are colleges. The Medical profession has been totally corrupted by business interests. And some of the biggest scandals, most of which could have easily been avoided, have occurred in church organizations. In the Judiciary,

"Prosecutorial misconduct is more pervasive than is generally realized."[19] Again, this book can do wonders in exposing and ridding jerks from these environments, however alternatives such as described in Chapter 10 need to be introduced to free up career choices for the work force, to really break the jerk stranglehold.

Chapter 12 examines one of the most jerk-challenged environments of all, the military. For any doubters, simply read the best military expose of all time, *A Glimpse of Hell*, by Charles Thompson, the bombshell revelations of the true story behind the 1988 explosion of gun turret #2 that killed 47 sailors aboard the Battleship USS Iowa and the Navy's subsequent criminal cover up of the outrage, which in the grandest of military tradition, continues to this very day. No doubts can remain on the need for major reform even if one only gets 40 pages into this stunning book. This kind of malfeasance and "cover up culture", which I saw on a recurring basis during my military days, is common and accepted in the military, which makes it one of the prime targets for urgent, lasting reform immediately.

Another bombshell book, *Silent Knights,* just published in 2002 by acclaimed Aviation Safety expert Dr. Alan Diehl, exposes the Pentagon's criminal cover-ups of the true causes of thousands of military deaths due to preventable accidents with weapons and aircraft – it will undoubtedly ignite a firestorm of calls for criminal judicial proceedings, and urgent reform of the military *now*.

The comments made on the Government sector apply here, but to an even higher degree. The solution to the Military's biggest problem is surprisingly commonsensical and simple, which will leave most readers asking, "What are they waiting for???" Since some 52% of the Federal Government's *discretionary* income is poured into the military's wasteful, bottomless appetite, after the virtual rape & plunder of much more productive educational, medical, and social programs, this issue is of major importance to all taxpayers and citizens. We want a competent, well run national defense that spends its budget wisely, not the pathetically managed, bloated, pork-barrel, white elephant we're presently saddled with.

Part V of *Jihad the Jerk at Work* opens up new vistas of reform: "Moving Beyond the Workplace: Emboldened to do More".

Chapter 13 invites readers to submit candidates for "best run" organizations and "worst run" organizations, based on the response of their mid-level and senior level managers to EAJ campaigns via this book. The candidates will **not** just be limited to business organizations. *Any* kind of organization is fair game. We will publish an annual summary of rankings of these organizations with some appropriate juicy particulars, a press release which we'll have highly profiled exposure in the *Newsweek*'s and *Business Week*'s of the media, which love to air this kind of mind-boggling insight. The honored and dishonored companies and Directors will be identified by name, obviously you will not, to protect your identity, nor will low-level target jerks. We will also annually present the Jeffrey Skilling Jerk of the Year Award , and the Dave Frasca Runner-Up Award (Dave was head of the FBI's radical fundamentalist unit, which buried *both* the Phoenix memo and the Minneapolis Moussaoui warrant request) to deserving candidates. This promises to be a lot of fun, for sure.

Chapter 14, "On to the Next Crusade" opens up a whole new arena: now that you've successfully reformed your workplace, you're freed up to accomplish more, if you so choose. Society and the Planet need people like you to weigh in and save them from the disaster we're careening towards. Despite the rantings of the nutty right wing in this country to the contrary, and so-called "moderates" who are anything but, September 11 was indeed a wake up call that we ignore to our peril.

As we'll see in Chapter 10, the federal government is a corrupt morass, utterly compromised by corporate bribe money. Only immediate and serious campaign finance reform can save it from dissolution by an enraged citizenry. This corruption has been the prime mover of our morally bankrupt foreign policies which have contributed significantly to worldwide environmental disaster, huge & dangerous global overpopulation, and endless unnecessary wars.

In our own country, criminal government corruption has led to the public health disaster of 41 million people without health insurance and the dictatorship of media conglomerates who are stifling diversity of opinion. We have a ravenous military dominance of the federal discretionary budget (52% goes to the bloated imperial US military – almost $400 billion a year). Meanwhile the public education system has all but collapsed.

Chapter 14 presents an innovative voucher-only schools system that levels the playing field & leaves no child behind – really. This will spur the development of tens of thousands of progressive schools, and foster the creation of a citizenry that will lead the country to true greatness.

Chapter 14 also plugs the reader into significant progressive media outlets, as well as political movements like the Green party that offer the only hope of real reform in the US. Readers will be inspired to become resolutely active, speak out, and reform society as effectively as they've reformed their workplaces.

Chapter 15, the Epilogue, continues the call for action, and reflects upon the impact all this reform will work upon society.

So much for the cook's tour of this book.

YOUR MOTIVATION AND INTENTIONS MUST BE PROFESSIONAL, NOT PETTY AND SELF SERVING

Before I close this introduction, it's a good time to discuss a key factor in successfully using the methodology detailed in this book. That is, what is your motivation for targeting and exposing the jerk in question?? There can only be one answer, and if your answer is different, don't do it. The answer has got to be that this is being done for the benefit of reasonably cleaning up your work environment for yourself and other decent fellow employees, it's for the benefit of your work group, and it's for the benefit of your company and customers and shareholders.

One of the justified and strongest motivations that has historically driven an "emergency" EAJ campaign is when word filters in, for

Heaven's sake, that a Jerk is a candidate for a *promotion*! Hopefully, you and your committee will not have allowed things to slide to this catastrophic point, but to be honest, I was once part of a committee that was energized by this very specter, and we conducted a campaign with such competence and zeal that the red-faced Director slipped the Jerk out of the Department quietly, with no promotion. On this motivational point, see Chapter 4 on the Enron rumored promotion that helped spark one of History's most famous EAJ campaigns (although nothing as effective & sophisticated as this book's method).

This is another good reason to go the anonymous route – then there can be no doubt or suspicion that anyone is trying to "claim credit" or grandstand for unseating the Jerk, or that anyone is trying to use this process get a promotion or to advance his career. This is also why the collective effort / committee approach is desirable, a genuine grassroots group effort rather than a solitary martyr's rebellion.

Be sure that your motivation for embarking on this campaign is as pure as the driven snow.

WHINERS NEED NOT APPLY

I hate to even have to broach this subject, but I might as well get it over with. You can probably tell by now that a classic principled EAJ campaign using the methods presented in this book is held to a high standard. In fact, it will work for you *only* if certain high standards are met. We've already covered them, *e.g.* no light and transient causes, all charges completely truthful, no exaggerations, principled motivation, no self-gain, in the best interests of the employees and company, *etc.*, *etc.*

It should be obvious that "Whiners need not apply" – these EAJ actions should **not** be conducted by, or even *contemplated* by, chronic complainers, incompetents, losers, whiners, backstabbers, jerks of any stripe. And make sure none of the above get on or even are aware of your Committee. We've got to keep these EAJ efforts pure and above reproach. In his excellent 1999 book, *Jerks At Work*, syndicated newspaper columnist Dr. Ken Lloyd gives some thought-provoking advice. Basically, he cautions us to make sure we're not acting like Jerks ourselves, which can be doubly bad since it could spread the Jerk mentality around even further. Food for thought.[20]

EAJ campaigns can only be conducted by the pure of heart: hardworking, loyal, decent, high performing, competent, reasonable, moderate, intelligent, caring, high energy individuals. 'Nuff said.

MATERIAL PROGRESS IS ONLY HALFWAY PROGRESS

The process you're setting in motion has to have the purest of motivations in order to succeed. And it is a truly revolutionary process, the cleansing of organizations from within. One of the major dichotomies that we have witnessed over the last 5 decades is how much progress we've made in the *material* world, and how little progress we've made in *human* interactions. Sounds like a Sunday sermon, but it's a truth that has much more impact on us everyday than we'd care to admit.

The roll call of relatively recent material and technical innovations is impressive and most welcome: credit cards, Xerox machines, touch tone phones, faxes, cell phones, voice mail, better antibiotics, cortisone cream for once-feared poison ivy, Allegra, FM radio, cable TV, "post-it" notes, car alarms, 4 wheel drives, laptops, HP desktop printers, the Web, microwave ovens, VCRs, e-mails, low maintenance Corolla's and Camry's, 100k radial tires, 9 minute snooze buttons on alarm clocks, invisible yard fences for dogs, Viagra (in moderate doses, mind you), and now even tele-zappers to defeat unwanted computer-generated sales calls at 7 pm home dinners. The wonderful list could go on for 1000 more entries, it's really amazing. When we set our minds to it, we humans can solve just about any tangible problem.

But in the sphere of *basic human interactions* in the workplace, we're still stuck in Medieval Times, in the year 1237 AD, where a few bizarre personalities can still paralyze a fear-ridden group or department, and the situation degenerates from the ridiculous to the absurd as a matter of course. The dichotomy could not be more stark, and to any progressive, rational human being, an embarrassment to our species. Can't we do a lot better than *this*???? Perhaps the crux of the problem can be found in the last sentence of the preceding paragraph, with the word, "tangible", which the dictionary defines as "actual – capable of being understood and evaluated, and therefore regarded as real". For the first time in human history, this book is putting an actual *face* on the plague of Jerkism, making it "actual", and at the same time prescribing a cure that works.

Feeble, half-hearted attempts by HR are a joke, and the best and brightest bail out without senior management having a clue as to *why*. Nothing has changed. Interpersonal relations in the workplace in recent decades have made little to no progress, and there is much evidence to suggest it's actually gotten much worse.

This is about to change dramatically for the better. The last Great Frontier is human behavior, human foibles, the dearth of effective communications, totally unnecessary *fear*, and the curious & absurd dominance of the mean-spirited hard core Jerk At Work. Right now it's an absurd mess, but with some common sense, some focused actions suggested by this book, and a little light shed on the subject, **A NEW DAWN IS FAST APPROACHING.**

LIFE IS JUST TOO SHORT TO TOLERATE JERKISM

As I close this introduction, but before we launch into the tactics of a successful get-rid-of-a-Jerk campaign, I'd like to once again engrave this thought indelibly on your mind: Life is just too short for you to allow a foolish jerk at work to ruin a week or a day or an hour or a minute of it for you. **DON'T DELAY** ... if there's a hardcore problem person at your workplace, regardless of his position, use this method to bounce the issue anonymously and safely up to an intelligent person in your company who can get rid of this idiot before he can do more damage. Clean house today. Start now!! Just do it. Read

Chapters 2 and 4 today, the Action Chapters, and lay out your plan of attack asap.

Actually, I fervently hope that you now work in a wonderful environment, with decent managers and employees, and that you have no need now, or ever will, for this book. But, sadly, I know the reality is quite different for many of you, and that your pain runs deep.

INACTION LEADS TO DOOM

A lot of Enron employees are bemoaning the fact they've lost their jobs, life savings, and 401K Plans. But all of them bought in to the Enron environment – they well knew they were part of an organization that exhibited little to no morality, a place that was so warped that the personnel system was dominated by a sick "rank and yank" regimen that created paranoia and mistrust. Illegal and shady deal making were standard operating procedure. Yet *none* of these employees, with the exception of VP Cliff Baxter (who many think was murdered to keep him quiet, not a suicide), company treasurer Jeff McMahon (who was quickly transferred) and Sherron Watkins (whose revelations came too late in the game to salvage the Company), ever raised any protest or tried to slow down the train wreck.[21]

Well, you guessed it, there's an obvious lesson to be learned here. Employees just can't sit on their behinds and do nothing, then complain about the awful company they worked for when the feces hit the fan!! You help create your own environment by your **inaction** as well as your action. Employees, *those who bear witness daily* to what's really going on in their own workplace, bear ultimate responsibility for correcting the obvious ills there ... *remember that.*

"Many a false step is made by standing still."

Resistance, *any* resistance, to evil and Jerkism has a far greater impact than meets the eye. The onset of any principled resistance triggers a loud tolling bell that terrifies the typical Jerk, foretelling his eventual doom. Outwardly, he may act unruffled, but inwardly, his stomach is in knots, as he realizes that the free ride is over, the game is up – someone has seen through the charade.

> *"Evil, once manfully fronted, ceases to cast its sickly spell; there is generous battlehope in place of dead, passive misery."* [22]

>> Thomas Carlyle
>> 1795–1881
>> Scottish-born English essayist, historian

A typical example of this principle is the resistance of various groups to the barbaric policies of National Socialism in Germany and Europe in the 1930's and 40's. Despite the Nazi's terrifying power, almost every time religious or community leaders protested against specific outrages (*e.g.* the Euthanasia program or eradication of Jews who'd converted to Catholicism), the fascist leadership became concerned about losing popular support, and often reversed the policy. Deep down, this cowardly group of swine knew what they were doing violated basic morality, and were worried that they'd be eventually exposed and punished … which they were, thanks be to God.

Deep down, the typical Jerk knows his days are numbered.

THE TIMES, THEY ARE A'CHANGIN

Your timing is perfect, the climate is really on your side. The wind is starting to shift in favor of decency and integrity in the workplace. The Enron, Priest Pedophile, FBI, and Worldcom scandals were the last straws – *no one* has any more patience or tolerance for the stereotypical greedy, jerky, tyrannical manager or psychotic employee. It's plain for all to see where this kind of guy, no matter what kind of impressive Ken Lay type of smokescreen he's hosing about, is leading organizations: to their doom.

There were signs, even before Enron, that the cutting edge of the business community is finally waking up to the need for house cleaning, fundamental ethics, and jerk reduction.

One need look no further than the recent #1 pick for the top MBA program in the nation, according to the *Wall Street Journal /* Harris 2001 Interactive Survey of Corporate Recruiters. And the winner was... Harvard? ... Yale? ... U. of Chicago? ... nope, #1 was the rather small Tuck School of Business, Dartmouth College, in rural New Hampshire.

And why tiny Tuck? The *Wall Street Journal* story by Ronald Alsop says it all:

> "'Tuck students are ambitious, certainly,' says Alexander Lejeune, a Tuck student from France, 'but they aren't greedy and aren't willing to kill anyone to get ahead.'"
> (my, that's a breath of fresh air, coming from an MBA)
>
> "... the Survey ... named Tuck the most collegial of all business schools and gave its graduates the best scores of any school for interpersonal and communication skills and teamwork abilities.
>
> 'Dartmouth people come with inherent humility and a team orientation; they don't have that arrogance that's all too common among MBA graduates,' says Reid Jackson, a survey respondent and 1996 Tuck graduate. Now a vice president at Commerce One Inc., a software company in Pleasanton, Calif., Mr. Jackson says there's a joke among recruiters that the only problem with Tuck is that they have to prepare several case studies for the student interviews. 'If a Tuck student felt he didn't do well in the interview, it's always possible he'll tell his classmates what the case study was to help them get the job,' Mr. Jackson says. There's this loyalty to the group that doesn't exist in any other business school.'" [23]

We have to pinch ourselves when we read this admirable place was chosen #1 by Corporate Recruiters, a hard boiled group not known for their touchy feely side.

So perhaps the cutting edge of Corporate America is actually starting to "get it". Be advised this occurred even *before* Enron hit the fan. The same *WSJ* article cites the reasons other top rated schools were selected, for producing graduates with "ethics and values", "bright risk takers – with a conscience", and "team spirit, thinkers".

SHARE YOUR SUCCESS STORIES

I know that by now, you're all pumped up, loaded for bear and ready to read on and plunge in to mapping your campaign for reducing the jerk count in your workplace by at least a factor of one – you're just itching to get to Chapters 2 and 4, where the triumphal battle is joined. But before you leap into the breach, a final request. You're a competent, focused individual, otherwise you wouldn't have made it this far into this book. Using your good judgment, and the powerful tools in this book, your chances of success with your EAJ campaign are very high.

YOU'RE DEPUTIZED

So at the completion of your successful operation, don't just forget about "The Cause" and the millions of work slaves out there, too many of whom are working for total jerks, or are having to put up with an obnoxious peer. Your experience will be **extremely valuable** in the 2nd Edition of this book, to that "80%" of good decent folks out there that thrive on inspiration and "lessons learned" – so let us hear from you about your own "rid-a-jerk" operation. We'll cloak you and your tale in anonymity to protect you and all the innocent & guilty parties, we promise, unless you request otherwise. Just make sure you put the *final* nail in the coffin, have driven the wooden stake through the heart, insure the jerk in question is truly gone or at least reformed (fat chance). We don't want Dracula springing back to life, do we? Or even worse, having *any* input whatsoever into your annual performance evaluation.

Anyway, E-mail, fax, or write us
        E-mail: rail128@aol.com   fax: (877) 386-5353
        write: Corporate Jedi
                  PO Box 438
                  Lake Hiawatha, NJ 07034-0438

with your experience. Nothing is more powerful than real-world examples. I've included many in this book, but more will ratchet up the momentum of this crusade and allow it to reach more and more people. The deeply satisfying feeling you'll have as you and your valiant committee bid a teary, fond farewell at the going-away luncheon as the hard core jerk departs, can be expanded a hundredfold, no, a ***thousand-fold, by sharing it with others*** who are considering launching their own noble EAJ Jihad.   After all, when all is said and done at the end of our short stay on this planet, if we can honestly say that we've left a much better world for those who follow, what better legacy is there?? In their heroic struggles over the past 300 years, our ancestors left a much better world for us. We now have a rare 21st Century opportunity to do the same, and that is truly exciting.

And, although it may sound trite and old fashioned, a *noble crusade* it is, and we all can feel very proud being a part of it.

Suggestions are also welcomed. The state of the rid-a-jerk art is advanced, but there is always room for improvement in any endeavor. Like those admirable MBA's from Tuck, let's pull together, we'll be unstoppable. I really do want to hear from you if you think I've missed any major concepts or even minor ones. We all need to team up to put a big dent in World Jerkism.

Finally, whether you have the opportunity to actually execute a jerk-dumping operation via this book's system or not, *spread the word* to co-workers and friends. When this book gets into the hands of the right people, the severe jerk-at-work problem in this country is quickly and dramatically going to be curbed (note again that I am not under the illusion it will be eliminated, because it's always going to raise its ugly head again – but *we'll be ready* for them. Eternal Vigilance is not too steep a price to pay, consider the alternative).

This knowledge also must be handed down from generation to generation. There must be no safe haven for jerks, no place to hide.

AND MAY THE FORCE BE WITH YOU

"A single idea, if it is right, saves us the labor of an infinity of experience." [24]

Jacques Maritain
1882–1973
French Philosopher, writer

Chapter One –
How Bad Is It??

"When you remove dross from silver, you have sterling ready for the silversmith. When you remove corrupt men from the King's court, his reign will be just and fair."
The Bible
Proverbs 25: 4,5

IS THIS FOR REAL?

One legitimate question that could be posed is "OK, so you've seen a large number of Jerks at Work in the past 30 years in different workplaces, and you've seen them cause a large amount of damage – but is it representative?? Is 'jerkism' really all that widespread?? Maybe you've just experienced anomalies, or had bad luck."

INVESTIGATIVE JOURNALISM'S SHINING MOMENT

If we can believe investigative journalists' statistics published widely in the print media recently, then damaging "jerkism" is not an anomaly, it's more like a thirty year long plague revisited every 30 years – it's pervasive. Remember the examples of jerk related behavior cited for the US in the introduction? It's also a serious *worldwide* problem!! In a recent feature article entitled "How To Handle a Toxic Boss" in *XL*, a popular British men's magazine, author Chris Dunkerley reveals just how huge a problem "Jerks at Work" are in England:

> *"The pit bull boss is running wild. A survey by Staffordshire University Business School in 1994 found that 53% of people had been bullied at work. Last April, a survey found*

47

that 2 out   3 middle managers felt bullying was a major cause of stress. ***If you don't have a bully at work, the chances are that soon you will.***"[1] (underlining & highlighting added by author)

The article proceeds to detail all sorts actual horror stories of tyrannical, "toxic" bosses, along with advice to workers on how to deal with these situations. While I don't disagree with a lot of the remedies proposed, the concrete system laid out by *Jihad the Jerk at Work* offers a faster, safer, more permanent, and much more effective process to get toxic jerks fired and out of the picture. In a hardball game, only clever and hardball tactics really work.

THE "DEAR ABBY" FOR JERK PROBLEMS

Some of the most dramatic evidence of the extent and seriousness of the Jerk at Work problem comes from Dr. Ken Lloyd, who writes an excellent workplace advice column in the United States and Canada. The column, "On the Job", runs in the *Los Angeles Daily News* and many other newspapers. Ken stumbled on to this massive phenomenon in an obvious way, best told in his own words:

"The questions (reproduced in his book, with his responses) *were originally mailed, e-mailed, or called in to my weekly advice column, 'On the Job' ... many readers submitted questions that were centered upon matters that could easily fall under the heading of 'all in a day's work' such as how to ask for a raise or make a résumé look better.* ***But there were far more questions that dealt with the problems created by jerks at work. Question after question focused on jerks as managers, jerks as supervisors, jerks as co-workers, ... jerks as subordinates*** *..."*[2] (my emphasis added)

In fact, the volume of jerk-related questions was so significant, Dr. Lloyd decided to write a book on the subject, *Jerks At Work*

(Career Press – Franklin Lakes, NJ), which he published in 1999 (thus stealing my first-choice title for my own book!). It's a great book that presents intelligent, common-sense ways of dealing with specific situations with idiots in the workplace in a Q & A format, and I highly recommend that you read it.

EVEN NEWSPAPERS AND TV HAVE CAUGHT THE SCENT

The massive problem of "Jerks at Work" has now caught the attention of major US newspapers. The *Boston Globe* recently featured an article, "Dealing With Bullies", by Diane E. Lewis, which highlights the problem with a probing analysis of the mindset of the typical jerk at work, and what can be done about it.[3]

Even major TV networks such as CBS and CNN have aired features on the jerks at work phenomenon.[4]

THE SURVEYS SPILL THE BEANS

A rash of recent surveys and studies also point to the gravity of the problem:

> *"In a 1998 study, the International Labour Organization noted that psychological aggression and bullying were the most frequently reported complaints among US employees."* [5]

Even health care workers are not immune from this plague:

> *"Social psychologist Loraleigh Keashly, director of dispute resolution at Wayne State University, reports in a new study of 147 health care workers that 82% have experienced some form of aggression from co-workers or supervisors."* [6]
>> (note, this abuse didn't come from *patients*,
>> it was from *co-workers* and *supervisors*, people
>> who are supposed to be on the same "team"!)

A survey by Walker Information, an Indianapolis research organization of 2,785 workers returning questionnaires divulged the somewhat shocking results that only half said they would recommend their employer to others seeking a job. That means that 50% of these employees were so disgruntled with their jobs they couldn't give it a positive referral! And only 24 % *"said they were committed to the company they work for and plan to stay at least two years"*![7] That indicates the other 76% were looking for a way to jump ship.

When I read between the lines of these surveys, based on my years of experience, I would hazard a strong guess that a major cause for this kind of skyrocketing unhappiness at work can be attributed to the unrestrained activities of a few jerky and tyrannical people in that workplace. ". . . the bullying boss or co-worker tends to drive talented staff away."[8]

As Diane Lewis reports in the *Boston Globe* article, ". . . many workers never report (the abuse from supervisors or co-workers) and *tend to internalize their anger*. As a result, a once loyal employee no longer gives 100% of his time. In more extreme cases, a worker may steal information, vandalize company property, sabotage projects, or explode in anger." (My emphasis)[9] One has to wonder if some scenario like this was going on a few years ago when it was discovered that disgruntled employees at a contract IRS processing firm in Philadelphia were just *throwing taxpayer returns away* (about 20,000) rather than process them, because they were swamped! The exact same scenario recently occurred in Phoenix when contractors working on INS applications just shredded the incoming documents, to "relieve" the workload. Smells like a huge dysfunction to me, a bunch of managers not watching the ball – I can imagine the Jerks at Work on this beauty. Since this was US Government-related, the whole scandal was swept under the rug and well hidden, a technique some bureaucratic Jerks in the federal government have elevated to a high art form and precise science (see Chapter 10 for more).

LINKAGE TO WORKPLACE VIOLENCE

To expand on the linkage theme of various serious workplace problems to rampant Jerkism, it doesn't take a mental giant to deduce that a lot of actual *violence* in the workplace could be defused and preempted if jerky behavior was significantly reduced. I've seen reasonable, decent employees so enraged over the duplicity of immature or unethical jerks, that violence was seriously contemplated. I am reminded of an article written by a military officer who worked in the Pentagon in the 1970's who recalls walking down the stairway in one section, and glancing at a painting of a prominent general, realizing that some upset staff officer recently just *spit* in rage on it, the saliva oozing down the face![10] A bad staff meeting perhaps? Knowing the incredible nonsense that goes on in peacetime militaries, it's anybody's guess (see Chapter 12 for how this book can help, even in that bizarre environment) .

There are some **two million serious incidents of violence a year** in US workplaces.[11] With the number of Jerks at Work greatly reduced via use of this book, it would *not surprise me to see the number of these incidents cut in half*, or more. And the linkage between jerkism and even more serious societal ills/disasters is also a relatively easy and chilling case to make – the next 14 chapters provide endless examples. It makes the case for strong action against Jerks at Work NOW all the more urgent.

BOOKS GALORE

Added to the volume of print and media material on Jerks in the workplace are a growing number of full length books on the subject such as *Bullyproof Yourself at Work, Disgruntled : the Darker Side of the World at Work*, and *Executive Blues: Down and Out in Corporate America*. All of these authors are decent people whose hearts are in the right place, and they are providing a great service to society by pointing out different aspects of workplace problems. But my sense is that they have not really gotten a handle on the essence of the problem, much less a dynamic, positive method to triumph over it. **Now, finally, that breakthrough has been made.** But the actual triumph will only occur when you, and thousands more like you, decide you've finally had enough, and resolve to sweep away that Jerk in your own workplace whose behavior can no longer be tolerated.

In addition, there are even web sites now, with chat rooms on workplace anger, that have popped up.

DILBERT IS ON TO SOMETHING

The phenomenal success of Scott Adam's "Dilbert" in the 1990's gives us a clue that he's tapped into a seething ocean of resentment in the workplace, much of it centered on the jerky behavior of bosses and co-workers. The cartoon themes of boss misbehaviors and coworker foibles are not-so-coincidentally divided about the same percentages as found in real life. No surprise there, since Scott draws on real life for all of his material, mostly from the flood of 350 e-mails a *day* he receives from workers eager to share the latest idiocy witnessed on the job.

"I use a lot of 'bad boss' themes in my syndicated cartoon strip, 'Dilbert,'" Adams told *Wall Street Journal* readers in a hilarious 1995 Op-Ed piece. "I'll never run out of material. I get a hundred e-mail messages a day *(Author's Note: three years later, by 1998, it had more than tripled to 350 a day)*, mostly from people who are complaining about their own clueless managers."[12]

Note that all these hundreds of thousands of rather damning complaints are being funneled to Scott Adams, **the cartoonist** – *a doodling **cartoonist**, for God's sake.* Because there's no real, *safe* avenue to route concerns to one's own Company directors ... **until now, with the preprinted forms in this book, attached to this weighty book itself, anonymously landing on a Director's desk.**

In an interview a few years later, Scott expounded on the success of his comic strip and books and the lucrative paraphernalia of the Dilbert empire:

"'There were about 35 million office workers in the US all having this shared experience, but not knowing it was shared,' Adams once told *Time* magazine, 'who were going home and not talking about it because they assumed it could not be this bad anywhere else.'"[13]

Note that *Jihad the Jerk at Work* is highly relevant not just to Scott's 35 million office workers, but to most of the 100 million workers in the US today, from janitors to technical workers to school teachers to managers to CEO's – plus another billion workers overseas.

Adam's Dilbert is humorous and entertaining, but it is clear he's "struck a nerve" with millions of disgruntled workers, as we discussed in the Introduction. (More on the dark side of the Dilbert approach in Chapter 3). Adams is a genuinely all-round funny guy, and a keen observer of human nature. And he doesn't have to make anything up – he joyously feeds on the reality that's piped to him by the truckload daily.

TWO PHASES

The "Jerks in the Workplace" problem is clearly serious and widespread, an extremely heavy problem that has, until the publication of this book, defied solution. For the next five to ten years, as many millions of people use this book to clean house, the problem will dramatically shrink to a more manageable, "percolation" level, down from the show-stopping crisis level it's at now, *anno* 2005, the Enron era.

It's going to be a lot more fun to launch these "clip-on book attacks" *now*, when workplaces clogged with completely clueless jerks won't know what hit them – kind of like the Dodo bird on Pacific Islands in the 19th Century, who allowed sailors coming to shore to drive them into extinction by clubbing them to death with their rowing oars. I call this attack period, "Phase I", 2005–2008. As time marches on, jerks will become quite gun shy, and shrink their profiles, but you'll still be able to nail them – it'll just take a little more sophistication and targeting. The very fact that they'll lower their once highly-annoying profiles will constitute a great relief in itself to all decent people of integrity in the workplace.

Actually, with the complete raving idiots purged, it will allow the targeting of the more deeply rooted, subtle forms of jerkism, if one so desires, that can be just as deadly to organizational performance. I designate this wave of cleansing as "Phase II", 2009-2012. Both phases will be a lot of fun, regardless, and very satisfying. Good hunting! Just make sure you are completely justified in conducting the operation, see Chapters 2 and 4, and you target only those that *clearly* must be excised.

A CLEARCUT PROBLEM

Many organizations have too many dysfunctional managers and workers walking around. For specific "fault lists" to identify these parasites, see Chapter 2. I've also sprinkled my favorite classic "Jerk at Work" stories throughout this book. I'm sure you have many cherished classic stories of your own. The disastrous consequences of this situation are detailed in Chapter 3. The failure of most companies "upward feedback" programs, that are supposed to detect, stop, and correct these behaviors is discussed in Chapter 9.

We can confidently assert that jerkism is a dangerous problem in the present-day American businesses and organizations of the era of Enron. It is also clear that, over and above the destruction caused at the employee level of unhappiness, weakening productivity, increasingly serious turnover, and loss of top flight employees is the blowback effect of ratcheting up corruption, scandal, criminal activity, employee abuse, and customer outrage which occur *always*, I repeat always, hand-in-glove with jerk-at-work behavior. Thus the immediate and sustained application of this book will significantly reduce these outrages because the jerks who perpetuate them will be exposed and fired, or otherwise marginalized.

TAKING CARE OF BUSINESS, FIRST

You'll note that to date, and throughout Part I of this book, we focus on the impact of, and how to destroy, "Jerks at Work" in the private business / corporate setting. This is done intentionally, like a Boot Camp, to develop a basic, "killer application" methodology that will succeed in decisively restoring decency, competence, and integrity to *any* workplace. Also, we've chosen the reform of the typical American business as target #1 because these corporations, and corporations like them based worldwide, effectively rule the planet in this era of increasing globalization, September 11 notwithstanding.

Corporations, with their huge and often corrupt lobbying power, virtually control all levels of governmental, academic, cultural, and military institutions. Even more frightening is the global corporate push to secretly ram through "MAI", the Multilateral Agreement on Investment, which would effectively destroy national sovereignty and allow corporations to ruthlessly dominate the globe 100%, without *any* restraints from those pesky, popularly elected parliaments and congresses, who actually are held *accountable* by real people who are affected by predatory corporate practices.

This nightmare scenario is beyond the scope of this book, but the threat of it underscores the urgent need to reduce the jerkism level in the corporate world from here on out, and keep it at a reasonably low level. This we will accomplish, we must accomplish, God willing.

THE SPREADING STAIN

If corporate "sickness", *i.e.* jerkism and corruption *á la* Enron and Worldcom and Global Crossing *etc.*, is allowed to continue and spread unchecked, then the "spreading stain" permeates and destroys our entire society. This process is in full gear now – one need look no further than the corrupt airline industry's ("an unviable industry run by incompetents" according to United's CEO) bribing a corrupt US Congress to do **NOTHING** about airline and airport safety and security in the 13 years following the 1988 Lockerbie disaster, when expert after expert came before "concerned" Congressional committees to testify that the US Airline industry was a security nightmare, and that disaster was merely a matter of time.

Congress gladly took its 40 pieces of silver (*i.e.*, the annual $20 million of airline lobbyists' bribes), ignored the experts, and openly invited the September 11 calamity with the horrible deaths of 3000 innocents. *Yet strangely, we read nor see not a peep of this outrage in our Corporately controlled media.* And even after 11 September, there are still many in Congress, and one of the major political parties, who **still** have the gall to fight campaign finance reform and expect to be re-elected, to boot. Find out your Representative's and Senator's position, and vote him out of office if he's one of these sleazes. I now climb off my soap box and return to the book at hand, but I owed the 3000 dead innocents at least this small gesture.

TERMINAL SELF-INFLICTED WOUNDS

There's also much evidence exposing business's own self-destructive impulse, to the point where now unbridled greed has allowed Jerks to severely punish even companies' *own* **watchdogs, researchers, and auditors** (!) when they competently do their jobs and honestly report corruption, bad accounting practices, and weak businesses. Incredible, and *it could only have been the doing of unrestrained hard-core Jerks at Work.* This is a disaster that may well destroy all the advances the capitalist system has made in the last 40 years, because it destroys investor confidence, the pillar of it all. The following examples are chilling, and not unrepresentative of the unmitigated rot that took hold in the 1980's & 90's on Wall Street, and we understand, *still is untreated and spreading* today:

> *"Owen Cheevers, 51, was head of high-yield bond research at the Bank of Montreal in New York when he wrote a cautionary report on companies in the radio industry. An experienced analyst, Mr. Cheevers was asked by investment bankers at his firm to make his report more glowing. He refused and pleaded with the bank's compliance department to intervene. He received no help.* ***Two months later he was fired.***

> *Joseph M. Mulder, 59, was a brokerage firm auditor with decades of experience, including identifying two money launderers who later went to prison. But soon after Mr. Mulder alerted his superiors to what he said were serious violations by a broker at Donaldson, Lufkin & Jenrette, **Mr. Mulder was fired. More than a decade later, the broker in question was accused by regulators of stealing $3.2 million from clients**.*"[14]   (highlighting by author)

It's no wonder investors have lost all confidence in the morons running Wall Street. In a similar case, one of dozens if not hundreds that have come to light as horrified investors realize what a corrupt fraud "the Street" is, Salomon Smith Barney fired analyst Kenneth Boss after he refused to change a negative report on "several office-furniture companies ... Boss claims in his suit that his investment banking colleagues were 'visibly dismayed and angered' after reading his draft report and demanded that the 'neutral' ratings assigned to Steelcase Inc and Interface Inc be upgraded to 'buy'."!

> *"It is common practice for Salomon Smith Barney to use the carrot of positive research coverage in order to secure lucrative investment banking business," he says in the suit, filed last week in Manhattan federal court.*[15]

The decay has set in, it's destroying our society, and we must purge it quickly before the cancer consumes us all. We must sweep the rot back and banish it from our culture. If enough readers eliminate just one jerk in their workplace in the next four year time frame, 60% of the battle will be won. (Again, I caution readers to initiate a EAJ Campaign *only* against certified hard-core Jerks.) Then with your success stories published to inspire others, we'll spur a second wave to eliminate many more undesirables in the following four years to get us to 90%. From this position of strength we can keep hammering the jerk population even lower indefinitely, always keeping vigilance. This is how decent people will triumph and make the 21st Century the brightest in human history.

BEYOND THE BUSINESS WORLD, IT'S EVEN WORSE

I would be remiss to limit the jerk at work problem just to private businesses, however important this sector may be. The problem is just as bad, if not much worse, in a whole host of other occupational areas to include all levels and agencies in local, state, and federal Government, law enforcement, judiciary, academic institutions, medical establishments, churches, and the military. The jerk at work problem is often *much worse* in these non-business areas, as we'll discover in Chapters 10-12, because of the monopolistic nature of these organizations and dead end, no alternative-choice aspects of careers there, that grip employees in a relentless vacuum of fear.

The abuses that occur due to jerk-dominated workplaces in these non-business fields are truly startling, and make the outrages in the corporate world look tame by comparison : from suicides in police ranks to the pettiness of academia where "a supervisor at a southwestern university assigned staffers she did not like to unairconditioned areas where the temperatures were more than 100 degrees in the middle of the day" [16], to outrageous and illegal conduct by prosecutors and judges in courtrooms, to the jerky blunders at FBI Headquarters in the 90 days leading up to 9/11, to grossly negligent actions of senior Catholic bishops and cardinals in ignoring & covering up devastating pedophilic crimes committed by hundreds of celibate, randy priests in the US and Europe, to criminal cover-ups of the FBI hierarchy in knowingly sending innocent men to prison for murders they did not commit to protect FBI informants who actually committed the murders, who kept on murdering while on the FBI payroll, to the gross lying of the CIA to Congress and its subsequent persecution of honest employees, to the incredible drumbeat of endless scandal and corruption and incompetence that permeates our budget-busting military establishments.

A hundred examples will be reviewed in Chapters 10-12, but it is obvious that while this book's methodology can go a long way towards cleaning up the "jerks at work" mess in NBO's (non-business organizations), the systemic problems there are so severe that this book, even with all its power, can't do it alone. There must be some fundamental structural, career-pattern changes, usually revolving around giving employees opportunities and training options for alternate career paths to free up those organizations from the stifling dead-end fear that institutionalizes such aberrant, jerky behaviors.

When asked "How bad is the jerk at work problem?" for the NBO sector, we have to respond, "You won't believe it could get this bad – it's mind bending."

We've got our work cut out for us, but at least the mission is clear-cut. Let's move on to tackle the problem head-on and triumph. Like the stiff, invigorating sea breeze of Trafalgar, the scent of resounding, liberating victory is now in the air.

Chapter Two – Traits and Characteristics of Jerks and the Nature of Evil

*"When we are born
we cry that we are
come
to this great stage of fools"*

Shakespeare
King Lear, IV, vi [1]

*"Human Nature is the same
all over the World."*

Earl of Chesterfield
letter to his son,
October 2, 1747 [2]

CHOOSE YOUR BATTLES CAREFULLY

This is an important chapter – read it scrupulously. Because in life it is very important to pick the battles you fight with great care. Fight only those battles which are truly worth the trouble, and those which are possible to win.

That means it's essential to know how to determine who really is, and who is not, a hard core jerk at work that must be eliminated, and whether or not you and your (potential) committee are the ones best suited to conduct the campaign. You *must* know in advance if your operation will be worth the effort.

NO "LIGHT AND TRANSIENT CAUSES"

One of the most memorable and succinct characterizations of this concept is set forth prominently in our own Declaration of Independence, a magnificent document that has inspired peoples throughout the world to throw off the shackles of tyrannical governments, both foreign and domestic. For continual inspiration, I sincerely urge you to read it at least annually. The parallels between the Declaration of Independence and the course of action laid out in *Jihad the Jerk at Work* are striking.

Most importantly, Thomas Jefferson makes the reasonable and logical point that one can't take such a drastic step as declaring independence – rebellion – unless things are so bad that it's absolutely necessary. He also makes the astute observation that by nature, folks will tend to quietly put up with tyranny and oppression over and over until it just becomes totally unbearable. Sound familiar?? Just like many 20th / 21st Century workplaces. Listen to Tom speak to us over the ages ...

> " ... *Prudence, indeed, will dictate that Governments long established should not be changed for light and transient causes; and accordingly all experience hath shewn that* **mankind are more disposed to suffer, while evils are sufferable, than to right themselves by abolishing the forms to which they are accustomed.** *But when a long train of abuses and usurpations, pursuing invariably the same Object evinces a design to reduce them under absolute Despotism, it is their right, it is their duty, to throw off such Government, and to provide new guards for their future security.*" [3] (my emphasis)

YOU OWE IT TO YOURSELF – AND SOCIETY

As well, we stress that a campaign such as outlined in this book should also not be undertaken "for light and transient causes". But note Jefferson's next point: on the other hand, if you determine that you and your allies are enduring insufferable tyranny, then not only is it your *right*, but it is your *"duty"* to correct the situation. Which is also one of the major themes of this book: **by resisting and exposing and eliminating a hard core jerk in your workplace, you truly perform invaluable and lasting service to society as a whole and human history.** It is your duty so to do. *"There are no passengers on spaceship earth. We are all crew."* Marshall McLuhan[4]

Jefferson then proceeds to brilliantly laundry-list all of the outrages perpetrated by King George III in a "Bill Of Indictment", which is the same as you'll be doing in your simple logbook of incidents transposed onto the easy-to-use complaint forms in Chapter 6.

MARTYRS NEED NOT APPLY

One other note of interest. The 56 members of the Continental Congress who signed the Declaration of Independence were brave men, who realized that by publicly defying the King of England, they were placing themselves and all they held dear, in grave danger. Indeed, many of these courageous souls paid a steep price over the following seven years as vengeful British (who'd had the previous 100 years to practice and perfect civic terrorism in Ireland and Scotland) and Tory troops torched their homes, destroyed their farms and businesses, and butchered their loved ones. Theirs was a selfless, necessary sacrifice, for which today we honor them and are deeply grateful.

But, take a hint. In your campaign, with this book's approach, there's no reason for you to martyr yourself!! In Chapter 4 we discuss further why your complaint form should be submitted *anonymously*. You don't want, or even need, to "fall on your sword" and join the pantheon of martyrs we see sprinkled throughout corporate and ecclesiastic history – your only goal here is to quickly and safely rid your organization of a malicious jerk.

A CAUTIONARY TALE

Let's repeat again one of Jefferson's major points in the Declaration: before you revolt against the King or the prince or the knave, make sure the situation really warrants your effort, or is appropriate.

I'll give you a personal example. In one large company I worked for, my immediate boss was rather well known as a "terror" – he could be very arbitrary, his hard work was legendary and he expected his people to also work with evangelical fervor, and he had no patience for slow progress. He was outspoken, blunt, and often downright rude. Too often he'd get overexcited and get off on the wrong track. There were times I would privately get angry with him for a stupid thing he'd say or do. People from other groups would ask me, "How can you work for this guy??"

So, was this a classic "Jerk at Work," deserving to be targeted and gotten rid of?? Nope, not by a long shot! He was one of the best bosses I ever worked for. He was courageous, always had the best interests of the company at heart, even in one of the most high pressure situations I've ever seen, ramping up production on a short fuse five billion dollar contract. He was fair, didn't play favorites, backed up his product managers *loyally* (yes, loyalty can also flow from top down, unless you're at Enron), had generally sound judgment, was keenly intelligent, and had a sharp sense of humor, which is a blessing in almost any tough place I've ever worked. Back to loyalty – a boss's unselfish, genuine *loyalty* to his own people is a rare trait in managers. Treasure a manager who exhibits this golden attribute.

TARGET WITH CARE

So you have to carefully assess every work situation, honestly tallying the pros and cons, and **only** (!) employ *Jihad the Jerk at Work* full force when it's absolutely clear that the object of your concern is an incorrigible 90 – 100 % *bona fide*, full time Jerk (for less serious situations, we present a whole range of less draconian actions that this book can assist in – see Chap 4 and 7). At the risk of sounding Politically Incorrect: if you're under 25, you may not have the depth of work experience to confidently make this judgment call. If you're 25 – 30, you still may not have the depth. In the personal example I just related, I had well over 15 years experience to realize that this tough boss was really a treasure, and I even persuaded a few others in the group to stay loyal to the boss and hang in there with him through thick and thin. I also vigorously defended him to Doubting Thomases in other Departments.

Be careful – just remember Tom Jefferson's "light and transient causes" admonition. I'm not trying to dis "young folk's" inexperience, it's just an important factor to consider. On the other hand, there are many 24 year olds who exercise far better judgment than some 44 year olds. After all, Jefferson was only 33 when he penned the Declaration of Independence. It's just that 35 and 45 and 55 year olds have a lot more yardsticks of experience with which they can gauge the relative seriousness of job situations. It can bolster your resolve if one or more of these "wise elders" join your *ad hoc* and very close-knit, discreet "Committee" (see Chapter 4).

Or, you can use high tech analysis to lead to the attack decision, namely, "If the fish stinks badly, it's time to toss it out."

TIPOFF – A "DRUMBEAT OF IDIOCIES"

A couple of missteps do not necessarily a jerk make. What clearly tips you off that you've entered a hardcore "jerk zone" is what I term the "drumbeat phenomenon", when you notice that your new boss, or someone else at work *constantly* is doing stupid, incompetent, absurd things 2 or 3 times a day, a pattern that *never* lets up or is never mitigated by superb performance. The depth and breadth of idiocies just goes on and on. This is a red flag that truly a "Jerk is at Work". After a few weeks or months, or however long you can actually stand it, you can give him enough rope to hang himself, whilst taking insightful notes, and you can confirm to yourself this is for real. Then you *must* decide on your response. In most cases I've seen, if you have any self respect, and value your sanity, you can a) decide to just leave the group – a wimpy way out, if you *actually like* the job you're in – or b) you can use *Jihad the Jerk at Work* to help you get rid of the Jerk quickly and safely. But *do* something, don't just sit there paralyzed. More on this response decision in Chapter 4.

VITAL NOTETAKING

In order to confirm the target and to properly focus an effective attack, you must keep an informal, *confidential*, written "logbook", simply documenting each Jerk-related incident you witness (date, short clear summary). From this, it's amazing how clear-cut patterns of misconduct emerge, making it quite easy to target the jerk-in-question (J.I.Q.) – not to mention preserving your own sanity! After a couple of weeks, or months if you're a patient type, the consistency and absurdity of the Jerk's behavior becomes crystal clear, and you start to wonder how he's gotten away with it this long!! (more about logbooks in Chapter 4).

From here, it's a quite easy step to check off the "fault's list" on the forms provided, and you've got yourself a mighty and righteous club!!

I can assure you this is much more than an academic exercise. Clearly defining, recording, and focusing in on jerk behavior is the vital process in exposing Jerks and *reducing* the terrible impact Jerks and their minions inflict on organizations.(*Eradicating* jerkism sounds like a better goal, but the stranglehold of jerkism on the human race is so profound, it will realistically take many, many years to reduce its impact even 25 to 50 to 75 per cent).

Wait, one may ask: won't everyone's definition of what constitutes jerky behavior vary?? True, there may be some variance, but my experience is that there often is a lot of agreement between a great majority of folks in the workplace as to where the major problems lay, and what constitutes unacceptable, jerky behavior. Up to this time, the "decent majority" has had to suffer in silence – but no more!!!

JERKS OMNIPRESENT

Also, one needs to be aware that jerky behavior can crop up *anywhere* in your organization. As we've mentioned before, it is often found in the management level just above you, or even at Director level, or more rarely at VP or CEO levels. Since these folks have more power, and power can have a corrupting influence, jerky tendencies can expand and become far more serious at higher levels. All the more reason to cherish and value those higher level managers who retain their basic decency and integrity despite the temptations of power. Indeed, it is this type of admirable person who prevents companies from traveling down Enron Avenue, and it's the same type you want to send your Jerk Complaint forms to for justice and action. They exist, and are the shareholders greatest equity in any corporation.

PEERS, SADLY

Sad to say, but sometimes it's one of your own peers that's a major problem Jerk. But just because he's at your level is no reason cut the idiot any slack. Even a relatively low-level Jerk can do a lot of damage to an organization, so fire away. A *lot* of good people will be glad you did!! I've seen incompetent moronic peers get away with dozens of behaviors on the "Faults List" (see further on in this chapter) for *years* because otherwise decent people were reluctant or even afraid to take action! The recent Jayson Blair fiasco at the *New York Times* is a classic example of this phenomenon. For years and years, both at the *Boston Globe* and the *Times*, Jayson Blair was widely known among his peers as a sleazy backstabber, an extremely annoying office gossip, fast & loose with the facts, and a selfish little twit to boot – *but he got away with it*, because nobody had the *chutzpah* to drop a dime on the moron.

With *Jihad the Jerk at Work*, no more excuses for inaction on twits like Blair! Now, with the Complaint / Fault forms attached to this book anonymously dropped on the Jerk's boss's desk, his career as a dangerous jerk will mercifully terminate posthaste. A peer jerk can be one of life's worst nightmares – it's just best to get rid of this sickening pestilence and enjoy one's job. **I have absolutely no sympathy or "solidarity" with peer Jerks.** (See Chapters 3 and 4 for some Classic Jerk examples to see why.)

Most of the techniques discussed in Chapters 4-6 also apply to this peer situation (*e.g.,* peer Jerks almost always have a shoddy history of past abuses worth unearthing) – but like all these EAJ campaigns, it must be handled carefully.

EVEN THE HOI POLLOI NEED WEEDING

Even lower-level people in your organization can exhibit jerk-like tendencies, and they must be dealt with *decisively* – if we're going to clean house, let's do it from top to bottom. You're doing your organization and its people a *big* favor by flagging jerky behavior, even at low levels, because all too often low-level jerks, unrestrained and undisciplined, can become high-level jerks in a breathtakingly short time frame. A stitch in time saves nine.

Just what happens when there is poor discipline in the rank and file becomes apparent in incidents like the Louima Case in the New York City Police Department in 1997. When a group of NYC Police illegally grossly brutalized a Haitian immigrant in a Police station-house, some patrolmen attempted a blatant coverup, even going so far as to threaten and intimidate higher-level police officers who were trying to unearth the truth.[5] For this kind of absurd environment to exist, it's obvious the NYPD needs to weed out a lot of Jerky patrolmen, as well as discipline an irresponsible, lawless, rogue union (as it was, this union, the Patrolmen's Benevolent Association, a sleazy organization if there ever was one, was forced to pay Abner Louima an extra $1.6 million – in addition to the $7.1 million NYC had to pay to settle the Police Brutality case – to compensate for its criminal role in this attempted coverup.[6])

Tyranny, corruption, and Jerkism at any level is unacceptable in any organization, but it's astounding and inexplicable when it's allowed to fester at the lowest levels. I would not hesitate to use *Jihad the Jerk at Work* to zap a lower level Jerk anywhere in my organization, unless I was his direct manager and could reform or fire or prosecute him outright.

15 MINUTES OF PLAYING GOD

If you take a gander at the simple pie chart on the next page, you may be tempted to stifle a yawn and prepare to flip the page . . . but wait, you may be in for a surprise treat. For on this simple chart you can actually "slot" or categorize everybody of importance in your workplace. Try it . . . just jot down names of people you're very familiar with in your workplace next to the appropriate pie slice. It's amazing how everyone actually has a comfortable "fit" on the pie chart. It's fun to either award people the lofty rank they deserve or else plunk them into the purgatory or howling hell they belong in.

The real value of the chart is that you can actually stack up the good versus the bad versus the fence-sitters – you may be surprised to find out you have more dependable allies and better odds than you'd imagined. Reliable committee members can assist you in getting a very accurate snapshot of the landscape. Also, there's a distinct security value to going through the "slotting " drill – you can carefully identify dangerous Quislings* and then firewall them off so they can't sabotage the campaign. Like the captain of a sailing ship, you *must* perform this drill, with help from trusted allies, in order to insure you *clearly identify* any dangerous shoals (*i.e.,* slimy quislings) to avoid during the upcoming voyage.

WE'VE GOT'EM OUTNUMBERED – THE GOOD, BAD, & UGLY

The most impressive take on this chart is, "Wow, the good folks have the Jerks outnumbered!!" Essentially *80%* of the folks in most workplaces can be categorized as decent, good people, and only 5%

---

*For the history-challenged, this refers to Vikund Quisling, the leader of the Norwegian fascist party who collaborated with the Nazi invasion of his own country in 1940. His name immediately entered the lexicon as a synonym for "slimy traitor" and "sycophant collaborator". He may have been shot for treason in 1945, but his toady namesakes inhabit every organization known to man. **Know who they are, and beware.**

listed as hard-core, dangerous jerks. Why, we've got'em outnumbered 16 to 1. Or at least 8 to 1! The important thing is to realize for yourself just how solidly the numerical odds are on your side.

Go ahead and slot all 20 or 40 or so key players in their pie-piece category – you can write in their names right on the page (but not in the copy of the book you send your director). Don't be surprised if other trusted committee members suggest shifting certain people to different categories, and they may be quite correct. At the end of the drill, you all will have learned much more about allies vs adversaries, and be much better prepared to conduct the campaign. It's a fascinating, and essential, exercise. Like MacArthur in the WW II Pacific campaign, you can bypass a lot of superfluous enemy islands and just attack the strategic one you need for "choke points and airbases". It's a little-known fact that MacArthur had one of the lowest troop casualty rates in the War, much better than Eisenhower in Europe. Fight smart, not foolishly.

And just how, one may ask, did our illustrious author arrive at the seemingly authoritative percentages of good vs. fence-sitters vs. bad? A Harvard Business School or Gallup Poll survey perhaps? Nope, just by doing the same drill, in many different workplaces over decades, slotting people I've known well in corporate battles, business triumphs and retrenchments, war and peace. It's representative of some real-world experience, not academic theory.

PIECES OF THE PIE : THE BAD

It's the panorama of the human condition. When I was cranking on this exercise, I was amazed to discover that the real hardcore "target" jerks made up only 5% of the pie, even though they've been responsible for untold misery to untold millions over the years. "Take out" *i.e.,* eliminate these parasites, and the whole workplace dynamic immediately changes dramatically for the better. We'll continue to analyze this choice group later in the chapter.

Allies vs Enemies in the Workplace
(typical %)

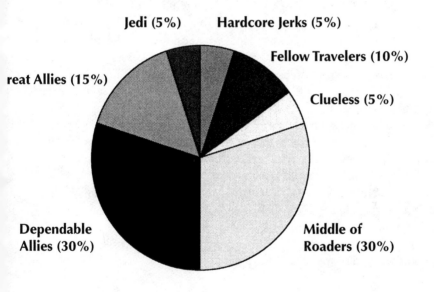

THE UGLY

Now let's continue on around our tour of the "pie" chart on the previous page. The next two groups comprising 15% won't help you and your committee at all – they're not as dangerous as the hard-core Jerk 5%, really not worth targeting at all, until the "A Squad" is eliminated, but they are "enablers" of Jerks, *de facto* allies. Of this gang of 15 %, two thirds (group of 10%) are "fellow travelers" . . . you know the type: opportunists, fence sitters, sycophants, toadies, quislings, Judases, often not very bright, foolish, back stabbers, "weak as water", slimy, lightweight etc. They haven't made it into the elite Jerk category, yet – they don't have quite the vicious initiative, and some actually possess a *tad* of a "sense of shame".

You *must* clearly identify these individuals to insure *none* of them gets the remotest *whiff* of wind that your committee is forming. Steer clear of this lot, they are dangerous, and *will not hesitate to betray* the noblest of causes. Often these swine are easy to identify, but every once in a while you'll run across someone you assume could never stoop to the depths he's actually very comfortably swilling about in already. A pleasant personality and winning smile can easily mask the soul of an absolute leech, the dregs of the earth. This is why having a reliable committee is so handy – Quislings can fool some people, but *never* those who work with them closely.

Consult closely with your trusted allies to insure this lethal group is clearly firewalled off. Don't assume from casual acquaintence you really know who the "fellow travelers" are. You may be surprised at who can and who *cannot* be trusted. **Be safe, not sorry**. Let me repeat this again:

Be safe, not sorry!!

You're entering a dangerous zone, you must proceed with great caution when you're dealing with the foibles of human nature. More on this and reasonable security in Chapter 4.

The other third of this group (5%) can be almost as dangerous to the effort, the "Decent But Clueless" clan. These folks have poor insight, are weak judges of character, tend to be somewhat amoral and gutless, exhibit indifference to the outrages perpetrated by Jerks, are prone to convenient self-delusion and the ignoring of reality. Sound like anybody you know?? They will *never* commit to the Effort and have absolutely no backbone – the real ticket puncher, time-server, pension striver mentality. These folks already have one foot in the grave. Included in this select group are folks so "nice" and naïve and mousy they couldn't bring themselves to resist *any* evil, however despicable. These people must be avoided like the Plague. Dante had a few choice thoughts about the eventual fate of these folk:

> "*The hottest places in hell are reserved for those who, in time of great moral crisis, maintain their neutrality.*"[7]

For convenience sake I've included in this group the "decent but dangerously incompetent". This well-meaning type might want to support the cause, but have such a bad reputation for sloth or poor judgment or indiscretion or whatever that their association with your effort can only damage it. Hate to be so brutal and "elitist", but we're engaged in a hardball game here, and we have to minimize risk. Firewall these folks off also.

THE GOOD

Now we finally arrive in friendly territory (whew!), the Grand 80% you've heard me gush warmly about, folks who are all quite decent and competent, and generally are disgusted with the behavior of the Jerk in Question and would be delighted to see him disappear forever. However, some of this rather large group will be far more useful to the effort than others, so you must slot these in categories *carefully*.

The first group, approximately 30%, I call "Middle of the Road-ers". These are decent, intelligent folks with fairly good insight. They know what's going on, but are loathe to commit to join any *coup d'etat* or effort until they know which way the wind is blowing, or the Jerk does something to them so outrageous (happens all the time), they cast their lot with us decisively and with a vengeance. So folks here can be strong contenders to shift up into the next more reliable group, "Dependable, Good Allies" – you and your Committee should always have an eye on Middle of the Roaders for good candidates to enlist in the cause.

In the "Home Stretch" phase of the campaign (see Chapter 4) when a higher level Director or Angel is gathering information which can finally destroy the Jerk, folks from this Middle group can be the decisive element that really clinches the outcome. Be attuned to them, they can actually win the war, but it helps to *feed them enough good info so they're reasonably tuned in to the picture.* They can sometimes be shaky and worried about Jerk retribution, but can be given spine-stiffening and confidence by shared confidential insights into the objectives and progress of the campaign. It's *well worth* the effort, see Chapter 4.

THE 50% "CORE GOOD" – THE COMMITTEE

Now we're getting deep into Hobbit Country! And the Hobbits outnumber the Jerks ten to one.

The next group of 30%, "Dependable, Good Allies" will be the mainstay of the effort. There are a lot of folks in this category, and if the Director has five or ten interviews with this solid group, the writing will be on the wall for the Jerk in Question (JIQ). I've seen it happen, and it's glorious. They call a spade a spade, are usually extremely competent and valuable to the organization, and are a joy to work with, day in and day out. Obviously, they will make solid committee members – they provide dependable eyes and ears to keep the committee and you alert to all relevant developments. Alert eyes and ears are key to the success of the campaign.

The next group (15%) are even more valuable – they're "Strong, Great Allies". These have a huge amount of initiative, are combative, and contribute killer app ideas. Often they are very considerate people and some have a great sense of humor. They usually possess, like you, a burning hatred for the JIQ, and can help the committee craft a strategy sure to unseat the same. All these folks need to be brought into the Committee as full-fledged members. They're in this for the long haul – make sure you keep them completely informed, and appraised of the progress and successes of the campaign. Their efforts should be given the credit and praise it richly deserves.

ALLIES IN EXILE

I should mention that in the two groups of allies just discussed, some of the most valuable players may well be solid, competent people who have *left* your organization out of sheer disgust with the J.I.Q. (Jerk in Question). Very often, the Director has no idea why these people *really* left, and is stunned when the actual reason is revealed. This is a Diamond Mine, don't neglect it!!

You must actively recruit these people into your Committee, and solicit their views. Go to the ends of the earth, if need be, to contact them. You'll find that the great majority are **delighted** someone is finally taking effective action to torpedo the Jerk. These folks are also excellent candidates to volunteer to be placed on the Director's "must interview" list for his private investigation. These departees have nothing to lose, since they've already left the immediate organization, and have high credibility, since their poor opinion of the Jerk has been underscored by their decisive action of jumping ship.

It's worth repeating . . . often, clueless Directors have *little to no understanding* of *why* good people have left their organiz-ation, and are shocked & disturbed when the truth comes out. I've seen more than one Jerk bite the dust when the Director finally gets this damage assessment!! **Don't pass this Treasure Trove up.** Also, it well be that some of these talented exiles long to return to your organization, once the Jerk has been deposed and banished. Out with the bad, in with the good.

The final group (5%), should you have the great fortune to find this rare breed, I'll call the "Jedi". It's hard to do justice to these saints in mere words, but I'll try. These are wonderful, principled people, with a sharp sense of justice. They possess high initiative, superb "combat skills", and have a shrewd intelligence. Most of all, they are keen judges of character, which is absolutely central to gathering a committee one can place trust in. They're also cool and courageous, and have such a rare competence that the organization prizes them highly.

They are outraged, as you are, at the antics of the Jerk, and are truly dangerous when aroused – that's what makes them such superb allies. They are not rash, however, they are realists which makes them formidable. (I assembled all these superlatives from the Chinese fortune cookies collected from my last visit to "Madarin Taste".) They're such a joy to work with, you'll never forget them, for the rest of your life. Surprisingly, they usually have a keen sense of humor, which goes a long way towards getting us all through this process, and even makes it fun, in a way you may only really appreciate in retrospect. Watching them in action makes it all worthwhile. No, they're not perfect people, they have their flaws, but their fiery purpose and cunning make them legendary achievers. The Jedi. Unforgettable.

A POWERFUL COMBINATION

The bottom line is, based on my last 30 years experience in the workplace, I can confidently project that over 50% of the folks in most workplaces can solidly support a well-run effort to oust a flaky jerk, with an additional 30% that may jump in during the Final Battle of Annihilation. We outnumber our target 10 to 1 – with a modest effort of teamwork and the methodology in this book, the chances are high that any jerk in the workplace can be gotten rid of, no matter what level he's working at. **"We can do this!"** I've seen the power of this approach in action. *It works and it works well.*

Let's get on to the main focus of this Chapter, *i.e.,* understanding the traits and characteristics of Jerks. We'll cover the basic causes of Jerky behavior, the nature and depth of the actual evil that permeates our world, laundry listing the typical characteristics of the hardcore jerk (always a fascinating exercise), analyzing the environments that allow Jerks to flourish, the façades and tactics and games jerks typically employ to try to stay afloat, and more.

FOUNDATIONS OF JERKISM

There are a wide range of behaviors clearly associated with jerks and their ilk – we'll list a hundred or so in a moment, grouped in categories, but I believe it's relevant to try to shed light on the key motivations that drive this aberrant misconduct.

It's rare to find a jerk that was not *excessively ambitious*. Now, ambition itself is not necessarily a bad thing – the old saying goes that "one should be known to have *ambition*, but not known to be *ambitious*" . In other words, one's ambition should be a reasonable, disciplined, principled ambition, part of that healthy mix of hard work, loyalty, social consciousness, business sense, integrity, caring, pride, competence, and decency that is the core makeup of any admirable professional or worker or human being anywhere.

THE ULTIMATE CURSE: THE DEARTH OF SENSE OF SHAME

But naked, selfish ambition unrestrained, and fueled by blind desire for wealth and status and power too often, or should I say *always* leads to a downward spiral of greed and corruption that easily descends into ever deepening levels of evil that's hallmark is the inability to possess any sense of shame, any sense of decency. I'll apologize in advance for sounding like the preacher on Sunday, but I feel that this fundamental understanding of the underpinning of Jerkism is essential to destroying it.

I first heard of the concept of "lack of a sense of decency." while viewing an old TV film clip of the Senate Army-McCarthy hearings of the mid-1950's. It's widely recognized that on June 9, 1954, when the head counsel for the Army, Joseph Welch, wearily and deliberately confronted the demagogue, witch-hunting Senator from

Wisconsin, Joe McCarthy with this withering blast . . . *"Until this moment, Senator, I think I never really gauged your cruelty or your recklessness . . . Let us not assassinate this lad further, Senator. You have done enough. Have you no sense of decency, sir, at long last? Have you left no sense of decency?"*[8]

it was such a powerful, heartfelt response that it marked the beginning of the end for this unstable, dishonest charlatan. (Welch was responding to McCarthy's wild "charge that a member of Welch's law firm had once belonged to a Communist front group".[8]) It really hit the nail on the head, and you could tell everyone in that Senate chamber room knew it, even Joe McCarthy himself, who had no coherent reply, but could only make a few sputtering, mocking facial gestures. It was truly a defining moment.

It was also seen on the new medium of Television all over the United States, thanks to a young Senator from Texas, Lyndon Johnson, who cagily understood that if the people of the country could actually see and hear the bully McCarthy at work, they'd react with disgust . . .

> *"'He (Johnson) knew what McCarthy was doing was a very dangerous thing for the country. And he knew that the newspapers alone and two minutes a night on television during the Army hearings wasn't enough. McCarthy had to be seen day after day during the entire hearings on the Army. He thought that would make people see what the bastard was up to."*[9]

Johnson was right, and McCarthy lost most of his popular support, was disgraced & soon history. Technology can weigh in on the side of truth and right once in a while! It's also key to the premise of this book: good people can effectively resist and destroy Jerks, *if they just make an intelligent, hardball effort to fight back – truth well articulated can easily dissipate smoke & mirrors.*

And when I reflect on the dozen or so of the *worst* Jerks I've known in the past, one salient characteristic they all jointly possess, the characteristic that defined the very core of their being, is that they indeed had a **profound lack of decency, or sense of shame** – there was almost no behavior too low for them to willingly sink to.

This gaping, fatal flaw led them time and again to incredibly evil, foolish, immature, arrogant, stupid behaviors. This became quickly obvious to dozens of decent, honest people who either had to work for these jerks, or worked with them as peers, or were involved with them via the matrix activity so common in business and other organizations. For more juicy, mind-boggling examples, peruse Chapters 3 and 4. I'm sure you could provide even better horror stories of your own.

"PEOPLE BORN WITHOUT CONSCIENCES"

The acclaimed author Kurt Vonnegut (*Slaughterhouse-Five*), in a recent (September 22, 2003) talk to students and professors at the University of Wisconsin in Madison, touched on a parallel theme. In his comments cited below, Kurt is of course alluding to the "Three Stooges" of the present pathetic administration (Bush, Cheney, Rumsfeld), but the insight is perfectly appropriate to *any* of the hardcore or cosmic Jerks I've personally seen in action. Speaking of several different short stories and books he highly recommends to everybody, he states,

> "... But I can hardly (fault you) if you had never even heard of the next book I want to celebrate. Practically nobody has, since it is basically a medical text: "The Mask of Sanity", first published in 1941 and written by the late Dr. Hervey Cleckly, a clinical professor of psychiatry at the Medical College of Georgia.
>
> Some people are born deaf, some are born blind or whatever, and this book is about congenitally defective human beings of a sort who are making this whole country and many other parts of the planet go completely haywire nowadays. **These are people born without consciences. They know full well the pain their actions may cause others to feel but do not care.** They came into

this world with a screw loose, and now they're taking charge of everything. They appear to be great leaders because they are so decisive. Do this! Do that! What makes them so decisive is that they do not care and cannot care what happens next."[10] (Author's emphasis)

THE COLD GRIP OF FEAR

Rarely do Jerks betray their true sickening characteristics to higher level executives, but 80% of their peers and subordinates are acutely aware of it. This situation almost always sparks an exodus of talent away from these jerky personalities, or a "silence of the lambs" as a stifling atmosphere of fear permeates the organization, like rigor mortis setting in on a corpse!! This, of course, allows the Jerk to continue and even expand outrageous behavior unrestrained. **BREAKING THIS CYCLE OF FEAR AND SILENCE AND TYRANNY AND ABUSE IS THE PRIME OBJECTIVE OF THIS BOOK AND ITS METHODOLOGY.** Read that sentence again.

Employees and managers and Directors and VP's and CEO's and Boards of Directors all have a prime responsibility to detect and eliminate these kinds of abusive behaviors that can and will wreck an organization quickly if left unchallenged. This book is to be used as a prime tool to destroy Jerks and jerky behavior. Start today. And never relax vigilance.

IT'S EVERYWHERE

I'll stress again that the scenarios described are quite common in large business corporations, mid and small sized businesses, professional practices in judicial, legal and medical organizations, local, state and federal governments and agencies, all branches of the military, schools and universities, and even religious organizations. The methods described in this book can be effectively applied to *all* of these workplace environments and many more. Jerks can and will be destroyed wherever they raise their ugly heads.

HISTORICAL PARALLELS

Students of history can find endless parallels between calamitous historical events and the jerky behavior of fools who were instrumental in triggering these episodes. This is important because a convincing linkage can be shown between the jerk at the office and the jerk who plunges nations into bloody unjust wars – this knowledge will help motivate you to wipe out small pools of jerkism before they can mushroom into something far worse.

Analyze any disaster in human history, and very often we find a jerk, or several jerks, were instrumental in orchestrating the event. Every evil and monstrous tyrant in human history also had the distinction of being a hard core jerk.

Joe Stalin immediately springs to mind. Cruel, brutal, dishonest, foolish, selfish, murderous, of course. But above all, *shameless . . .*

>   *"Stalin was gradually eliminating shame.*
>   *Fear is stronger than shame."*[11]

In the 70's, 80's and 90's the standard Indonesian saying was, "The Suhartos have everything . . . airlines, hotels, TV stations, companies . . . everything except a sense of shame."[12]

Every Hitler, Mao, Pol Pot, Kim Il Sung, Lenin, Pinochet, Somoza, Robespierre, Tojo, Mussolini, Michael Milikin, Mobutu, Henry Kissinger, Ceausescu, Oliver North, Chainsaw Al Dunlap, Milosevic, Jeffery Skilling, Ken Lay, *etc.,* was also a consummate jerk personality, who's lack of any sense of shame brought corruption, misery and/or death to hundreds of millions. Ditto for the thousands of faceless bureaucrats and party hacks and death squads and business associates who executed their slimy agendas.

All of these swine started out as piglets, mini-jerks, in some obscure organization. Too bad this book wasn't around then to put the kibosh on their sorry careers and pre-empt all the subsequent, unnecessary tragedy!!

> *"An evil at its birth is easily crushed, but it grows and strengthens by endurance."*[13]
>
>   Cicero

UNDERSTANDING THE NATURE OF EVIL

In order to more effectively employ the methodology presented in this book, it helps to acknowledge one inescapable fact: that Evil, represented by the 5% Jerks and 10% Enablers, is alive and powerful in the World, that it knows no boundaries, is unrestrained by any depths, is sickeningly amoral, and shows no mercy. If you understand this key reality, then it makes it very easy for you to resolve to help reduce and destroy evil, and evil people, in its lair, and to play such a resolute game of hardball that they are driven from your organization without remorse or pity.

THE UTTER DEPRAVITY OF EVIL

A few examples demonstrate the utter depravity the worst human elements are capable of. Executives in the tobacco industry in the United States are some of the worst scum imaginable, who for 60 years lied about the dangers of their product while tens of millions were poisoned by it and died. As a Congressional aide pointed out,

> *"The (tobacco) companies had evidence that their product killed people. They deceived Congress and the public about that evidence. They kept it completely hidden."*[14]

One of the "deepest secrets" of the tobacco industry for 30 years was the use of ammonia to boost levels of nicotine to the brain to compensate for lowering levels of tar. They needed the "free nicotine" produced to keep smokers addicted to cigarettes.[15] Recently it was proven in litigation what many had long suspected – that since 1985, tobacco companies have been desperately and systematically destroying thousands of documents that reveal their criminal and deliberate activities in "hooking" consumers into the deadliest habit of their lives.[16]

These flag waving, "God fearing" crooks in suits and ties, and the hundreds of slimy Congressmen they've bought off in Washington, have killed and are killing to this day, more people worldwide via painful, horrible cancerous death than Stalin and Mao ever did in all their nightmarish gulags. "There are about 1.2 billion smokers worldwide, half of whom will die prematurely from cancer, heart disease, emphysema or other smoking-related diseases, research has shown." That's 600 million people! The more legitimate studies that are made on cigarette smoking, the worse it's impacts are seen. In 2002, from the International Agency for Research on Cancer: "Tobacco smoke is even more cancerous than previously thought, for both smokers and non-smokers who breathe in the fumes, causing cancer in many more parts of the body than previously believed, a panel of specialists has concluded."[17]

Evil and abject corruption in certain people know no limitation – never forget this when dealing with any human jerk. (I'll interject to remind you that I believe this sick evil has a grip on only 5 to 15 % of the workforce. 80% are quite decent people, who refuse to prostitute their integrity and honor. Remember the percentages, I don't want you going all depressed on me! *We can do this."*).

JERKS, EVIL, & STUPIDITY – THE INSEPARABLE TRIUMVIRATE

Other amazing examples of the utter depravity of certain jerks are the numerous crimes committed against the public by the automobile industry. For 15 years, Ford withheld information and lied to the US Government and public about the heat-related failures of thick film ignition, TFI (a computerized ignition system attached to the engine's distributor) in it's automobiles, which caused cars to *completely quit running (!!)* in traffic, causing numerous injuries and deaths.

This is a classic tale of the gross stupidity of Jerks at Work. Conscientious Ford engineers for **years** argued in vain for a changed placement of the TFI so it wouldn't be exposed to so much heat. This was rejected by various jerky, criminal managers at Ford in the 1980's and early 1990's to save a few bucks. But Ford finally ended up spending billions and billions of dollars in the late 1990's to fix the problem and to settle lawsuits from all the maimed and mauled Ford customers, not to mention the suits filed by survivors of the dead.

Special Note:　　*Hello*, **see the message here?? Most Jerks I've known were also** *extremely stupid people.* **They bluster and they intimidate and they try to impress you that they're very clever, but they're just pathetic losers. This is important to grasp, because if you're aware of it, and play your cards carefully, it makes it that much easier to get rid of them.**

"Ford had engaged in a huge corporate cover-up, concealing from both regulators and consumers a design flaw affecting 22 million cars produced between 1983 and 1995, almost 15 million of which remain on the road."[18]

The more that's revealed about the inner working of Ford, the easier it is to understand why the Company continues to slide downhill . . .

　　"Michael E. Ballachey, the California Superior Court judge who ruled against Ford, blamed Ford for a corporate culture in which the ***careers of executives can be ruined*** *by reporting design defects to higher-ups."*[19] (author's emphasis)

More about workplace environments soon . . .

So the continued fiascos at Ford over the belated "recall of 6.5 million Firestone tires after dozens of deadly crashes involving Ford Explorers" should come as no surprise. Here's a Company completely saturated with amoral Jerks, through and through. Jerks and

evil and crass stupidity are an inseparable trio, hopelessly inter-
twined.

A WORLDWIDE PROBLEM

Just so you don't think I'm implying that massive evil is just
linked to the Lower 48, I'll give you a few reminders to illustrate the
presence of unmitigated evil worldwide.

The French have recently concluded a series of trials, which, to
their credit, dispels the myth that the Germans were the *sole* perpet-
rators of heinous crimes in Europe during World War II. It turns out
that a high-level French bureaucrat, Maurice Papon, sent 1,560 Jews,
including 223 children, to certain death to German Concentration
Camps from their homes near Bordeaux between 1942 to 1944. He
was only one of too many Frenchmen who gladly collaborated with
their Nazi overlords – this kowtowing to evil is an all too human
failing . . . in the same circumstances, I'm afraid many Americans,
Brits, Brazilians, *etc.,* would have disgraced themselves likewise.

This trial is especially interesting because it exposed the utter
banality that characterizes so much of the evil that jerks perpetrate,
and the seedy role that stupid, insipid, blind ambition plays. "Like
many French wartime bureaucrats, Papon was 'neither an anti-
Semite nor a xenophobe', said Marc-Oliver Baruch, a French
historian. Instead, he was an ambitious, well educated, and discreet
civil servant who was praised in a 1943 German report as 'an
administrative specialist, able and zealous, who works quickly and
gets to the bottom of things.'" [20] And, I might add, typical of all Jerks,
an amoral, soulless pimp destined and deserving to roast in the eternal
fires of Damnation in Hell.

> *The Evil that Men do gladly*
> *Astonish Lucifer himself.*
>
>   E.M. Fergusson, 2004

And to clearly demonstrate that mind boggling evil-doing is not
the sole province of Americans and Europeans, endless examples

emanating from the Third World demonstrate its unfortunate universality.

Due to some liberalization in China as a spin off of market reforms, Chinese journalists now feel bold enough to uncover festering scandals. Recently, a cabal of slimy mine operators in Nandan County of the Guangxi Region, in cahoots with some corrupt local Communist Party officials, desperately tried to cover up the deaths of at least 81 mine workers by drowning on July 17, 2001, when mine officials violated all safety procedures and negligently conducted blasting operations near manned mine shafts. This gang of murderers tried to cover up the facts that *any deaths occurred* at *all* by trying to bribe the families of the deceased into silence!![21]

The relatives were outraged, and brought in out of town reporters, who in turn were threatened by the cabal. After wide publicity, including web site postings, the Central Government finally stepped in, drained the mine shafts, discovered the "decomposed bodies of 78 miners"[21], and arrested all the culprits. The story is a great example of what can happen when decent people refuse to cave in to corrupt jerks, is a tribute to courageous investigative journalists, demonstrates the power of the Internet to let the cat out of the bag, and bodes well for the future of China. But it also does illustrate the depths of depravity Jerks will go to make an illegal buck and to cover up their slimy activities.

A year later, on June 22, 2002, a similar incident occurred in Shanxi Province, Fanzhi County, Yixingzhai village when a fire started in a gold mine. The workers asked to leave because of the danger but the mine operators ordered them to keep working. Explosives ignited, killing 38. The operators only admitted to 2 dead, and secretly hauled 36 bodies away in trucks, dumping them in local ravines. Again, these corrupt Jerks were only exposed when relatives of deceased miners, streaming into town from a poorer province to the south, refused to take hush money and demanded justice. The corrupt operators are currently on the run from the police. It is estimated that as many as 10,000 Chinese miners *a year* die in underground accidents![22]

Evil runs deep in the world, it is *everywhere*, and can only be overcome by courageous, good people willing to play smart and tough hardball.

EQUAL OPPORTUNITY JERKISM

Some politically correct folks won't like to hear this, but it needs to be said to clear the air. Jerkism and evil behaviors are not confined to the sole province of white American men over 40. There are many admirable female, asian, black, latino, young, progressive, and handicapped people in the world, but these various groups also exhibit their fair representation of terrible Jerks. Evil and Jerkism know no particular race, gender, age, or creed. And there's nothing worse than a Jerky person trying to hide their evildoing behind some kind of minority or "oppressed" status. It won't wash. Don't fall for it.

In order to effectively destroy jerkism, you need to understand just how deep evil runs in the world, the destruction it causes, and to summon the resolve to destroy it down to and including its *roots*. Ridding the workplace of a hardcore jerk is truly holy work, possibly one of the greatest contributions a good person can bestow upon society. *We count ourselves fortunate if a severe jerk at work situation never presents itself and we work in a blissful environment, but we consider it a high honor to successfully conduct a rid-a-jerk campaign if the situation warrants.*

You are the hammer, *Jihad the Jerk at Work* is the anvil.

WHAT'S YOUR BEEF??

We now arrive at the heart of this book. You've worked hard to keep a diary-style list of incidents/times-dates-places. It has tallied up to quite an impressive picture, I'm sure. And you notice certain behaviors repeated over and over. If you're lucky enough to have some discreet allies, their lists will probably tally closely with yours.

When I've composed these type of lists on hardcore jerks, I've always been struck by the incredible variety and depth . . . it's truly astounding!! Some of these guys (and gals) could keep an entire *firm* of psychiatrists busy for years, and half of the shrinks would probably go batty themselves trying to get a grasp on the idiot in question.

These people are poster boys for dysfunction, but we can't complain, because the sheer depth and breadth of the idiocy make it child's play to hang a "better get rid of this guy before he destroys my Company and my career" on the Jerk that any intelligent Director or VP can easily read and act on without hesitation.

Obviously, it's very central to the Complaint Package that's forwarded to higher to be thorough and fair in listing all the problems that this jerk manifests. No exaggerations necessary, just the facts, ma'm. The Jerk will give you *plenty* of rope to hang himself, as it is.

THE FUN BEGINS HERE

In the preprinted forms I've provided for your use (if you choose to use them, which I highly recommend) in this Chapter and in Chapter 6, I've laundry-listed some of the more common idiocies displayed by the classic jerk at work. You can merely check off those appropriate, add some juicy narrative details if you desire, and even add more faults to the list – have fun!!!

It gives your Complaint more *credibility* if the Director or boss or whomever can see that these behaviors are so commonplace that they can be listed on a preprinted form, as well as attached to an entire *book* on the subject (this one). You can also reference pages and passages in the attached book with yellow Post-It Notes to provide additional insight and credibility to the complaint. A Director might pooh-pooh a one-page handwritten complaint, but he has a hard time doing that, and even a harder time *losing*, a ten-page tome attached to an *entire book* on his desk!! Not to mention the fact that you're giving him a **30-day deadline** to resolve the Jerk problem intelligently, before the entire ball of wax finds its way to *his* boss's desk!!

A thorough fault list gives the Director substance to investigate. Some Directors may want to try the "counseling" approach with the Jerk, but by now most experienced Managers know that although this *may* work with younger, more malleable employees, the probability of success decreases as the jerk grows older and more set in his ways.

THE PEN IS MIGHTIER THAN THE SWORD

The important thing is that a deadly accurate picture is painted that can be verified by others in the organization, and that gives the Director the ammunition he needs to take appropriate action. I've also included sample filled-in forms in Chapter 6 that demonstrate **the power and impact that a well prepared Complaint can have**. Remember our example of the American Declaration of Independence discussed at the beginning of this chapter. Jefferson's lucid description of the King's abuses was so impressive, a large segment of the House of Commons openly expressed sympathy with the Colonies, and it's a matter of record that some respected English military officers refused commands in the British expeditionary forces sent to quell the rebellion. Some, like General Jeffrey Amherst, already had a high regard and respect for the Colonists from French & Indian War experience, but the brilliance of the Declaration of Independence reinforced their decision to opt out of **this** particular war. The pen is indeed mightier than the sword.

Below is a copy of the "Fault's List", which reflects a real-world snapshot of the behavior of Jerks at Work. Enjoy, I'm sure you'll see some all-too-familiar behaviors!! Remember, don't exaggerate or check off behaviors that do not honestly reflect the actual observed behavior of the Jerk in Question. Be rigorously fair and balanced. It may be a good idea to have your allied "shadow committee" agree on a list that is complete and accurate and appropriately indicting. Others may have deep, and thoroughly damning insights you may have missed. Note the convenient numeric tally of deficiencies that summarizes the severity of the Jerk's condition:

Inclosure 1 – **Observed Deficiencies Of** _____
Page 1
   (marked with an "x")

Deficiency Summary (check one) of _____

___ 1 –10 major deficiencies		= "Regular Jerk"
___ 11–20 " "		= "Major Jerk"
___ 21–35 " "		= "Hard-Core Jerk"
___ 36 and over "		= "Cosmic Jerk"

_____'s total score: _____

Basic Traits:

____ No sense of shame	____ A hypocrite
____ Displays poor judgment	____ Uncooperative
____ Shortsighted	____ Immature
____ Lacks intelligence, slow,	____ Manipulative
not bright	____ Lightweight
____ Devious	____ _____
____ Greedy	

Character / Performance:

    ____ A sycophant, an obsequious ____ Dodges
       toady   responsibility for own
                                                  actions
    ____ Solely concerned with superficial appearances to higher,
       unconcerned with substance
    ____ Is using position merely as stepping-stone to promotion,
       does not care about improving or strengthening his
       organization

____ a ticket-puncher	____ a cover-up artist
____ not loyal to own employees	____ cannot be trusted
____ has no respect for others	____ overambitious

Page 2 – **Observed Deficiencies of** _____

____ screws over own people and unfairly fawns over other organizations to gain brownie points

____ not a team player, loves to ____ cowardly politico
grandstand

____ no backbone, runs scared ____ counterproductive "change for change's sake"

____ addicted to irritating fads and meaningless corporate buzzwords

Interactions With Others:

____ Tries to intimidate and bully people

____ Extremely arrogant

____ Ill tempered

____ Loud

____ Rude, offensive personality

____ Arbitrary, unfair in dealings

____ Employs undeserved verbal abuse

____ Insults people regularly

____ Plays favorites

____ Doesn't bother to get both sides of the story

____ Is a bull in the china shop

____ Incapable of listening to criticism

____ Petty

____ Intemperate (lack of self control)

____ Mean-spirited

____ Vindictive

____ Has severe negative attitude

____ Inveterate back-stabber, slimy

____ Has "not invented here" syndrome

____ Excessive finger-pointing

____ Loves to "Shoot the Messenger"

____ Is verbally abusive to employees

____ Unstable; can be violent and dangerous

____ _____

Managerial Ability:

Page 3 – **Observed Deficiencies of** _____

_____ Ingratitude; does not recognize or reward good
        performance
_____ No filtering of unreasonable demands from higher,
        he actually amplifies it
_____ Does not provide constructive, meaningful counseling
        to employees
_____ Is a poor judge of character _____ Won't delegate tasks
_____ Is a micromanager, to   _____ No meaningful
        detriment of organization   communication
_____ Excessive meetings,   _____ Not respected by
        clumsy communications   employees
_____ Not respected by peers   _____ No positive vision
_____ Afraid to discipline misbehavior of employees; gutless,
        whimpy
_____ Generates meaningless busywork, wastes company time
_____ Does not care about   _____ Is despised by employees
        employees   _____ A danger to this
_____ Unfit to manage people   organization

Fundamental Character:
_____ Egocentric   _____ A moral coward
_____ Completely selfish   _____ No self discipline

Personality:
_____ Humorless   _____ Completely unhelpful
_____ Bizarre! Needs psychiatric   to others
        help   _____ Pompous
_____ Flaky   _____ Inbred

Integrity:
_____ Has no integrity, personal   _____ A brazen liar
        or professional

Page 4 – **Observed Deficiencies of** _____

_____ Is A fraud				_____ Leadership "façade"

Job Competence:

_____ Is incompetent			_____ Blunders with customers

Potential to Reform:
_____ Incapable of reforming self or improving

Impact on This Organization:
_____ Good people leaving the		_____ Has caused employee
department because of his		morale to plummet
actions
_____ Good people actually		_____ His behavior has caused
leaving the Company			employees to lose their
because of his actions			initiative
_____ Has generated huge		_____ People are now afraid to
dissatisfaction among			do their best
employees
_____ Has done harm to customer relations or business
_____ One of the worst managers we've ever seen
_____ Is the worst manager we've even seen

Rate _____ on a scale of ten (highest) to
one (lowest), comparing to peers: _____

Individual's performance in past jobs, if relevant:

_____
_____
_____

Page 5 – **Observed Deficiencies of** _____

_____

_____

Any Actual *Criminal* Behaviors Noticed:
_____ Can be violent and   _____ Physical abuse of
     dangerous   employees
_____ Venal (corruption)   _____ Sexual abuse of
  specify: _____   employees
_____ Engages in criminal activity
  specify: _____

Miscellaneous:
_____ Personal problems adversely impact job performance
_____ Disloyal to this organization
_____ Prejudiced against races or religions

Additional Problems Not Listed Above:

_____   _____
_____   _____
_____   _____

Other Comments:

_____
_____
_____

    This Form can be found on our website,
www.upublishing.com/forms.htm—just check off categories, add
comments if you desire, and "PRINT."

You get the idea – I'm sure you could easily expand this list tenfold. As long as it's a truthful and accurate picture of the Jerk In Question, definitely go ahead and wax poetic. The goal is to convince the Director or whomever you send the Complaint Package to **that this is a serious matter**, it's not just going to fade away, and that he has to take decisive action within 30 days or his own boss will be involved.

So why did I bother to include a check-off jerk faults list in the Chapter Six "Complaint Package"?? The same reason I have a generic "Letter to the Director" that just asks you just to fill in the blanks . . . one of the goals of this book is to present a fairly *easy* way to get rid of the jerk, *not have you try to reinvent the wheel and spend a lot of time on paperwork*. You can expend as little or as much effort as you desire.

HEAVY BAGGAGE

You'll undoubtedly recognize that a **lot** of these traits apply to your "Jerk." You may wonder if he has a twin brother out there, it's so uncanny. In fact, hard core jerks I've known possess *20 to 30* of these traits simultaneously – "Cosmic" Jerks can soar to 40 or more. It's a marvel they don't collapse in a heap just from the exertion of carrying all this baggage around.

So when you're ready to assemble your package, just check off the appropriate blocks on the "fault list" form in Chapter 6, add any pertinent comments, and you're well on your way.

LATE 20TH CENTURY EVOLUTION OF THE "COSMIC JERK"

There was a time when most organizations actually expressed embarrassment when rogue managers or employees engaged in jerk-like behaviors. This kind of boorish, "low class" activity was frowned upon and discouraged.

However, in the 1980's and 1990's, all this changed. Too many business and government organizations evolved into ultra-greedy, vicious entities that encouraged the "greed is good" mindset. This resulted in Enron, Arthur Anderson, the 9/11 blunders and cover-ups, the Priest pedophile scandals, Worldcom, *etc., etc., ad nauseum* . . . basically the meltdown of corporate America and society.

A major spinoff of this corrupt mindset was the nurturing and evolution of a new super-strain of hard-core Jerk, namely, the "Cosmic Jerk." Here was a abberation of Jerk so vicious and venal that it left the traditional hardcore jerk looking like a Boy Scout in comparison. Thus, in this book, when we speak of hard core jerks, realize that fully 30% of these are actually Cosmic Jerks of the very worst sort. If you tally up 35 or more deficiencies for your target jerk on the fault's list, you're definitely dealing with a Jerk of the Cosmic variety, and must insure he's run out of your organization pronto before he can destroy it. This disturbing snapshot can easily be conveyed to the Director via the fault's list tally.

A FEW POSITIVES DO NOT A JERK UNMAKE

One key thing to keep in mind: even the worst of Jerks may have some positive attributes, but if the negatives are so numerous and deep, don't be distracted. It's often a favorite tactic of that 10% group of fellow travelers / opportunists who tacitly or openly support hardcore jerks to say, "Oh, Barry may be an SOB, but he's just great in negotiations with customers", or some other weak defense. Once you've compiled your lists and determined that "the Jerk must go", don't get softened and be disarmed by quibbling minutia. Keep their feet to the fire until they're kicked out!! You must honestly ask yourself, "Will this place be better off if the Jerk is gone??" If in the affirmative, waste no time, don't second-guess, *launch the campaign* to rid this scourge from your organization.

ENVIRONMENTS WHERE JERKS THRIVE

There's always been the eternal debate on the causation of crime, malfeasance, and tyrannical behavior: what's the culprit, genetics or circumstance or environment?? It's always been obvious to me that raw DNA genetics has a huge influence, but it's also undeniable that environment plays a major role.

NO RESTRAINTS SPELL T R O U B L E

Far and away the largest environmental problem that breed major jerkism is the one where bizarre and excessive behaviors of jerks are *not mitigated in any way by superiors, peers, or subordinates.* This occurs far too frequently, and is just an *unacceptable failure of weak management* – and this is why this book had to be written!! No one ever "calls" the Jerk on his flaky behavior, and there is even encouragement from higher because the jerk seems to "get things done."

In these type of terrible organizational environments, fear rapidly takes over, and it's a slippery downhill slope from there on. Decent people of integrity are quickly destroyed in this bottomless cesspool. Just look at Enron, and Sunbeam under Chainsaw Al Dunlap and the Diocese of Springfield Massachusetts, where the decent Parish Priest of Amherst, Mass, the Rev. Bruce Teague, was fired in 1997 for trying to protect his Parish children from a visiting, *convicted* pedophile Priest, the notorious Rev. Richard Lavinge. Naturally, the *good* priest got severely *punished* by the Hierarchy and the criminal priest was protected and kept on the payroll, the *modus operandi* of the Catholic Church,[23] as well as too many other organizations. **"No good deed goes unpunished"!!!**

The whole thrust of this book is to confront this type of morass before it gets to an Enronesque critical mass, and smash it with the light of reason and truth. Jerks must be rooted out and obliterated, one by one. Then, vigilance must be eternal – you can never allow your organization to creep back into this abyss.

Many factors, besides the obvious genetic aberrations of the jerk himself, can contribute to the enabling of jerkism. Difficult business environments, overwork, "overachievement" hype, family problems at home, workaholics with no other life, basic greed, poor or nonexistent checks and balances, **no genuine upward feedback program** (see Chapter 9), and upper management negligence in detecting obvious problems. But none of it excuses disgusting, jerky behavior – thus our standing orders to be ruthless in stamping it out before it destroys the host organization and its people, are sacrosanct.

Various corporate situations contribute. One chronic problem in many organizations is stagnation / inbreeding. This can be seen most clearly in large organizations that have little turnover or new blood in and out. Like a stagnant pond, a corporate culture evolves that's so bizarre and counterproductive, it astonishes the small number of new folks who enter the organization.

STAGNANT ORGANIZATIONS

I had the opportunity to experience this firsthand in one large corporation I joined. First of all, the place was so stagnant, people were amazed to even meet a mid-level "new hire." "We haven't hired anybody new in 15 years" was one comment I actually heard. You could almost feel the cobwebs brushing against your face as you walked through the place. Some of the company "cultural" customs were stifling and obviously counterproductive. Needless to say, the weird varieties of jerks incubated in this mouldy hothouse stretched the credulity of the imagination.

Fortunately, due to market factors and technology breakthroughs, this technical company started experiencing huge growth, and many new hires soon after my arrival made it easier to effect positive changes. Also, the stagnated culture and high density of jerks mentioned above engaging in mutually destructive, mindless battles made it obvious to even the densest of senior managers that constructive changes had to be made, and made quickly, if they didn't want to continue to lose top talent to competitors. They even instituted a very effective (although short-lived . . . see Chapter 9 for more) Upward Feedback program. But it took them five years to improve a messy situation that *application of this book in force could have much better resolved in six months.*

As it was, many of the newest employees were floored and upset by some of the more archaic and idiotic corporate customs, and were vocal about it. This emboldened even older employees to agree and speak up. Senior management then made a serious attempt to understand the discontent, and to the company's credit, many positive changes were made, if for no other reason to attract and retain valuable employees necessary to sustain growth. But they never managed to really clean house and sharpen up the organization to encourage peak personal performance – the influence of cultural stagnation and the pervasive grip of Jerks was still too strong.

YOUNG FOOLS, OLD FOOLS

The question also arises: Where is the most jerky behavior manifested? In older established employees and managers, or in organizations that are in the throes of explosive growth with relatively young and inexperienced people being given rapid promotions?

I've seen that jerkism can arise *anywhere*, in almost any situation. In the latter category, with young folks in their 20's being promoted to manager, director, and even VP with large responsibility being thrust on the relatively inexperienced, ripe opportunities for major managerial errors and blunders are created, especially if blind ambition further clouds the judgment of immature minds. The parallel turbulence of new markets and rapidly evolving organizations can act as a force multiplier to the destructive impact of unrestrained Jerky behaviors. Some of the resulting aberrations are worthy of books, non-fiction and fiction, unto themselves (for now you'll have to settle for some of the astounding tales found in Chapters 3 and 4).

There's no substitute for thoughtful, calm, decent, intelligent attributes of the experienced manager. But it seems the flashy, self-promoting types often get promoted over these better kinds, which may seem like a good short term fix for desperate CEO's, but too often backfires in the long run.

In any case, the application of this book by employees disgusted with the high-jinks of adolescent "managers" is an excellent way to put the brakes on this type of short-sighted judgment of senior managers who ought to know better, a sharp reminder to them to more carefully consider whom they tap for greater responsibility.

THERE'S NO FOOL LIKE AN OLD FOOL

But lest I stand accused of blind prejudice towards up and coming twenty-somethings, I'll hasten to add that jerkism can also be deeply ingrained in older managers, 40 to 50 to 60 years old, who should know better, but have fallen into very bad managerial habits that seat them firmly in the "maximo jerko" camp. Again, mature age is no defense, they must be ruthlessly rooted out before they can continue to hopelessly corrupt the organization. As we've previously pointed out, there are just too many excellent managers and potential managers floating about as replacement candidates to tolerate retention of Jerks in positions of responsibility, or in *any* position, for that matter.

Bottom line is, seriously jerky behavior knows no particular age, race, gender, pay level, nationality. It can and will pop up anywhere, and must be aggressively rooted out. There are ten excellent, decent candidates to replace each jerk that's deservedly removed – there's no reason to delay.

TURN DEAD-ENDS INTO THRU STREETS

Another "hothouse" work atmosphere that enables jerkism to spread like the bubonic plague are organizations and career fields that are *dead-ends and have no visible alternative career "outs."* Most of the business world is spared this through the dynamics of competition, headhunters, and ambitious companies vying for talented employees – this deadly problem is found most often in monopolistic entities like government and the military (and in some cases, academia and hierarchical churches) and is covered in Chapters 10–12 with suggestions of injecting alternate career options to loosen this deadly systemic institutional logjam.

THE MAGIC THREE

To review, there are only three effective ways to mitigate and destroy jerkism: 1) effective HR Upward Feedback programs. 2) this book and its methodology (by far the quickest and most powerful antidote to jerkism). 3) in dead-end government, military, and monopolistic organizations, ensuring that employees are trained in an "alternate civilian career" program that creates a dynamic "Israeli Defense Force" type atmosphere.

FAÇADES JERKS ERECT – GAMES JERKS PLAY

This little section has two objectives. By alerting you to some of the typical tactics employed by Jerks: 1) you can confirm your suspicions (if the 100 "Observed Deficiencies" characteristics we just listed are not enough!!) and 2) you can employ countermeasures to shield yourself from the sick games jerks play to try to intimidate people, so you can safely get on with the urgent business of ridding this cancerous wart from your workplace posthaste.

I'll start by asking a rather odd question – you'll quickly come to understand why it's so central to the issue. That is, "Do jerks have any self-awareness, do they actually *know* they are Jerks, what a pox they are on decent humankind???"

You may quickly answer, "No, how could they, how could they *stand* themselves if they really knew??" This may be somewhat true for younger jerks I've known, in their 20's, blinded by all sorts of self-delusion and bizarre world-outlooks. But I'm convinced by the time jerks reach their 30's and 40's and 50's it dawns on them, to some degree, just how screwed up they are, and how they're loathed by the 80% of humankind I label "decent folk."

DEEPENING PARANOIA

And since they're genetically programmed as hard core jerks, with dozens and dozens of glaring, deep-rooted personality defects, as they grow older their paranoia deepens . . . as well it should (!) since as more and more people come to despise them, they become a much larger target. They also become much more dangerous . . . they'll swiftly strike out in revenge, often violently, to any perceived threat, real or not. They know well just how flaky they are, and how vulnerable they are.

In fact, I've seen evidence that many jerks are surprised at how much they can get away with by intimidation and playing on people's fears. They are actually amazed that normal people suffer under their obnoxious behavior, as Thomas Jefferson well understood, without complaint, for as long as they do.

PROCEED CAREFULLY IN A DANGER ZONE

This is why I admonish those undertaking the destruction of these cankers to keep a low profile, to *very* carefully gather powerful allies, to choose the complaint package recipient judiciously (as one who has the power and the guts to fire, or get rid of, the Jerk), to submit the complaint package *anonymously*, and to play a very ruthless game of **hardball**: giving the jerk's boss a *fixed amount of time* (usually 30 days) to get *rid* of the scourge, or have identical complaint packages bounced up to *his* VP boss as well as to the VP of Human Resources. And, you must be well prepared to ratchet it up to the CEO and Board of Director level. Once this process starts, do not expect and do not grant *any quarter* at all. Eliminate the Jerk, and do it *ruthlessly* and *swiftly*. The chances are high that you and your decent allies will win. Evil is real, it's powerful, it's out there, it must be dealt with without pity or remorse. Evil is truly vulnerable, it can be trounced.

JERKS IN QUICKSAND

As I've mentioned before, one of the unexpected side benefits of using the methodology described in this book is that often, when the jerk realizes he's been exposed, and his boss vainly tries to counsel him to be more moderate and reasonable, **he'll do exactly the opposite!!** He'll start lashing out at any and every thing – he does us the kind favor of hanging himself.

I saw this graphically illustrated in one company I worked for when a committee I helped form submitted a complaint to a Jerk's boss. The Jerk in Question was grossly and tyrannically mismanaging his employees, persecuting some unmercifully (one, we deeply suspect, because he was a Muslim). After the Director counseled the Jerk, the latter flew into a rage and really started ranting at the poor Muslim guy, who, after informing the Committee exactly what was going on, in turn directly complained to the Director!!

The Director commented to a valued Committee Member (the Director did *not* know she was a committee member) in another geographical location 1,000 miles away, "It's not working out for "Ralph" (the jerk), is it??" To which she understatedly replied, "No, Paul, it's not." Note the value of cunning, well informed, strong allies, anonymous, far and wide, with their ears to ground, and ready to weigh in at decisive moments!! **Patient preparation and planning always pay off.** From that moment, the Jerk was *doomed*, his days numbered. Soon the Jerk was transferred out – he did *not* get his expected promotion, his wings were severely clipped, his career in that company was in deep trouble. If we had *not* acted to expose him, he had been blowing so much smoke that he might well have been *promoted* and taken over our very Department!! *Fate favors those who ACT, not those who cower and whine.*

So sometimes all that's needed is a stiff breeze to cause the rotting structure (the Jerk) to come crashing to earth. Jerks inherently are unstable people. All that may be required is a little nudge to propel them over the edge. Nudge away, don't delay. "Time Wounds all Heels" they say, but why not fast forward it a bit and obliterate the bastard now???

OSCAR NOMINEES . . . FAÇADE FRENZY

Never underestimate the extent some jerks will exert to erect a false image of themselves as a really great and caring person. The hypocrisy and pretense exuded by many Jerks would draw breathless admiration from the slickest of Hollywood actors.

Jerks love to put up a Big Front. I'm reminded of one of the biggest Cosmic Jerks I've ever known (who was also engaged in crassly criminal conduct, and got caught in the act) who was arrogant, loud, boastful, deceitful, and totally cynical and abusive of his employees. In his office, on his desk was a prominent sign proclaiming "I'm Their Leader – Now Which Way Did They Go? " – the idea was to project how wonderfully modest he was, how he humbly admired his employees' proactive initiative and willingness to get the job done with little direction from the Great Man. Of course, this was all a farce – he was infamous for brutalizing decent people, and had not a shred of personal or professional integrity, among 50 other gross faults one could check off on the "List." It truly made his employees nauseous to have to look at his sign every time they entered this fraud's office.

Another incredible Cosmic Jerk I knew had a sign on *his* desk that admonished those blessed with entrance to his office to "Spend each day as if it's the most important day of your life" or some such lofty sentiment. This guy was a notorious pinhead whose callous, stunningly selfish mismanagement ran a good organization into the ground.

The lengths jerks will go to erect a smokescreen cloaking their true selves is breathtaking – although the façade does indeed come crashing down once the Complaint Package hits their boss's desk, bless the day.

TRUTH BE SWEET, SWEETER STILL ITS REVELATION

Jerks also are fond of cloaking themselves in an aura of success, corporate buzzwords, and anything that apes their boss's latest pearls of wisdom. Also, to Jerks, substance takes a *remote* back seat to image, the smokescreen of "progress" at the expense of substance. Image and illusion are everything – **they expect to move onward and upward to higher posts before the reality of their ineffectiveness can catch up to them in their lowly present job.** Of course, this Ponzi Scheme eventually collapses, often destroying the organization that has been duped by it. Enron, Sunbeam, Global Crossing, and Worldcom are but a few examples. What decent people can do, with this book, is to expose this game, stop Jerks in their tracks, clip their wings, and blow them out of the water *now* before they can do further damage.

GAMES GALORE

I can think of three favorite tactics jerks use to try to keep decent people off balance and to protect their corrupt tenure. First, they'll employ psychological tricks to try to unnerve people. They enjoy *intimidation and ridicule*, to make good people doubt their own self worth. Jerks are so insecure, they can only take pleasure at making others feel even more insecure. Don't let it faze you, better yet, don't make yourself a target.

In his article on "How To Handle a Toxic Boss" for the British magazine *XL*, Chris Dunkerley sums it up precisely:

> *"Why does the pit bull boss bully? . . . Tim Field of the National Workplace Bullying Advice Line says,* **'The purpose of bullying is to hide inadequacy.** *Good managers manage, bad managers bully. Bullying is an admission of inadequacy, and bullies bully in proportion to their inadequacy. They project their inadequacy on to others to avoid facing up to it themselves, or to divert attention from it. In an insecure workplace, this is how inadequate and incompetent people keep their jobs.' Got it?"*[24] (my emphasis)

Secondly, I've seen some jerks attempt to use a twisted kind of humor to make themselves untouchable. One manager I knew used glowing self-depreciating humor in which she described how she "sucked up (*i.e.,* fawned over)" to those in power to get ahead. This fell really flat with her employees because she was describing *exactly* what she really did and why. She was widely known as solely concerned about immediate image. Real substance was of no concern. Her employees were not amused or deceived, and she was widely detested in the corporation as being a hollow, unethical, untrustworthy ticket-puncher. Was it pure coincidence that this person's meteoric rise to the highest positions in this corporation was followed shortly thereafter by one the fastest and greatest loss of stock value (over $20 billion), by that very corporation, in the *recorded history of business*?? We think **not**.

Thirdly, insecure jerks are infamous for their casual use of hyperbole and exaggeration as a tool to eliminate perceived threats, such as "Well, I've never seen anything like this in 20 years." Don't fall for it, they use this line like a broken record to intimidate decent people.

There are many more such games, but you get the idea. Again, the best defense is, don't become a target. Launch quietly and anonymously, gather strong and reliable allies, play hardball, and get it over with in 30 days or less, if possible.

We now cover a few more aspects of the traits and characteristics of jerks before we close this key "know thine enemy" chapter.

CAN A JERK BE REFORMED??

Can a jerk be reformed, or reform himself? Can he be counseled, and then do a sincere about face, never to revert to his idiotic ways?? I'd like to say yes – certainly, I've seen a few people in their 20's change immature behavior and "grow up" after being strongly disciplined by perceptive senior managers.

However, once people enter their 30's, they become more set in their mold – they are who they are who they are. And considering the large number of faults the typical "5 %" hardcore jerk is plagued with, I've seen little evidence that jerks can actually be reformed and return to the fold of decent humanity. They're too far gone, too corrupted, moral wrecks – the hurdle is just too high to scale.

Regrettably, what I've seen repeatedly is that **"the Leopard does not change his spots."** This is why a Director who chooses to use the 30-day deadline period to try to "counsel and reform" the Jerk is taking a *very* risky path that may be harmful to his own career, with a second wave of complaint packets landing on the desks of several VP's above him. "Born a Jerk, die a Jerk."

If presented with a truthful, strong case on a Jerk, the Director is usually far better off just getting rid of him altogether (ideally, booting him out of the Company rather than foisting his problem child off on some other unsuspecting Department – however, transfers seem to be the most common response of spineless Directors. At least *you* don't have to put up with him anymore! And with this book, it's a easy matter to conduct a simple "pursuit" to his next Department, and get him booted out of the Company there . . . see Chapter 5, "Advanced Jerkbusting Operations").

ANY JERKS TUNED IN??

To any certified jerks who accidentally stumble on to this book: if one truly desires to reform, sincere humility and a real sense of shame are good places to start. I'm not a Catholic, but the Church stumbled on to a great idea when it set up the first Confessional. The odds of one's actual reformation are slim, but go for it anyway. Again, I would strongly recommend Ken Lloyd's thoughtful book, *Jerks At Work*, for intelligent discussions of the many aspects of stupid behaviors at work and how to correct them.

Here's another powerful motivation for all hard core Jerks: if one doesn't reform their dysfunctional ways soon, chances are high the offending party will be "booked" in the near future by this publication, and can contemplate his stupidity and miserable existence whilst pumping gas in sub-zero temperatures for a living.

THE WORK PERFORMANCE OF JERKS

It's true that often jerks are hard-working and ambitious, and many are known to "get results." Does this mean their work performance is superior to the "decent 80%"?? If one factors in the incredible damage done to the corporate fabric by the typical unethical, arrogant, shameless, selfish, shortsighted hard core jerk, the answer is a re-sounding, no-brainer " NO!" The damage done to the organization as good irreplaceable people flee to competitors, and bonds of trust are shredded, is incalculable. "Chainsaw Al" Dunlap ran up impressive inflated earnings at Sunbeam in the 90's as he fired 1000's of dedicated staff. Then the entire Company collapsed. Jeffrey Skilling ran Enron into the ground before he plundered it and jumped ship. Jerks bring only chaos and disaster to organizations – get rid of them asap!!!

PERSONAL LIVES A MESS

This is a really sensitive and explosive topic, but it's advisable to be aware of it, nonetheless. Often, not only is the work life of a jerk reprehensible and disastrous, but also his/her *personal* life is a real mess. Can we really be surprised?? If someone is so screwed up that an ad hoc committee can list 3 dozen serious faults manifested daily at work, can we actually believe this guy undergoes a magical transformation as he passes the guard's desk and exits the building, and turns into a loving stand-up spouse who lives an exemplary home life?? Don't think so.

Very unlikely – in fact, personal lives of jerks are often a train wreck in progress: divorces, assaults, child problems, instability, abuse . . . the domestic "faults" list, just like the "work faults list", can be bottomless. I knew of one jerky person at work, a rather strange twenty-something "shooting star", who was infamous for his bizarre personal life – at one dramatic point, one of his jilted girlfriends actually tried to *kill* him (unsuccessfully). Believe me, she had no idea of the immense favor done her by parting from this clown.

The ruthlessly work-blind ambitious can be quite callous about slighting the welfare of their own family – some of the scenes I've witnessed are so sad, I will not relate them here.

It's rather amusing to see arrogant, aggressive managers preaching values and objectives to their worker bees, when it's widely known their own personal lives are a disaster. Reminds me of the 1970's-era song " . . . he can't even run his own life, I'll be damned if he'll run mi . . i . . i . . ine . . . "

SPOUSES FROM HELL

Especially amazing, and perversely quite humorous is some insight into the spouses of the typical hard-core jerk. No surprise, they often tend to be incredibly hardcore jerks themselves, with their own baggage train a mile long. Truly, these people richly deserve one another, and these marriages from Hell are often doomed from day one. The resulting messy divorce is hardly a surprise. Of course the real victims are the children of such unions, whose early lives can hardly be imagined. But we must remember that even good people can get into difficult and even tragic home situations, and our purpose here is not to gloat, only to be aware.

SO WHY DO WE CARE?

So why is this even important? Why do we care? Well, first of all, a highly unstable home life can make any employee a danger to his co-workers and company – there's many a tale of folks who have snapped at work due to home pressures. The danger becomes magnified when this person is a hard core jerk, and even worse if he's at any level of management.

YEP, WE'RE PLAY'N HARDBALL

If you and your action committee are targeting such a person, it can be advantageous to pick up this kind of knowledge, if it's handled properly. It may sound callous, but if the personal-life-disaster info is very credible, and it clearly is a factor in the jerk's work performance, you may decide to include this information in your complaint package. After all, this jerk *is* making your life, and the lives of many others, miserable. Sharing this with "the Director" can speed his resolve to remove the jerk from the workplace. In fact, it often adds a panicky twist to his already terror-stricken reaction to the Complaint Package. You may be doing the Jerk in Question a big favor if all this results in his getting serious psychiatric care, or marriage counseling, if it's obvious these things could help him wherever he ends up next.

After all, our first goal is the dramatic improvement of the workplace environment by getting rid of obnoxious jerks. If they also end up getting much needed counseling as a consequence which ends up making them a better person (don't hold your breath!!), so much the better. Frankly, after seeing the sickening damage these callous people have inflicted, and the careers and lives of decent folk they've ruined, I'd just as soon see the bastards fired and dumped on the street – but work situations do tend to vary, so we sometimes must be flexible and reasonable in this regard.

THE PLUS SIDE TO JERKISM

Now, as we draw to a close on this chapter on the traits and characteristics of Jerks, we feel confident we have a better understanding of the evil we face, which gives us much better odds in smashing its stranglehold on the workplace. Jerkism casts a dark cloud on human existence, and its demise, or at least sharp curtailment, is long overdue and will be roundly applauded by decent people everywhere.

There is one paradox, however, about the existence of deep-rooted jerkism. It's not entirely a negative story. Think about it . . . if we didn't have knowledge of the utter depravity all too many humans are capable of descending into, could one ever be as appreciative of the "decent 80%", those employees and managers and Directors and Vice Presidents who courageously refuse to sink to low levels of Jerkism, who struggle (their personal *Jihad*) to maintain their integrity, their quiet competence, their basic goodness despite all the pressures and temptations of power in the modern workplace?? Probably not.

Our awareness of the bottomless depths of Jerkism makes us treasure even more decent people in society. We value them more, we admire them more, we feel blessed and enriched by them. It grants to life itself that much more depth and sacredness. I suppose we've bumped into yet another example of the ancient Buddhist concept of Yin and Yang . . . if pure evil didn't exist, then neither could unadulterated good.

We still maintain, however, that jerks and the evil they perpetrate have grown *far too powerful*, and that it's high time to greatly diminish their awful influence, if not outright domination of the workplace. This brooding Yin needs to be countered by the enlightened Yang. *Let's begin our work now, let's Yang'em, and be rigorous about it.* This is a sacred Crusade, an admirable Jihad, that is unstoppable and just. There, we've invoked three of the World's major religions in the last two paragraphs – that ought to earn our Campaign some well-deserved blessings by the Almighty, His Prophets and Scholars, enough to send Lucifer "slouching back to Hell."

Chapter Three –
Consequences of Jerkism
Unrestrained

"By the way, just in the event you do not know, let me furnish you the Websters definition of 'careerism – the policy or practice of advancing one's career, often at the cost of one's integrity.' Maybe that sums up the whole problem."[1]

> FBI Agent Colleen Rowley, in her bombshell May 2002 Memo to FBI Director Robert Mueller and the US Congress exposing the FBI's 9/11 blunders and attempted cover up of those blunders.

THE DEVASTATING IMPACT OF JERKS RAMPANT

I've mentioned the excellent work of syndicated columnist Dr Ken Lloyd, who has commented that one of the biggest surprises he's seen in 20 years of dealing with Questions & Answers on jobrelated problems is the large percentage of complaints relating to "Jerks at Work." In his 1999 book, *Jerks At Work*, Ken reminds us of just how huge the negative impact is of Jerks on the Workplace:

*One properly placed jerk at virtually any level of an organization can be linked to a **vast array of problems** that include leadership ineptitude, widespread unfairness, abysmal teamwork, resistance to change, twisted feedback, conflict escalation, pointless meetings, communication breakdowns, employee stagnation, muddled decision-making,* *inequitable rewards, staff rebelliousness, and a very uncomfortable environment. And, as the number of jerks increase, so increase the number of problems . . .*

. . . As tough as work is, particularly in light of the long and arduous hours that men and women are now putting into their jobs, **work can be turned into sheer torture** *by the presence of just one jerk. Even sadder is the fact that many organizations and even many departments would rejoice if they only had one jerk.*"[2]   (my emphasis added)

HOLY COW -- NIGHTMARISH HEALTH CONSEQUENCES OF JERKISM FINALLY REVEALED

Dr. Lloyd hits the nail on the head when he equates the impact of Jerks as "sheer torture" to decent employees – after 25 years of receiving thousands of complaints nationwide he's well equipped to hone in on the reality. The "sheer torture" creates massive amounts of unnecessary, counterproductive, debilitating stress on decent employees – and as we'll shortly see, *recent major medical studies* have conclusively proved that this abnormal, **prolonged "chronic stress" causes or contributes significantly to a whole host of serious medical problems and emergencies, to include "heart disease, rapid aging, depression, rheumatoid arthritis, diabetes, high blood pressure, hardening of arteries, damaged blood vessels in heart and brain, increased vulnerability to diseases & strokes & infections, inhibition of the immune system, serious damage to brain nerves that control memory, and mental disorders."** [3]

Jeez Louise.

Reuters has just reported that a major medical study (by the Medical College of Wisconsin and the University of South Carolina) has confirmed that hypertension rates (high blood pressure) in the US increased dramatically in the 1990's. Certainly some of the increase was due to increasing obesity rates, but it would not surprise me if a lot of the increase was due to the increased activities of Jerks at Work.

Almost one in three US adults had high blood pressure at the end of the last decade, reversing a downward trend and raising another warning flag about American's health, researchers said yesterday.

The prevalence of high blood pressure, which is a major risk factor for cardiovascular disease, rose to 29% among adults, up 4% since the last survey in 1988–1991 . . . [4]

To cut to the chase: employees and hapless managers in organizations that negligently tolerate and "suffer jerks gladly" **pay a grievous price, a price *far too high* to humanly bear.** We must end the madness.

In this chapter, we'll drive this theme home – for in order to possess the burning desire that can readily see an EAJ Campaign *all the way* through to unconditional triumph, it's helpful to have a fire-tempered motivational perspective that extends beyond one's immediate horizon.

THE SPREADING STAIN

What is the dynamic when a "Jerk at Work" is *not* resisted or challenged in any effective way, shape, or form??? Simply the dynamic of disaster piled upon catastrophe. It's a domino effect of decay and rot, that can spread so fast that an organization can be ruined within *months*, not years.

In one company I worked in, my boss was well-known as a ticket-punching self promoter, a lightweight whose byword was "form over substance." As "Lucy" moved up the corporate ladder, she infected each organization she took over with the same cancer. Managers of her departments who once gladly and intelligently cooperated with engineers suddenly became gun-shy and obsessed with covering their behinds. The climate of showmanship, which was her trademark, choked off the teamwork which for many years had been the towering strength of the Corporation. Suddenly, top talent could not *wait* to bail out of this stagnant, dead-end company. Naturally, with the best and brightest departing, contracts were lost and profits plummeted, posting $29 *billion* in losses within 3 years. A once-mighty company, a legendary institution famed worldwide, lost 95% of its market value, and had to lay off 71% of its workforce in two years.

POWER OF EXAMPLE

The best way to clearly see the damage that hard-core jerks inflict on organizations is to look at various snapshots of Jerks at Work and the massive damage they do, destroying the motivation of one employee at a time, rending the fabric of trust and teamwork into a pile of shreds.

In my group at "Wiretech", we were blessed with dozens of superb engineers. One of the very best, "Fred" worked for us way out West, and eventually ended up working for a different department in the Company that acquired jurisdiction there, but I kept close contact with him for years afterward.

He continued to have many dealings with the departmental group which my former "Lightweight" boss took over in her relentless rise to the top, which led to its eventual oblivion. What had been a top performing group, with unshakable standards, admirable initiative, and proud morale rapidly morphed into a sniveling, groveling nest of ineffective sycophants. "Fred" called a product manager during the "Lucyized" era to get some information on customers – in the past he'd worked closely and effectively with PM's to nail down lucrative contracts.

"What are you calling me for?" whined the PM, obviously infected with "Lucy" disease. Fred was stunned. Soon after, another shaky PM accused Fred of "panicking" on a conference call. Fred just had a cold, but the PM was so paranoid, she flipped out. Thanks to Lucy's gross incompetence and foolishness, an entire Department went down the tubes, and quickly, dragging the entire Company with it.

Fred couldn't believe this nonsense was coming from people who were supposed to be the brains and driving force behind the corporation, and resigned in disgust. In our Western locations, as elsewhere, customer and engineering relations unraveled soon after, and we lost huge contracts to savvier competitors. As we've already observed,

"Jerks are bad for business – it's that simple."

MORE FALLOUT

A contemporary of "Lucy", "Pat", was another example of what occurs to organizations when Jerks go unchallenged. He also rose rapidly in rank and created an entire Department known for it's bad attitude, surliness, and general ineptness. He was a driving force in killing off one of the few good things the Company had going for it, an effective Upward Feedback program, which he didn't like because it clued him in to the fact he was increasingly considered to be a boorish prima donna by large numbers of his employees!! Hey, if you don't like the Message, just vaporize the Medium.

"Pat" was a big promoter of one of the most insane, idiotic "counseling" systems I saw in 30 years, a "cascading objectives" approach, which was so stupid and superficial that several good project managers left the Company to get relief from the madness.

THE CALCULATED DESTRUCTION OF TEAMWORK

But the collapse of an organization can be precipitated from other sources than higher management. In one company I worked for, a low-level manager in a group close to mine created such a paranoid atmosphere that ordinarily competent engineers who would once gladly share information to solve technical problems in multiple locations suddenly "clammed up" and refused to interact for fear of alienating their moron boss, who didn't want "his" people "contaminated" by contact with "alien" groups. Such counterproductive, destructive paranoia is a sure tip-off that a hardcore jerk is operating at full tilt.

THE BOTTOMLESS PIT OF JERKISM

The incompetence of Jerks can often lead to massive waste and profit loss. In one company a good friend of mine, "Ben", worked for, one piece of equipment was failing in the field at an alarming rate – in fact, the Company was replacing, *for free*, 100% of Customer's stocks, just so their complaints wouldn't reach the ears of it's own VP! A design change was clearly called for, and fast.

However, this turkey piece of equipment was the brainchild of a powerful executive in the company, "Vince", who also happened to be a Mega-Jerk of the Omega (Cosmic) Class. He had convinced the VP to buy off on this terrible design, provided by a shady "low bidder." Ego-driven Vince, and his idiot sycophant henchman "Marv", couldn't tolerate *anyone* questioning their Holy Infallibility.

After huge and unnecessary infighting, the Company finally admitted to itself that the design of this equipment was indeed a catastrophe, and that it had to be replaced. But Vince the Jerk never forgot the role my friend Ben played, and clearly planned to "get even" one day. That he did, as Jerks always do, **if you allow them to survive**.

Even after the decision to change designs was made, "Vince" and "Marv" dragged their feet so stupidly that a whole batch, a year's worth (!), of the old worthless equipment was ordered, even though they well knew it would be scrapped, at huge cost to their own company. Meanwhile the new equipment arrived on time and was a major success, with rave reviews from Customers. In fact, within six months of being received by customers, this equipment played a major role in saving the lives of hundreds of people – had the original flaky design not been replaced, serious disasters would have occurred.

"Ben", the hero of the tale, never got any credit for his courageous action. In fact, several years later, Vince, the mega-jerk, got Ben fired on trumped up, false charges. The moral of this (true) story is that if Jerks are not destroyed posthaste, they **will** in turn destroy good people, and eventually the very company they work for!!

THE GHOST OF CHRISTMAS FUTURE

In fact, if you really want your Director (or the Jerk's boss, whoever he may be) to **experience the ultimate Scrooge-like revelation of the consequences of failing to get rid of the Cosmic Jerk** who's screwing up your organization, *make sure he reads* the following startling e-mail, forwarded to me by a high-ranking executive in a very large corporation. This close friend thought I'd be interested in the scenario which resulted in his company's loss of a billion dollar contract because the Senior Manager of the proposal team was an abysmal leader and a chronic Jerk who was detested by anyone coming in contact with him. Here's a classic example of the damage Jerks do to their own organizations.

Note that this is a *real* company and an *actual* event. I've changed all the dates and names of people & companies to protect the guilty, but the bulk of the e-mail is exactly as received. Unfortunately, the folks who had to tolerate this Chuck Heydrich moron for the past 25 years didn't have a copy of *Jihad the Jerk at Work*, otherwise his sorry career could have been terminated long ago. But all this is about to change:

ENTERING DISASTER ZONE
(ACTUAL CORPORATE-DISASTER E-MAIL)

Subj:	**Thanks for the "Complacentitis" Briefing Last Night!**
Date:	10/13/2003 10:46:17 AM Central Daylight Time
From:	JOSH.K.PERKINS@disksoft.com (Perkins, Joshua K.)
To:	marksd@US-Wheaton.mail.disksoft.com (Marks, David S. ll)

Dave,

As one of those on the Hagerstein Group's proposal team for the Central Electric Upgrade (CEU) contract, I enjoyed your interesting (and often scary) briefing, "Don't Catch Complacentitis" last night. Thank you for your efforts to steer us clear of the dangers of complacency and focus us on the things we need to do to win this important contract for Disksoft against our competition.

As a former member of the Software Upgrade Group, *aka* the Heydrich Group, I was most interested in your frank comments about why Disksoft / Laserlite lost the North-corp Contract competition. I was not surprised when you mentioned that they had lost this contract well before the RFP even came out because of problems in keeping the team together under Disksoft as the prime and Chuck Heydrich angering key subs like Cabletran and SIPA with his arrogance, *etc*. I admit I was surprised by your comment that they also lost because they did a very poor proposal and that the customer really did not think as highly of them as Chuck Heydrich and other SUG key players assumed they did. Classic complacentitis it would appear, despite Heydrich's frequent claims of preparing vigorously for the contract competition for at least two years before the RFP came out, including courting John B. Napier, the Northcorp CEO and other senior Northcorp executives.(I know John Napier well and I have a feeling he does not care for Chuck Heydrich, never did, never will. Heydrich's efforts to get to Napier may have actually backfired and in any case, as you reminded us last night, the people who evaluate proposals for Northcorp are usually the engineers, accountants, and business analysts, not senior VP's and Directors!)

I know only too well **how extraordinarily arrogant and demeaning Chuck Heydrich can be in his treatment of others, how hated he is by many of those who have worked for him, and what a huge ego he has.** He may have been a good marketing rep (and many of my market-ing friends will dispute this), but I am convinced from everything I know about him that **he has very poor lead-ership qualities**. In short Chuck Heydrich is not the kind of person who normally reaches VP level in our corporation. He is not the sort of executive I would want to serve under in any tough or stressful situation. Finally, he is simply not a leader, and in my humble opinion he was promoted far beyond what he deserved, both at Cobrands and at Disksoft.

I have 25 years of experience at Disksoft, including P&L responsibility in manufacturing, sales, and engineering departments. Hearing about Heydrich's reputation in marketing and also when he was on the CEO's staff, I could never understand why Cobrands promoted him to marketing director and put him in such key positions **except for the fact that he was smart, clever, and always managed to please his bosses no matter how terribly he treated his subordinates and how obviously self serving he was**. I had the same amazement about his meteoric rise within Disksoft. In the two years I spent in the Heydrich Group (1998-2000), **I had a strong feeling that eventually Heydrich's arrogance, poor leadership qualities, and lack of integrity would catch up with him. And that is exactly what appears to have happened.** Apparently he has been forced out as VP of the Software Upgrade Group by Carl Holden and moved up to the sector level as a precursor to his departure from Disksoft. Good riddance!

Please send me the 30 page report you told us about last night on the Northcorp loss. Thank you.

Josh Perkins
X63440   (author's emphasis added)

Need we say more? Now, with *Jihad the Jerk at Work*, the careers of hard-core Jerks like Chuck Heydrich can be cut mercifully short long before they can assume positions of high authority & wreak so much damage to their own organizations.

Good riddance, indeed!!

NO CAREER FIELD IMMUNE FROM JERKS

One of the key themes in this book is that hard-core Jerks don't just flourish in corporate business settings. Even in lofty institutions such as Academia and the Judiciary, unchecked Jerkism can lead to horrific abuses. Organizations of any stripe can easily devolve into hellish, fear-ridden environments (especially if employees feel trapped there, and perceive that they have few, or zero, alternative employment options), where hypocrisy and gross stupidity lock up and suffocate the entire works.

TALES OUT OF SCHOOL

A classic example of institutional insanity recently occurred at the famed Groton school, the elite prep school 40 miles northwest of Boston. Young students there were routinely sexually harassed by older students, to include incidents such as

> *"Three or four boys will often pin a single boy down, grab his testicles, shove fingers up his rectum, then lick his face."* [5]

according to one complaint, which was verified by three dozen students. One young victim was "sexually assaulted 15 times, starting on his 3rd day of school."[6]

The blue-blood, stellar administrators, headmaster, and trustees of Groton tried mightily to sweep the whole affair under the rug, and employed the time-tested tactic of all too many bureaucracies and institutions: "smear the victim." No disciplinary action was taken, and Groton blatantly lied to the Commonwealth of Massachusetts DSS (Department of Social Services) that all the victims were over 18, when in fact many were 16, and subject to DSS intervention.[7]

The Jerk-Rot was so pervasive at Groton that an English teacher at the school

> *"called Mr. Hawkins* (one of the victims of these criminal
> attacks) *stupid and arrogant for complaining about
> 'behavior that some find pleasurable' !!!"*[8]

Hello, do we detect **Unrestrained Jerkism** on the loose at this institution for the elite?? If you check out the "Characteristics of Jerks" faults list in Chapter Two, you'll see prominently listed the endearing trait of "Gross Hypocrisy." One of the favorite axioms of Groton is "Character is what you do when no one is looking." The school prides itself as the prep school of FDR and McGeorge Bundy . . . although Bundy's prominent role in stupidly pushing the US into the Vietnam Quagmire[9] is surely nothing to be proud of (on second thought, maybe this reveals a *lot* about the Groton of the last 50 years).

This blatant hypocrisy parallels Enron's hawking noble Corporate Values such as "Integrity", "Respect", and "Loyalty" whilst it's sleazy executives plundered the Company and abandoned its employees. Unrestrained, unquarantined Jerkism races through an organization like the bubonic plague, sweeping all before it.

It's also obvious that Groton's hierarchy suffers from not just one or two Jerks, but from an entire cabal of fools who have clustered together over the years until the critical mass of Jerks obviates any common sense, any decency, any sense of responsibility to its own young students. **Unrestrained Jerkism is cataclysmic, every time, everywhere – no exceptions. Where there is no resistance to Jerks, disaster will strike the organization.**

The fools running Groton were slapped with a multimillion dollar lawsuit by enraged parents, were investigated by a grand jury[10] for their shameless lying, and succeeded in irrevocably staining the reputation of the school – who'd want to send their son there now, blueblood or not?? The main point here is that the decline and fall of another legendary institution didn't just occur overnight. Jerks infiltrated and eventually came to dominate the top Groton administrative and faculty positions, gradually pushing out those of integrity and competence. The cumulative effect of 40 years of unrestrained jerkism is the *de facto* destruction of the organization . . . so it be everywhere.

DISORDER IN THE COURT

One of the great surprises I encountered as I researched this book was discovering the general pervasiveness and seriousness of the problem of hard-core Jerks at work prominent in *professions I thought might show some immunity*, such as the Judiciary.

Oh, sure, we all watched "Perry Mason" in the 50's and 60's, and saw the Prosecution portrayed as bumbling, dense fools. But even Hamilton Burger was a basically honest DA, and I always clung to the belief that flawed they can be, the people's advocates are an honorable bunch with the best intentions of justice and truth at heart . . . folks who would **never stoop** to base or degrading criminal behaviors, just to bolster their conviction record to sordidly and shamelessly advance their sorry little judicial careers, perhaps to some day snare a fat judgeship on easy street.

Hello, what planet was I from??? Jerkism triumphant worms its way into every nook and cranny whence human DNA abides. Unrestrained, it'll rot out each nook and each cranny.

In Pennsylvania in 2001, a sensational example of corrupt prosecutorial misconduct exploded into public view. Eleven years previously (1989), a mentally retarded man, Dennis Counterman, was convicted and sentenced to be executed in Allentown for setting a fire in his house that killed his three sons. He'd been in jail ever since, on Death Row – during the 90's he was nearly executed several times (the pitiless Execution orders signed by clueless Governor Tom Ridge . . . oh, wonderful – and this clown was until recently in charge of protecting you and me against terrorists – screw up and move up) but was saved by the intervention of dedicated public defense attorneys.

It has now been revealed that the prosecutor on the case, Assistant District Attorney Richard Tomsho, **deliberately withheld from the Defense** half a dozen statements gathered by the police which clearly exonerated Mr. Counterman, and clearly implicated his oldest son, who, it turns out, had a history of setting fires!![11] Tomsho, in his criminal effort to nail a perpetrator whether innocent or guilty, went so far as to actually *white out* portions of Mrs. Counterman's initial police statement that exonerated her husband before giving it to Defense Attorneys!!! Yep, this DA whipped out his bottle of Paper-mate Liquid Paper & just blotted it out – something he learned in Law School, or from a kindly DA mentor, perhaps? From watching *Law and Order*? This "public servant's" immoral, unethical behavior is just unbelievable.

Tomsho blatantly lied about his role to the Jury. After his stellar record of sending innocents like Counterman to death row, Mr. Tomsho was naturally promoted – he now works in the Pennsylvania Attorney General's Office, who fervently hopes everyone will just forget about this former DA's crimes . . . as does Governor Ridge.

> *"Death penalty lawyers say that the Counterman case illustrates that **prosecutorial misconduct is more pervasive than is generally realized. 'This is only the tip of the iceberg,'** said George Kendall of the NAACP Legal Defense and Educational Fund, Inc. 'Few Courts are willing to do much about it.'"*[12] (author's emphasis)

This truly reeks of unrestrained Jerkism, and demonstrates again the high penalty society pays when DA's like Tomsho are given a free pass to commit criminal acts without penalty.

Surely several dozen police and paralegals and DA staff were well aware of this District Attorney's criminal conduct in trying to railroad an innocent man into the electric chair, yet none came forward, even anonymously. Here is Jerkism truly unrestrained.

The methodology in this book allows anyone with a shred of conscience and decency to anonymously and safely expose this kind of gross corruption. *Carpe Diem.*

THE DOMINO EFFECT

The quote at the beginning of this chapter from Dr. Ken Lloyd on the devastating effect a hard core Jerk can have on any organization can only be topped in the horror category by an even more chilling fact: that the typical Jerk will **attract and hire even**

more Jerks into the organization, which always sets it on the road to perdition. Like the Black Plague in a remote medieval French village, nothing survives except the Priest's lame dog, Hortense.

In one company I joined, one notorious department (not mine, thankfully) was already saturated from top to bottom with blithering Jerks. In fact, as a naïve newcomer to this organization, I was startled to find that even the mere *mention* of the offending Department's name in polite company triggered a collective wrinkling of noses and little gasping sounds as if some great putrefaction was being released. I discovered soon enough that no less than four (4) *entire management levels* within this pariah department were saturated with moronic jerks.

It got so bad that good field agents working with subcontractors who became enraged at the stupidity perpetrated by this cabal of Jerks actually flew thousands of miles back to our home base just to meet with senior management to vent their complaints. The corruption and rot emanating from this septic nest was so pervasive that even its secretaries were surly and their Xerox machines were notoriously obnoxious, always malfunctioning – the collective stench was total, and awful to inhale.

This truly is the inevitable product of unrestrained Jerkism: *complete rot*. Jerks *like* other Jerks. Jerks **hire** other Jerks. Jerks even marry other Jerks. Any way you cut it, Jerks beget Jerks. Good people bail out of these infested organizations like the Titanic after midnight. This is the "Domino Theory of Jerks" – organizations are terminally doomed when Jerk-like behaviors go unchallenged and become the norm.

MILITARY ROT

In 1999 Seymour Hersh, of My Lai fame, did an long, eyeopening piece for the *New Yorker* on a military unit in the Gulf War that fell prey to this very plague. The commander, a notorious Jerk, put "his" people into most key command and staff slots, forcing decent, thoughtful, experienced people out. This commander was just *itching* to actually engage the Iraqi enemy and really draw blood, come hell or high water, and was frustrated that the foe just melted away from his forces. At a crucial period, two days *after* the February 28, 1991 Gulf War cease fire went into effect, all the weaknesses of this unit coalesced and it ended up irresponsibly (many say criminally) placing a murderous fire on large numbers of retreating Iraqi troops who posed no threat to US forces, and who were in complete compliance with the terms of the truce . . . in fact, they were clearly motoring home with gun turrets in the "lock and travel" administrative convoy mode. 700 vehicles were destroyed and probably thousands were gunned down, to include soldiers, civilians, and even some women and children. All were quickly buried in mass graves and no media visited the scene.[13]

Some US staff officers who tried to prevent this tragedy were shoved aside and ignored. The military officially tried to cover up the entire affair, but numerous soldiers of all ranks, disgusted by the lies and crimes, refused to keep silent, and the whole story came out. The bloody incident cast a pall over the US victory and was a disgraceful stain on the honor of the US military, especially the shameless cover up. This atrocity is well known in the Middle East and has helped fuel hatred of the US in many Muslim countries there . . . as if we didn't have enough of a PR problem already.

So the point is made again: Jerks are **hugely bad news** for *any* organization – allowing them to get a foothold spells disaster – each and every time!!!

ENRON DOMINOS

A classic case of the Domino Theory of Jerks comes from our favorite dysfunctional corporation, Enron. This investigative report from *Newsweek* on March 11, 2002 captures the spreading stain of jerkism with chilling clarity:

> "*While Mark* (Rebecca Mark, a rival VP, who was an honest power plant builder, as opposed to Skilling's sleazy smoke & mirrors accounting games) *globe trotted, Skilling was filling Headquarters with his own troops. He was not looking for 'fuzzy skills', a former employee recalls. His*

recruits talked about a socialization process called 'En-
ronizing'. Family time? Quality of life? Forget it. Anybody
who did not embrace the elbows out culture 'didn't get it'.
They were 'damaged goods' and 'shipwrecks', to be fired
by their bosses at blistering annual job reviews known as
rank-and-yank sessions."[14]

If Enron employees had this book back in the 90's, they possibly
could have saved the Company from the clutches of Skilling and
Fastow. But with no such restraints, the organization was doomed.

THE BLEED-OVER EFFECT

There's another disastrous impact visited upon organizations
when jerks are allowed to operate unrestrained and unchallenged.
When the level of Jerkism reaches a certain, sickening Critical
Mass, their poisoning of the organization can become so pervasive
that it extends even to decent, good people and managers who
haven't managed to get out in time, or who *don't have the backbone
to courageously fight back.*

I saw this up front and painfully close in one company I worked
in. One Jerk manager in a sister organization literally ruined a decent
(but rather weak) manager in another organization. By the time the
intimidation and poisoning had run its course, the previously decent
guy was a mere shell of his former self, shaken and contrite. It was a
sad, pathetic sight to behold. **With the advanced Jerk-elimination
techniques at your service in this book, this scenario does not
have to befall your company.** It's so much easier to destroy Jerks
posthaste *before* they can inflict these cancers on unsuspecting
workplaces and destroy any decency that remains.

JERKS CAUSE *MAJOR* DAMAGE TO EMPLOYEE
HEALTH

We've seen that experts widely agree that Jerks cause the
"unnecessary, abnormal stress index" in organizations to jump

way off the charts. Now, from a series of recent major medical studies released in 2002, performed by distinguished researchers nationwide, we know the huge toll this "chronic stress" takes on the *physical*, as well as the mental, health of employees. The proof is finally in, and it's stunning.

The New York Times, arguably one of the best newspapers in the world, has just published a blockbuster analysis by the *Times'* Science writer Erica Goode, "The Heavy Cost of Chronic Stress" (December 17, 2002), of these studies that summarizes the deadly damage severe stress wreaks on people. (This reporting was based on detailed research performed by "Dr. Bruce McEwen, director of the neuroendocrinology laboratory at the Rockefeller University; Dr. Ronald Glaser, immunologist at Ohio State University; Dr. Janice Kiecolt-Glaser and Dr. Timothy Loving; Dr. Robert M. Salpolsky, a professor of neurology at Stanford; Dr. Elissa S. Epel at the University of California; Dr. Cohen of Carnegie Mellon; Dr. Michael Meaney of McGill University; Dr. Charles Nemeroff, a psychiatrist at Emory University "[15]) Excerpts follow from Erica Goode's landmark article:

> ### *"The Heavy Cost of Chronic Stress, a Key to an Assortment of Illness"*
> #### *By Erica Goode, New York Times, 12/17/02*
>
> *"Prolonged or severe stress has been shown to weaken the immune system, strain the heart, damage memory cells in the brain, and deposit fat at the waist rather than the hips and the buttocks (a risk factor for heart disease, cancer, and other illnesses), said Dr. Bruce S. McEwen, director of the neuroendocrinology laboratory at the Rockefeller University and the author of a new book, 'The End of Stress As We know It'. **Stress has been implicated in aging, depression, heart disease, rheumatoid arthritis, and diabetes, among other illnesses.**
>
> *Researchers have known for many decades that physical stress takes a toll on the body. But only relatively recently have the profound effects of psychological stress*

on health been widely acknowledged. Two decades ago, many basic scientists scoffed at the notion that mental state could affect illness. The link between mind and body was considered murky territory, best left to psychiatrists.

But in the last decade, researchers have convincingly demonstrated that psychological stress can increase vulnerability to disease and have begun to understand how that might occur.

... The more researchers have learned, the clearer it has become that stress may be a thread tying together many illnesses that were previously thought to be unrelated.

. . . Central to this new understanding is a novel conception of stress, developed by Dr. McEwen, who has been studying the subject for more than three decades. According to this model, it is not stress per se that is harmful. Rather the problems associated with stress result from a complicated interaction between the demands of the outside world and the body's capacity to manage potential threats.

That capacity can be influenced by . . . the piling on of normal stresses to the point they overload the system.

In moderate amounts, the scientists argue, stress can be benign, even beneficial, and most people are equipped to deal with it.

*. . . When stress persists for too long, or becomes too severe, Dr. McEwen said, the normally protective mechanisms become overburdened, a condition he refers to as allostatic load. **The finely tuned feedback system is disrupted, and over time it runs amok, causing damage.***"

Laboratory animals were placed in difficult situations and displayed . . . *"the effects of chronic stress. They grew anxious and aggressive. Their immune system became slower to fight off invaders. Nerve cells in the hippocampus, a brain region involving memory, atrophied. The production of new hippocampai neurons stopped."*

Studies have shown that people are likewise affected.

> *". . . So it is not surprising that when the stress system is derailed, the brain is a target for damage. A decade of research has demonstrated that sustained stress and **the resulting overproduction of cortisol can have chilling effects on the hippocampus, a horseshoe-shaped brain structure intimately involved in memory formation.***
>
> *. . . But it was not until the 1980's and early 90's that scientists began to discover the mechanisms that might lie behind the mind and body link. Investigators uncovered nerves that connect the brain with the spleen and thymus, organs important in immune responses, and they established that nerve cells could affect the activity of infection-fighting white blood cells.*
>
> *. . . Yet in some cases, it seems, cortisol does not properly shut down the immune system under stress, allowing the continued production of cytokines that promote inflammation. These cytokines **have been linked to heart disease, depression, stroke, and other illnesses.***
>
> *. . Stress also seems to make people more likely to contract some infectious illnesses . . . findings offer strong evidence that stressed people are more likely to become infected and had more severe symptoms after becoming ill.*
>
> *. . . Recent studies have provided increased support for the notion that stress contributes to heart disease, and **researchers have tied psychological stress, directly or indirectly, to diabetes, rheumatoid arthritis, fibromyalgia, severe depression and other mental disorders."***[16] (my emphasis)

The *Times'* article was very long and detailed, so I can just give you the few excerpts above to convey the high points, but you can catch the drift. **The chronic stresses induced by Jerk behaviors is *extremely serious stuff*, and *it's ruining the health of innocent millions*. To allow Jerks to operate unhindered to wreak this sick havoc on decent folk is an OUTRAGE – start the game plan to oust your local hard core Jerk *today* – delay no longer!!**

A jerk unrestrained is a *mortal threat* to our health, happiness, our very existence!!

MORE JERK-RELATED *SERIOUS STUFF*: VIOLENCE AND SUICIDES

We now discuss a topic that some may view as speculative, yet my past 30 years of workplace experience convinces me strong connections can be made. To what degree does serious Jerk-like behavior of managers and peer employees help provoke or actually cause high rates of workplace violence and suicide?? We know that "about two million American workers are victims of workplace violence *each year* ", according to the US Department of Justice. "Other Federal statistics show workplace violence costs $36 Billion **annually**."[17] Rival statistics claim the cost is nine times higher than that!!

Jerks can precipitate this violence in many ways. One commonly seen scenario is when a Jerky boss establishes an "I don't want to hear about problems" atmosphere. This is a commonly found sign-post *en route* to Hell. When workers notice flaky "Bob Edge" acting even more strangely, they clam up – no one wants to give the boss, or even HR, the bad news. No disciplinary action or counseling or intervention is triggered, so the situation continues to deteriorate. And then one day ol' Bob waltzes in to work with 3 hidden handguns and in ten minutes 4 workers are dead and 5 more wounded seriously. And everyone says, "Gee, we never saw it coming.."

Another scenario, that from reading many news accounts is not unusual, is when a hardcore jerk boss screws over a hapless employee so ruthlessly that the guy snaps and takes his revenge.

I've also seen some people working in Corporations that are truly walking time bombs, just waiting to explode (see Chapter 4). It's scary just being in the same room with these loonies. My advice is to anonymously "book" them with this book asap and get them out of your organization *now*. You'll be doing yourself and your coworkers a huge favor.

I have yet to see a serious study on the jerk-related aspects of workplace violence, probably because Companies fear lawsuits from irate survivors and families of victims. For now it all remains a dirty little secret – this is inexcusable, and must be aired.

DAMAGE JERKS INFLICT KNOWS NO BOUNDS

So we see that jerks clearly can contribute to the level of violence at work in many ways. It's also been well established that they precipitate large turnover in companies as good employees bail out to get away from their obnoxious behavior:

> *"Nevertheless, Francis notes that success is often tied to company support. 'For coaching* (of jerks) *to work someone in the company, someone at a very high level, must perceive that the individual has a problem,' he says. 'And usually, with bullies, that problem is* **turnover.**"[18]

The varieties of idiocies the Jerk will resort to are relative – often the incidents seem petty and trivial, but their consequences can still have major negative impact. One stupid, unreasonable manager at a contract training company not only insisted that all her employees *had* to attend the company picnic, but that they were *required* to wear bathing suits! This made a lot of employees very uncomfortable, "so they just left the company", related a witness. Since nobody had this book, or even any upward feedback program (see Chapter 9), Clueless Management couldn't figure out why they had such high turnover. The *complaint forms* in Chapter 7 would definitely bring them into focus, and quickly. Use them liberally. Just like in Mayor Daly's Chicago on election day, "Vote early, and vote often."

It's well known that Jerks cause severe loss of customers to companies. You can gauge the level of power Jerks exert in companies just by talking with Customer Service reps from your local HMO or AOL on the phone – when they refuse to pass on your negative comments about poor corporate performance (their Jerky bosses don't like to hear bad news, remember?), you simply fire your HMO, and dump sloppily run AOL for Earthlink.

There is some evidence to indicate that jerks are directly involved in job-related suicides. Suicide is a complex personal subject that doesn't lend itself to sweeping indictments. However, some reporting has mentioned that bizarre office politics may have possibly contributed to the high rates of suicide among police officers. "Police are twice as likely to kill themselves as to be killed by a criminal," a little-known fact that police departments nationwide would rather you did not know. (Many police who die "accidentally while cleaning their handgun" are really suicides – great classification for survivor benefits, but hampers localities in instituting preventive programs.)[19]

How many suicides can be traced to the sleazy actions of Jerks at Work?? In a newspaper interview, a New Jersey businessman who has become locally famous for his support of disadvantaged children, recounts his happy childhood ending abruptly via a Jerk at Work:

> " 'I had a great childhood,' he says.
> It didn't last as long as he wished. When he was a teenager his father, a lawyer, was given an opportunity he couldn't refuse. Lasser won't be specific, but it had to do with the movies and required moving to California.
> 'I had to leave all my friends and go out there, but my father was so certain we'd be all set for life.'
> Then something happened.
> 'All I know is he was asked to do something unethical. He refused and lost his job. He was in his 50's, broke, and unemployed.'
> The family returned to Jersey. Stu's friends had all left for college. Within months, his father was dead.
> 'I hung on thinking about how happy I was as a kid. I told myself if, I ever had the chance, I'd try to make other kids happy, too.' "[20]

Jerks' behavior can be a major factor in work-related violence and death and suicide. **If you have any hesitation about ridding your workplace of a Jerk, that thought should dispel it instantly.**

PROTECT YOURSELF – NOBODY ELSE WILL

In the wake of a horrendous on-the-job killing spree at a small software company near Boston in December 2000, when a disgruntled employee massacred 7 employees in 10 minutes, a lot of soul-searching took place. How can companies prevent this type of atrocity?? One criminal justice professor wrote,

> *"The overriding goal (for companies) should be to make civility and decency in the workplace as critical as profit. Companies need to upgrade and humanize the way in which they deal with employees every day, rather than just to focus narrowly on how to respond to the one who has made threats or fits a profile. Long term planning with strong HR programs will greatly improve the workplace climate and employee morale. A study conducted for Northwestern National Life Insurance concluded that Companies with effective grievance, harassment, and security procedures also reported lower rates of violence."*[21]

Noble sentiments, but can you afford to *wait around* for your company to see the light?? You're better off taking this book *now* and safely purge Jerks, both managerial and peer wack-o, out of your organization. If you do not take this relatively easy initiative, then you well could be placing both yourself and your family needlessly at risk.

IT'S NOW OFFICIAL: JERKS CAUSE *WARS*!!

A book just published catapults the consequences of jerkism unrestrained to the Alpha Level. All during the 90's I looked forward to reading the incisive dispatches of *New York Times* reporter Chris Hedges from the war-plagued Balkans. He was known as a front line muddy boot reporter, as opposed to the "hotel room" variety. Now Chris has thrown in the towel on 15 years of combat reporting, and written a book reflecting upon what he learned from it all, *War Is A Force That Gives Us Meaning.* His insights into the incessant post Cold War conflicts of the last decade are startling, and clearly relevant to *Jihad the Jerk at Work*. From a review by Abraham Verghese in the New York Times Book Review:[22]

> *"It comes as a surprise when Hedges discounts the notion that wars are born out of pure ethnic or religious differences; most wars, he believes, 'are manufactured wars, born out of the collapse of civil societies, perpetuated by* **fear, greed, and paranoia,** *and they are run by* **gangsters, who rise up from the bottom of their own societies** *and terrorize all, including those they purport to protect.'"*[23]

In other words, Jerks are *prime instigators of modern day violence, depredation, and war.* Societies who allow Jerks to rise to power pay the price in spades. After four stupid, bloody, unnecessary wars in the 1990's, it would be too easy just to point to Serbia and Slobodan Milosevic as poster children of this sad truth – however, recent revelations clearly point to all sides in the Balkans, to include Franjo Tudjman of Croatia and even the supposedly "saintly" Alja Izetbegovic of Bosnia, both guilty of criminal, murderous behaviors.[24]

Diana Johnstone's recent book, *Fool's Crusade: Yugoslavia, NATO, and Western Delusions* (Monthly Review Press, 2002) exposes the major blunders of Germany, NATO, and the US – accompanied by the self-serving, dishonest complicity of the Western Media – in unnecessarily igniting the Balkans hellhole of the 1990's.[25] Go to Chapter 14 and see how this kind of "peeling back layers of the onion" relates, if you decide to do more after you've cleaned up your own workplace. You'll never know what's really going on by relying on mainstream corporate-controlled US media.

CARPE DIEM

Getting rid of Jerks at Work, whether in your company, your engineering group, your factory, the police department, the state department of highways, your military unit, the junior high school faculty, or your political party, is **not** a trivial, unimportant matter – it never will be. It may well be the most important and far reaching crusade you ever embark upon. **So, if it needs to be done, do it, do it now, do it with cunning fury, and nail it !!!!**

DILBERT, THE GREAT FRAUD

Three chapters back, in the Introduction, I mentioned that although it's clear that Scott Adams has presciently tapped in to a mass of seething worker resentment, the Dilbert comic strip strays from real truth, and actually does more harm than good. In this chapter on the consequences of unrestrained jerkism, I'd like to explore this rather unsettling viewpoint.

Like all of you, I've read my share of Dilbert comic strips, and chuckled at many – but I've always had a vague uneasy sense that something was very wrong with the entire Dilbert mindset. Then, an Op-Ed piece in the *Boston Globe* in 1997, "Dilbert the Diffuser", by Norman Solomon, snapped on the light.

"THE CULTURE OF EYE-ROLLING CAPITULATION" [26]

Norman is a nationally syndicated columnist of "Media Beat", a prolific author, media critic, and the executive director of the Institute for Public Accuracy. In the article, he strikingly made the point that the mega-problem with the whole Dilbert mindset is that it **glorifies "the culture of eye-rolling capitulation"** and encourages workers just to give up trying to improve workplaces – just shrug and accept things for what they are, says Dilbert. Naturally you'll find some of biggest fans of Dilbert are jerks who are delighted with this unconditional surrender, which signals they'll be allowed to romp and stomp unfettered and unchallenged until their golden retirement years. What a marvelous windfall!!

Norman hits the nail on the head. More from his brilliant op-ed *Globe* column:

> " . . . *In Dilbertland, where sarcasm is the preferred mode of expression, little can be done about on-the-job frustrations. . . . Dilbert and his colleagues are reduced to acid quips and feeble wisecracks. The Dilbert phenomenon is part of a social environment that acclimates people to cynicism and ironic passivity. Idealism is chronically inappropriate; strong solidarity among co-workers is out of the question. The savvy response is always to take care of No. 1 and let others fend for themselves.*
>
> *More than ever, Dilbert is a common fixture in our daily lives. Yet any substantive critique is likely to be met with the argument that 'it's just a cartoon.' At a time when millions of people are acutely aware of oppressive working conditions,* **Dilbert feeds into a culture of eye-rolling capitulation.** *But we are urged to believe that the Dilbert tales are without consequence.*
>
> *'Industrially produced fiction has become one of the primary shapers of our emotions and our intellect in the 20th century,' writer Ariel Dorfman has observed. 'Although these stories are supposed to merely entertain us, they constantly give us a secret education.'*
>
> **Despite its irreverent pretensions, Dilbert is a media product that teaches us how not to rebel.** *That helps to explain why corporate America finds Dilbert so delightful.*"[26]   (my emphasis)

Obviously, the book you're now reading, *Jihad the Jerk at Work*, has a philosophy 180 degrees away from Dilbert. You *can* do a lot about your workplace, and quickly, with major success!!

DILBERT EXPOSED!!

In 1997, Norman also published his devastating exposure of the whole Dilbert scam, *The Trouble With Dilbert*, which brilliantly explains how we've been *had*. I highly recommend you get a copy (Common Courage Press – 1997 – Monroe, Maine). Here are some juicy tidbits (highlights by me):

p 50 *"Throwing stark light on unpleasant absurdities **without the slightest hope of solutions for the common good**, Scott Adams digs the readers into a deepening trough. In his estimation, the only way out is an individual escape. . ."*[27]

p 55 *"Millions of people are frustrated on a daily basis. **They'd do something about it if they knew how.**"*

"'The real story of Dilbert is the basic disregard for his dignity as a human being, which is the biggest problem in workplaces generally,' Scott Adams said in an interview with Inc magazine."[28]

p 59 *"No wonder the people who read Dilbert feel powerless. The strip actually **contributes** directly and constantly to making them feel that way."*[29]

p 63 *"Of course Dilbert is popular. It vents anger while subtly sharing the operating assumptions of management. It's a safe way to thumb your nose at the boss **WITHOUT ACTUALLY TAKING REAL ACTION THAT MIGHT JEOPARDIZE, OR IMPROVE, YOUR OWN POSITION.**"*[30] Right on, Norman!!

p 83 *"In real life, many of us are Dilbert. And statistics about on-the-job stress prove it. According to the US Department of Labor, the workplace is the greatest single source of stress, no matter what you do or how*

> *much you earn. The New York based American Insti-*
> *tute of Stress reports that as many as 75 to 90 percent*
> *of visits to physicians are related to stress – at a price*
> ***tag to American businesses of 200 to 300 billion a***
> ***year.***" [31]

p 95 "*Pessimism and disillusionment have also led some*
> *to a further retreat, with an abandonment of the*
> *desire as well as hope for progressive change . . .*"[32]

> "*Like his colleagues, he (Dilbert) is reduced to*
> *feeble wisecracks and asides, the gallows humor of*
> *a man sentenced to live the corporate life.*"[33]

Get this book, it's superb.

ONE ISSUE DEVIL INCARNATE SCOTT ADAMS IS RIGHT ABOUT!

I partially agree with Scott Adams on one issue, however. Norman Solomon bashes Adams for saying that a huge problem in corporations is too many employees creating too much useless bureaucracy and stifling "programs" that waste people's time and clog effectiveness. Adams believes that corporate downsizing is actually *good* since the bullshit level decreases as superfluous bureaucrats in HR and other places are laid off.

Naturally, Norman is outraged at this heartless betrayal of the proletariat.

I humbly suggest an intelligent compromise between the two positions. I will have to say, after many years working in large corporations, that Scott Adams is accurate in pointing out that the BS level rises in corporations that are bloated with employees. In companies that are expanding and doing well and hiring, year after year you sadly see the level of excessive sensitivity programs, redundant equal opportunity initiatives, "values" programs, "GROWS" programs, corporate goals surveys, excessive PC password changes, suffocating numbers of useless meetings, disastrous "peoplesoft" HR data flops, PC "help" operatives 2,000 miles away, engineers who cannot speak intelligible English, myriads of corporate buzzwords crescending to such a suffocating level that I actually have witnessed top-notch, high producing employees quit the company to get relief from the insanity. It's a serious reality that Norman may not be aware of because he has not experienced it personally. At Pac Bell, Scott obviously did, and he's correct to blast it.

Back to my humble solution: don't *fire* this 10% of employees generating all this useless bullshit, but *shift* them to jobs within the corporation that are *actually useful*. Often, companies can use a lot of help in research, secretarial work, project management, administrative aides, and jacks of all trades that take burdens off of engineers and key employees. Top management should occasionally gauge the "BS Level" in their companies in order to discern when it's time to execute this resource shift.

And how do good employees alert senior management that the BS level is intolerable and it's time to move some of the workforce into more productive roles?? Just use the Suggestion and Complaint forms (anonymously and with 30-day deadlines) in Chapter 7 – go ahead and **deluge** your VP's with demands for *relief*, and relief now.

Now I return to bashing Scott Adams and his turdy dwarf minion, Dilbert.

THE SLAVE MENTALITY OF DILBERT

In *Jihad the Jerk at Work*'s Introduction, we discussed the curse of the slave mentality in the workplace, and its key role in keeping jerks secure no matter what outrages they perpetrate. Norman Solomon correctly portrays Dilbert as a key player in keeping workers in chains. Dilbert is the ultimate "realist."

From our history books we can see just how often a retreat to the blind acceptance of "reality" can be a dangerous house of cards. In his 1988 book, *Mission To Civilize*, Mort Rosenblum's refreshingly different history of modern France, the author describes the dangers of caving in too readily to "reality", and how the French nation nearly destroyed itself via that mindset. He quotes the memoirs of a young French soldier who surrendered to the Nazis in 1940, and soon, Dilbert-like, turned his back on the only honorable French faction remaining, the Free French led by General Charles DeGaulle. He turned instead, as most Frenchmen did, to the Quisling General Petain, who sold France and her honor out to the detested *Boche*:

> "... *In short, we were, according to the word that had such success later,* **realists**.*We preferred to accommodate to reality than to change it.*
>
> ... *The word realism is mainly a polite translation for cowardice. . . . In the best of cases realism leads to mediocrity; in the worst (the more frequent) it leads to the grave. There are circumstances where prudence is the worst of follies. It is by realism – lack of imagination – that men accept slavery. By the maxim, 'Better to be a live dog than a dead lion,' one descends to the rank of dog, which is precisely our case today ... '* "[34]

The author proceeds to document the sickening collaboration of all too many French with their Nazi occupiers, including their betrayal of 76,000 French Jews. As Hitler remarked, "Petain, with his police, replaced 15 divisions for me."[35]

BETTER LATE THAN NEVER, BUT EARLIER IS BETTER YET

It's stating the obvious, but a powerful factor in really restraining / pre-empting / destroying Jerkism is to expose the Jerk's game *early on.*

A disturbing example of the tragedy of tardy disclosure is revealed to us with Patrick Tierney's shocking book, *Darkness in El Dorado: How Scientists and Journalists Devastated the Amazon*, published in 2000. In the 1960's, discovery of some stone-age tribes of Indians, the Yanomani, deep in the Amazon forest triggered a tidal wave of anthropologists and journalists eager to cash in on the story.

In the subsequent thirty years, these hustlers, "who published in the most reputable journals and rose to the heights of their professional societies"[36], managed to infect a peaceable, stable tribal society with ruinous wars, disease, prostitution, the exploitation of criminal gold-miners, and a whole litany of horrible evils. Only very slowly did the truth leak out, finally culminating in Tierney's broadside in 2000.[37]

His *exposé* revolves around one of the greatest criminal frauds of the 20th Century, the American anthropologist Napoleon Chagnon, who sold millions of books boasting of his exploits in "civilizing a brutal stone age people", when in fact **he** was the brute who perverted and destroyed a peaceful, happy society which would have been thrice blessed never to have encountered this blithering charlatan. Chagnon's prime motivation, a classic jerk tactic, was to make a huge publicity splash so he could attract big financial grants from anal, ignorant, deep-pocketed institutions.[38]

We arrive at the bottom line: **why did it take *40 years* for all this evil to be exposed??** The damage to these innocent Yanomani peoples could have been greatly minimized if the exposure had been done in 1970 or 1980 or even 1990 instead of 2000. Most great consumer fraud, sleazy corporate financial crimes, political corruption, academic shenanigans, and military cover-ups are *well-known at the outset* by many folks, some of whom are decent to the core, but happen to be working for corrupt jerks – and could be nipped in the bud by either a jerk-busting campaign (Chapter 4), a bombshell scenario (Chapter 8), or even a pre-emptive complaint (Chapter 7) – all anonymous, of course. I hasten to add that I certainly do not fault Tierney – he should be lauded for his courageous book. My point is that there were undoubtedly hundreds of others who knew early on the horrors perpetrated, but chose to remain silent.

The moral of this story is of tremendous importance to all principled "Jerk-Busters" – *don't let Jerks slide*, **don't let them get away with it for another *day*!! Launch your attack *now*, do not delay.** Remember what disclosure delay did to the devastated Yanomani tribes of the Amazon.

Always remember:

JERKISM UNRESTRAINED IS JERKISM TRIUMPHANT.

A JERK INTELLIGENTLY CHALLENGED IS A JERK DOOMED.

Mantra (to be chanted by each member of your EAJ Jihad
Committee when he/she wakes up each morning
during the 30-day attack phase)

"Good people can be tough
we have to be . . .

Good guys can win
we can do this.

Good folks can be smarter and tougher
than Jerks
Jerks can be soundly beaten,
scattered
And this will happen
now

Remember the ravaged Yanomani!!
Strike NOW,
Show the Jerk no mercy."

(Author's Note: No illegal activity or violence of any kind is
intended to be conveyed or advocated by this
"Mantra" or in any other way, shape or form in
this book. Such activity is unnecessary and
counter productive, since the powerful tools in
this book can do the job much more effectively:
legally, ethically, and peacefully)

"No propagation or multiplication is more rapid than that of evil, unless it be checked; no growth more certain."[39]

Charles Caleb Colton
1780–1832
English writer, clergyman

Part II . . .

Execution of Successful "Eject-A-Jerk" Operation

"Now that I know she wrote this mystery memo, I would say I have a newfound respect for this person. Because it's not easy to stand up and point out things that are wrong in corporate America. It's much easier to let it go." [1]

> Houston Accountant Chris Cagley, on Enron VP Sherron Watkins' anonymous letter to Enron Chairman Kenneth Lay, detailing financial abuses.

Chapter Four – Let's Roll:
Laying the Groundwork /
Planning the Attack / Attack
Execution

"Resistance to tyrants is obedience to God."
>   Thomas Jefferson,
>   motto on his seal . . .
>   original author unknown[1]

FINALLY, ACTION!

The time's finally arrived, which you've been impatiently waiting for, when we actually plan and execute a real Eject-A-Jerk (E.A.J.) campaign. In Chapters 4, 5, and 6 you'll find the step by step road to the successful ousting of any hardcore Jerk from your organization.

FIGHT, OR FLIGHT??

As you begin to realize you have a serious specific Jerk at Work problem on your hands, and as you're beginning to take notes and gather relevant facts, you are of course grappling with the obvious question, "What am I really going to *do* about this situation??" As you get more and more insight and information, and observe the landscape, one of the following five (5) solutions usually will become the obvious Way Out of the Woods:

(Note! Go through this analysis *carefully*; it may spare you a lot of wasted effort in the near future!)

Option # 1) Sit on It:

Do nothing – you discover the issue(s) is really rather trivial; you decide you can easily weather the problem by letting nature take its course.

Option # 2) Reason It Out:

Work out the problem(s) with the person – you find that just by talking to the problem person, differences can be smoothed over, and life can proceed normally. By your being diplomatic and sorting things out, or just by your working harder and smarter, the issues become non-issues. Works well with reasonable and competent people, even if they are sometimes "difficult" or demanding.

> Advice: If you decide to choose this low key reasoning approach, or the next approach # 3, "Mild Counseling", I highly recommend you procure and read Dr. Ken Lloyd's excellent book, *Jerks at Work* (Career Press – 1999 – Franklin Lakes, NJ) in which he presents 100 difficult job situations given to him by fans of his nationally syndicated work advice column in US and Canadian newspapers, and his very effective answers. The intelligent methodology and thought process he uses are excellent and worthy of emulation – you may even find your specific problem addressed.

Option # 3) Mild Counseling Approach:

You discover the problem person is somewhat of a blockhead, but is not really "dangerous" *per se* and could respond to some counseling. A possibility could be to fill out the fault forms you PRINT off from Chapter 6, and either give them directly to the problem person, or to his boss. Attaching this book is a possibility. Doing it openly or anonymously is your call, as is the use of a modified cover letter of the type you see in Chapter 6. It demonstrates to them that this is a serious problem, but that you have confidence they can reform and resolve. *But you have to be careful . . .* this should be a relatively benign situation where there's little to no danger of a flare-up, or a vicious counterattack. You obviously don't want a malicious, unstable person applying *jujitsu* on you and retaliating by "booking" *you*. Just be cautious. When in doubt, keep it anonymous.

Option # 4) Hard-Core Jerk, But Not Worth the Effort:

In this case, you easily recognize that the person really is a serious hard-core jerk. Perhaps he's your new boss, and is a real head case. If, at the same time, you realize you're actually not enthralled with your job's scope *anyway*, and you can arrange for a transfer to a department or job that you'd be much happier in for as much or even more money and opportunity, then go for it. Nobody's asking you to bat your head against the wall, if it's really not in your best interest.

From my observations, this is one of the most *widely used end games in the workplace*. In one large company I worked for, we had nine folks, all very good people, working for a dynamic boss. The good boss was shifted to higher responsibility, and a new manager was moved in. The first week seemed promising . . . then we all suddenly realized we were working for one of the hugest incompetent fools any of us could imagine. The guy was a total moron – the "drumbeat of idiocies", discussed in Chapter 2, was incessant. In the space of two months (!), *six* of our original group had found other jobs in the same division, leaving only three original people left. Then after another 2 months, one of the last 3 couldn't stand it any longer, and also jumped ship, even though he was handling one of the most sensitive and demanding programs in the entire Department. It was so obvious what was going on, it was comical. Our analogy was "nine turtles lined up on a log, rolling off into the pond to other logs floating by, one by one." The seven folks that departed were *very happy* they'd done so (I stayed), and were very fulfilled in their new positions. No fuss, no muss.

Option # 5) Get Rid of the Jerk at Work:

But what about the situation where you're extremely *happy* working in your present job, you have no desire to go job hunting in other parts of the company, and you realize you're doing vitally important work *right where you are*?? Also, you see that "the new boss", or a manager in a nearby group, or some sensitively placed person in your organization, is doing a huge amount of damage.

This is the most difficult situation, but it's ready-made for this book – **it's why this book was written.** It occurs quite often and is a prime situation for the application of a classic "Get Rid of a Jerk at Work" operation. The motivation to act decisively is powerful, often driven by multiple reasons to act . . . kind of like the Second World War, "the Good War" – it's just darn necessary.

(Special Note: Emergency Jerk-Busting)

Another classic case for this combative approach could occur if a "hotshot" manager in your group, or even an associate group you work with closely, has pulled the wool over senior management's eyes but is well known in the ranks as being a destructive, dangerous (or any combo of 80 other faults listed in Chapter 2 and 6) hardcore Jerk. Reliable rumor has it that this hotdog is in line for *promotion* in the near future, perhaps even to take over your whole department. You may well desire to offer your services, armed with this book as a trusty sword, to a discreet action committee in the group (or organize one yourself) to eject the jerk posthaste – naturally, the "promotion" gets deep-sixed as collateral damage, so two birds are obliterated with one stone. This is a classic, clear-cut case for fast action, if you have enough guts and smarts to pull it off.

In the recent Enron debacle, Sherron Watkins did exactly this with her August 2001 letters and e-mails to Chairman Ken Lay – one of her prime motivations was to kill off the impending promotion of the mega-crook Andrew Fastow (her own boss) to fill the departed super-crook Jeffrey Skilling's shoes as Enron CEO. In this she succeeded brilliantly – even anyone as dense as Ken Lay could see the game was up, that the rogues needed to be shunted away before even more damage was done, although by that time the corporate ship was already 90% sunk, with 85% of the lifeboats already incinerated as firewood.

It's instructive to note that Sherron's action was the *only* brake applied on Enron's 10-year slide to disaster, where Skilling's "Mighty Men" Jerks At Work* ran amok with no restraint whatsoever.[2] Too little, too late, but the courageous symbolism of principled resistance to evil and jerkism struck a chord throughout America, and made Sherron a household name – not to mention a *Time* "Person of the Year 2002". Even more importantly, she set a courageous, high profile example. It would not surprise me in the least if it didn't inspire another admirable woman, the FBI's Colleen Rowley, to send her bombshell memo from Minneapolis to Congress and FBI Director Robert Mueller on May 21, 2002 , that blew the lid off the FBI's cover up of it's blundering on the 9/11 terrorist pilot-training clues handed it on a silver platter in July and August 2001.

And this particular positive domino-effect of courageous resistance to stupidity and Jerkism did not even end with Colleen! As I'm writing this section of this book, I read in *today's paper*, June 6, 2002, that one of the principle investigator's of the FBI's blundering in the 9/11 fiasco, Senator Bob Graham (D-Fla), states that Colleen's professionalism in airing the truth about 9/11 is leading others to also speak out about problem areas:

Newsweek did a mind-boggling exposé of Enron in its March 11, 2002 issue . . . "Out of Control Corporate Culture that ultimately wrecked the Company". Jeffrey Skilling, Enron's immature, corrupt CEO "would take his favorites (employees), 'the Mighty Man Force' ... on macho adventure trips. They raced across Mexico on a 1,000 mile bike tour. While tearing through the rugged Australian Outback, the overexuberant Mighty Men trashed several expensive SUV's they'd rented." The links between overt immaturity and crass corruption are not casual and coincidental. Over the past years I've seen this perplexing mix linked together time after time – I've concluded they can both be traced to the root behavior of just plain unvarnished STUPIDITY. Be alert for it, and show these type of idiots no mercy, before they **destroy** your organization.

"'As this investigation gains more public attention, and particularly as people like Ms. Rowley do courageous things, it stimulates others who think they have information that might be relevant to come forward with it, and we are getting an increasing volume of volunteered information,' Mr. Graham said.

He added that if the new information was confirmed, it would demonstrate that there were 'additional pieces of the puzzle' that should have been put together by intelligence officials before September 11."[3]

This illustrates the same point I made it both the Introduction and Chapter 2 . . . the real impact of a successful EAJ campaign comes *afterwards*, when people *actually realize that they now control their own destinies*, and never need to fear the threat of irrational Jerkism again. **It's a wonderfully liberating moment, one which millions of Americans are going to experience in this first decade of the new Millennium.**

I've personally taken this "prevent a hard-core Jerk from being promoted" action several times, and to this day I'm very proud I did it. It truly can change the course of corporate and human history for the better. Just like the theme of the Michael J. Fox 1980's movies, "Back to the Future (I, II, & III)", ousting Jerks early-on inserts a cascading positive effect on history, that mounts to a crescendo, happily influencing dozens and then hundreds and thousands of key events for weeks and months and years into the future. It's a bit mind-bending, but absolutely true. With this book we'll see thousands of campaigns like this, and the world will be a far finer place for it.

Keep in mind: this is **always** the way it works in real-life – if *you* don't step forward to destroy the Jerk, then **no one** will. After you strike, then all sorts of people will emerge from the woodwork, emboldened to do battle with Jerks. *You*, however, must lead the way and take the first step. This is called, *"Leadership"*.

CASTING THE DIE

The next several paragraphs are the most important in the book – pay attention! **We're going to walk through the key decision making process for deciding how to deal with a hard-core jerk.**

If you determine that you're dealing with a *hard-core Jerk*, and he happens to be your new boss, you must decide between course of action # 4 (leave) or # 5 (get rid of Jerk). "Doing Nothing" is *not*, I repeat **not** an option. Doing Nothing is a clear-cut course of action that will only insure disaster. *The only job security in today's workplace is working for and around good, high quality, top-notch people.*

I say again . . . *The only job security in today's workplace is working for and around good, high quality, top-notch people.* If you allow yourself to work for a Jerk, you're simply screwing yourself, your career, and ultimately your loved ones and family. I'm not expressing academic theory here – I've seen this validated a hundred times over the past 30 years observing the experiences of friends, acquaintances, and many others, not to mention my own. And if you decide to opt for Option #5 (get rid of the Jerk), do it with a fury and cunning that will make the heavens gasp – this Jerk is going to screw up your *Life* if you don't act ruthlessly first. **Let's Roll!!**

IT'S NOW OR NEVER

The Editor of the British Magazine *XL*, John Westlake, puts it bluntly in his January 1998 issue that features the dynamic exposé of "Toxic Bosses" we quoted earlier in Chapter 2:

> *"None of these solutions are easy. They require vast portions of determination and courage. But what comes out clearly in the case studies is the importance of **doing something – anything**. The longer your plan of action stays in your head, the more the cretin will wear you down, and*

the harder it becomes to do anything about it."[4] (my
emphasis)

I would hasten to add that with *this* book, now it's much easier to
safely get rid of the Jerk than ever before.

TIME WOUNDS ALL HEELS??

Advocates for the "do-nothing" approach are fond of the "Time
wounds all heels" philosophy. But it's clear for many reasons stated
before that this is not fast enough for effective workplace cleansing.
If you're taking the Option #5 path, you must act, and must act **now**.

THE LEOPARD DOES *NOT* CHANGE HIS SPOTS

The "Counseling" approach, while useful for constructive behavior modification on moderate, reasonable people, is completely useless when dealing with a hard core Jerk. If the JIQ's characteristics
resonate with five or ten or more of those listed on the "faults list" at
Chapter 2, chances are he truly is a dangerous idiot, and counseling
will at best only create a temporary respite from jerk-like behavior.
"The leopard does not change his spots." Any progress made is only
illusory, as the Jerk drifts back to his natural asinine behavior pattern,
time after time.

I saw this graphically demonstrated in one Company I worked
for, where for three years (yowsa', 3 years) we tried to counsel and
collaborate with and try to nudge a truly Jerky boss back to reasonable
behavior. I can recall three different episodes where he received very
vigorous feedback from his employees and even his boss (!) on his
jerk-like behavior. For a month or two he'd dramatically improve.
"My, " we'd naively think to ourselves, "we've actually reformed this
moron". But then in months 3 and 4 he'd visibly drift back towards
the old bad habits, and by month 5 and 6 he'd be worse than ever. It
was a fool's game, an utter waste of time, to even *attempt* to reason
with this idiot.

"Temporary suppression" just doesn't work. Lousy managers just **don't** get better. If you decide to deal with a hardcore jerk rather than move jobs, don't take prisoners, go for the jugular – use this book's anonymous methodology and get rid of him in 30 days or less. No half measures. There's no substitute for victory.

Being "nice" to Jerks just doesn't work . . . never has, never will. Also bear in mind *not to give jerks any time to exact revenge on you and your committee*. Even though you're anonymous, you've got to kick him out in 30 days, or at least 60 days, so he has no second wind to counterattack. You can be assured that a Jerk will attempt to strike back hard, unless the Blitzkrieg you unleash kicks him out so fast his head never stops spinning. Give Jerks **NO QUARTER**, and never ever trust them in anything.

It's been stated previously, but bears repeating: Once you've made the decision to oust the Jerk, don't go all soft and mushy if he suddenly displays some nice qualities and seems to change. It's an act. Beware of Fellow Travelers who tout the Jerk's finer qualities. Remember, THE LEOPARD DOES *NOT* CHANGE HIS SPOTS. Be ruthless, or be devoured. Just do it!

TIMING IS CRUCIAL

As with most successful endeavors, the *timing* of your operation is very crucial. You don't want to launch too soon, and you'll suffer unnecessary pain if you launch too late.

If you and your committee initiate the attack too soon, you may not have enough damning evidence to get the Jerk ousted. In other words, be sure to "give him enough rope to hang himself". How much time is enough?? My experience indicates that within 2 to 4 weeks you can clearly establish the fact that a "Jerk is at Work". In another month or two, you and your allies should be easily able to compile a damning indictment. So within a total of three months an effective campaign could be credibly launched. Ideally, a devastating EAJ attack with a 30-day deadline should be launched 3 to 6 months after a Jerk has been discovered "on the job". If you can do this faster than this, so much the better. Strike while the Iron is Hot.

Also, the advantage of striking early is that a "new Boss" jerk is usually under a 6-month probationary period anyway. Directors and VP's are very watchful when a new manager is placed, and a "Clip-on Book Attack" at this vulnerable stage is usually enough to send the probationary Jerk packing. What a relief.

After 6 months, the longer a Jerk is allowed to hang around unchallenged, the more opportunity he has to dig in and ingratiate himself with the powers that be. Not that you can't oust a Jerk after 1 or 2 or 3 years (just think of the depths & varieties of incidents – think of the legions of enemies the Jerk's made) – you just have to build a much stronger case.

THE DANGERS OF DELAY

Also, three major factors to bear in mind. The longer a Jerk is allowed to hang around, the more damage he'll inflict on your organization:

1) the more good people will jump ship, "turtles rolling off the log".

2) the more clone Jerks he'll bring on board (remember Chapter 3 on the Consequences of Unrestrained Jerkism, and the Domino Effect of Jerkitis?)

3) If jerk behavior goes *unchallenged*, I *guarantee you* he'll morph into an even *bigger*, *malicious* jerk as time passes. I've seen too many cases of your basic hard core Jerk evolving into a screaming criminal monster (*i.e.*, a Cosmic Jerk) with no restraints. It's like feeding roasted chopped livers to a piranha . . . they just grow bigger teeth.

Getting rid of Jerks is like weeding a garden – the longer you put it off, the bigger and more pervasive the weeds are.

Mantra

"Never fear a hardcore Jerk,
Only fear your own failure
*to deal with him **quickly** and **ruthlessly**."*

Re-read that Mantra. And in turn, quote it to your committee members every time you conduct e-mail, phone, or face to face conversations. Your EAJ Campaign must be crisp, clear-cut-objective-and-deadline driven, and end-game conscious. Don't drag it out. Nail it and bag it! *What are you waiting for*??

THE POWER OF "KEEPING BOOK"

The foundation for success in your EAJ Campaign is the taking of reasonably precise daily notes on all incidents that demonstrate the Jerk's unsuitability for your workplace. In the typical "drumbeat" scenario, a hard-core jerk can screw up 2 or 3 times a day. Document time / date / place / people involved & witnesses / brief event summary in writing, in your "logbook". Doesn't have to be elaborate, just understandable so you can use it in the near future. Also, keep it absolutely *to yourself* that you're even compiling such a record, until your Committee is well established and you can share this with folks you can *absolutely trust*.

You'll collect a lot of incredible fodder from the outrages the Jerk perpetrates on other poor sods beside yourself, so include any and every thing that's relevant to this Jerk's behavior and performance. Accurately document each and every incident. You'll be amazed at the huge volume of damning material you'll collect in even just a few weeks time.

Collect any e-mails, documents, phone conversations, incidents in meetings, trips, hallways, *etc.* – anything that sheds light on what's really going on in your workplace. Especially detail information that may indicate criminal activity or gross negligence taking place. Written documents, and in particular printed e-mails with time/date stamp, can be damning, irrefutable sources.

PEARL HARBOR CONTINGENCIES

The intent of all this event-capturing is for use in an anonymous complaint package to be sent to a mid-level Director of a department, keeping everything quietly in-house and allowing management to perform intelligent housecleaning duties as envisioned by senior management and shareholders. However, in the rare case of an Enron-style corporate corruption scenario that evolves into a high-stakes lawsuit, this kind of primary source insider information can become **priceless**, a litigator's dream come true.

A close friend of mine used this kind of information once in a scenario which spun into a huge lawsuit in which his lawyers totally defeated two large frightened and very criminal corporations, who had clearly been taken over by mega-jerks, that quickly pleaded with them to settle out of court. Their facts and information were just too overwhelming. With a 3" thick Complaint Brief shotgun pressed to their temple, brimming with damning evidence, they were quite generous, the sleazy bastards. Afterward, it was conservatively estimated that public disclosure of this information in court would have cost these slime balls over $ 10 billion in stock devaluations, had their criminal conduct been revealed to investors. So, you never know. Take notes. Much better odds than the Lottery. (By the way, the proper authorities *were* informed early on – the US Attorney General and the Department of Justice were so outraged at the criminal activity of these Corporations that they also officially joined forces with my friend in his Lawsuit.)

HUGE OPPORTUNITY FROM DESPAIR

So the power of "keeping book" is truly awesome. Don't get *depressed* about your strange or stressful work situation, *take notes*! It can, it will, be *devastating* to the career of the hard-core jerk, the very thing he fears above all else: exposure to the light of day. Think of it. *A nightmare situation in any workplace is, in actuality, a huge opportunity*! And the worse the nightmare, *the bigger the opportunity* – I guarantee it.

BE SAFE, NOT SORRY

By the way, before I forget, let me remind you of the obvious. *BE SURE* to have copies (if not the originals themselves) of ALL of the documentation mentioned above – *all of it*: notes, logbooks, e-mails, documents – taken **off campus**, *away* from your workplace and secured at some safe place. You don't want to have your treasure trove trapped at work if a worst-case scenario unfolds. *Just a necessary precaution*. Also, be diligent about keeping your "safe files" **routinely updated**. E-mails can be specially ephemeral – they have a way of being conveniently erased when the shit hits the fan – always print out and copy damning e-mails and stash in your off-campus trove.

Be safe, not sorry! If things spiral out of control into WW III litigation, or a Chapter 8 - style bombshell approach, your eager, competent lawyers will reward your foresight with whoops of delight at the gold mine of documents you lay at their feet.

CONNECTING THE DOTS

And a pile of treasure all your notes surely are. I'll share with you a little technique that greatly simplifies harnessing all this data towards power-launching your Complaint Package. Xerox off all your logbook notes, e-mails, commentary from 3rd parties, documents, *etc*. With scissors clip out distinct incidents, character traits, faults, observations . . . and place each into it's appropriate category pile. You'll notice the piles begin to grow, clearly revealing the worst weaknesses of this particular clown you're having to cope with.

Soon you'll see his "display of poor judgment" pile grow, next to his "dodges responsibility for own actions" pile, adjacent to his "ingratitude – does not recognize or reward good performance" stack, next to his mountain of "incompetence" examples, butted up against his "extremely arrogant" notations, bordering the "names of good employees who left his group in disgust" slips, and on and on and on. Rapidly, you'll have a damning snapshot of a Master Jerk at Work, priceless insights that will force all but the most incompetent and corrupt of Directors to take decisive action to get rid of the scourge.

PSYCHOLOGICAL LIFT

I can also assure you that a *very important* spin off of this drill is that the burden of the situation is suddenly lifted from **your** shoulders. The 20 or 30 piles you see before you, like trusted advisors, speak volumes:

"No, you're not crazy, this guy really is a serious Jerk"
and,
"Hey, let's get our Committee together, fill out the
anonymous complaint forms in Chapter 6, and get rid
of this idiot"   and,
"Yo, what are you waiting for, hoss??"

Yep, those piles of paper slips are sending a clear message.
You become *empowered* and excited when you realize that soon, if you just play your cards right, the Jerk will be History, long gone. This is truly is a liberating feeling, the fresh breeze of emancipation imminent.

HE'S GOT A LITTLE LIST (AND NOTHING WILL BE MISSED)

Print several website copies of the Complaint Forms so you can prepare a draft. You'll be amazed at how fast a damning faults list can almost effortlessly take shape. After you've compiled yours, you may wish to consult with a very few *deeply trusted* allies to expand upon it. You'll be amazed at the *priceless info* they can contribute to the Complaint Package. Have fun.

A LITTLE BACKGROUND DIGGING CAN A GOLD MINE UNEARTH

Here's a little gem of advice that most folks might not consider in preparing an EAJ Campaign, namely: I can *guarantee* you, if you have a hard-core jerk on your hands, *I promise you* that like a lot of pedophile Catholic Priests, "He has a History". The guy (or gal) didn't just magically become a Jerk overnight. Ten to one odds are that you can look into his past job(s), either in your Department or in another Department or company, and unearth all sorts of significant Dirt on this Bum.

You and your Committee can discreetly probe around, and chances are you'll find lots of folks willing to tell all about the Jerk's sordid past. Many times they're amused, fascinated, impressed, and even enthusiastic that somebody at long last is finally going to *nail* this Jerk. In any case, it's always a revealing exercise. And usually you'll discover that one or more of the Jerk's former managers *failed to do their supervisory job* to either counsel or mold or fire the idiot from the Company, *a la* Cardinal Bernard Law with dozens of criminal priests in Boston in the 80's and 90's – ditto with hundreds of fellow Bishops and Cardinals. Supervisory negligence and incompetence are rampant in our society – and often the driving force of it is either moral cowardice or sloth, or both – but you just don't have to put up with it any more, now that you have *Jihad the Jerk at Work* in your clutches.

CASH IN YOUR CHIPS, BIGTIME

So how does all this juicy past history on the Jerk help now? You may well discover that his screwups were so colossal and behavior so outrageous, that his *present boss*, the very person you may be sending the Complaint Package to, was *grossly negligent* in failing to discover any of this mind-boggling conduct **before** he hired the Jerk for your group. In other words, he didn't do due diligence, didn't do his job. Happens all the time when Directors are in a hurry to fill management slots – and regular employees get screwed as a result.

MAKE THE DIRECTOR AN OFFER HE CAN'T REFUSE!

Think of what this means. This puts massive pressure on the Director. If he diddles and squanders his 30 days, and fails to get rid of the Jerk, your Committee's 2d wave Complaint Package to *his* boss, the VP , and the VP of HR will highlight this hiring negligence, as well as the present work scandal – the Director will **really** look bad! This often clinches the issue right there – if the Director has a prayer of halting disclosure of all this highly embarrassing information, he's got to comply with your Committee's very legitimate request to get rid of the Jerk *pronto* – end of story.

Don't forget – an effective part of your Complaint Package is to mark appropriate pages in *Jihad the Jerk at Work* with yellow Post-It notes, and highlight pertinent passages. The paragraph above, in the right situation, may be a good candidate. So whip out your yellow highlighter, and go to town.

RUB SALT IN THE WOUNDS

Notice in the "Sample" Cover letter to the Director in Chapter 6, in the Postscript, PS, section, we use the space to remind the Director of his negligence in hiring the Jerk without first checking out his background.

This particular Jerk will truly be History, and soon.

SPEED DEMON – SHORTCUT TO VICTORY

You'll observe we have a prominent section of the "Fault's List" reserved for presenting the *past* job performance of the Jerk. If you unearth a cesspool on this category, use it without mercy – it is conceivable that confronted with all this damning evidence, the Director will wisely forego lengthy investigation and just get rid of the Jerk far before his 30-day deadline is up. In fact, we're running a contest on an annual basis to see which Jerk gets canned the fastest, and what was the decisive factor (current record is 25 days, I'm sure some of you can easily beat that). See the address and fax and e-mail

LET'S ROLL: ATTACK EXECUTION

lists enclosed to send in your entry, which may discreetly make future editions of this book, as well as the annual "Jerk at Work" contests listed in Chapter 13.

JERKS WITH HISTORIES

At this juncture, I'll have to share two hilarious, eye-opening "past history of jerks" stories with you, just to illustrate what an incredibly powerful but "best kept secret" this weapon is. Both pertain to "peer jerks", guys who were so bizarre and screwed up, I just had to learn what Rock they slithered out from. Sure enough, they both had job histories so twisted it's a wonder they weren't pumping gas already.

"WIRETECH'S TOP TEN LIST"

One fellow I had the grave misfortune to have to work with (I'll call him "Stan Rajput") was a bizarrely uncooperative type who was a lazy, extremely stupid, incompetent, habitual backstabber and game-player type. He was about 40 years old, and still at a very low level in the Company, so that's very revealing right there. I often wondered, am I the only one who sees through this idiot??

Then the revelation came . . . a friend from a distant, but very large, location related an amazing story that clinched the issue. At a going-away luncheon for a well-respected executive at this location, the organizers read off a David Letterman-style "Ten Reasons why Joe won't miss working at 'WireTech' " list. High on the list, around #2, the reason was,

"Because Joe won't have to work with Stan Rajput any more!" which elicited thunderous laughter from the crowd, because all were aware what a total Jerk Stan Rajput was. My friend explained to me how despised he was, and how much damage this idiot caused during his career at WireTech, which confirmed everything I had witnessed about Stan at my own location. Remember, **your gut instinct about people is right 99 times out of 100.**

With this book, you can quickly and easily and *safely* get rid of the Stan Rajput's of the world, who are overpaid and ruining job environments left and right. Do it today – *you just don't have to put up with the nonsense any more.* Trust your gut instinct – if you feel that an individual is acting like a hardcore Jerk, chances are astronomically high he truly *is* a hardcore Jerk, and has been so consistently for 5 or 10 or 20 years. And that 500 outraged co-workers would lynch him if they had the opportunity.

> *"If it walks like a duck, talks like a duck, looks like a duck*
> *. . . chances are high the damn thing's a duck."*
>   an old law enforcement adage

"ONCE A JERK, ALWAYS A JERK"

The second story that demonstrates the power of a little digging revolves around a bozo I had to work with in a different Company. I quickly realized that this guy was a certified psycho that I suspected was on some kind of psychotic drug, because he could become insanely violent at the drop of a pin. Ol' "Hal Greenglass", a true freak show – and he even looked the part.

Folks on our office floor seemed strangely terrified and deferential to this Jerk, or at least avoided him whenever possible.

I thought to myself, "This sick-o has got to have a History." And sure enough . . . turns out ol' Hal, who was only 33 or so, already had a horrible reputation from previous jobs in the Company. As a manufacturing supervisor at another location, he became infatuated with an attractive woman who worked on his shift. She intensely disliked him, but he pestered her incessantly. After being rebuffed a dozen times, slimeball Hal decided to impress the girl big time. (There never was a Ruder Pest, slimy Hal from Budapest.) He put her photo on a huge poster promoting "manufacturing safety", and had it plastered at 60 locations all over the plant. The infuriated woman complained to HR, who hastily shifted "Hal" over to our location, well away from manufacturing and vulnerable female employees. What a Jerk. What a typical mousy HR response.

> I repeat, *"ALL JERKS* HAVE A *HISTORY* – DIS-
> COVER WHAT IT IS, AND USE IT MER-
> CILESSLY TO PURGE THEM FROM
> YOUR MIDST. "

The Director will fall all over himself hastening to get rid of this stinking albatross around his neck.

THE MAJOR BENEFITS OF ALLIANCES

I've often mentioned the formation of a "Committee", a very discreet alliance of good, solid people that all desire to get rid of the Jerk in Question. If you can maintain trusting, strong relationships in your Committee, there truly is strength in numbers. "More hands make light the work." The most successful foreign engagements we've undertaken as a nation (*e.g.*, WW II, NATO in the Cold War, the Gulf War, *etc.*) were built on strong alliances, not unilateral action. Any competent analyses of the messes we've gotten into in Vietnam and Iraq 2003 demonstrate the folly of unilateral action.

Most Americans are blissfully unaware that if the Soviet Army hadn't tied down – and then smashed – 80% (!!) of the *Wehrmacht's* combat divisions on the Eastern Front (1941-45), today we'd all be humming Wagner on the *Fuhrer's* birthday and christening our first-born with names like "Reinhard", "Heinrich", "Tojo", and "Benito". Strong alliances are just as important in getting rid of a Jerk at Work.

"EYES AND EARS" WIN WARS

The Rid-a-Jerk alliance has many key functions. Its members morally *support* one another, and also collaborate to craft the most truthful and damning Complaint Package possible to send anonym-ously to the Director. They are the crucial early warning "eyes and ears" that detect everything that's going on during the intense 30-day rid-a-jerk first wave campaign. As we've seen already in previous chapters, crucial and timely information can deliver a quick knockout blow to a Jerk, sometimes to the delighted surprise of all.

A COMMITTEE OF ONE

Forming a trustworthy Committee of 4 or 5 folks is a big plus, but what if you're working in such a fear-saturated environment that even decent people are so terrorized they'll lose their jobs that the concept of even an *anonymous* collective protest is unthinkable?? Yet you're convinced that a hard-ball EAJ Campaign is exactly what this organization desperately needs??

Well, in that case, (and this ain't theoretical, I actually worked in one company where I saw it for real . . . boy, it's not much fun) you'll just have to form an anonymous "committee of one". Sherron Watkins did at Enron. You don't have to advertise these numbers to the Recipient Director, or anyone else – just proceed as if you had a Jedi and powerful Committee of Seven. You well may pick up allies and *bona fide* members along the way. And just think, your vetting and security concerns will be greatly diminished. You alone will have to make the crucial decisions such as whom to place on the "list of people or organizations to talk to" in the Cover Letter to the Director. You gotta do what you gotta do.

WHO WILL BELL THE CAT??

Back to the Committee of greater than one. As the Committee begins to build mutual confidence and trust, you may find more and more members will happily volunteer to have their names listed on the Complaint Form to the Director, *not* as Committee members (names of Committee participants *always* remain anonymous) but as reliable folks the Director can consult to verify the Jerk's behavior and performance.

This can be a sensitive subject: Who do we list on the Cover Letter to the Director as "People you should speak to" to confirm the Jerk's ineptitude for his present job. Many, many factors come to bear on this decision – it boils down to the consensus judgment of you, your trusted Jedi, and faithful committee members. Factors such as personality of the Director (is he reasonable and open minded, or is he a pinheaded, moronic terror?), the workplace atmosphere, the personalities and experiences of individuals involved.

It's been my experience that highly motivated and energized Committees can easily resolve all these issues. High motivation is the key to dynamic, successful committees. As committee members share information about the extent of damage the Jerk has foisted on the organization, a cool anger, a steely grim determination, a fanaticism even, takes hold that sweeps away all obstacles in the path of the objective . . . exiling this Jerk to the very depths of hell. Your role is to energize the Committee and then harness this fury to accomplish the mission.

SHARPENING THE LIST

Often, coming up with a dynamite list of folks the Director, or VP, or CEO needs to consult about the subject at hand is really a no-brainer. Sherron Watkins, the Enron finance VP who sent the anonymous letter to Chairman Ken Lay in August 2001 raising the Red Flag on Enron's shaky financial schemes, merely laundry-listed a whole host of folks she knew had intimate knowledge of the financial partnership problems and were as concerned as she was. It obviously was an excellent list, because after a few inquiries, Lay realized how correct Sherron was, and he quickly drew back from promoting master crook Andy Fastow to CEO (it also convinced Lay, who was a sleazy crook as well, to unload $10 million of his personal Enron stock immediately).

I have worked with Committees where establishing a very precise contacts list presented no problem at all. The 6 or 7 Committee members all had such an intense hatred of the JIQ that they eagerly volunteered to have their names listed as Director contacts. However, I've seen other work environments where good people were so terrified of unpredictable, strange managerial behaviors (very justifiably, I might add) that it was better just to tell the Director to discuss the problem Jerk with "people in the Quality Control group and Marketing group" or whatever, and to let the die fall where they may. In this case, no one in this stinking cesspool of a Company had their delicate individual neck sticking out. However, the exceptions may be those priceless exiles who've already left the Department and have nothing to lose. *Be sure* that the Director personally talks with all these folks; they should be able to single-handedly torpedo the Jerk, if they understand their **key role** in the EAJ Campaign.

I saw one Director try to shirk his responsibility and conduct a shallow investigation to attempt to whitewash a Jerk – we didn't let him get away with it! To lessen the probability of the Director even *considering* this old tired ploy, notice on the Generic Cover Letter to the Director we list two categories of folks he needs to consult:

1)   People he *must* talk to for his investigation to have any credibility whatsoever.
2)   Other folks he should talk to.

If he tries to run a whitewash scam and ignore knowledgeable witnesses, he'll have a lot of explaining to do to several irate VP's. He can count on it. Your Committee can easily determine how sincere his probe was.

CREATING MOMENTUM

This key area is where your skills as a "ringleader" are most important. Folks obviously can't be coerced into risking a higher profile, nor would you desire to exert any coercion. You need to establish the most secure and optimistic conditions so they'll gladly desire to come forward: strength in numbers, a strong united front, a devastating Complaint Package, a confident sense of humor, the appropriate no-nonsense warnings to the Director that bullying tactics will immediately backfire and result in Complaint Package escalation to higher levels, *etc.* Operate from unassailable positions of strength.

Let me return to the "confident sense of humor" passage. I've found out over the years that his may well be one of the most effective weapons in your EAJ Campaign. Nothing revs up the troops more than sharp-edged, hit the nail on the head, incisive humor, if it comes to you naturally. Use it freely – and best of all, Jerks seem to have little sense of intelligent humor, only boorish banter.

SINGING FROM THE SAME SHEET OF MUSIC

Given the Jerk's sordid performance, he's made a large number of serious enemies, so it should be also relatively easy to identify stalwarts outside the immediate Committee to add to the contacts list. Usually if people understand there's a very large list of eager dime-droppers, they have no problem signing on because their own risk is small to non-existent. As we've mentioned, the more and better all these people are briefed as to the game plan, the better the chances they'll present an accurate, damning picture of the Jerk's activities to the Director, if and when he asks to discuss the matter with them.

Needless to say, there's no point in their discussing any ties to, or even the existence of, ringleaders and committees. Their only role is to honestly discuss the Jerk's performance and behavior with the Director, so he can get an accurate picture of what's really going on. They should *always* be prepared to honestly advise the Director, should he ask, of the *appropriate resolution of the problem.* (*e.g.* "Well, I'd kick him out of the Company for what he's done, but at *least* get him well away from this Department – *please.*") Since you and the Committee have shared information with the contact, he probably will honestly and gladly line up with your recommendation, and thus be a decisive element in the success of the Campaign. It just has to be an open and honest effort. Honesty and integrity are central here – no EAJ Campaign can succeed without adhering 100% to each.

This entire drill is probably the *decisive* element in really getting the Jerk canned. It's all about having knowledgeable people convey "truth to power". Don't slack off on this effort. Success in lining up a solid, vigorous, truthful, courageous, united front of opinion can alone seal the fate of the Jerk at Work.

A BIT OF ADVICE

As the coordinator who's orchestrating all this truth to power, it's probably not a good idea for you to be on the Director's talk-to contact list. You need to be keeping an eye on the big picture, directing the flow, not be sweating it out exposed on the hot seat in the Director's office.

TIMELY FEEDBACK

Also suggest to all your allies that they discreetly debrief you once the Director has met with them. This feedback should be immediately passed on to all committee members, and all other key parties, to keep everyone up to speed. Knowledge is power and security. E-mail is a rapid way to disseminate **as long as** you're *absolutely sure* of the loyalty of the distribution list, and that you clearly request on the e-mail that the message is *"Read only. Not to be forwarded or disseminated. Confidential."* You must *carefully control* electronic communications, or they can destroy your efforts.

Also, in this day and age when many folks have their *own private laptops* and a private e-mail account, all the e-mailing might be conducted on non-company assets, to preclude Corporate snooping. Especially consider this if you work in a KGB-style organization.

This kind of close communication is always great for boosting morale, because it lets everybody know what's going on at a very sensitive time, and prepares them for any "surprise questions". This all sounds like a lot of work, but it's really not – it's just common sense, good unified communicating psychologically spine-stiffening tactics when it's most crucial. The effort will seem gold-gilded, time well spent, when the Jerk is actually gone for good.

The Committee creates its own momentum. You don't necessarily have to lead it from start to finish, you may be fortunate to find a Jedi to power the movement.

SECURITY IS CRUCIAL

Just be sure that you *very* carefully build the Committee with people you can **absolutely trust**. You must discover who the Quislings are in the landscape, and give them *wide berth*. As we just discussed, be especially leery of broadcast e-mails. The Committee must exercise the discipline to **seriously limit and firewall e-mail distribution**, and observe high security at all times. Loose lips sink ships.

Looking at our trusty pie chart again on the next page, it's obvious that Fellow Travelers, the Clueless, and even Middle-of-the-Roaders be excluded from the committee – that also means they must have no clue that such an organization even exists. You will base it on "Dependable" and "Great" Allies, and, of course, the occasional Jedi. Avoid shaky lightweights with any ties whatsoever to the Dark Side.

We've already mentioned absolutely including folks who've left the group in disgust to get away from the JIQ. They're pure-spun Gold – they can often help sink the Jerk almost single-handedly. Also, anyone, anywhere who has done business with the Jerk should be discreetly sounded out – his peers, associates, customers, *etc*. You'll never know where the MLODI (Mother Lode of Damning Information) will pop up, but, rest assured, **it's out there**, this El Dorado, waiting for discovery.

KEEP ALL TRUSTED ALLIES WELL INFORMED

The most important order of business with the Committee is keeping all members fully up to date. Of course, let them join in the fun of selecting "Fault List" categories – they'll astound you with priceless, damning insights into the depravity of the Jerk. Let them know when you plan to submit the Complaint Package to the Director, as well as the target window of the 30-day grace period.

This way they'll be mentally prepared to respond to any investigative queries from the Director.

They'll also be alerted to watch for any unfolding developments, so they can keep the entire Committee current. This alertness to what's happening, or not happening, can make or break an EAJ Campaign. This vital exchange of information can often easily ensnare the Jerk in his own foolishness and hasten his demise, not to mention bolstering the confidence of all trusted allies.

OPRAH'S BOOK CLUB

It's a great idea to get a copy of this book *to each and every one* of your trusted Committee members, long before H-Hour commences (*i.e.*, when the Complaint Package hits the Director's desk). It will greatly aid them in binding to the team, and help stiffen their resolve. Obviously, folks should treat it as a Confidential Document, and not just leave it lying around the office.

BLESSED ARE THE PEACEMAKERS

Be sure to smooth out any disputes between Committee members asap. The last thing you need is any kind of infighting between the good guys. Yet sometimes ridiculous clashes can materialize out of nowhere, and you and your Jedi must be alert resolve them pronto – the Committee's efforts must be focused *entirely* on ousting the JIQ.

BIGGER FISH TO FRY

In the same vein, don't allow you or your focused EAJ Campaign to get sidetracked or derailed by other minor issues that pop up – I'd be willing to bet *nothing* will be as important as dumping this hard-core jerk that's destroying your work environment. Impart this sense of urgency to all on the EAJ Committee. Remember . . .

Allies vs Enemies in the Workplace
(typical %)

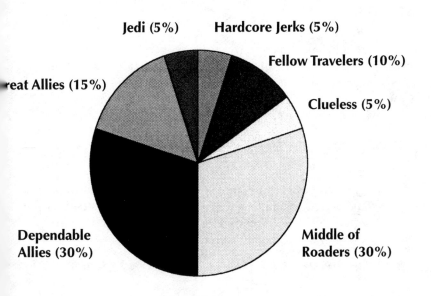

The wisest sage
on this green earth
Twixt the Sun and the Sea
and the Sky,
Is one who eschews
the ego-frivolous fray
*When he's got **bigger fish***
to fry.

"The Sage"
E. Fergusson
2005

ANONYMOUSNESS IS NEXT TO GODLINESS

All through this book you've heard us harp on the **absolute need** for you and your Committee as an organization to remain "anonymous" throughout this entire Rid-a-Jerk campaign, and even beyond. We'll now discuss this extremely essential key to your EAJ effort success in depth – you must understand the concept completely so that:

1) you can be successful without getting destroyed in the process (avoiding a Pyrrhic victory)
2) you can easily blow away objections to the anonymous method from any quarter, and also counterattack so effectively that the complainers will be embarrassed they even broached the subject.

Don't skip this section, it's VITAL to the success of the effort!!

IT REALLY IS A JUNGLE OUT THERE

I'll once again remind you: this is a high-stakes game we are playing. You must *never* become complacent, even after the Jerk has been successfully exiled to Timbucktoo.

First of all, always remember that the higher level you deal with in any organization, the more powerful the Manager is, the more high-dollar, high-pressure, high-stakes issues the executive has to deal with on an *hourly* basis, and the more dangerous the atmosphere becomes to those who question, prod, and otherwise rock the boat. Also, the less time and patience the manager has to spend on aspects of your EAJ effort. That's why I *always* recommend getting the issue resolved at the **lowest** possible level in the company you can find a manager of integrity and intelligence. He'll have more time and motivation to really delve into the key specifics, and should be quickly able to see the validity of the Complaint Package and act on it.

PIRANAH-LAND

Just remember, from Director level on up, the guy you are dealing with can and will *fire anybody with the flick of his wrist.* They do it all the time, without a qualm. It's part of their job description. So when the Complaint is made, **let the *Package*, and the Jerk**, take all the Heat (cover letter & list of faults paper clipped to this book well annotated, with generic letter from yours truly, your favorite author). Let the *burden* of the deliberation and decision fall *squarely* on the Director's shoulders, where it belongs.

Because if it becomes known that *you* are the ringleader, or the structure of the committee or identities of members is disclosed, chances are that the Director, no matter what a *great guy* you thought he was (so much of the benign image thing is just fluff, when the going gets rough) will do what typical human beings do the world over – he'll

TAKE THE PATH OF THE LEAST RESISTANCE,

which in most corporations and organizations translates to

SHOOT THE MESSENGER, *ERGO* THE PROBLEM GOES AWAY

Criminy, it seems so primitive and brutish and pathetic, but then *this is how the real world works* – it's just so much easier that way

(at least in the short run, and most business executives are under so much pressure, the short run always looks sooo attractive)

SO, WHAT TO DO ...

So, wise ringleaders are keenly tuned in to this hard fact of life. Your goal then, is to put a *box* around the Director, to set up the situation so that **THE PATH OF THE LEAST RESISTANCE IS TO GET RID OF THE JERK, AND DO SO SPEEDILY.** You set this up by . . .

> ⟶ submit the Complaint Package via a *committee* of concerned workers (anonymous)
> ⟶ remain *strictly* anonymous, always (you and all committee members)
> ⟶ submit a *dynamic* Complaint Package
> ⟶ make a clear-cut *recommendation*
> ⟶ give the Director a strict *30-day deadline* to perform
> ⟶ *ruthlessly* escalate the Package to two VP's if the Director screws up in any way
> ⟶ repeat the same procedure with the VP level – never let up the pressure! and if needed, on up to the CEO and up . . .

I'm going to repeat the key sentence in this entire book . . .

Your goal as ringleader is to create the condition that the **PATH OF LEAST RESISTANCE FOR THE DIRECTOR IS *SIMPLY TO GET RID OF THE JERK, AND QUICKLY.***

If you do not create this "path of least resistance" condition, you will fail, it's that simple.

THE WAY IT IS

Let's review the real-world of organizations . . .

Golden Rule of most Corporations, Agencies, and other Organizations:

> *"He who makes the accusation, no matter how truthful or justified, gets automatically tarred with a **filthy black brush** – always shoot the messenger, then there'll be a lot less uncomfortable messages floating around."*

So, keep anonymous, and vigorously ridicule anyone who suggests otherwise. Show them these passages, if you think it will help them see the light.

THE 10% SOLUTION

Oh, and if your identity becomes known to the wrong people (*any* of your bosses) you might not get canned right away. But if you have *any* experience in business organizations, you know that *every* organization, even if they won't admit it, has a "bottom 10%" list, a pre-selected group slated to be *laid off* if business slows down, or there's a need to impress brilliant Wall Street analysts (the same crew of mental giants that were bullish on Enron and Worldcom right up to, and even during (!) their gory implosions) on the Company's great cost-cutting program. Remember, today's feel-good boom is tomorrow's dowdy bust – don't get yourself slotted in that bottom 10% list, if you can help it.

You're not on this shit list now, you're a top performer, but you'll definitely be placed there if you're identified as a "troublemaker". You don't need all this hassle, so simply remain anonymous and explain to your loyal committee why – they'll understand, and support you. End of problem.

Homily: *anyone representing himself in a court of law has a fool for a client*
anyone sacrificing the protection of deep anonymity in the midst of an EAJ campaign is likewise a fool

stay anonymous . . . be safe, not sorry

HARDBALL

In the generic "Cover Letter to the Director", you'll notice we have quite a prominent little section that lists situations in which the Director's 30 day "grace period" to kick the jerk out, can be yanked (at which time the entire Complaint Package goes directly to his boss, the VP of _____ – engineering, or whatever – and to the VP of Human Resources). Before we discuss these, let's explain first why we call the 30-day period a "grace period". Are we being flip or disrespectful, or what?

There's a simple reason we call it a grace period – mainly, if the Director had **really been doing his job,** he never would have let the workplace atmosphere in his Department deteriorate to the point where employees had to resort to the extreme of having to present a package of grievances against a manager or employee as serious as you're submitting. He just hasn't been watching the ball – he already has two strikes against him. But instead of going over his head to several of his VP and CEO bosses, your Committee is giving him a last chance to fix his screw ups so well that not only will his bosses *not know* how badly he stumbled, he can *actually make himself look good*, like a pro-active Executive who's in charge, knows what's going on, and makes decisive personnel changes when appropriate. In my generic letter to the Director, which I recommend you send in your Package, I diplomatically point all this out to him.

So, in effect, you're doing the Director a big favor in pointing out this disaster in his organization, and you're giving him enough time to fix it. If he screws up the opportunity, truly a "grace period" in every sense of the phrase, then *he* may be more of the problem than all initially thought, and he'll have to answer to higher authority for his own incompetence.

How can he blow it?? We clearly list the ways in the Letter. One is if he in any way tries to discover the identities of Committee members. You and your Committee members cannot afford to put up with these games. To paraphrase President George W. Bush, "Either the Director **is** sincerely trying to resolve the issue, **or he isn't.**" If he's trying to identify Committee members, you can bet he's angling to "shoot the messenger" – and that's when you cut him off at the knees and get his VP boss involved, as well as the VP of Human Resources.

"Expect no mercy, show no mercy"

BE ULTRA-SECURITY CONSCIOUS!!

By the way, now's a good time to mention the obvious. For the good guys to remain anonymous, and thus protected, the "faults list" comments and other components of the Package should be sanitized of any obvious clues that would give away identities – pointing to you as the ringleader, or any other key members of the Committee, such as the Jedi or "strong allies". With a little thought and mild editing, this should not present any problem. Obviously, it will be much safer to use our website forms rather than the hard copy forms in Chapter Six. And, if you're working in a real corrupt, paranoid Enron-type organization that hires ex FBI, CIA, NSA, DIA, CID, KGB, *Sicherheitsdienst*, SAVAK, and Gestapo thugs to snoop and probe, you might not even desire to leave fingerprints. Just use your best judgment about what level you wish to take security precautions.

CUT THROUGH SMOKESCREENS

You may run into some resistance from some in going the anonymous route. Most of the time the motivation for this resistance is a smokescreen for an effort to brush off or derail the Complaint Package using the Counterattack philosophy of "Ridicule is the most effective weapon." Don't fall for this *old ploy*. You can Xerox off or tear out pages from this book, highlight, and discreetly send to offending parties, to show them their tactics will backfire, your alliance will *not* back down, and that you're *on* to their game. Put the fear of God into them.

Why do all Human Resources "Upward Feedback" programs have **anonymity as their cornerstones**?? Because any competent

HR professional knows employees wouldn't *dare* to fill out a criticism form going to higher management without the **guaranteed protection** of anonymity. Why are all credible democratic elections conducted via secret ballot?? It's the same principle with the EAJ Complaint Package, which is merely a more dynamic manifestation of Upward Feedback.

Initially, the Independent Board investigating NASA on the Columbia disaster had *extreme difficulty* getting *anyone* in that agency to willingly be interviewed. It was **only** after the Board promised complete anonymity to all interviewees did they get any cooperation.[5] Why?

Lower and mid level employees in any organization are *extremely vulnerable*. If they take the initiative to honestly and sincerely present truthful information that exposes incompetence, jerky behavior, or even more serious charges leveled at another employee or manager, it is their *right* to do so anonymously. It is legitimate management's obligation to senior management and shareholders to investigate in good faith and take appropriate action. ***Do not let anyone ever suggest to you otherwise.*** If somebody does, inform them that yours truly, the Author, will be soon coming over to kick his ass. That ought to shut him up.

Seriously, your right to anonymity is sacrosanct. Never give it up, or allow others to cast dispersions on it. Their motivations for doing so can be traced back to the Dark Side, and the Jerk himself.

DON'T MESS WITH US (share with anyone whining about anonymity)

I'll share a real-world story with you on how to ruthlessly combat the anti-anonymous mindset. Once a Committee of mine forwarded an EAJ Package to a very powerful Director we mistakenly *thought* would immediately take professional action. Instead, we discreetly found out from his secretary that he contemptuously tossed the entire Package in the trash because he "didn't deal with anonymous people".

Like bad, Jerky managers everywhere, this selfish fraud had not *one whit* of concern about the pain and terror his employees were undergoing.

So we immediately forwarded an identical package to his Vice President in the organization (with an additional commentary on the Director's precipitous and intemperate trashing of our appeal), who was intelligent enough to take it seriously. He conducted a swift and fair investigation, and concluded not only that our complaint had merit, but that we'd actually **understated the seriousness of the damage the Jerk had inflicted on our organization** (note the awesome power of understatement again – actually I've found it's easy to do, since the *full damage* a Jerk perpetrates often only becomes known when further investigations uncover massive amounts of travesties, and a lot of different people come forward). The Jerk was quickly transferred to a distant location in an embarrassingly nondescript job (we learned that 8 months later the Jerk resigned from the Company – finally saw the writing on the Wall).

But this story gets much better. Four months after our Complaint Package hit the VP's desk, the original Director who'd arrogantly distained our original Package abruptly "retired". They had a big tearful luncheon for him and all, but the word was out that a *lot* of folks were relieved to see the back side of him. He'd just gotten too cocky, too detached, too arrogant, too *sanctimonious* for his own good, and he paid the price. Reliable scuttlebutt had it that his VP boss was furious that he was not carrying his own weight, that the VP had to use *his* valuable time to resolve issues the Director could have easily handled. The question eventually boiled down to, "Well, why *am* I paying this guy $ 250,000 a year, plus stock options and benefits????"

> *Feel free to pass this little cautionary tale on to whomever – in today's high-speed world, folks who are rigid, inflexible, sanctimonious, and lazy end up on the dustbin of history, often a well-deserved fate.*

DON'T LET'EM SLOW ROLL

An occasional Director may raise his eyebrows that a Complaint Package is anonymous, but he's taking a huge risk to his *own* career by displaying *any* kind of bad attitude, or showing any indication he's not sincere in fairly solving the problem. Any whining on the subject is a sure sign the Director is looking for a way to sweep the problem under the rug – don't let him get away with it. Have your two "2d Wave" packages ready to go at a moment's notice to his VP boss and VP Human Resources. It's psychologically vital for you and the Committee to be **fully prepared to escalate the Complaint** if the Director starts foot dragging. You must be absolutely ruthless and decisive. In fact, *expect* to escalate to Wave Two and even Wave Three – you can be pleasantly surprised if the Director actually does his job.

EASY STREET

If any readers believe I'm being too cynical about the professionalism of Directors or mid-level managers in Corporations and other organizations today, just recall the driving factor that dictates behavior routing in 98% of human brain synapse grooves . . .

"The Path of Least Resistance"

So make *SURE* you stack the deck so this path for the Director is clearly marked "Get rid of this Jerk yesterday".

I'll now give you three quick real-world examples of the absolute imperative to keep your anonymity during EAJ Campaign (and well beyond).

DANGER – JERKS AT WORK

The first we've already alluded to: the famous one-page note and follow-up six-page letter Sherron Watkins sent to Enron Chairman Ken Lay raising the red flag on Andrew Fastow's criminal partner-

ship financial schemes which ran Enron into the ground. The first
1-page memo was *anonymous*. What's really chilling is how fast it
was from the time she actually identified herself and handed over
the long six page letter to Ken Lay[6], to the time a cabal of Jerks in
Enron were actively trying to get her ruthlessly FIRED.

She gave the long letter to Lay at a private meeting on 22 August
2001. I surmise that he immediately sent a copy to her boss (probably
with a panicky note that said "Is all this stuff true??"), the crook Andrew Fastow, and that within 4 hours (!) Andy was actively plotting
to fire Sherron – note that only 2 days later, August 24, e-mails were
flying around between *outside* legal counsel (the notorious Vinson &
Elkins lawfirm) and Enron's in-house lawyer (Sharon Butcher, aptly
named) about strategies to terminate the employee.[7]

Sherron Watkins also stated that once her identity became
known, she feared for her personal safety for many months
afterward. Fastow even tried to seize her computer. The message is
crystal clear – the very minute a Jerk can identify who's doubting his
superhero status, a vicious firing scenario is being actively plotted.
Don't make it easy for the Jerk. The damning Complaint Package
must emanate from an anonymous, principled, no-nonsense, hard-
hitting Committee that strikes terror into the heart of the Jerk, and
commands deep respect from the Jerk's boss, the Director.

The Associated Press article of February 18, 2002 detailing this
sordid scenario is so classic, it should be required reading that will
be a frigid dash of ice water in the face of any employee with naïve
illusions about the realities of Evil in Corporate and Organizational
worlds. Representative Billy Tauzin (R-La) did a great job in his
Congressional Committee's investigation at penetrating Enron's
smokescreen, and exposing just how sleazy and corrupt this Company
was. (Although Tauzin, several years earlier, eagerly pimped for the
accounting industry by leading the corrupt effort to successfully gut
the SEC's power to police the sleazy financial practices of
corporations.[8] There are very few of unquestioned, consistent integrity
in the Congress of the US, and Tauzin is not one of them).

EFFECTIVE, BUT ANONYMOUS

Examples 2 and 3 of the need for anonymity both coincidentally deal with sexual harassment, but they're valuable to all of us because they illustrate most employees' (very correct) perception that they dare not *openly* complain about important, serious issues to their Company. It makes all the more urgent the method presented in *this book*, for Concerns to be raised in an **effective but anonymous** manner.

Example #2: In a 1998 magazine interview, "Dilbert" creator Scott Adams was asked about some of the massive numbers of e-mails he receives daily. Scott says,

"Occasionally, a woman will write and say, 'I can't take this (sexual harassment complaint) to the authorities – I need my job (!). But please do something about this so that I can at least get some satisfaction in your comic strip."

Q. *" Do people often write you for that type of help? "*
A. *" They do. Sometimes I'm the court of last resort."*[9]
(author emphasis)

Wow.

The American Workplace, Anno 2005, has descended to this abysmal level – the employee fear level is so elevated, serious issues can only be aired to syndicated cartoonists! We've finally reached the absolute bottom of the slag heap, and now we must climb our weary way up and out. Let's roll, without delay.

TARGET FOR RETALIATION

The 3rd and final example comes from the incredible Astra USA scandal of 1996. To make a long story short, high-level executives of the Swedish pharmaceutical company Astra's American subsidiary routinely practiced a vicious, predatory form of sexual harassment on their female employees through the 1980's and early 90's. The magazine *Business Week* did a superb job exposing this scandal. A passage from the May 13, 1996 *Business Week* exposé illustrates the crying need for a safe, anonymous method to quickly surface serious problems in organizations (a need to which *Jihad the Jerk at Work* provides the answer):

> *"As the Astra case suggests, few people have the fortitude or the financial wherewithal to blow the proverbial whistle. Some Astra employees were daunted by the prospect of taking on a deep-pocketed corporation – especially since those who did complain allege they were **targeted for retaliation**. Economic need meant others put up with behavior they felt was degrading. Many of those interviewed also said they feared complaints would only result in a **reputation as a troublemaker** – something that would haunt them on the job market. 'If another pharmaceutical company knows you're involved in something like that, your chances of being hired are slim,' says Mary Ann Lowe, a former rep who left in 1991.*"[10]
> (emphasis added by Author)

The drawbacks to being openly identified as the complainee are obvious – it's the same old story: "targeted for retaliation", "identified as a troublemaker" – Without the protection of anonymity, employees who ask for justice are dead meat, it's that simple. Just DEAD MEAT. Again, if anyone gives your EAJ effort any static about being anonymous, please forward copies of these pages to them and kindly ask them to stuff it.

WHAT'S THE *OBJECTIVE*???

Let's see: we've decided to fight, not flee; we've taken comprehensive and damning notes, collected incriminating e-mails; done probing historical research and selected the time to strike; established strong alliances and coordinated all parties; erected layers of security firewalls and kept the entire effort anonymous. What have we left out? Just the most important element of all . . .

Sometimes, during all the preparations for sending the Complaint Package, the Committee forgets to clarify one absolutely key area, namely: What *result*, or set of results, will signify a **clear success** of the operation, which would signal termination of the effort, calling off the Hounds of Hell? And conversely, what scenarios would be unacceptable, and trigger 2d wave escalation to higher levels, until the minimum acceptable result is achieved??

In Chapter 6 you will notice that in our generic "Cover Letter to the Director", we have a section in which we check off our recommendations. This is vitally important, and *these recommendations must be made clear to all parties*, because it will determine whether the issue is peacefully closed after 30 days, or the warfare is escalated to higher levels in the Company.

Note there are four levels of ratings of "Job Performance linked to Committee Recommendations" ranging from mild counseling all the way to termination from the Company. You may wish to add other categories as you see fit.

DRAWING THE LINE

There may be some cases in which you and the Committee would *like* to see a certain outcome ideally, but would accept as a *minimum* a lesser outcome. The classic case is where the faults list clearly indicates the Cosmic JIQ should be terminated from the Company – however, to speed up the Jerk's removal from your department without a ruckus or involving the VP's and HR, the group reluctantly agrees they'd accept the Jerk's **total removal** from your Department, to another Department far away, so at least he'd be gone quickly. Usually the litmus test for the distance of removal is that he's "so far detached that he can have no possible input on our annual performance (and bonus) reviews". This concept is called "compromise".

The possibilities of combination leveraging & compromise are endless. You could indicate to the Director that you'd accept mere removal if he promptly acts in 30 days, but that if you have to escalate to VP level, you'll up the ante and demand the Jerk's unconditional termination from the Company. But you can't just posture, you have to carry through. This gives the Director another *strong incentive* to contain the scandal and act promptly. And **Scandal Containment, as we all know by now, is the keystone of managerial behavior in any and all organizations, bar none.**

This concept of "minimum acceptable result" is not necessarily a cop out. It may be the shrewdest way to really dump the Jerk. Once the Jerk is pawned off on some unsuspecting other group (who's Director must be at least as incompetent, if not more so, than yours, since he'd have to neglect due hiring diligence), it's an easy matter to contact trusted associates in that group, get them a copy of this book, and fill them in on the situation. When the Jerk starts screwing up again, "Bam" – they can "Book" him again, this time out of the Company for good. The Jerk is in a weakened condition, ripe for destruction (see "Pursuit" in Chapter 5).

Every EAJ Campaign has a different twist, so you'll have to tailor the Objective to fit the situation. **The important thing is that the team has a *clear-cut objective*, and a firm commitment to escalate until that objective is reached.**

CHOOSING THE RECIPIENT

The obvious first choice of whom to send the Complaint Package to is the Jerk's direct boss. This keeps it simple and at the *lowest level possible*, always a big plus. We'll call this person the "Director", although it could be many different titles or levels.

But things get more complicated if you and the Committee feel that this particular Director is *part of the problem*, who won't give your Complaint a fair and honest hearing. He may even start a scathing witch hunt to identify and Shoot the Messengers. In that case, you may be better off choosing a Director or Executive in another position and try to push the case with a decent individual. If your Company is the exception and not the rule, and you have an intelligent, gutsy HR VP, you could try that route – but still, keep it

anonymous. Always. Or you could just jump over the Director's head
to the Jerk's VP.

You could send the Complaint the traditional route to the
Director in the expectation you'll escalate to VP's within days, and
thus kill two birds (jerks) with one stone! But you have to judge
whether you'd be asking for trouble by biting off more than you can
chew. After all, the most successful EAJ Campaigns limit their target
to *one* Jerk at a time, for maximum impact. It's the judgment call of
you and the Committee.

AGAIN: THE BEST KEPT SECRETS OF U.S. CORPORATIONS

It's worth repeating: the *Best Kept Secret of US Corporations*,
indeed all organizations, is that there is always someone in power
(excepting utter disaster zones like Enron) who will take your
Complaint Package and act properly on it. Find that person, create the
proper atmosphere (committee complaint, anonymous, a strong
honest case, clear recommendation, 30-day deadline, set to elevate
higher, *etc.*), and you will succeed in getting rid of the Jerk in
Question (or whatever your minimum stated objective is).

Also keep in mind the *Second Best Kept Secret of Organizations*:
there **is always incessant infighting and friction between managers
in any organization, especially if one of them is a certified hard-
core Jerk** (or better yet, a *bona fide* "Cosmic Jerk" . . . see Chapter
2) **, and your Committee Complaint may well tip the balance to
the Jerk's ouster** – the proverbial straw that finally breaks the
camel's back. Good executives highly value insights from lower-
level employees – especially when they realize it's a truthful, selfless,
courageous act taken in the very best interests of the Company. A
damning "Committee Report" could very well sink a Jerk outright.

Especially remember that the recipient Director has one overrid-
ing goal: *the health of his own career.* He will act to protect it, even if
it means burying his own mistakes, which could well entail getting rid
of a protégé Jerk who has created a mess in his own Department.

THEY *KNOW* YOU'RE SERIOUS WHEN . . .

To the typical Director, receiving a devastating Complaint Package is unnerving enough – he becomes *even more* concerned when he discovers it's a *group* of employees and not just a lone wolf. He truly realizes he's dealing with pros when it becomes clear they will not present easy targets for his wrath and will remain anonymous . . . but what really sends him to his Prozac bottle is the **30-day deadline you give him** . . . solve the problem correctly in *30 days*, or this baby is rocketing up to his very unforgiving, impatient VP bosses.

Only then, he suddenly understands that he can't slow-roll, the clock is ticking, that he's being observed by many critical eyes, that any attempt to bluster and intimidate on his part will have catastrophic consequences as the Package gets catapulted to several Vice Presidents above him.

You will be astonished at how swiftly he moves – **if** you set, and rigorously adhere to, a firm 30-day deadline (calendar days, not working days). **If you** *fail* **to set a deadline, he'll treat the whole thing as a joke.**

PAINT A CLEAR PICTURE

Notice on the Generic Cover Letter to the Director we provide for you in Chapter 6 (easiest method is to simply fill in the blanks on our website forms and our website "Faults List," "PRINT," and send as is all paper-clipped to the front of this book. You *really* do **not** have to spend a lot of your precious time on this EAJ Campaign) there is a clear- cut section where you *let the Director see exactly each level of power the Complaint Package is going to*, Wave by successive Wave, if he squanders his Grace Period. For example, the levels can be ratcheted to:

> **2d Wave:**   *** his boss, the VP of _____ (eg Engineering, or whatever)
> *and*
> *** the VP of Human Resources

and
*** the company ombundsman, if your organization is fortunate enough to have a competent
one

3rd Wave: *** the President of the Company
and
*** the CEO

4th Wave: ***   key player on Board of Directors, major
stockholder, *etc., etc.*

5th Wave: ***   media outlets, trade groups, *etc.,*
only limited by your imagination

THE SECOND WAVE

Take another look at the *2d Wave* Complaint Package scenario. It seems to make logical sense to ratchet the Complaint up to the Director's immediate boss, his own VP, *and also* to the VP of Human Resources. This puts a *double whammy* on a recalcitrant Director who refuses to do his job. Notice that we have *not* involved HR until now – we've given the Director a chance to clean up his own mess in his own Department quietly, without involving a lot of heavy breathers. If he's too dense to grab the opportunity, then he richly deserves Double Whammy VP involvement. Often if two VP's are involved, they try to outdo one other in seeing who can land on the issue with the most tons of bricks. Bumbling Directors who allow matters to deteriorate to this point often end up getting squashed by falling masonry and mortar.

And you might as well make it a Triple Whammy by sending a third package to your Company Ombundsman, if he exists – but keep it anonymous with him also, no matter what.

BRAINSTORMING – TARGET INFLUENTIAL PEOPLE

But here's a related factor you should make a high priority to discuss with your Jedi and Committee. Oftentimes there are *strong personalities* in the Company that have influence far greater than their official title would suggest. They may be a close personal friend of the CEO, or have a special charisma or wisdom or insight that lends tangible respect to their views. It could be Jane Reynolds, the savvy VP of Marketing, or that lowly Director of Operations, John Cobb, whom the smart money is on to eventually lead the Company. Every organization has some of these "mega-influence" players.

It could even be an executive you know that the Jerk has pissed off. Payback plays a major role in the daily life of all organizations. Never underestimate the stunning power of a seething desire to take revenge.

Brainstorm this with your team – if you come up with one (or more) candidate(s), you may well consider sending an additional Complaint Package to him *as well* in the 2d Wave. Let's face it . . . if your Director drops the ball in the 1st Wave, the kid gloves come off and you will feel no reluctance in unleashing the Dogs of War to quickly resolve all this nonsense. Your Committee has patience, but there are limits to patience, and the Committee does not suffer fools gladly. You and your Allies must think "out of the box" so a stunning *Blitzkreig* is always mapped out *well in advance* that will be unstoppable. You have the insight, the power, and the motivation to do it, as well as the wise guidance of *Jihad the Jerk at Work*.

THE TURNING OF THE SCREW

Again, *you must establish a firm deadline for the Director to perform*. Otherwise he'll just slow roll and slow roll . . . if you let him get away with it, the Path of Least Resistance channels him to slow rolls. This is a classic tenet of "Business as Usual" management . . . "delay, delay, and it will all blow away " . Don't fall for it. Once the Complaint Package has been submitted, **Never let'em up for air**.

There are endless examples, in the Business World and other organizations, of naïve, trusting employees who foolishly think higher management will constructively take action, *without a hefty sledgehammer hovering over their skulls*. To show you how pathetically common this is, and how the principle applies to all walks of life, I merely turn to *today's newspaper* (April 18, 2002, *New York Times*) for an classic example popping up on page one of the *"Arts"* section, no less.

A DISCORDANT SYMPHONY

Apparently there has been great friction between Montreal Symphony Orchestra players and their autocratic conductor, Charles Dutoit, during the past decade. By all accounts, the Conductor's rude and humiliating treatment of orchestra members has been patently outrageous. Here clearly is a Jerk At Work . . . abusive, harassing, rude, disrespectful, intimidating, exploitive, insulting, shooting the messenger – the same old litany.

Orchestra members have complained to no avail (even though they're unionized!) As the *New York Times* article reports,

> *"Members of the Orchestra said they had become increasingly frustrated that senior management **had not acted on several letters and petitions they had sent in recent years complaining of Mr. Dutoit's behavior**."*[11]
> (emphasis added by author)

Whoa!! Several **years**! Quick, what's wrong with this picture???? If you've been paying attention to the advice dispensed so generously in this tome, it's obvious. If you've identified a hardcore Jerk in your workplace and you truly desire strong resolution of the problem, you **must** set a *30-day deadline* for resolution to the Director along with the Complaint Package (that's 30 calendar days, not business days – 4 weeks is plenty long enough for any Director who's remotely serious about reform).

Then, if he *does not perform* in that time period, the Complaint must be automatically ratcheted up to higher levels, each 30 days, level by level, until the pressure becomes unbearable to the power structure – each escalation intensifies the terror. In the case of the Montreal Symphony, Wave 2 could be two key members of the Board of Trustees who hire & fire senior managers, and Wave 3 might involve a major financial donor and a major political supporter. Wave 4 escalates to several media outlets.

Spell it out clearly to each and every recipient where the next set of Complaint Packages is going, if he fails to act intelligently within 30 days. And never try to fake and bluster – follow through and do *exactly* what you say you'll do.

There must be a relentless "turning of the screw" until the problem is justly resolved. The Complaint Committee *must* sit down *beforehand* and cold-bloodedly map out the most effective progression of attacks, level by level, wave by wave – where are the *real* levers of power and influence??? This must be done **well in advance** of launching the 1st wave. This method would have resolved the Montreal foolishness in 30 – 90 **days**, not five years. The essence of it all is to be wonderfully creative and ruthless in cranking up the pressure in getting rid of a hardcore Jerk.

READY TO ROLL

So all the groundwork has been laid. You simply fill in the following forms found on our website, (www.upublishing.com/forms.htm) and "PRINT."

1) Cover Letter to Director
2) Faults List
3) the Author's generic Letter to Director

The Package is **paper-clipped to the front of a copy of this book**, *"Jihad the Jerk at Work"* – you place post-it notes on choice, relevant passages in the book that you specially desire the Director read . . . yellow highlight choice sentences . . . write blistering commentary in the margins. Whatever strikes your creative fancy. No Director alive can resist the urge to page to all the post-it notes to see just how jacked up his department really is.

Your recommendation and 30-day timetable is made *crystal-clear.*

Of course, make copies of everything you send in case they're needed for Waves 2 and 3 up to VP's and CEO's.

All Allied parties are briefed, especially those you believe the Director will contact to interview.

You're all prepared.

You send the Package anonymously and discreetly to the Director (or whomever the 1st Wave recipient may be).

THE FIRST 30 DAYS

Be prepared for *anything* during the crucial first 30 days. It is most important that key Committee members and close Allies be in *constant*, daily communication, to share *any* and *all* developments in the case. All Allies have their eyes and ears open, all are on alert, all resolute to stand fast, come what may.

THE FAT'S IN THE FIRE . . . BE ON YOUR TOES

Having gone through this nerve-wracking 30-day period a few times, let me give some advice on what to expect, and how to handle it:

When the Director starts interviewing people in his investigation, it's to your great advantage to find out *what* he's asking, what his *real attitude* is. Therefore, make every effort to debrief each "interviewee" and pass on the info to all potential interviewees, and your Committee.

You and your Committee must be **alert, flexible, and smart**. You must all be and remain very **strong**, and keep morale very high. You must stay on top of all developments, so that a full court press can be applied, 24/7. Don't allow either the Jerk, or his Director, up for air.

THE FURY OF THE DAMNED

The Complaint Package landing on the Director's desk is a huge personal and professional blow to the Jerk In Question. It well may be the *first* time this asshole has had *any* brakes applied to him in his entire gilded career. You may safely assume that the Director will immediately call him in to discuss it with him. This will be devastating to him, and desperate, moronic people have been known to do very weird things . . . **be prepared**.

The Jerk will spend every waking moment trying to get out of his predicament. It's like flushing quail in south Georgia – Jerks can "flush", *i.e.* react, in many different and bizarre ways. I've already mentioned the case in which one Jerk started berating one poor guy even more than before, despite the Director's admonition to cool it. Another Jerk reacted by suddenly acting like Mr. Nice Guy, swerving a laughable 180 degree turn in personality. Don't fall for it, it's all a pathetic act. Another Jerk went around to each of his employees in a panic, trying to find out what they thought of him (2 years too late). Remember that hardcore Jerks *just have no sense of shame*, no concept of basic decency.

In any case, you can be sure that the Director's receipt of your masterful Complaint Package will create waves which will cause some interesting things, to "float to the surface", in the manner feces float to the surface of a pond. Be alert and prepared to work all these to the advantage of the prime objective.

KEEP UNREMITTING PRESSURE ON THE DIRECTOR

We've mentioned the bizarrely immature reaction of one Jerk, who even after being counseled to back off by his boss the Director, intensified his harassment of an innocent employee (I knew the victim well, he was extremely competent and undeserving of this inexcusable treatment). When the abused angrily complained to the Director, the Director sent out feelers to employees in the group, who under-statedly confirmed that the Jerk was *totally out of control* and beyond the pale. End of Story – End of Jerk.

But what should be done when events transpire during the 30 day period that are masked from the Director as he wrestles with his decision of how he's going to handle one of his rogue managers??

Simply send a **"second broadcast"**, an anonymous update that
ratchets up the ante. For example,

> *" To Ralph Noceros, Director:*
>
> *We've just been informed that Chuck Heydrich has
> again disregarded your instructions, and has verbally
> abused Raoul D'Amato. This conduct is typical of Chuck,
> and we urge you to control this rogue manager.*
>
> *You may rest assured that if Chuck is not gone by July
> 27, this **additional** outrage will be added to the master
> Complaint Package that will be forwarded to Doug Prick-
> hard, VP of Engineering, as well as to Tom Hartless, VP of
> Human Resources.*
>
> *Sincerely, Business Effectiveness Committee,*
> *WireTech "*

In other words, gladly assist the hardcore Jerk in digging his own
hole. This type of rapid-response communication is guaranteed to
send a chill up the spine of any reasonably intelligent Director
who's interested in keeping his job.

BE WELL PREPARED TO SMASH SERIOUS COUNTERATTACK

In the military, ground combat officers (infantry, armor,
artillery, cavalry, marines) are *religiously indoctrinated* that once an
attack has overrun the Objective, always always *always* consolidate
your position and immediately *prepare to repel a strong enemy
counterattack.*

The tendency in amateur or poorly led combat units is to breathe
a sigh of relief and let down its guard once Hill 509 has been taken.
Well-led enemy forces know this, and history is replete with examples of over-confident friendly units being blown away by strong
enemy counterattack.

So take heed. Even if things seem to be going swell during the first 30-day period, DO NOT LET DOWN YOUR GUARD UNTIL THE JERK HAS BEEN PHYSICALLY REMOVED FROM YOUR DEPARTMENT AND LONG GONE.

Keep the firewall of anonymity strong and intact. Imbue your Committee with the discipline of professionals. Resist the impulse to stroll over to the Director's office to cheer him on to his final decision. IT AIN'T OVER 'TILL IT'S OVER.

Especially be prepared to ruthlessly squelch any counterattack launched by the Jerk himself, or even the Director, or even HR, if those imbeciles blunder into getting involved on the wrong side. Insure your Committee has steeled itself to detect and destroy any negative activity at all. "Loose Lips Sink Ships" – keep security tight throughout. Beware of fellow travelers and quislings (whom of course, you long ago identified via the Pie Chart drill) sent by the Jerk or other hostile parties attempting to penetrate your organization – train all your allies to report these "probes", or attempts to gather information on shadow committees. Deal with these traitors subtly but harshly – instill in them the Fear of God.

ALWAYS KEEP IT LEGAL AND ETHICAL

Having said this, I hasten to clarify that in no way am I condoning *any* violent, illegal, or unethical means be applied against anyone, even if he's a disgusting Jerk or Jerk's proxy. Such means are unnecessary, and totally counterproductive. The ethical and legal tools described in these pages are so powerful and effective, the career of any Jerk in its sights will be curtailed in short order. The pen is far mightier than the sword.

GETT'N COLD FEET

There's an unforgettable scene in the classic movie, *The Caine Mutiny* – you may have seen it. As you might recall, some decent officers on the USS *Caine*, a scruffy Naval supply ship in the Pacific during WWII, decide that their Captain (brilliantly played by Humphrey Bogart) is dangerously unstable and deranged, and is a threat to the lives of all on board. They summon up the courage to send a delegation to Admiral Halsey's command aircraft carrier to complain. When they arrive on the Carrier, there's the classic scene where they gaze around at the iron discipline and perfect order and smartly uniformed sailors, mechanics, and pilots lined up at rigid attention on the flight deck, and deeply worry that this crusty, iron-spined Admiral will laugh them off the boat, or worse, with their "petty complaints". Then Fred MacMurray cravenly wimps out.

This is called "getting cold feet", and is quite common in any EAJ Campaign, no matter how justified that Campaign may be. You and your Committee should discuss this phenomenon long in advance of H-Hour, and be **mentally hardened and prepared** to shrug it off when it arises so you can blitz along unhindered during the entire Jihad. After all, you've carefully considered the facts, you've established the reality that you're truly dealing with an irresponsible, dangerous Jerk, that he *must* be gotten rid of. Don't let doubts and second thoughts slow you down. Rock Steady. Your cause is righteous and just. If you cave in to self doubt and fears now, *you'll forever regret doing so. **Strength. Courage. Now** is the time for steadfastness.* Glorious Victory lies just over the horizon, one can see the tips of Her wings glinting in the probing rays of dawn.

(By the way, *The Caine Mutiny* is considered one of most underrated novels of all time, by many observers. It is highly recommended, inspirational reading for those about to undertake any form of EAJ Campaign.)

EVEN ATTILA THE HUN HAD ADMIRERS

Also, keep in mind that in my experience, even the worst Jerks imaginable seem to always attract at least a few dimwitted admirers. So expect to witness this phenomenon, but don't be surprised or swayed by it. There will always exist that pathetic 5 to 10% element of fellow travelers and quislings that possess *zero* ability to judge character or integrity. Ignore them. The decent 80%, *your* 80%, have an uncanny knack of correctly identifying winners and losers, stalwarts and Jerks. Stick to your guns, you'll be glad you did. Trust your native common sense and gut instinct – where people are concerned, it'll be right 99 times out of a 100.

THE HOME STRETCH

In a well-orchestrated EAJ Campaign, the more the Director digs into allegations against the Jerk, the more powerful evidence he'll find to indicate that the Jerk must be gotten rid of posthaste. It's been my experience, **over and over again**, that the behaviors you've witnessed are *only the tip of the iceberg* – most Jerks leave a trail of disaster, wide and deep, in their wake. An honest inquiry given some focused direction usually exposes amazing amounts of stunning incidents, grossly inappropriate behaviors, and sometimes even criminal activity. Once people feel they can honestly testify without fear, the cat's out of the bag. This is why Jerks try so hard to tighten the lid down via intimidation and terror – they well know that once the leaks begin, the dam begins to give way.

If all goes well, the Jerk will quietly disappear before the 30 days are up. Mission accomplished. Don't make a big fuss, don't reveal your role in the ouster. Just disappear back into the woodwork as if the whole thing was just a passing dream. And then enjoy the magically improved new atmosphere in your workplace. Revel in it, exult in it . . . you earned it, you changed things for the better.

"LAST CHANCE" BROADCAST

But what if the Director decides to stonewall or otherwise fail to do his job??? You have two choices:

1) As you promised in the cover letter, you can immediately bounce full Complaint Packages to two powerful VP's above the Director.

2) You can make one last good-faith effort to keep the action at a low level. As we've stated, it's always easier and quicker to solve a Jerk at Work problem at the *lowest possible level* of supervision. If the Director starts to waiver, shows signs of weakness or gutlessness, actually tries to identify Committee members (!) (obviously this leads to shooting of messengers), **but** you think he's smart enough to respond to a little shock therapy, you can issue a "Last Chance" Broadcast. In an anonymous note, you simply reveal that you're aware he's screwing up, that he's angered the Committee, that his career is in *deep* trouble unless he delivers asap. Then you tighten his noose by informing him his "Grace Period" has been curtailed, he's only got a week left to deliver instead of two (or some such time penalty). See the sample "Last Chance" Broadcast below. It will be obvious to even the stupidest of Directors that he's in the process of tightening the noose around his own neck. Directors tend to find the inspiration to suddenly start doing their jobs, when faced with cold wills of steel and the smoldering menace of explosive escalation.

It's worth a shot – it could well wrap up the entire EAJ Campaign successfully in one week as opposed to it dragging on for six weeks and involving a gaggle of VP's.

Example of "Last Chance" Broadcast memo to a wavering Director:

To: Ralph Pattela
Director, WireSat Engineering Dept
WireTech, Inc

You've really disappointed a lot of people in botching the Tamar Kalhid investigation by trying to discover the identities of the Business Effectiveness Committee instead of faithfully focusing on the problem manager. Also you have displayed some

attitude problems, which, quite frankly, has surprised many. Ordinarily, in this type of situation (consult the book we sent you, *Jihad the Jerk at Work*), we'd proceed to seriously damage your career by immediately terminating your Grace Period, and forwarding the Complaint Package to VP of Engineering Doug Ralston and VP of HR, Susan Hightower.

But we feel these slip-ups are *out of character for you*, so we'd like to give you one last opportunity to resolve this issue quietly in the Department. Why ruin your career for an incompetent like Tamar, when there are so many superior managers you could replace him with?? By now you've surely discovered he's totally unfit for the job, and will give you nothing but grief from here on out.

However, the penalty you've now incurred is a reduction in your allotted grace period. Instead of the two weeks left spelled out in the original cover letter to our Complaint Package, we now require that he be gone, completely gone, from this department not later than one week from today, *i.e.*, by COB July 26. Then the entire issue will be closed and not mentioned again.

If this does not occur, the two packages will be sent to the two VP's on July 27, annotated with your inappropriate actions and behaviors.

This is your last and final chance. You have greatly disappointed us, but we harbor some confidence you will quickly rebound. You will receive no further slack on this issue from this point forward.

> **Committee for Business Effectiveness**
> **Wiretech, Inc**

(Example "Last Chance" Broadcast Letter to Director)

LAUNCHING THE 2nd WAVE

If you are forced to escalate the Complaint Package to a higher level (for example, to VP level), it will take another 30 days to resolve the issue, but there is a big bonus (one of the great secrets to EAJ success is the motivation derived from always seeing the bright side of any situation).That is, not only will you eventually get rid of the Jerk, but your efforts have revealed the fact that the Director is an idiot also, far flakier than anyone could have imagined, a fact that will NOT be lost on the recipient VP's. The Director's career may well be seriously harmed by the revelation to higher management of his ineptness in handling a no-brainer personnel issue. It's true – more bang for the buck, kill two birds with one stone. Just remember, these folks have **done this to themselves** via their own ineptness – they can only blame *themselves.*

Therefore both your Corporation, and Society at large, get twice or three (or twenty) times the benefit from your EAJ Campaign. When Jerks and flaky executives are exposed, it merely makes their competition, other managers who have not blundered, look that much better, and provides more opportunity for truly competent, decent people to advance. It's kind of a Darwinian analysis, but I've seen it play out this way time and again. It's hard to appreciate this grand aerial view of the struggle when you're down in the trenches battling against abject idiots, but it's absolutely real. It's really healthy for organizations, and it demonstrates the priceless value-added of EAJ Campaigns to real human progress. In the next few years, look for a sea-change in progress in the United States.

But, we can always hope that in your particular EAJ Campaign, your Director will be decent and competent, and he will intelligently solve the problem at his level, making such a second wave escalation unnecessary.

THE MOMENT OF TRUTH

In any case, when Day 30, the witching hour, rolls around, there will exist one of two outcomes. Either,

1) **Outcome # 1**: The Director has not produced, and you have to escalate the Complaint Packages to two Vice Presidents with added comments on the Director's failure to perform. You simply access our website forms again and "fill in the blanks." on an entirely new "Cover Letter" and add a section on the Director's specific failure to deliver (eg, "did nothing", "tried to intimidate employees", "tried to cover up the Jerk's behaviors", "failed to faithfully execute his duties as Director", "exhibited bad attitude", "extremely arrogant", and so on.) Attach a copy of the entire original complaint, with all enclosures and, of course, an annotated copy of this book. I'm not trying to sell more copies of this book, it will just make a huge impression on them to have "the Book" thrown at them! Really. You know how swamped most executives are – a package attached to a dynamic book on the very subject is *much less likely to get lost on their desks*, and will dramatically hold their attention. The squeaking wheel gets the oil, and believe me, they'll hear your wheel loudly squeaking.

2) **Outcome #2:** The Director does a good job, and the Jerk is gone. You may decide to send the Director a nice anonymous note thanking him for his efforts and noting that the Committee considers the entire matter closed. Or perhaps you'll do nothing of the sort. You may reason that the Director was merely correcting a major mistake he'd made, and it was high time, and we have nothing to thank this guy for. Sometimes dead silence carries a lot more weight. It's up to you and your Committee to make this decision.

GOOD JOB, YOU'VE DONE IT!!
AND YOU'VE MADE HISTORY IN DOING SO
ENJOY YOUR IMPROVED WORKPLACE
    ATMOSPHERE

****   and don't forget to *immediately* send us your story at rail128@aol.com or via regular mail to:

> Corporate Jedi
> PO Box 438
> Lake Hiawatha, NJ 07034-0438

or fax to (877) 386-5353

> And keep us updated as related developments occur.
> Your example will inspire *many others* to clean up
> their workplaces.
> The positive and constructive ensuing domino effect
> will be *enormous*.

At this point, if the Jerk has been merely transferred to another Department, I would strongly urge you to consider a "pursuit" action detailed in Chapter 5. Might as well help put the *final nail* in this clown's floundering career, if he truly deserves it.

AN EXPECTED BENEFIT

"Once Burned, Twice Shy" – once the Jerk is ousted, and the Director is searching for a replacement manager, you should be able to *reasonably expect* that he will be much less sloppy, and much more careful, to hire a manager who is a decent human being, as well as being competent.

He'll take the trouble to carefully check his background, and he'll obtain strong personal recommendations from other Directors he has confidence in. Chances are, the replacement for the Jerk will be an infinitely better manager. I'd call that a win-win scenario, wouldn't you??

And so ends our discourse on the "basics", the practical aspects of an effective Eject-a-Jerk Campaign. I know you'll manage it well. All the forms you need are in Chapter 6, and our website.

Happy Trails to You . . . . . . Godspeed.

"These people don't belong to you,
they belong to God."

> The Reverend James Nutter, of the Palmer Memorial
> Episcopal Church in Houston, in a letter to Enron
> CEO Jeffrey Skilling, after hearing so many an-
> guished complaints from unhappy Enron employees
> about their sick, exploitive workplace atmosphere.[10]

Chapter Five –
Advanced Jerkbusting Operations

"Misfortunes one can endure. They come from outside, they are accidents. But to suffer for one's own faults – ah! There is the sting of life."[1]

Oscar Wilde

Having mastered the basics of getting rid of a Jerk in your organization, in Chapter 4, and having all the necessary pre-printed forms to help you do so in Chapter 6, let's pause in this chapter to reflect on some more advanced techniques to get the most out of your new-found skills.

PURSUIT – IF YOU NEED TO COMPLETE THE JOB

Because Directors and higher management are typically reluctant to fire a Jerk outright, oftentimes the Jerk will be transferred from your Department to another Department, hopefully far removed. You and your Committee can take great pride in striking a great blow for decency and the future of your organization. If you are all completely happy with this arrangement, then it's end of story.

However, if you'd very much like to see the Jerk bounced out of the Company for good, there's a very simple, low-effort remedy – it's called "Pursuit". All you have to do is to contact or establish a trusted acquaintance in the Jerk's new Department, fill him in on the whole story, hand him copies of your entire Complaint Package, and get him a copy of this book. If you don't know anybody personally in that group, chances are one of your Committee members does – it all boils down to finding someone there of high quality that you can *trust* to carry on the mission. Naturally, you must continue to maintain a high degree of security in all your liaisons with this new organization, and instill it with them as well. It's probably better to conduct all this business off campus, to insure an impenetrable firewall.

If the Jerk actually turns over a new leaf and performs decently and well in his new role, then there's no point in conducting a witch hunt . . . the effort is simply put on ice. But it's been my experience that

THE LEOPARD DOES NOT CHANGE HIS SPOTS . . . 9 times out of 10, the Jerk will revert to his old disgusting ways, and he'll dig himself another deep hole. The new group can form an EAJ Committee, fill in the appropriate forms, and make sure the entire package is sent to the Jerk's new boss with the 30-day deadline demand that the Jerk be fired entirely from the Company. All the escalation rules apply.

The Jerk, being in a new Department, is in a vastly weakened position – chances are, he'll be History, and soon.

This truly is the easy way to finish the job while memories are fresh and all the good guys are on a roll. It eliminates the chance you'll keep bumping into the Jerk for the next 20 years . . . why not *finish* the job when the momentum is there?? Just like Bush Senior should have done in Iraq in 1991, instead of criminally allowing Saddam to slaughter another 30,000 Shiites around Basra. (This is an overly simplistic viewpoint, of course. Since Bush '41 pledged to fully adhere to the UN mandate to only push Saddam out of Kuwait, and knew full well the US would not deal the knockout blow, he was criminally remiss in encouraging the Shiites to full rebellion – and doubly criminally negligent in allowing the Baathists free hand in massacring Shiites without restraint.)

"Never let a Hard-Core Jerk up for air"

"ALL THE LONELY JERKS, WHERE DO THEY ALL BELONG?"

The answer to this line paraphrased from the Beatles "Eleanor Rigby" (1966) can be answered rather easily, applying a little insight, on a State by State basis. Once a hard-core Jerk is finally canned by a Company that's been shown the light, where can the poor sot find employment?

In the State of New Jersey, for instance, there's a perfect employment opportunity for your typical hardcore Jerk. Because of insurance law restrictions, all gas stations are required to have attendants who must physically dispensed all fuel pumped – no self service allowed. Traditionally, these plum jobs have been held by immigrants from Turkey and Bulgaria, who are clearly overqualified.

Ergo, these immigrants should be encouraged to apply for business jobs leading up the corporate ladder and they should be replaced at the pump by hardcore Jerks recently terminated from your company – it's a perfect match. There is some risk involved, since the newly hired jerk will be required to handle gas customer's credit cards, but with proper training and motivation (say, the threat of deportation to Rafsanjan) the jerk can learn quickly.

You get the idea – there's a perfect job match for every hard-core Jerk bounced out of your organization. No need to harbor any guilt about their transition to more appropriate employment where they can do no more rapacious damage to the social fabric. And the best news is that there are plenty of these minimum wage job opportunities available, so hard-core jerks can be joined at the gas pumps by Directors and other middle and upper-level executives who fail to properly exercise their managerial responsibilities within allotted 30-day grace periods. This is the true genius of the economic flexibility of unfettered capitalism, on display for all to admire.

THE PRE-EMPTIVE STRIKE

Now that you've mastered the tactics of effective Jerk-busting, and perhaps even gotten rid of a major jerk in your department, you and your Committee would be wise to be watchful on any strategic or looming threats to your neighborhood.

Preventive medicine is *always* easier and more effective than treating symptoms and an entrenched disease. Let's look at an example:

Say you and your allies are quite happy where you are, and contributing excellent service to your company. Then a rumor starts floating around, that your much beloved Director is being moved to another assignment, and the biggest asshole in the company, whom all know and despise, is slated to be moved in to take his place!! Holy Cow!!

Unfortunately, too many people will complacently muse, "Well, once Vince the Viper takes over this Department, he'll grow up and reform, things will work out OK."

Wrong Answer.

If I've learned anything in the past 30 years, it's this: "A jerk is a jerk, will always be a jerk, and will become a *bigger* jerk with the passage of time." It's the blunt truth. Drop all the self-delusion, right now.

If you're ever in this situation, get off your duff and launch a pre-emptive strike to prevent the movement of *any* jerk into your area of operations, especially at manager or Director or VP levels. With your Committee, figure out who's really making the decision to move this moron in, then fire off an anonymous Complaint Package, with this book attached, to him asap. Prevention is by far the best cure.

All the same EAJ rules apply. Really sock it to'em with the pre-printed faults list, cover letter, 30-day deadline, escalation clause, *etc.* Pre-plan for 2ⁿᵈ and 3ʳᵈ Wave escalation. Obviously, the Cover Letter will need to be slightly tailored to fit the bill – the Chapter 6 pre-printed one can be used as a general guide. In this kind of sensitive case, it wouldn't be a bad idea to also send an identical submission to the HR VP simultaneously – getting a couple of VPs wringing their hands and worriedly conferencing over a projected disastrous management change could be the most effective tactic of all. No VP wants to screw up in full view of his peers.

Most importantly, just like we do in order to get rid of a standard cosmic jerk: do your due diligence and find out who this high level jerk's *worst enemies* are in the organization. You can easily get this info, and then either laundry list these folks in your cover letter as people the CEO needs to consult, or make sure each gets a copy of the complaint package. In either case, the resulting firestorm alone may well firewall your department off from the impending jerk transfer in perpetuity.

Also, don't forget the company's in house "gurus" and "wise men", who have powerful influence – he/she could easily tip the balance in the decision-making huddle. But one has to be diplomatic with these types, no hints of escalation. Perhaps the company has an Ombudsman – you might try also exerting pressure there, but always anonymously.

Take heart. Remember the *2nd Best Kept Secret* **of corporations**, and all other human organizations: **there's always** *major infighting* **going on among higher levels of management (all levels, for that matter).** A strong missive from anonymous employees is always a shocker, so unheard of that it has to be taken seriously!! Enemies of the Jerk – and Jerks *always* have enemies, often numerous & powerful – may well see this kind of shocking resistance as a golden opportunity to really do the idiot in. Your pre-emptive Complaint Package just may be the ticket. Remember,

"A stitch in time, saves nine."

A pre-emptive strike barring a Jerk from even *entering* your Department could well be the most effective and easiest EAJ campaign of all . . . we'll call it a PAJ Campaign, "Prevent a Jerk". Always keep this weapon ready to employ at a moment's notice.

THE "OUTSIDE ANGEL" ROLE

Here's an aspect of the EAJ effort to consider. If another group is suffering from the impact of a Jerk, you may at least quietly let them know about the *Jihad the Jerk at Work* methodology. Your role could range anywhere from casual advisor to actually orchestrating the EAJ Campaign in its entirety – it's your call. Obviously, it's better if the other group shoulders the entire burden – after all, it is *their* group, *their* fight. The key here may lay in finding a strong leader or Jedi within that group to power the campaign. But they may be unaware of our methodology, so clue them in asap.

Onward, to Chapter Six and all the pre-printed forms you'll need to launch a sizzling EAJ Campaign.

"The only thing necessary for the triumph of evil is for good men to do nothing." [2]

Edmund Burke

Chapter Six –
The Clip-On Book Attack:
the quick n' easy forms

*"The despot, be assured, lives night and day like one
condemned to death by the whole of mankind for his
wickedness."*

Xenophon, Hiero
430 – 355 BC[1]

TOOLS OF THE TRADE

This chapter and our website provide you with all the forms
you'll need to *quickly* and *simply* launch your Eject-A-Jerk
Campaign, and save you a lot of time doing so. The Generic "Cover
Letter to the Director" and the "Fault's List" are here that will make
assembling your Complaint Package a snap. I'll first provide you
with a filled in *sample* cover letter and *sample* Enclosure One fault's
list, so you can quickly get into the spirit and fun of the Campaign,
and get a glimpse of the myriad of possibilities for effectively
presenting your case (anonymously & safely, of course) to the
"Director", or whomever you choose as the package's recipient,
a.k.a., the Actionee.

Further on in the Chapter are the blank generic forms - you could
use these, but it's much easier and more secure to just fill in the
blanks on our website, and "PRINT."

Also, I've included a generic "Letter From the Author", a
communication from me, yours truly, *directly* to the Recipient of
your Complaint Package. All you have to do is fill in the Director's
name in the "To" blank. This letter is self explanatory, but the ob-

vious intent of this "honest broker" missive is to put the Director (or whomever) in a positive frame of mind so he can give your Complaint Package serious, rigorous, honest consideration. It's up to you and your Committee whether to use it or not – knowing the mindset of the typical senior executive and manager in organizations, I believe it will be of constructive assistance, and may hasten the just resolution of your Complaint.

WHY JERKS MUST BE CANNED

Ideally, in situations of this sort, you, your Committee, and the Director are really on the *same team*. You all desire a competent, well-run organization with a productive work environment. That's why I suggest you name yourselves the "Business Effectiveness Committee" (or if you're in a government agency or university or military unit, *etc.*, something similarly appropriate). In fact, in the absolute peak-performing, profitable organizations I've worked for, many in the workforce can't wait to get to work in the morning, are even reluctant to leave at the end of the day and often work late on weekdays and nights so they can **excel** at the task at hand, are extremely happy in their work, take professional initiative to boldly & courageously solve problems, and bend over backwards to mutually support co-workers and their managers. This *only* can occur when management itself reaches, and is sustained at, a high level of excellence, and is held in high regard by workers at all levels. *Ergo*, Jerks at any level in this organization MUST be gotten rid of, and gotten rid of quickly – we do not have the luxury of Jerk Toleration in high performance organizations. Period.

RECAP: LAUNDRY LIST OF CHAPTER 6 FEATURES

Here's what follows:
- Master Control Checklist to use to guide a typical "Eject A Jerk" Campaign
- *Sample* Forms (examples filled in to give you a flavor of the possibilities!):

      ** *sample* cover letter to Director
      ** *sample* fault's list (*a.k.a.*, "Inclosure 1")
   – Generic Forms to be actually used (easiest method is to fill in forms on our website and "PRINT").
      ** generic cover letter to Director
      ** generic fault's list (Inc 1 to cover letter)
      ** the Author's advice letter to the Director (Inc 2 to cover letter)
   All of the above, when finalized by you and the Committee, would be paper clipped or otherwise *attached to the front of a copy of this book*, *Jihad the Jerk at Work* (Inc 3 to cover letter), and sent on to the Director.
   (Author's recommendation for the most effective Complaint Package)

So, best wishes on your EAJ Campaign. Remember:

1) keep anonymous throughout
2) keep tight security – firewall out quislings and fellow travelers
3) communicate closely and often with allies and committee members
4) give the Director a strict *time deadline* to perform by!
5) escalate ruthlessly to Wave 2 if he fails to perform, or shows attitude problems
6) keep the faith, brush off "cold feet"
7) believe that what you're doing will save the corporation or organization, save society, save the planet – it will. *"There are no passengers on spaceship earth, we are all crew."*[2] Marshall McLuhan
8) attend the hard core jerk's going away party – but keep a very low profile before, during, and after.

We've thrown a lot of information at you in the last six chapters, so here's a simple checklist to keep your Eject A Jerk Campaign on track:

Eject-A-Jerk Campaign Checklist:

____ You detect that a Jerk may be at Work
____ Take notes, gather evidence, sort behavior
        patterns into categories, connect the dots, discuss with
        very trusted allies.
____ Touch base with reliable fellow employees
____ Classify seriousness of Jerk at Work problem –
        choose 1 of 5 alternatives

If it's Option # 5, "stay & fight":

____ Investigate Jerk's past work performance history
____ Conduct "Pie Chart" analysis to determine work-
        place allies vs non-allies
____ Form discreet EAJ Committee
____ Determine *Objective* of Campaign (counsel, transfer,
        or fire the Jerk?) VERY IMPORTANT!!!
____ Fill in and collate Complaint Package on our website
        (faults list, cover letter, annotate book, *etc.*)
____ Select Recipient – *also carefully plan 2d, 3rd, 4th
        Wave strategy & Recipients* VERY IMPORTANT!!
____ Establish action deadline (usually 30 calendar
        days)
____ Remain anonymous throughout, and beyond!!!
____ Coordinate all allies on plan/objective – give all
        heads up on H-Hour and 1st
        Wave time period
____ Send Package to Director
____ Director conducts inquiries – keep allied team well-
        briefed on all developments – receive constant
        feedback on progress

↓	↓
↓	↓
Director transfers Jerk	Director ignores Package
↓	↓
↓	↓

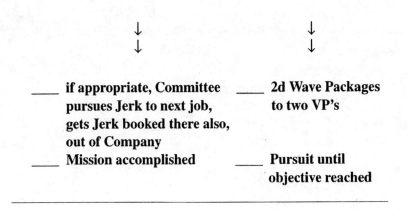

The following section has two *sample forms* filled in to give you a flavor of the possibilities:

OBSERVED DEFICIENCIES LIST (ie, list of the Jerks faults)
COVER LETTER TO DIRECTOR

(EXAMPLE ONLY!!)

Inclosure 1 -- Observed Deficiencies of _Shaheen Gublmar_
Page 1
(marked with an "x")

Deficiency Summary (check one) of __Shaheen___

___	1 -10 major deficiencies	=	**"Regular Jerk"**
___	11-20 " "	=	**"Major Jerk"**
___	21-35 " "	=	**"Hard-Core Jerk"**
_xx_	36 and over "	=	**"Cosmic Jerk"**

__Shaheen__'s total score: _45_ !!!!

Basic Traits:

__x_ No sense of shame   *really!*   ___ a Hypocrite
     none at all!!

__x_ Displays poor judgment often   __x_ Uncooperative   *looks for*
                                            ways to constantly foot-drag

__x_ Shortsighted   __x_ Immature *has the emotional*
                                            maturity of a 9-year old!!

__x_ Lacks intelligence, slow, not   ___ Manipulative
     bright   *we have to explain*
     things to him over and over
___ Devious   ___ Lightweight
___ Greedy   ___ _____

Character / Performance:

__x_ A sycophant, an obsequious toady
     spends 80% of his time sucking   __x_ Dodges responsibility for own
     up to his Director!!   actions *never admits his screw*
                                            ups, always tries to shift blame
                                            onto others!!

__x_ Solely concerned with superficial appearances to higher, unconcerned
     with substance
__x_ Is using position merely as stepping-stone to promotion, does not care
     about improving or strengthening his organization
___ a ticket-puncher   ___ a cover-up artist
__x_ not loyal to own employees   __x_ cannot be trusted *a habitual*
     undercuts his own people constantly   *backstabber!!*
__x_ has no respect for others   ___ overambitious

Page 2 -- Observed Deficiencies of __*Shaheen*_____

  __x_ screws over own people and unfairly fawns over other organizations
to gain brownie points *never backs up his own people – sells them
out!!*

  __x_ not a team player, loves to   _____ cowardly politico
grandstand *if he can't grandstand
at a meeting, he just doesn't show up!!*

  _____ no backbone, runs scared   _____ counterproductive "change for
change's sake"

  _____ addicted to irritating fads and meaningless corporate buzzwords

Interactions With Others:

  __x_ Tries to intimidate and bully people   __x_ Petty *plays silly games with good people*

  __x_ Extremely arrogant   __x_ Intemperate (lack of self control)

  _____ Ill tempered   _____ Mean-spirited

  _____ Loud   __x_ Vindictive

  _____ Rude, offensive personality   __x_ Has severe negative attitude

  _____ Arbitrary, unfair in dealings   __x_ Inveterate back-stabber, slimy

  _____ Employs undeserved verbal abuse   _____ Has "not invented here" syndrome

  __x_ Insults people regularly   __x_ Excessive finger-pointing *constant!!*

  _____ Plays favorites   _____ Loves to "Shoot the Messenger"

  _____ Doesn't bother to get both sides of the story   _____ Is verbally abusive to employees

  _____ Is a bull in the china shop   _____ Unstable; can be violent and dangerous

  __x_ Incapable of listening to criticism   __x_ *__has created a hostile working environment for own employees*

Managerial Ability:

  _____ Ingratitude; does not recognize or reward good performance

  _____ No filtering of unreasonable demands from higher, he actually amplifies it

  __x_ Does not provide constructive, meaningful counseling to employees

Page 3 -- Observed Deficiencies of _____*Shaheen*_____

____ Is a poor judge of character	____ Won't delegate tasks
____ Is a micromanager, to detriment of organization	____ No meaningful communication
____ Excessive meetings, clumsy communications	_x_ Not respected by employees ***his own people despise Shaheen***

_x_ Not respected by peers ***tries to backstab peers at every opportunity!!***

____ Afraid to discipline misbehavior of employees; gutless, whimpy

____ Generates meaningless busywork, wastes company time

_x_ Does not care about employees   _x_ Is despised by employees
pulled Helmut Kramer back   *just ask!*
from vacation in Ukraine, when
he wasn't really needed here
at all

_x_ Unfit to manage people   ____ A danger to this organization

Fundamental Character:

____ Egocentric	____ A moral coward
_x_ Completely selfish	____ No self discipline

Personality:

_x_ Humorless ***incapable of communicating with real people***	____ completely unhelpful to others
____ Bizarre! Needs psychiatric help	_x_ Pompous ***thinks he knows it all***
____ Flaky	____ Inbred

Integrity:

_x_ Has *no* integrity, personal or professional	_x_ A brazen liar ***incapable of reliable truth-telling – distorts truth constantly***
____ Is A fraud	____ Leadership "façade"

Job Competence:

_x_ Is incompetent	_x_ Blunders with customers

Page 4 -- Observed Deficiencies of ___*Shaheen*_____

Alienated Jaspar (Wyoming) operator to the point they just wanted Wiretech to pull out our software and use our competitors – Shaheen was unresponsive and arrogant to the max – unbelievable

Potential to Reform:

__x_ Incapable of reforming self or improving

Impact on This Organization:

__x_ Good people leaving the department because of his actions

__x_ Has caused employee morale to plummet

____ Good people actually leaving the Company because of his actions

__x_ His behavior has caused employees to lose their initiative

__x_ Has generated huge dissatisfaction among employees

____ People are now afraid to do their best

____ Has done harm to customer relations or business

____ One of the worst managers we've ever seen

__x_ Is the *worst* manager we've even seen

Rate __*Shaheen*____ on a scale of ten (highest) to one (lowest), comparing to peers: ___*1*__

Individual's performance in past jobs, if relevant:

_-- *Several of his past employees in Systems Group stated Shaheen was* ___*the worst manager they'd had in 20 years (how on earth could you have hired him, Ralph??)*_____
_-- *Two peer managers there said Shaheen was infamous for his inability* ___*to cooperate with anybody at all.*_____

Any Actual *Criminal* Behaviors Noticed:

____ Can be violent and dangerous   ____ Physical abuse of employees

Page 5 -- Observed Deficiencies of ___*Shaheen*_____

____ Venal (corruption)
    specify: _____   ____ Sexual abuse of employees
____ Engages in criminal activity
    specify: _____

Miscellaneous:

____ Personal problems adversely impact job performance
____ Disloyal to this organization
__x_ Prejudiced against races or religions *has openly disparaged Muslim people – really hates Islamic people. Shaheen Gublamar is an embarrassment to WireTech*

Additional Problems Not Listed Above:

____   ____
____   ____
____   ____
____   ____
____   ____

Other Comments:

_____
_____
_____
_____
_____
_____
_____
_____
_____
_____

(EXAMPLE ONLY!!)

To: **_Ralph Pattela_____**
              _Director, WireSat Engineering Department

From: Business Effectiveness Committee
              _WireTech, Inc_____

Subject: Job Performance of **__Shaheen Gublamar_**
                              __Technical Manager, Software
                              Deployment
              and Action Required

Date: **__July 11, 2004_____**

Suspense Date:__August 15, 2004___

1. The employee Committee for Business Effectiveness (CBE) is committed to resolving workplace issues at **_WireTech, Inc** in house, early-on, before issues can cause serious damage that can adversely affect profit, functioning of the Company, employee effectiveness, and workplace integrity.

2. Based on the employee evaluation compiled by our CBE, found at Inc 1, your employee's job performance, and your action required, is indicated below:

_____ **Acceptable**, but needs counseling and guidance.

_____ **Unacceptable**, but has some potential; needs *major* counseling and guidance asap.

Our minimum recommendation:

___x__ **Seriously unacceptable**; must be transferred *well away* from this Department *immediately*. Counseling can not undo the damage done to your group.

Our primary recommendation:

___x__ **So Poor** that termination from this Corporation is the only option.

3. Please study the evaluation at Inc 1, which details observed job performance and behaviors, as well as the resulting impact on our organization.

4. We assume that you may wish to conduct your own inquiry, unless your observations to date lead you to *already fully concur* with our findings *and* recommendations, making an inquiry unnecessary.

   a) Any serious inquiry on your part will require your consultation with the following individuals / groups. **The Committee would judge your investigation "not thorough"** if *all* these sources are not closely consulted*:

   ___*Employees who've recently left the group, in disgust:*
   _____*Sarah Miles* ___*Horst Vandel*   *Chang Lee Doi*___
   _____*Roger Collins*_____*Page Michaels*_____
   ___*Any of our Jaspar, Wyoming customers: Sam Hollister,*
        Joyce Lu
   ___*Trudy Brooks in Marketing*_____*Don Pizzo, manager of*
                                        hardware development

   b) We also *suggest* you consult with:
   ___*Dick Renfern in Lab 2E*   *Tom Petit of Brazil deployment*
   team
   ___*Toby Marchand, supervisor of financial audits*_____

5. Your Action Required:
   Today is *_July 11, 2004*. 35 days from this date, *_August 15,*
   *2004_*, one of two events will have occurred:

A. You will have competently executed your responsibilities as an executive of this Corporation, and the subject, *_Shaheen Gulbamar*_____, will have been dealt with per **at least the *minimum* level recommendation of** the Committee for Business Effectiveness. Upon the realization of this outcome, the CBE will regard the issue as "closed" and will take no further action within this department.

B. If outcome "A" has not occurred, for whatever reason, the Business Effectiveness Committee will forward this identical package, with added commentary on your action or lack of action to:

> _Doug Ralston, VP Engineering_____

and

> _Susan Hightower, VP Human Resources_____

We will escalate the matter to even higher levels, if it is necessary to satisfactorily resolve the issue.

6. The Committee grants you the aforementioned 30-day grace period to resolve this issue in-house, and sincerely desires this be accomplished quietly at your level. However, the Committee reserves the right, and *will, escalate this Package **immediately** to the above named parties upon the discovery of any of the following events:*

*** any attempt to determine the identity of Committee members (which would be interpreted as a prelude to "Shooting the Messengers")

*** any moves to threaten, or otherwise intimidate any employees over the raising of these recommendations.

*** obvious lack of good faith in the pursuit of fair, honest inquiry into this matter.

*** any actions or statements indicating contempt for this method of Complaint, or negative attitude towards, or intent to blatantly disregard said Complaint.

*** any indication of gameplaying, tapdancing, unprofessional conduct, "slow-rolls", stonewalling, *etc., etc.*

7. Please find at Inclosure 2 a letter from Mr. Edward M. Fergusson (author of Book at Inclosure Three), who offers some helpful, constructive insights into these type of situations.

8. At Inclosure 3, please find a book entitled *Jihad the Jerk at Work,* which is an in-depth study of common workplace problems, and has many helpful passages pertaining to the situation in your organization, the pages of which we have noted and *highlighted for*

your perusal. See particularly pages *12_* , *_20_, _101*, *_138,* and
_209_.   **Read this book – you'll learn a lot!!**

We thank you for your immediate attention to this important
matter, the resolution of which is key to the continuation of
progress and profits at ___*WireTech*_____.

                          Sincerely,
                          Committee for Business Effectiveness
                          ___*WireTech, Inc*_____

Inc -- 3

PS. ___*Ralph,_*

We also have to impart to you our sincere outrage and
stunned disbelief that Shaheen is still a manager within your
Department!!__It's a shocking travesty. His performance is
absolutely the worst we've seen in our collective 133 years of
professional engineering life.
  What were you thinking??
  _____*Get him out of here and do it now.*_____
Note our discovery of Shaheen's abysmal performance in his
last job with Systems Group. Why didn't you find this out before
you hired him to come here?? Why did you inflict this ludicrously
substandard manager upon us?? Cut your losses now to prevent
the need for higher management (your boss, Doug Ralston) to get
involved in this sordid affair.

_____*The Committee*

Clip-On Book Attack

Chapter 6

GENERIC BLANK FORMS SECTION, AND WEBSITE FORMS ACCESS

You can either tear out the generic forms found in Chapter Six and Xerox & enlarge them and then fill in manually **OR**, even easier, just proceed to website http://www.upublishing.com/forms.htm, user id: "reformer" password: "progress," fill in the forms you desire, "PRINT," and you're all set. Then, just paper clip them to the front of this book and send anonymously to the jerk's boss.

(NOTE: You may find it wiser to access this website via a privately owned PC and internet access provider, since some companies/organizations don't hesitate to monitor – OK, spy on – company-owned PC's and internet transactions! Better to be safe than sorry.)

All the generic forms (8) in *Jihad the Jerk at Work* can be found on this website, just pick n' choose.

** **COVER LETTER TO DIRECTOR**

** **INC 1 -- "FAULTS LIST"**

** **INC 2 -- ADVICE LETTER TO DIRECTOR FROM AUTHOR**

To: _____

                       _____
From: Business Effectiveness Committee

                       _____
Subject: Job Performance of _____

                                           _____
                       and Action Required
Date: _____
Suspense Date:_____

1. The employee Committee for Business Effectiveness (CBE) is committed to resolving workplace issues at _____ in house, early-on, before issues can cause serious damage that can adversely affect profit, functioning of the Company, employee effectiveness, and workplace integrity.

2. Based on the employee evaluation compiled by our CBE, found at Inc 1, your employee's job performance, and your action required, is indicated below:

_____   **Acceptable**, but needs counseling and guidance.

_____   **Unacceptable**, but has some potential; needs *major* counseling and guidance asap.

_____   **Seriously unacceptable**; must be transferred *well* away from this Department *immediately*. Counseling can not undo the damage done to your group.

_____   **So Poor,** that termination from this Corporation is the only option.

3. Please study the evaluation at Inc 1, which details observed job performance and behaviors, as well as the resulting impact on our organization.

4. We assume that you may wish to conduct your own inquiry, unless your observations to date lead you to *already fully concur* with our findings *and* recommendations, making an inquiry unnecessary.

   a) Any serious inquiry on your part will require your consultation with the following individuals / groups. The Committee would judge your investigation "not thorough" if *all these sources are not closely consulted*:

_____   _____
_____   _____
_____   _____
_____   _____
_____   _____

    b) We also *suggest* you consult with:

_____   _____
_____   _____

5. Your Action Required:

Today is _____20__. 35 days from this date, _____, one of two events will have occurred:

    A. You will have competently executed your responsibilities as an executive of this Corporation, and the subject, _____ _____, will have been dealt with per **at least the *minimum* level recommendation** of the Committee for Business Effectiveness. Upon the realization of this outcome, the CBE will regard the issue as "closed" and will take no further action within this department.

    B. If outcome "A" has not occurred, for whatever reason, the Business Effectiveness Committee will forward this identical package, with added commentary on your action or lack of action to:

       _____   _____

    and

       _____   _____

    We will escalate the matter to even higher levels, if it is necessary to satisfactorily resolve the issue.

    6. The Committee grants you the aforementioned 30-day grace period to resolve this issue in-house, and sincerely desires this be accomplished quietly at your level. However, the Committee reserves

the right, and will, escalate this Package **immediately** to the above named parties upon the discovery of any of the following events:

    *** any attempt to determine the identity of Committee members (which would be interpreted as a prelude to "Shooting the Messengers")

    *** any moves to threaten, or otherwise intimidate any employees over the raising of these recommendations.

    *** obvious lack of good faith in the pursuit of fair, honest inquiry into this matter.

    *** any actions or statements indicating contempt for this method of Complaint, or negative attitude towards, or intent to blatantly disregard said Complaint.

    *** any indication of gameplaying, tapdancing, unprofessional conduct, "slow-rolls", stonewalling, *etc., etc.*

7. Please find at Inclosure 2   a letter from Mr. Edward M. Fergusson (author of Book at Inclosure Three), who offers some helpful, constructive insights into these type of situations.

8. At Inclosure 3, please find a book entitled *Jihad the Jerk at Work,* which is an in-depth study of common workplace problems, and has many helpful passages pertaining to the situation in your organization, the pages of which we have noted and highlighted for your perusal. See particularly pages ___ , ____, ____, ____, and _____.

We thank you for your immediate attention to this important matter, the resolution of which is key to the continuation of progress and profits at _____.

                 Sincerely,
                 Committee for Business Effectiveness

                 _____

                 _____

Inc -- 3

PS. _____

    _____

    _____

Inclosure 1 -- Observed Deficiencies Of _____

Page 1
        (marked with an "x")

        Deficiency Summary (check one) **of** _____

        ___ **1 -10 major deficiencies = "Regular Jerk"**
        ___ **11-20   "   "   = "Major Jerk"**
        ___ **21-35   "   "   = "Hard-Core Jerk"**
        ___ **36 and over   "   = "Cosmic Jerk"**

                _____'s **total score:** _____

Basic Traits:
_____   No sense of shame   _____ A hypocrite
_____   Displays poor judgment   _____ Uncooperative
_____   Shortsighted   _____ Immature
_____   Lacks intelligence, slow,   _____ Manipulative
         not bright
_____   Devious   _____ Lightweight
_____   Greedy
                                        _____ _____

Character / Performance:
_____   A sycophant, an obsequious   _____ Dodges responsibility
         toady   for own actions
_____   Solely concerned with superficial appearances to higher,
         unconcerned with substance
_____   Is using position merely as stepping-stone to promotion,
         does not care about improving or strengthening his
         organization
_____   a ticket-puncher   _____ a cover-up artist
_____   not loyal to own employees   _____ cannot be trusted
_____   has no respect for others   _____ overambitious
_____   screws over own people and unfairly fawns over other
         organizations to gain brownie points

Page 2 -- Observed Deficiencies of _____

____ not a team player,   ____ cowardly politico
      loves to grandstand
____ no backbone, runs scared   ____ counterproductive "change
                                              for change's sake"
____ addicted to irritating fads and meaningless corporate
      buzzwords

Interactions With Others:

____ Tries to intimidate and bully   ____ Petty
      people
____ Extremely arrogant   ____ Intemperate (lack of self
                                              control)
____ Ill tempered   ____ Mean-spirited
____ Loud   ____ Vindictive
____ Rude, offensive personality   ____ Has severe negative attitude
____ Arbitrary, unfair in dealings   ____ Inveterate back-stabber,
                                              slimy
____ Employs undeserved verbal   ____ Has "not invented here"
      abuse   syndrome
____ Insults people regularly   ____ Excessive finger-pointing
____ Plays favorites   ____ Loves to "Shoot the
                                              Messenger"
____ Doesn't bother to get both   ____ Is verbally abusive to
      sides of the story   employees
____ Is a bull in the china shop   ____ Unstable; can be violent
                                              and dangerous
____ Incapable of listening to   ____ _____
      criticism

Managerial Ability:

____ Ingratitude; does not recognize or reward good performance
____ No filtering of unreasonable demands from higher, he
      actually amplifies it
____ Does not provide constructive, meaningful counseling
      to employees
____ Is a poor judge of character   ____ Won't delegate tasks

Page 3 -- Observed Deficiencies of _____

_____ Is a micromanager, to detriment of organization

_____ Excessive meetings, clumsy communications

_____ Not respected by peers

_____ No meaningful communication

_____ Not respected by employees

_____ No positive vision

_____ Afraid to discipline misbehavior of employees; gutless, whimpy

_____ Generates meaningless busywork, wastes company time

_____ Does not care about employees

_____ Is despised by employees

_____ Unfit to manage people

_____ A danger to this organization

Fundamental Character:

_____ Egocentric

_____ Completely selfish

_____ A moral coward

_____ No self discipline

Personality:

_____ Humorless

_____ Bizarre! Needs psychiatric help

_____ Flaky

_____ Completely unhelpful to others

_____ Pompous

_____ Inbred

Integrity:

_____ Has no integrity, personal or professional

_____ Is a fraud

_____ A brazen liar

_____ Leadership "façade"

Job Competence:

_____ Is incompetent

_____ Blunders with customers

Page 4 -- Observed Deficiencies of _____

Potential to Reform:

____   Incapable of reforming self or improving

Impact on This Organization:

____   Good people leaving the   ____   Has caused employee
         department because of his   morale to plummet
         actions

____   Good people actually leaving ____   His behavior has caused
         the Company because of   employees to lose their
         his actions   initiative

____   Has generated huge   ____   People are now afraid
         dissatisfaction among   to do their best
         employees

____   Has done harm to customer relations or business
____   One of the worst managers we've ever seen
____   Is the worst manager we've even seen

Rate _____ on a scale of ten (highest) to one (lowest),
comparing to peers: _____

Individual's performance in past jobs, if relevant:

_____

_____

_____

_____

_____

Any Actual *Criminal* Behaviors Noticed:

____ Can be violent and dangerous   ____   Physical abuse of
                                                   employees
____ Venal (corruption)

Page 5 -- Observed Deficiencies of _____

      specify: _____ ____ Sexual abuse of
                                                    employees
____ Engages in criminal activity

      specify: _____

Miscellaneous:

____ Personal problems adversely impact job performance
____ Disloyal to this organization
____ Prejudiced against races or religions

Additional Problems Not Listed Above:

_____   _____

_____   _____

_____   _____

_____   _____

_____   _____

Other Comments:

_____
_____
_____
_____
_____
_____
_____

Inclosure 2

To: _____   Date: _____

     _____

From: Edward M. Fergusson
             author, *Jihad the Jerk at Work*

Subject: Comments on Attached "Complaint Package"
             from your employees

Dear _____ ,

This letter is intended to accompany a Complaint Package sent by a Committee of concerned employees to a respected executive in an organization, who can investigate and take appropriate action.

The Committee has carefully selected you as the recipient of their Complaint. They have explicitly placed their trust and confidence in you and your judgment. In the often distrustful world of work today, they are paying you the highest compliment possible. In my past positions of responsibility, it always gave me a good feeling when employees asked me to resolve serious workplace problems long before they reached the boiling point. As an experienced executive, you're very aware it's healthy for an organization to surface and solve problems early on.

Of course, I am not privy to the specific Complaint, or the individual or issue being addressed. But I would like to pass on some comments you may find helpful.

It has been my experience in managing large numbers of people, that if employees feel strongly enough about a situation or person in the workplace to band together to submit a complaint, anonymous or not, chances are the situation is serious indeed. Thirty years of work experience in high pressure corporate, government, and military environments have taught me this. I urge you to place a high priority on investigating and resolving this issue in a timely manner.

Also it has been my experience that there may be much substance to allegations of this type, to the point that the problem is even worse than stated. A fair, honest, non-threatening, vigorous investigation by you can determine the actual situation rather quickly. In some cases, you may be well aware of the issue, and can take immediate action without delay.

If, based on your investigation, action clearly needs to be taken, I urge you to resist the temptation to do nothing. It's better to resolve the problem quickly rather than let it fester and hope it will just "go away" on it's own. It won't. Look closely at the Committee's recommendation. It may be the correct solution. After all, employees are living with the situation, day in and day out. You may find it rewarding to read the attached book, *Jihad the Jerk at Work*, for some insights into problems you are not facing alone – they are pervasive and widespread in today's workplace – *all* workplaces.

If you still harbor any doubts about the serious *consequences* of tolerating or retaining a substandard, "jerky" manager or employee in your organization, please read the e-mail in Chapter 3, pages 119-121, in the attached book, *Jihad the Jerk at Work*. It was recently copied to me by a senior corporate executive detailing his company's loss of a *billion dollar contract*, a contract they were *incumbent* to! They lost it because the proposal manager, a very senior guy, was an arrogant, self-serving "jerk" who mistreated his people and was in turn despised by them . . . and who antagonized his own customers. Jerks are bad for business, it's just that simple.

You'll notice several aspects of this Complaint action. The Committee is anonymous. *I fully endorse this approach.* After thirty years in both employee and management positions, I have sadly come to the conclusion that too many good, decent people have adverse things happen to their careers when they openly point out problems in organizations. It shouldn't be that way, but it is. You know it and I know it. One positive aspect of anonymity is that you can focus on the facts discovered, and not get bogged down in personalities and careerist agendas.

Anonymous or not, it takes a great deal of personal courage and genuine concern for the well-being of an organization for a group of people to submit a Package like this. You can honor that courage by refraining from trying to identify or harass Committee members. You should concentrate on the issue at hand, and its just, swift resolution.

Also you will *notice a timeframe, a suspense date, for action.* It has also been my experience that, sadly, there are too many people in executive positions who defer taking timely action to resolve serious problems. This is inexcusable, and can only be dealt with via an allotment of a reasonable timeframe to get the job done.

If I may be even more candid – there *may* be even another reason to take very pro-active action on your employees' request. It *could* be that if even *half* of the allegations presented are true, it could signify that you have fallen short in some areas of your own responsibilities. Having been a manager myself, I know it's difficult to do everything perfectly – things do slip between the cracks, all the time.

But instead of running to your boss, the VP of _____, and the VP of Human Resources, your loyal employees are giving *you* the opportunity to fix the problem, *quietly and in-house.* In fact, you will even look good fixing it – it will re-enforce the perception of you, held in many circles, as a no-nonsense executive who knows what's going on in his organization, and who is not hesitant about fixing problems that need attention.

Hence the reference to your 30-day "grace period" in the cover letter – they're giving you an opportunity to fix problems, minus finger pointing in any direction (excepting their perception of the main source of the problem, of course).

I apologize in advance if you in any way feel my remarks to be condescending or simplistic. My only desire, as it was when I wrote my book, is to assist both you and your remarkable employees in resolving a difficult issue in the most positive, but rapid manner. I've seen too many unnecessary workplace tragedies that could have been easily avoided by better, unfettered communication between decent employees and decent managers.

You should be, and probably already are, proud to have employees who have the guts to want to improve their organization, and even prouder that they trust you to do the job.

Best wishes to you, your employees, and your organization. Working together, you'll build a legendary operation, *that all around you will hold up as an example of how to get it right*. Life is short (I know,.I've buried too many dear friends lately) – might as well work in an atmosphere of happiness, trust, and high achievement. Why not??

Edward M. Fergusson

CONCLUSION TO CHAPTER SIX, THE "FORMS"

So ends the direct action, the Primary EAJ Campaign portion of this book. We hope you get a chance to also look at Parts III - V of the book, which expand on related themes that may help out in your efforts to evolve to a more intelligent workplace:

Part III: Chapter 7 is a more moderate "Suggestions and Complaints" approach for workplaces that need just a little tweaking. Chapter 8 is for use when the entire Company or organization is a disaster and emergency measures must be taken for the common good. Chapter 9 examines the problems and failures of HR departments to implement effective Upward Feedback programs.

Part IV: Chapters 10, 11, and 12 discuss work areas beyond private business that tend to become paralyzed due to their monopoly status and dead-end nature of careers, with pro-active solutions proposed (government agencies, academia, church, medical, military, *etc.*).

Part V: Chapter 13, lots of fun, reviews our various annual contests (Jerk of the Year award, Corporate Hall of Shame, Non-Corporate Hall of Shame, Most Responsive Directors & Companies, *etc.*). Chapter 14 suggests some activities for you to undertake after you've straightened out your own workplace . . . why not go ahead and reform your town, state, society, and nation for the better?? Why not?? Chapter 15 invites you to tell us your own story.

Again, best of luck – and as they say in the Army Field Artillery, "Keep up the Fire!!!"

HOMILY -- "FOREVER CHANGED – BLESSED CHANGE"

**Understand the sway of Evil in the world
it's insidious ways, it's arrogance
the needless fear that grips men's hearts
knots in stomachs
shreds the Soul, degrades the workplace
turns lions into jackals.
Learn how Evil can be unmasked**

fatally weakened
by courage, light, and reason
Truth to power spoken, calmly
without fear
Now the world is forever changed
for the better
the wicked flee in confusion
their schemes in shambles
Lucifer slouches back to Hell
nothing is as it Was
it is changed forever.
"there are no passengers on spaceship earth
we are all crew"
The Moon shimmers, the spirit soars
Wisdom restored to her holy throne
but watchful!
reason and peace doth reign
Hope takes wing
as it was meant to be.
"Behold I tell you a mystery: we shall not
all sleep, but we shall be changed in a
moment, in the twinkling of an eye, at the
last trumpet."   *I Corinthians XV: 51,52*
"The trumpet shall sound . . . and we shall be
changed. For this corruption must put on
incorruption, and this mortal must put on
immortality."   *I Corinthians XV: 52,53*

                              E.M. Fergusson
                              anno 2005

"Tyranny, like hell, is not easily conquered;
yet we have this consolation with us, that the
harder the conflict, the more glorious the
triumph. What we obtain too cheap, we esteem
too lightly; it is dearness only that gives
everything its value."

Thomas Paine[2]

Part III . . .

Options: Various Levels of Action . . . and the Magic of Basic Upward Feedback

"Managers seem to have little knowledge of their own managerial strengths and weaknesses."[1]

Corporate Research Report
Survey Research Associates

Chapter Seven – Pre-Emptive Strike:
Low Key, Suggestions and Complaints Mode

"When people cease to complain, they cease to think." [1]
Napoleon I

IT'S TIME TO TURN THE TIDE

One little thing I've happened to notice over the past 30 years in the workplace: due to plain human nature, or just plain constricting atmospheres, it's getting harder and harder merely to make an honest suggestion or innocuous complaint without folks (typically the Jerk and fellow-traveler minions) getting all defensive and sensitive about it. In some dysfunctional organizations, people who desire to really improve the place are viewed with deep suspicion. Too many bosses "don't want to hear the bad news" – those that "complain" are summarily labeled and slotted for the approaching 10% layoff, creating a chilling effect on any progress, to say the least.

Needless to say, this kind of constipated atmosphere creates a fertile breeding ground for many varieties of Jerks. It permeated Enron, and paralyzed the FBI and CIA before 9/11. Once people are reduced to cowering, Dilbert-like nonentities immobilized by cynicism, silence, and fear, the hard-core Jerk has an open running-field.

ROCKING THE BOAT

So many examples of this paralysis, and the terrible resulting consequences, come to mind, it's hard to know where to start.

One friend of mine is attending a large, well-known music conservatory in Europe. He's young, competent, and idealistic, and when he sees something that's screwed up, he speaks out about it. He noticed that the conservatory's musical library, although very well-funded, had the wrong type of musical scores – nobody was using the scores they had; the students all went elsewhere to procure the right ones, at crushing personal expense to impoverished students who can least afford it. What a waste.

As a member of the student advisory committee, my friend made the suggestion, in the monthly meeting, to revise the collection to accommodate the students. Unbelievably, the Director of the Library, a typical hardcore Jerk, got very angry with my friend for making this constructive suggestion. The infallibility and perfect wisdom of the Jerk must never be questioned, especially in public.

After the meeting, some friends pulled my young acquaintance aside to caution him on his frankness. "Be careful," they ominously warned, "the music world is a small world."

What bullshit. We've all seen too much of this nonsense, and we know to what dark pit it always leads.

Another example in a similar vein comes from another young friend – I think it's significant to point out that when young, idealistic people are stymied and discouraged from contributing to effective reform, it's a compounded tragedy for society: not only is the immediate problem not dealt with, but the cold rejection can easily turn intelligent young people into hardened cynics, effectively snuffing out their motivation for contributing to progressive change for the remaining 30 to 50 years of their professional lives!! Anyway, this young man, a very bright college senior, worked last summer in a "Children with Disabilities" program in a northeastern state. It was very satisfying work, but one of the major problems both he and his immediate supervisor experienced was that there was *no minimum standard of discipline in effect* in working with their client children.

They both suggested a moderate, common-sense set of guidelines to their director, but *got absolutely no support* whatsoever from this clown.

The Director apparently was so concerned about covering his political ass, cravenly worried about causing any ripples with parents involved, that he squashed the initiative, effectively ruining the program. Consequently, the program was rendered impotent, and my young friend was extremely disgusted at this ineptly run effort. It's hard to stay motivated when managers make no attempt to do their jobs. In my view, an immediate application of a Chapter 7 suggestion form to high levels could quickly clear up this nonsense. And if the fool who stonewalled the reform figures out who made the suggestion, so what? We need to train our entire society to boldly tackle and solve problems early on – working this constructive process *needs to be included in the core curriculum of all high schools and colleges.*

ROCKING THE BOAT ANONYMOUSLY AND SAFELY

So now in the New Millennium we have the perfect solution to this dilemma – simply check out the form at the end of this chapter -then locate in on our Website, fill it in, and "PRINT." Send it anonymously to the appropriate manager. Don't let anything pass, *anything at all pass*, that needs correcting. Send 10 different suggestions for 10 different problems to four different mangers. Do it today. Never let'em slide, never let'em up for air.

Notice that there are many similarities to the "rid-a-jerk" approach of Chapters 4 and 6. It's also anonymous. With more serious problems, you give the manager a fixed period (14 days or 30 days) to resolve the issue, then you may or may not elect to escalate the problem to higher levels – it's your call. If you take a gander at the forms at chapter's end, you also have the option of sending a copy to HR or an ombundsman or whomever. Use of an ombundsman is not a bad idea, if your organization has one. I'd still keep it anonymous, however.

CATCH MORE FLIES WITH HONEY

Of course you may desire at first to keep the "suggestion" process entirely friendly, with no time deadline or intent to escalate or copy to HR. If you can get continual effective action via a non-threatening, totally positive approach, then there's no need to play hardball. This makes it easier to send numerous suggestions, without any associated rancor.

You also have the option of attaching the suggestion to the front of this book and sending it all, as is detailed in Chapter 4 and 6. If it's a low key request, and your organization is otherwise fairly well run, then perhaps it would be unnecessary overkill to do so. However, if there are a lot of serious problems and the organization is on a downhill trajectory, then perhaps this stronger medicine *is* appropriate. For the "suggestions and complaints" mode there's usually not a major hardcore jerk that spawns all the problems. The sources may be varied . . . perhaps the existence of stupid company policies, or areas management has overlooked, or just plain good ideas you have to improve things.

Again, you *could* openly sign your name – but it's risky, for reasons previously stated. And it could make it difficult for you at some future date to launch an EAJ Campaign if needed. Why blow your cover?? And, let's be frank about the two-faced nature of all too many managers: they may *say* they welcome suggestions, but may well *still* privately categorize "complainers" as "folks to be gotten rid of eventually". Be careful, it's just not worth exposing yourself.

THE *EFFECTIVE* SUGGESTION

One obvious element of successful complaining/suggestion making: *always* **have one or more intelligent, well-thought-out** *solutions* **to the problem.** Oftentimes it helps to chat with one or more trusted, competent fellow employees to get their take on the issue. There, you've just formed a "Business Effectiveness Committee". Really.

Note on the enclosed generic suggestion / complaint form that there is a prominent section for "Proposed Solution (s)" – good managers love it when employees present constructive ideas to *solve* problems, beyond just sitting around and grousing. Always propose workable, reasonable solutions.

But in today's screwed-up, flaky work environments, I'd still keep it anonymous.

GOING NUCLEAR

There are occasions when the suggestion / complaint will cover very serious territory, and be of major importance. A large nuclear reactor in Oak Harbor, Ohio (just a Chernobyl gust of wind away from Toledo's 600,000 people) –Davis Besse – has just been closed down because "water was leaking from two nozzles on top of the vessel. The water contained boron, a chemical used to regulate the chemical reaction, and the boron . . . ate away about 70 pounds of steel."[2] Disaster was a mere quarter inch of steel away!

It turns out that maintenance workers were afraid to *openly* point out corrosion problems at the plant for the past 20 years due to a "culture of mistrust" at the nuclear facility. This would be a perfect situation to deploy the suggestion / complaint forms in this chapter. Anonymously alert management to the problem areas, and if they took no action in 15-30 days, simply escalate it higher, to the NRC (federal Nuclear Regulatory Commission) or even local / national media if the Feds were their usual spineless, ineffective selves, in bed with the very industries they're supposed to be regulating.

EVEN LITTLE THINGS COUNT

There are numerous, wonderful examples of how a little anonymous complaining can improve things immediately – things that often strike very close to home.

I had a good friend who worked for IBM. Being an alert individual, he noticed that the Company's cost-cutting programs were going way overboard . . . the quality of the toilet paper in the company restrooms (for the hoi polloi at least!) went from poor to absurd. The rolls were literally slick, plastic-textured shards of rag that had the feel of industrial-grade sandpaper, manufactured by a low bidder from Slovakia.

THE ULTIMATE ENVELOPE-STUFFING

So my friend, not one to suffer fools gladly, blew a fuse. One day he erupted, grabbed a handful of this pathetic "toilet paper", stuffed it into an inter-office envelope, and sent it, anonymously of course, "Personal-Eyes Only" to the Senior VP based at his location site with a caustic note, "Bet you don't have this junk in your executive washroom – here, try using these shards to wipe your ass. We demand better toilet paper – have some shard of respect for your employees."

My friend proudly related that two days later, *every* toilet stall in his building was nattily sporting luxuriant, downy-soft, quilted, five-star toilet paper – employees were stunned at this sudden turnaround. And it was permanent – he worked at the location for three more years, wallowing in Four Seasons gourmet toilet tissue.

Whatever works. **The squeaking wheel gets the oil**. If you don't complain, and complain vigorously, to management, they assume everything is just hunky dory.

JERK-PROOFING

Looking at it from another angle, it is very possible that a consistent barrage of suggestions and complaints could well *prevent* tyranny and jerkism from ever gaining a serious foothold in your organization. People who might ordinarily drift into the Jerk mode of operation are given a dash of cold water in the face, and suddenly realize that the Jerk approach to management practice will land them in endless hot water. Also, if you and your faithful allies make the environment hostile enough for Jerks, they well may voluntarily bail out to seek a slimier, more compatible stinkhole to habitate.

A steady, constant stream of suggestions and complaints can contribute to establishing the proper atmosphere in the workplace. Managers suddenly realize that their employees are really *not* mindless Dilbert clones, that management is under serious scrutiny at all times. This keeps management where it's paid to be: on its toes, looking out for employees as well as the bottom line. A new healthy *respect* for the rank and file is born, and none too soon.

So if you're sick and tired of uselessly having to change your PC password every week because the security gurus like to generate make-work for themselves, or you observe that three different lower and mid-level managers nearby are starting to space and burn out because none has taken a vacation for the past two years, or you notice that half your engineers can't speak coherent English and are in dire need of English as a Second Language lessons . . . anonymously zip a Suggestion / Complaint form over to the nearest Director *today*. And hold his feet to the fire.

That's another key factor to effective "suggestion / complaint" change: don't delay, just fire it in now, otherwise it'll never happen! "Procrastination kills off progressive change". If you get in the habit of *immediate submissions*, you'll make a huge positive impact on your organization – and it might even steer you into exciting pathways that you couldn't have otherwise imagined.

Every employee has a big role to play in creating his or her proper workplace environment. *Never forget this.* Just ask the thousands of acquiescent, complacent Enron employees who sat on their behinds and did *nothing* as a corrupt management systemically destroyed the social and ethical fabric of the company – *partially* due to their own sloth, now many are out of jobs, and looted of their 401K savings.

THREE OBSERVATIONS

It's tempting to dismiss "suggestions and complaints" as a minor, undramatic tool of workplace reform, but consider these three thoughts:

1) few people take the trouble to effectively complain, even
   though they'll moan endlessly about it to co-workers who
   really can't influence outcomes.
2) consequently, most workplaces have too many problems
   that go untouched for years due to neglect.
3) often the subject problem is absurdly easy to fix.

There are two forces driving all this: *sloth*, and *fear*. Sloth can
easily be overcome by self discipline – now with the power of *Jihad
the Jerk at Work*, fear can be greatly reduced, if not eliminated.

If you're not making 3 or 4 good suggestions a year at work, my
guess is you could be missing out on one of life's greatest pleasures,
and one of society's crying needs. I still maintain, however, that
management can never be entirely trusted, and you're better off going
the anonymous route – I've just seen too many good people get burned
by going the open path. "No good deed goes unpunished" is more
than a wry joke, it's a sad workplace reality. To myopic, pollyanish
managers and CEO's who disagree with my observation, I have but
one reply: Stuff It . . . with Slovakian toilet paper.

THE FORMS

Here is the generic suggestion / complaint form. Fill it out on our
website (www.upublishing.com/forms.htm, user id: "reformer" password "progress") and use it regularly to keep your workplace decent
and viable. **"Use it or Lose it"**:

Suggestion / Complaint / Solution Form

To: _____

_____

From: Business Effectiveness Committee (BEC)
             (an informal employee advisory group)
             _____ Inc

Date: _____

Description of Situation or Problem:

_____
_____
_____
_____

Suggested solution (s) :

_____
_____
_____
_____

page one

Only Check Box or fill in if Applicable:

Urgency of ...   ____ urgent
                          ____ very high
                          ____ high
                          ____ moderate
                          ____ low

____ *You are requested to resolve this within ____ days,*
      NLT _____.

____ *If it is not resolved by this date, then the BEC will*
      escalate to _____ .

General Comments:

____ *This is an isolated issue . . . otherwise we feel this*
      organization is well run.

____ *This is just one of many problems in this organization.*
      Other problems are:

      1) _____
         _____
      2) _____
         _____
      3) _____
         _____

____ Attached is a copy of *Jihad the Jerk at Work*.
      Suggest you study it thoroughly.

____ Our organization is plunging downhill fast –
      suggest you turn this around, and quickly!!
      Seriously.

____ Other

      _____
      _____
      _____

Copies Provided:

_____ *No copies provided to other parties in our organization.*

_____ *to HR*

_____ *to Ombundsman*

_____ *to _____*

_____

DO NOT SUFFER FOOLS GLADLY

Oh, by the way, the same rules we use in a Chapter 4 EAJ Campaign apply . . . don't tolerate any whining by the recipient about anonymous submission of a suggestion / complaint (S&C). You can immediately send him portions of this book that knocks down that straw-man, or you may desire to send the entire book, with marked and annotated pages. You don't have to put up with the nonsense. If he won't do his job, notify his boss and escalate the S & C there. There's nothing worse for a Company's health than a manager who negligently tries to shirk his responsibilities.

LEAD THE WAY

And just like a standard EAJ Campaign: with regular S&C's if *you* don't do it, *then nobody will*. It's all about leadership . . . you must lead, if your workplace is ever going to emerge from the darkness. In this fear-ridden, pathetic, Dilbert-saturated society we inhabit, gutsy decent people must emerge from the shadows and *lead* – even if it's prudently anonymous, taking principled action in any form is truly leading the way.

As we commented, you can form an informal, anonymous Committee to generate the Complaints / Suggestions – this makes a lot of sense because members can pool their experience and formulate better recommendations with more depth. Or, you can hand out forms to trusted allies . . . then folks can deluge management with appropriate comments on a wide range of subjects.

Either way, be careful – *only trust* those you *know well* and have absolute confidence in, folks who are known for their discretion. Use the same high security standards you would for an EAJ Campaign (see Chapter 4).

Remember – good, consistent S&C's can create a positive, proactive atmosphere in a workplace, and even preclude Jerks from gaining a toehold. This should be a fixture in your workplace from here on. Try it out, you may be amazed at the benefits.

    "We boil at different degrees."[3]
                       Ralph Waldo Emerson

Chapter Eight – Enron City:
The Bombshell Mode

"Each time a man stands up for an ideal, or acts to improve the lot of others, or strikes out against injustice, he sends a tiny ripple of hope, and crossing each other from a million different centers of energy and daring, those ripples build a current which can sweep down the mightiest walls of repression and resistance."[1]

Robert F. Kennedy
speaking in South Africa, 1966

SOMETIMES MEGA-SHOCK EFFECT IS NEEDED

This is one of the two chapters in this book (the other is Chapter 14) that wasn't originally envisioned – not until the "stunning ten months" of 2001-2002 engulfed our society (Sept 2001- June 2002). The wave of disaster and deep-rooted scandal that hit us in this period – the 9/11 attacks, Enron, the Catholic Church pedophile revelations, Worldcom, Arthur Andersen, Adelphi, Global Crossing, the FBI/CIA 9/11 blunder coverups, *etc.* – have shaken the core of society in a way we haven't seen since 1968 (the Tet Offensive, assassinations of Martin Luther King and Robert F. Kennedy, the riots & protests). We have yet to really sort out the profound impact all these events have made, and are still making, but some "lessons learned" are crystal clear.

Even after "all that", I still hold to the general premise of *Jihad the Jerk at Work*, that in most organizations, one can submit a well-thought-out, anonymous complaint package to a decent Director/Executive, and get a hardcore dead-end Jerk fired, or at least ousted or transferred. *I've seen this done, and the benefits to both the workplace and employees is wondrous and inspiring.* However, after the stunning events of 2001-2002, it's obvious to me that there are too many of those bizarre organizations like Enron and the Catholic Church and even the FBI, in certain dire situations, where hapless employees must employ faster, medicine *far stronger* and ruthless than the standard EAJ Campaign presented in Chapter 4.

HIGH STAKES HARDBALL

In these extreme cases, the organization involved is **so corrupt**, and the problem at hand is **so severe**, that only *emergency measures, a bombshell approach*, can hope to avert disaster, can hope to have a measurable impact, can hope to save lives, prevent gross abuse, halt major criminal activity. There's no time to diddle around at lower levels – the Complaint Package must go to the *absolute top* of the Company, with the 30 day grace period followed up or even simultaneously paralleled to escalation well outside of the corrupt organization. The CEO or Cardinal or Agency Director must understand that if he doesn't act **IMMEDIATELY**, he will very likely be exposed and held criminally liable for his actions, or lack of action.

The "Bombshell Form" at the end of this chapter is self explanatory. Clearly, a copy of this book should accompany the Package to multiply the shock effect on the Jerk / Decision Maker it's being sent to – we don't want *this* package lost on some executive's desk.

There's clearly a big difference in the goal of the Bombshell Attack and the standard EAJ Campaign. In the normal, Chapter 4 -type EAJ operation you're quietly getting rid of a Jerk, in-house, in order to improve the workplace atmosphere. In a Bombshell Assault, you're shocking the head of an organization, CEO or Cardinal or Agency Director or whomever, into dramatically ceasing a criminal activity (*e.g.*, protecting grossly pedophile priests and reassigning them to unsuspecting parishes) or preventing a Company from self implosion (*e.g.*, enlightening a dull-witted CEO to the corrupt machinations of Skillings & Fastows) or exposing gross incompetence (*e.g.*, revealing

FDNY – Fire Department New York – incompetence with skyscraper disaster response to include radio & repeater upgrades, aviation use, and interdepartmental coordination).

With the Bombshell, you may well get one or more Jerks ousted, but the thrust is usually much broader than that.

Well, then, why not just go to the Media right off the bat and skip trying to deal with idiot CEO's or Cardinals??? The answer follows one of the basic tenets of this book – it's worth trying to *fix the problem at the lowest level it can be effectively fixed.* It's amazing how fast a terrified CEO or Cardinal can move if he's aware his game is about to be exposed. The newspapers are full of stories of the powerful and influential suddenly getting religion – the irony of the phrase does not escape us here – and acting properly on key issues when the whole bag of worms is about to revealed to the public eye. Often they can do a cleaner, more rapid reform if they're not also in the immediate glare of public scorn and revulsion.

WHEN *SPEED* IS IMPERATIVE

There are some issues that dictate speedy resolution to limit damage done – for instance, a quick change of the Boston Archdiocese's policy of coddling pedophile priests in 1984 (or better, 1974) would have spared hundreds of innocent children the lifetime agony induced by their rapacious molestation by dozens of criminal priests throughout the 1980's and 90's. The firing of both Skilling and Fastow in1996 or even 1998 could have easily spared Enron from collective immolation.

EXAMPLES TO PONDER

Let's take a look at some hypothetical examples to see how the Bombshell Scenario could make a huge difference in society:

Example # 1: Let's say the year is 1997 and you're the Fire Chief of Ladder Company # 14 in Lower Manhattan. You experienced the first World Trade Center bombing in 1993, and you're well aware how incredibly screwed up your mobile radios perform in tall skyscrapers. You're also disgusted that the New York Fire Department *never* has observers riding along in the numerous Police Department helicopters that flock to disaster scenes, and you're astonished that the Fire and Police departments don't set up Joint Disaster coordination at emergency sites. You're appalled that the Police and Fire Departments never even share a common radio channel. You have a gut feeling it's all just a disaster waiting to happen, a time bomb that threatens your life and the lives of your men.

It's been *four years* (!) after the 1993 bombing, yet nothing has been done to solve these huge problems. There haven't even been any joint exercises conducted!! You know that Thomas Van Essen, the City's Fire Commissioner, is a typical incompetent New York City bureaucratic fool who doesn't have the balls to tackle these challenges.

The solution is obvious. You take the Bombshell Form in this Chapter, fill it in and send it with *Jihad the Jerk at Work* anonymously to Mayor Rudi Guliani. Guliani is not exceptionally bright, but he's a political survivor. If he doesn't announce a concrete plan within 30 days that decisively solves all these problems within *one year*, you'll send an identical package to the *New York Times*, who will gladly blow the whole story wide open.

After closely following all the disasters of 2001-2002, I'm convinced that this methodology is the *only* way concerned, competent employees and managers can proactively save their organizations from horrible disaster **EARLY-ON**, without getting fired by vengeful Jerk bureaucrats. It's estimated that *several hundred* New York City firefighters *needlessly died* on 9/11/01 due to faulty radios and nonexistent coordination with the Police Department. A lot of courageous firemen saw it all coming, but felt helpless to influence events – and ironically, many died agonizing deaths in the hellish infernos of the north and south World Trade Towers.

With *Jihad the Jerk at Work*, and Chapter 8, all this helplessness can be channeled into proactive action, that doesn't endanger any careers and livelihoods.

Example # 2: In 1982, Margaret Gallant sent a letter to Cardinal Humberto Medeiros of Boston, complaining that her Parish Priest, John J. Geoghan, had molested *all seven* of her young nephews!! All seven, my God.

Due to the Catholic Church's criminal gross negligence, and total lack of concern for it's own parishioners, this monster Geoghan was merely transferred from that Parish to many more, where he molested literally scores of innocent children, ruining their lives. He, and dozens more like him, were carefully protected by both Medeiros and his successor, the infamous Cardinal Bernard Law – **it took another agonizing sixteen (16) years before the inept Catholic Church finally defrocked Geoghan, in 1998!,** only after he wreaked incalculable damage upon society.[2]

In hypothetical hindsight, Ms. Gallant would have been far more effective in using the Chapter 8 bombshell forms, paperclipped to the front of this book, to demand that Geoghan be defrocked and criminally charged within 30 days – or have all of it exposed to the *Boston Globe*, with the Cardinals thrown into the clink with their criminal Priests, to boot.

The deadline must be firm, and acted upon.

This would have been the only way to get sponge-brained Catholic Cardinals to do their job up front, and to protect hundreds of innocent young children from the horrible fates they suffered.

The lesson here is to **never trust "organization men" to do the right thing** in explosive issues like this. They will always act to *cover up*, unless threatened with damning media exposure that would ruin their own precious careers. I have been *personal witness* to the way all too many powerful people do business in the world – the first two questions they ask, when pondering how to resolve ethical/ business dilemmas is, **"Will we be caught? Can we safely get away with it?"** I've seen them openly discuss these questions in executive meetings, as a standard factor in the decision-making process!! *It's the way it's always been, and it's the way it will always be.*

And based on the complete collapse of morality and decency among the elites in business, finance, religion, government, and society in the 1980's and 1990's, the trend is ever worsening. The massive sex scandals worldwide in the Catholic Church, but even worse, that institution's disgusting attempts to cover it up, have been the last straw in the revelation of stunning institutional stupidity, cowardice, and greed for all to see. I foresee widespread use of Chapter 8 type bombshell attacks for the next decade (2005-2015), until institutional madness has been reasonably curbed. We must fight *fire with fire*, and *do it now*, before these wolves devour us all.

Example # 3: As you might expect, the incredible Enron 2001 debacle provides us with endless speculative "what might have been" fodder for a Bombshell Package. There were hundreds of Enron employees who were not at all happy with the dishonest, rotting mode of the Company under con artist Jeffrey Skilling in the 1990's (remember from the end of Chapter 4 the quote from the Houston Episcopal Priest's letter to Skilling when he admonishes him, "*These people don't belong to you, they belong to God.*"?). But from my analysis of the situation, they felt helpless, without the proper tool to reasonably deal with this terrible workplace environment. It's no different in thousands of businesses, government agencies, and other organizations today – *until Jihad the Jerk at Work* **was published.**

When doctors try to treat cancer, they initially employ a shock dose of massive chemotherapy to halt the rot and begin its destruction. That's exactly what the spineless, incompetent CEO of Enron, Ken Lay, needed, about 1996 or not later than 1998, to get rid of slick financial mega-crooks like Jeffrey Skilling and Andrew Fastow, and return the Company to honorable, decent people like Vice Chairman Cliff Baxter or CFO Jeff McMahon or even honest players like power plant construction VP Rebecca Marks.

A Bombshell Package to Lay threatening to expose all the Skilling / Fastow book-cooking schemes, as well as blasting the sick "rank and yank" elimination of good employees, could well have saved Enron from total destruction. Obviously, the company was so screwed up that a classic Chapter 4-style EAJ Campaign would not be sufficient – however, elements such as the "Fault's List" could be used to build a case against Skilling and Fastow.

The Bombshell Package would have to give Lay, say, 30 days to announce major changes, 60 days to fire and replace Skilling and Fastow, as well as to revise the personnel evaluation system in parallel. If he didn't perform, the entire scandal in all its sordid dimensions would be turned over to *Business Week* and the *Wall Street Journal* and the *New York Times* to feed upon, which would have been a **huge service** to the millions of naïve Enron investors who would be defrauded of *billions* from 1997 to 2001.

TOO LATE, AND YOU MISS THE TRAIN

But notice this Bombshell Package is delivered in "1996" or at the latest, "1998". Sherron Watkin's August 2001 memo to Chairman Lay, courageous though it was, was far too late – Enron was already six feet into the grave. So the timing of the Bombshell Package is key . . . the earlier it's launched, the better chance that it can have a meaningful impact. Faint heart never won fair lass.

Again, **staying anonymous** protects you from the attacks and intimidation of Jerks, and puts huge pressure on the powerful to get their acts together to do the Right Thing.

THE BOMBSHELL MODE FORM

OK, so here's the generic "Bombshell" form. You'll also find it on our website, very easy to use. Hopefully, you'll never be in this difficult a situation, but if you are, feel free to contact us for advice and moral support!! Anybody as courageous as you are deserves the assistance of man, God, superman, and the brotherhood of Jedi everywhere.

In fact, as a parallel to the Military's "Medal of Honor" Society, we at *Jihad the Jerk at Work* hereby announce the formation of the "Bombshell Society", membership limited to those courageous souls who have launched legitimate Bombshell campaigns on organizations, out of the kind of dire necessity described in this chapter. You may nominate your candidate on the form in Chapter 13.

You could form a supportive Committee, but due to the explosive nature of this quest, your security measures must increase tenfold.

Bombshell Form

To: _____

From: Business Effectiveness Committee (BEC)
                    _____ Inc
Date: _____

The following situation in your Organization has come to our attention:

_____

_____

_____

_____

*This is absolutely **intolerable**. It can result in only one of two possible outcomes:*

    1) You must immediately:

        _____

        _____

        _____

        _____

This must be accomplished within ____ calendar days, not later than _____.
If this outcome does not occur, on time, the BEC of _____ will:

    2)   _____

        _____

        _____

        _____

____ *Attached is a copy of "Jihad the Jerk at Work", which will give you added insights to aspects of the seriousness of you and your organization's present circumstance.*

Chapter Nine – The Magic of a Good Upward Feedback Program *(and how most are sabotaged by bumbling "Human Resources" Departments)*

> *"During my site visits, I had many long-term service employees, at their own initiative, tell me that this was the best thing they had seen management do . . . ever."*[1]
>
> Jim Styring
> AT&T Vice President of Engineering
> Initiated cutting edge Upward
> Feedback Program in his Group
> in the early 1990's

"THE PILL TAKES ONLY THREE SECONDS TO ACT, HERR FELDMARSCHALL"[2]

Field Marshal Erwin Rommel was worried. Recovering at his Heerlingen estate in southern Germany from wounds received in an Allied aircraft strafing of his staff car in Normandy three months before, he was concerned that a failed attempt on the *Führer's* life at his East Prussian Wolf's Lair and the abortive *coup d'etat* in that same July of 1944 would somehow be traced back to him. Numerous plotters had been rounded up and tortured by fanatical SS interrogators. And, inevitably, the Nazis uncovered indicators that these patriots had planned to ask Rommel, a German war hero idolized by the nation, to head the replacement government.

265

Suddenly the quiet at Rommel's country estate was shattered by a knock on the door. Two German Generals in full dress uniform invited Rommel to join them for a "drive in the countryside". As their Mercedes sped through the rolling hills near the Danube, General Wilhelm Burgdorf explained to Rommel that if he quietly took cyanide capsules now, his family would be protected, and he'd be given a hero's burial, after "dying from war wounds". Rommel agreed, and Burgdorf handed him the pills.[3] This spared the Nazi regime the embarrassment of a People's Court trial of the popular soldier.

General Wilhelm Burgdorf was the "Director of Human Resources" ("head of the Army personnel department, and armed forces adjutant at OKW headquarters") of the German Army.[4] The weasel Burgdorf, like so many of his fellow HR Directors worldwide, was a consummate liar – the cyanide pills took a full five minutes, whilst the noble Rommel died an agonizing death, writhing like an animal on the back floor of the HR Mercedes – another "Human Resources" department eliminates another one of it's "problems".

And so goes the typical role for Human Resources Directors . . . toadies for upper management and the CEO. Fittingly, Burgdorf committed suicide in the *Führerbunker* six months later, along with his CEO master, Adolf Hitler.

I admit it – I've generally never liked or respected HR types, except for a smattering of decent ones. Most I've seen have been clerical toadies, spineless and demonstrating little concern for the welfare of employees. The prime role for most HR Departments is to keep the lid on and ensure that employees don't rock the boat, stifling any constructive change in organizations. As mentioned in the Introduction, the disgusting performance of Enron's criminal HR VP in her pathetic testimony to Congress in February 2002 was a shameful, embarrassing blot on the reputation of HR departments everywhere – institutions whose reputations' were already lower than whaleshit.

HR has the most important function in organizations, but is typically staffed with the least competent people, with the worst attitude problems. Even Scott Adams and Dilbert via Catbert got that correct. And why are HR Departments so ineffective?? Because they generally do not have a clue as to what one of their most important responsibility is – not a clue.

THE COMPANY'S CROWN JEWEL: GOOD UPWARD FEEDBACK

And what's one of HR's most important responsibilities?? It's the creation and sustainment of a simple, direct, effective Upward Feedback Program (UFP), where on an annual basis each group of six to twenty employees via an anonymous survey constructively tell their *immediate* manager just exactly what he's doing right, and what he's doing wrong.

THE MOST DANGEROUS THREAT TO ORGANIZATIONS DEFUSED

So *why* is providing a constant, non-threatening, reliable flow of upward feedback to *managers at all levels* so incredibly vital to the health and effectiveness of organizations?? Because far and away the biggest threat to companies are the fragile egos and the blind, unrestrained arrogance of managers, Directors, VP's, CEO's, and leaders at all levels.

Even good decent managers can and will fall prey to this pervasive disease, and it can quickly lead to rot in any organization. I've actually seen this occur on too many occasions. The only antidote to this disease, besides this book itself, is the reliable, honest, non-threatening, anonymous flow of **annual** upward feedback from employees – it will preclude 70% of an organization's major operational / personnel problems from mushrooming out of control. Naturally, I think highly of the power of this book, *Jihad the Jerk at Work*, to clean the stables. . . but if more organizations had effective, simple Upward Feedback Programs, the need to employ EAJ operations would be reduced by over 50%!! **Prevention is so much easier than the cure.**

And when we say "upward feedback", that means upward feedback to *every* manager or supervisor or person with responsibility for over six or more people. They **must** get upward feedback from their direct reports annually. Must. That means even *Directors* and *VP's* and *CEO's* will get vigorous, honest, anonymous upward feedback from the managers or directors who report directly to them – **no one** is exempt, no matter how thin their skins, or gigantic their egos. No games, no politics, just simple upward feedback.

SIMPLE UPWARD FEEDBACK WORKS WONDERS

The positive impact a good Upward Feedback Program can have on a company or organization is major and undeniable. I'll never forget the look of wide-eyed amazement that one senior manager had as he explained to me his upward feedback experience of a few months prior (I had just joined the company as a mid-level hire). "I thought I was doing just fine, but the blunt upward feedback I received took me by surprise," he exclaimed. "I guess I've really got to try to moderate some of my interactions with my folks, and listen to them a lot more."

This upward feedback program is really great, I thought to myself. He *had* moderated his behavior, and he was a much more effective manager for doing so! Coming from the military, which had – and to this day still has – absolutely no upward feedback program at all, for which it suffers grievously (see Chapter 12), I was truly impressed with this proactive corporate innovation. Wow, think of the benefits anal-retentive field grade and general officers could reap from honest but low profile subordinate assessment.

THE NATURAL, CRUCIAL NEED FOR UPWARD FEEDBACK

It's true – the reason a well run Upward Feedback program is so priceless is a no-brainer: 95% of employees learn to become very hesitant about openly voicing *any* suggestions or criticisms at all to their direct supervisors. Anyone who does eventually gets burned in large or small ways.

And, of course, this constricted atmosphere is the perfect breeding ground for the hard core Jerk, whose destructive behaviors as a result are *unrestrained* and *rampant*. The work environment becomes more inbred, more negative, more disastrous. In this sick, deteriorating atmosphere, the best and brightest quickly bail out and move to other companies and careers.

On the other hand and bright side, in the few companies existing today that have excellent Upward Feedback programs that meet the minimum acceptable standards outlined in the chapter, and have stuck to their guns for 3 and 4 and 6 and 10 years with a consistent program, there is much less of a need for employees to launch Chapter 4-style EAJ campaigns. Much of the classic worst managerial behaviors have been moderated by effective employee upward feedback.

I'll also mention once again that a good UFP can help even the very *best* of managers. There are always some areas of their performance that good managers can improve upon, and upward feedback will often point the way.

NOT HR-DRIVEN, NO SURPRISE

It's interesting to note that one of the best UFP's I've ever seen at a large corporation was initiated and developed into a runaway success (that was lauded by both employees and management alike) *not* by a Human Resources department, but by a dynamic Engineering Vice President and the Business Training School of the corporation.

REFORMING HR, BUT DON'T HOLD YOUR BREATH

This is no great surprise, since most HR people tend to be ignorant, incompetent, squirrel-like clerics. In fact, when the UF program was mistakenly handed off to them a few years later, they quickly killed it off via their natural incompetence, lack of motivation, and carelessness. More on this later. You'd think that the creation and management of a decent upward feedback program is *clearly in the*

HR field of responsibility, but the typical HR person's lack of experience in line operations hinders them from any understanding of how the real world functions. That's why one of my prime recommendations to CEO's and other organizational heads is to move only good people & managers & directors into HR after they:

1) have proved their competence in line operations in the organization
2) have attended a dynamic training course in which they are indoctrinated and completely schooled in the UFP approach described in this chapter.
3) have proven they have "fire in their belly" about the incredible importance of competent HR and UFP's to their company, and want to excel in HR in order to really make a difference. No time servers or slackers need apply.

If the CEO feels his HR department is still not up to snuff, then he should turn over all UFP responsibilities to another group . . . say, the training school, or an *ad hoc* organization, to get the job done. Meanwhile, he should purge and fire within the HR department until all the deadwood is cleared out. Perhaps a *name change* would help break the stranglehold of mediocrity – it could be called the "Dynamic Human Assets" group, or whatever.

THE PROBLEM WITH UPWARD FEEDBACK PROGRAMS

So if upward feedback is so great, and the author has seen several examples of it working so well, what's the problem?? The problem is, that to be truly effective for the long haul, a company must institute a good UFP and **then, for God's sake, *stick with it year after year* after *year* without diluting it or screwing it up.**

Most companies and their dimwitted HR Departments just can't handle this simple task! I have personally witnessed two Fortune 500 Corporations institute excellent UFP's that almost immediately made significant improvements that all workers and management could tangibly see and feel, only to have both programs terminated or made unrecognizable, *i.e.*, destroyed, within 2-3 years of inception!! Companies just **can't seem to bring themselves to *stick* with a good thing that actually works**, or even *recognize success when it's blossoming right under their noses.*

How can this happen?? How can companies and their HR Departments act like such blithering, mindless morons??

THE GOLDEN FUNDAMENTAL OF UPWARD FEEDBACK

The major reason HR Departments and CEOs screw up upward feedback programs is that they don't understand the #1 dynamic of wildly successful UFP's: the major goal of the UFP is to open up a reliable, long-term, honest information flow from employees to their **immediate** manager (also from managers to *their* immediate Director, and so on). No, we didn't say "employee to director", or include quizzing employees on their concept for the direction of Corporate strategy into the next decade, or employee surveys on corporate innovation and customer relations.

Simply, we want 6 to 12 employees to funnel their impressions, in a non-threatening, anonymous way of how their immediate manager is doing – the good and the areas needing improvement. That's all. Tell me why human resources departments and directors can't grasp this simple, frigging concept, and we'll all understand why HR is clogged with such pathetic, ineffective clerks. The damage they inflict on the American workplace is monumental and tragic (replicated worldwide, I'm sure).

A GURU WORTH LISTENING TO

Perhaps you don't agree with my 30-year assessment of the crucial nature of the employee-direct manager link. Then peruse what one of the premiere experts on corporate productivity has to say, Marcus Buckingham, Gallup Poll consultant and guru:

*". . . Our research tells us that the single most important determinant of individual performance is a person's relationship with his or her **immediate manager**. It just doesn't matter much if you work for one of the '100 best companies', the world's most respected brand, or the ultimate employee-focused organization. Without a robust relationship with a manager who sets clear expectations, knows you, trusts you, and invests in you, you're less likely to stay and perform.*

I admit, it seems like the most obvious point in the world. but do we revere the role of the middle manager? Hardly. We don't even like the term! We'd rather transform everyone into grassroots leaders, change agents, intrapreneurs. We look at managers as costs to be cut – or, at best, as leaders-in-waiting, people who are putting in time before they get the big job."[5]

PAY ATTENTION – THE ESSENCE OF UPWARD FEEDBACK

If you can't send this entire book, xerox the page above and the following page and send anonymously to your idiot HR Director today. If the fundamental link in any organization is that between employees and their **direct** manager, then the **crucial benefit of an excellent UFP comes when employees realize that, on a regular basis,** *some* **of their suggestions are being taken to heart by their immediate manager, and they can see tangible evidence that he's altering,** *i.e.,* **improving, his behavior / leadership style / whatever in response.** They key word here is *response* – there's some *positive response* to employee input. This is *hugely important* to foster a heartfelt employee belief that he works for a company that's so intelligently run that it continually demonstrates it's capable of listening and acting on constructive feedback . . . and does so year after year, regardless of business climate, acquisitions, divestitures, management turnover, *et al.*

(highlight the previous 5 lines so your clueless HR director
can't miss'em)

Alan Walker and James Smither published their notable "Five
Year Study of Upward Feedback" in 1999 in *Personnel Psychology*,
in which they astutely pointed out via scientific study what I've
noticed firsthand for 15 years: that the greatest value in instituting a
good upward feedback process is that employees are really impressed
that management *cares enough about them that they actually ask for
their opinions*. This alone is enough to help boost their productivity
and work satisfaction. This is called "the Hawthorn Effect" after a
famous study at manufacturing plant boosted employee productivity
just because folks were so impressed that management cared about
the optimal level of lighting, they were inspired to work harder. The
workers were working at top form *even when the lighting was
experimentally set so low, it was almost dark in the plant*!! Such is
the power of psychology, caring for employees, and positive strokes
. . . and such is the power of healthy upward feedback.[6]

It's like electricity – a healthy circuit flows to the light, then back
to the source. It's a complete *circuit*. The effect on employee morale
and productivity is immediate and profound. It creates an atmosphere
of trust and hope and decency that allows any organization to reach
peak operating performance, and stay there, year after year. Make
sure your moronic HR Director sees these paragraphs . . . if he can't
grasp their essence, get him replaced with at least a half-wit who can.

More on the documented success of UFP later in this chapter.

These are such obvious truths, that it mystifies me why HR folks
feel compelled to continually barge into sound employee-direct manager UFP's and proceed to screw them up so royally. Here are three
informed guesses:

WARPED MINDSETS

1) One theory I have can be gleaned from the mounds of garbage
management fad books published in the last decade. It's the "if it ain't
broke, go in and totally screw it up" philosophy of the 1990's. CEO's,
Presidents, VP's and HR Directors just can't stand to stick with a

simple UFP that's working well. To embellish their annual fitness reports they've got to "tweak" and change and "improve" any and every thing. "Change for change's sake" has destroyed thousands of excellent UFP's and left formerly hopeful employees shaking their heads. This entire ticket-punching mentality, "form over substance", led directly to the hell of Enron, Worldcom, Arthur Andersen, and the collapse of the aura of corporate infallibility in the United States.

MINDLESS DESTRUCTION

I personally witnessed a classic example of this in one large corporation, who "improved" a very good UFP into oblivion by totally eliminating the direct employee – to – immediate – supervisor annual upward feedback, replacing it with a watered-down, meaningless "employee corporate opinion" survey.

In a long winded e-mail to disbelieving employees, the HR VP gave his ludicrous rationale for destroying one of the last really good programs in the company that was actually working, and replacing it with a useless "official corporate survey" that will be "significantly improved and streamlined" and which will "provide leading indicators for critical business results" – what crap, and the guy couldn't even express himself in direct English without lapsing into terminal buzzwordspeak. This "HR Business Partner" should have been given a "leading indicator" alright . . . a boot in the ass out the door.

Incidentally, less than two years after promulgating this nonsense and trashing their excellent UFP, this same huge Company lost 99% of its market value and was trading at 56 cents a share on the NYSE. Can anyone connect the dots???

One lesson can be gleaned from this fiasco. A solid UFP should be considered *sacrosanct*, and firewalled off from HR's narcotic urge to peddle useless "Corporate Opinion Surveys" – let HR conduct voluntary surveys all they want, but they must be directed to keep their incompetent paws off the core Upward Feedback Program.

Continuing on with reason UFP's get killed off . . .

2) Another way CEO's and the geniuses in HR have found to demolish good UFP's is that they allow it to become threatening (or even the perception of threatening) to individual managers. Big mistake. This is one of those areas where micromanagement backfires badly. The program starts out correctly as good, anonymous *private* feedback to the manager, *for his professional use only* in improving his performance. It's quiet, he can select one or two items to focus on, at his own pace. It's ideal, it's win-win. As already mentioned, the resulting immediate change and improvement has an electric, positive effect on employees, and their respect for their manager and company increases.

BUT THEN what happens? Inevitably, some idiot Director or HR manager on the make, grandstanding in the weekly D-level meeting, intones, "Well, why don't we *improve* this UFP, and require the manager to show his Director the list of criticisms received in the UF survey, and his plan to correct the problems??"

Then, not to be outdone, the Special VP for CMV (Corporate Millennial Vision) chimes in with, "Oh, this is great, now we can encourage Directors to use all this upward feedback as an assessment tool to rate his managers and peg annual bonus levels." The assembled gifted executives murmur assent, and bask in the glow of their collective business genius and matchless savvy.

What a disaster. You can see where this is leading . . . the instant any manager feels that data on the UFP could be possibly used by his boss to *rate* his effectiveness as a leader, the *entire* UFP will go down the tubes. I've seen it happen firsthand. Managers will begin to pressure HR Directors to water down and then deep six the UFP – and HR Directors, being the lily-livered toadies that most are, will readily cave in. The UFP is toast! It's dead in the water. I personally witnessed this scenario unfold in *two* separate, large Corporations. The UFP died within six months. It was an outrage!! Don't let this happen in your organization. Insist on UFP *purity*, sacrosanct.

CAN'T MAKE A PURSE OUT OF A SOW'S EAR

3) The third major reason for the untimely demise of even the most outstanding UFP lies at the very core of the problem with HR itself: the ingrained moral cowardice and spinelessness of most HR people & their Directors (coupled with the indifference, lack of oversight, and ignorance of many CEO's). Let a flaky manager, whose hyperinflated ego bruised by accurate UF from his own people, come into the office whining about "unnecessary employee feedback", and your typical weak-as-water HR Director, wanting to be popular with all potential movers and shakers, promises to "take care of it", and torpedoes the UFP.

This problem could be easily pre-empted by a vigorous company-wide training effort that vividly explains the crucial, non-threatening nature of good upward feedback. Simply nip the thin-skinned carping in the bud. UF is just too important to be derailed by this kind of jerky sniping.

INSIST ON HIGH-QUALITY HR

But for useful upward feedback to survive long term, HR Directors and people must have *fortitude* and actually *care* about the future of the company, the meaningful professional development of its managers, and the sanity of its employees. I urge you to pressure, anonymously of course, your CEO to keep firing his HR Director until, like Lincoln finding Grant in the Civil War, he finally finds one who's worth a shit, has a spine, and "gets it". This should be a high priority for all employees who want to work in a sane company that has a real future, that's trying to build a decent workplace environment. After hearing a complaint about Grant's heavy drinking, Lincoln famously quipped, "Find out what brand of whiskey Grant prefers, and send a bottle to each of my Generals! This man fights!"

Similarly, we need HR Directors who'll stick to their guns and fight for a decent Upward Feedback Program – indeed, who'll abruptly resign from any organization foolish enough to resist having the UFP system ingrained in their culture.

Send this book, anonymously, with these paragraphs highlighted to either your CEO or HR Director, or *both*, today. Tell them to get with the program, *now*. Upward Feedback is not rocket science . . . it's easy to do, and sustain, and the benefits are long-lasting and profound.

A BRIEF PRIMER: FUNDAMENTALS OF A GOOD, BASIC UFP

It's not my purpose in this chapter to engage in a lengthy dissertation on what constitutes a worthwhile Upward Feedback Program. There are several good detailed works by experienced, respected professionals available, which tend to agree on the basic fundamentals and which show the pitfalls to avoid, which I'll refer you to. But I would like to highlight some of the essential elements of good UFP's, so you can gauge whether or not your Company is either getting on solid track, or is heading towards hellish oblivion.

General elements:

- ****just do it once a year;** it'll be enough to open good feedback channels. It's surprising how fast that year rolls around. No need for overkill.

- ****every manager**, director, VP, CEO *etc.* who has at least six people *directly* working for him/her **gets feedback.**

- **keep the survey **concise** – limit it to 30 or so very important areas.

- **obviously, it's **strictly anonymous**
  (this is important. One study of respondents found that "When asked 'Would you have rated your boss . . . any differently if feedback had not been given to them anonymously?', 24 per cent indicated *'yes'*."[7])

- **in my view, don't pussyfoot around with this, this is not a voluntary form to fill out, **everybody's got to do it . . . mandatory**. This is too important to waffle on. Too many folks will blow it off if given the chance – they'll eventually be glad they were 'drafted' into participation!

- ****results are for the "rated" manager's eyes only**: This is *non-threatening* input designed to *help him to personally improve his leadership skills.*

(Possibility of negative managerial reaction to upward feedback can be minimized by the non-threatening approach and is "the major reason why the
results are often used only for developmental purposes. When managers know that the results will not
be shared with their supervisors, the *managers may
be more willing to view them constructively*, and
raters will be more willing to provide accurate feedback."[8] In a research survey of upward feedback
raters, "When asked, 'Would you have rated your
boss any differently if your feedback would be
shared with his/her supervisor and used for performance appraisal?', *34 per cent* indicated '*yes*'. As one
person explained, 'I like my boss and would be less
likely to give negative feedback if it would hurt.'"[9]

keep the UFP constructive and low key, and **never let it lapse
– it must be kept going strong for 3 and 5 and 8 and 12 years
hence. Don't allow anyone to kill it off after 2 years "because
it's time to move on to something else". *The strength of
upward feedback is that it's continuously there, year after
year.*

**all employees and managers must be given a **thorough
understanding** of the UFP and it's value.

I'd **limit the program to employee feedback to their direct
manager only. I see no need for "peer inputs" because peers
already freely and frankly talk to one another on a regular
basis. Also I've seen some *really weird stuff* and cosmic jerk
games go on when peers start "rating" one another. It's minor
value-added, or worse.

Tips for Recipient Managers:

****relax & enjoy it!** Use upward feedback as an golden opportunity to improve your management skills, at your own pace.
Don't try to improve everything at once – **just pick out the**

one or two feedbacks that seem important to you, and quietly go about acting upon the suggestions. If you can get to several more during the year, so much the better. Remember, actions speak louder than words! **Don't talk about it, just do it.** Your employees will admire you for acting on their feedback. And, once you become a true believer in the power of a good UFP in improving an organization's functioning, remember this when you take over as Director or CEO of a company that has none, and crank one up asap.

if you think some of the suggestions are absurd, perhaps they are. A strong clue can be found in the numbers: if ten out of eleven of your direct reports agree on a certain feedback, you should look at it closely. If only one person expresses the concern, then maybe it can go to the bottom of your "to do" list. **Let common sense show the way.

we're not after perfection here – what's more important is that feedback from employees to higher is solicited, and *some of it is acted on,* year after year. This **precludes things getting too weird in companies, keeps people's feet on the ground! Regular UF is like regular hand washing . . . it's healthy.

no one is going to "check up" on you to see your "action plan" to respond to the feedback. You naturally work on the feedbacks because you're a professional and it makes common sense to act on constructive, honest advice from **those who know you best – your direct employees.

CEO and HR Responsibilities:

the CEO **should personally champion the UFP and make sure it's a smooth running fixture in his organization. CEO's who fail to do this simply aren't doing their job. Period.

the Director of HR, and every HR employee, **should personally champion the UFP and make sure it's a well run program in the company. HR Directors who fail to do this *should be immediately replaced.* Period.

HR should institute a company wide training program designed to genuinely motivate employees and mangers to have a positive attitude toward upward feedback. Don't forget to indoctrinate *new* employees. **Good UF is an integral part of any world class organization's culture – make sure it's part of yours.

Just as important, HR should conduct a brief (mandatory) survey of all employees and managers *six months after* the annual UFP to get insights as to how effective the UFP was for that year. If the response is enthusiastic, which it should be, this inspirational news should be broadcast to the company **to continually reinforce the positive benefits to all. If, on the other hand, the survey reveals problems, fix the problems fast, don't can the UFP. HR should constantly be looking for ways to quietly strengthen the UFP – but remember, don't screw it up by meddling too much. Use direct quotes, transmit the genuine amazement and enthusiasm of both managers and employees, *especially those cynics who were won over by seeing how upward feedback improved things in real time.* See the next section, "Does UF Really Work?"

** don't be shocked to find that your Upward Feedback program is a **huge success in the first year** and extremely popular with both employees and management. Most intelligently run UFP's are. It's absolutely amazing. What you must be on guard for are the myriad ways that nameless schmucks in the company will try to botch it up, even the well intentioned! The real **challenge is to keep it going strong**, simple and unadulterated, for 5 and 10 years and more. The longevity record for any good UFP I've seen is 3 years, before "improvements" destroy the noble effort. So if you reach 4 years or more, and the UFP is still pure and effective, *contact me asap* so I can cart out some champagne to your location and we can celebrate. (Naturally, I'll need proof in the form of heartfelt testimonials gleaned from your annual follow-up survey, x years in a row).

if HR, or some other department wants to survey employees on Corporate Goals 2010, or Customer Driven Objectives or whatever, insist that the UFP be **firewalled off from all this drivel. UFP should always be given **the highest priority**, and employees precious time should be jealously shielded from too many frivolous surveys.

for God's sake, **leave corporate buzzwords and any references to the latest bullshit management fad **out** of the damn UF survey. You're trying to *engage* employees and managers, not utterly turn them off. Puuleeze! You catch more flies with honey, not strychnine.

**if you happen to be tasked to set up a UFP for your organization, I strongly recommend you read a study entitled "A Feedback Approach to Management Development", by Manuel London (State University of New York at Stony Brook) and Arthur J. Wohlers (Survey Research Associates), or perhaps more recent publications. This paper was published in the "Journal of Management Development", 1990.

FOR MUCH MORE CURRENT INFO ON UPWARD FEEDBACK . . .

Do a web search, of course. You'll find under "upward feedback for managers" over 22,000 pages of entries. A lot of it is really good info: "HRZone" has a 30 item questionnaire all laid out, excellent stuff. There are scads of books and articles available to aid in setting up a process. Many articles are published which can add to your upward feedback insight. There are even companies offering their services to set up a turn-key UFP in your organization.

... BUT BEWARE

However, one caution: a lot of the UF items being peddled seem to be overkill to me. As already mentioned, the purpose of a good upward feedback process is **not** to create the perfect "360 degree manager evaluation tool", or even to mold perfect managers. It's real purpose is to create a constant, reliable flow of employee-fueled ideas and impact to their direct managers, to increase the "health" of the organization. It's other main achievement is to insure the inflated ego's of managers are swiftly brought down to earth before they inflict major Enron-style chaos on the corporation. And the real challenge to UFP's, not mentioned in any of the 22,000 web hits, is the fact that UFP's die out unnecessarily in the toddler stage, 2-3 years, due to sloth and neglect by CEO's and HR incompetents.

Also, I see little mention of lower level manager upward feedback to directors, and director feedback to VP's, and 10 VP's giving the CEO an anonymous kick in the pants – these feedbacks play *just as vital* a role, if not more, in preventing an organization from "going weird". Just look at Enron, the FBI, the Catholic Church, and Worldcom. All those CEO's, Directors, and Cardinals needed blunt, dutch uncle-type upward feedback, but it didn't happen. The upward feedback guru community has missed the boat on this one. **It's clear to me that our society has got to really get moving and serious on UFP's everywhere,** with UFP's that are backed up by the white-hot evangelical fervor of the converted. Time to get movin', time to blitz.

But most importantly, once the ball is rolling, **stick with it** – *don't allow* your UFP to die out, as too many do.

Don't wait for this to magically appear from on high – **you**, dear reader, will have to be the change agent. **Get cracking!** Send all this info (anonymously) to your CEO and HR Director today, *NOW*!! Whip out your trusty yellow highlighter again, and do your thing.

BUT DOES THIS UPWARD FEEDBACK PROCESS REALLY WORK?

Well, I've mentioned that I've personally witnessed that it worked spectacularly in two separate, very large corporations I worked for (and my major beef is that these companies let both wonderful programs lapse, which was inexcusable, considering how positively received they were by management and employees alike).

But don't just take my word for it, consider this report from another Fortune 500 Company, who outlined the progress of their relatively new upward feedback process in a newsletter. The most striking thing about it is the *way even initially deeply skeptical folks were won over when they saw the beneficial changes unfold before their own eyes*, in their own workplaces. For brevity, I'll list some excerpts:[10] (my emphasis)

→"(Company) line managers typically had 20 plus years of experience with the company, and they weren't used to giving or receiving verbal feedback. In the old environment, that was a risky thing to do."

→"The general inability of managers and their reports to communicate led to alarmingly poor results in the Supervision category" of the Company Opinion Survey.

→To get the process on the right track, a team of facilitators worked on "not only accustoming managers to receiving Upward Feedback without becoming alienated or threatened, but also obtaining constructive feedback from their direct reports . . . *Preparation in ensuring everyone knows what to expect is key.*"

→After the first year of this UFP, the senior VP of the division reported, **"During my site visits, I had many long-term service employees, at their own initiative, tell me that this was the best thing they had seen management do . . . ever."** (my emphasis)

→One of the facilitators commented, **"The managers who resisted us the most are now our greatest advocates."**

→Another participant comment: **"It was one of the most valuable experiences I ever had, and *I could see that the relationships here did nothing but improve."***

→"Through Upward Feedback we've improved trust and communication, something that was lacking before. **There are now a lot of believers in the process because it really does work."**

And from the *Journal of Management Development* article previously cited:[11]

→"Managers seem to have *little knowledge of their own managerial strengths and weaknesses."* (emphasis mine) Thus the strong need for a non-threatening, constructive, confidential upward feedback process.

SO, WHAT KIND OF ORGANIZATIONS CAN BENEFIT FROM UFP'S??

All of them!! *Every organization known to mankind* has a crying need to provide a non-threatening channel of communication, on a regular basis, whereby people can safely let their direct supervisor know how he's doing. Just by looking at the % of opinion on various subjects, that manager can easily figure out what his reform effort priorities should be:

- •Businesses: large, medium and small (**hint**: Enron and Worldcom had no UFP in place)

- •Government Agencies: local, state, and federal (**hint**: the FBI & CIA have no UFP in place)

- •Political organizations, Academia, Judiciary, Non-profits, Medical, law enforcement, Religions (**hint**: the Catholic Church has no UFP in place)

- •Military

(wait a minute, would upward feedback in the military undermine discipline?? Not in any way . . . remember, the manager confidentially get his feedback to use in ways he sees fit. And, God knows, **the more autocratic and hierarchical the organization is, the more it truly needs upward feedback**. When I think of the generals and colonels and majors and sergeant-majors I've known who could have tremendously benefited from some honest, blunt UF, the list could stretch to the moon and back. Their effectiveness would have doubled as a result.)

EVEN THE LOFTY PROFESSION OF ELITE JOURNALISM

can not escape the fundamental, dire human need to have regular Upward Feedback in place!! The recent noisy scandal at the prestigious, brainy *New York Times* is a classic lesson of the *universal* mandate for some two-way communication, yes, some humility even (!), in organizations who've always felt they were "just a tad above all that" and who "don't need to stoop to plebian practice". After all we're Mensa geniuses, we're immune from the foibles of mere mortals . . . aren't we? Please tell me we are . . . . .

What, so these guys don't pull their trousers on one leg at a time?

I refer, of course, to the Jayson Blair scandal of 2003, when a young *NY Times* reporter was caught systematically fabricating "facts" for his articles, which were then published, sometimes on Page One of the "newspaper of record", the *Times*. There are two major components to this story. One is that if employees had Chapter 6-style EAJ forms from *Jihad the Jerk at Work*, they could have easily, safely blown the whistle on Blair during the previous five years when it was widely known he fudged the facts and was a major Jerk on the press floor – both at the *Boston Globe* and the *New York Times*.

But the second component is much bigger. This occurred after the J. Blair story blew wide open, and *Times* Executive Editor Howell

Raines gathered the *Times* staff on the press floor and naively invited them to vent their feelings. All the frustrations about Raines' autocratic and domineering management style of the past several years ("bullying, playing favorites, micromanaging coverage, alienating valued staffers") burst forth – Raines and managing editor Gerald Boyd were shocked at the hostility of the staff, so shocked that they both resigned shortly thereafter to try to save the institution. The well was just too poisoned to linger on.

And of course they were taken by surprise – the *Times* has always felt it's never needed an Upward Feedback Program, so management was flying blind when it came to their awareness of staff morale and true feelings. A world class newspaper that had just won seven Pulitzer Prizes (mostly on 9/11 coverage) and prided itself on probing investigative journalism *didn't even know what was going on under it's own roof* . . . and in fact had to establish several crash investigative committees to find out!! But it was far too late for Raines and Boyd.[12]

This truly is a classic cautionary tale about institutions who feel they're above having to institute an Upward Feedback Program. They're just kidding themselves. **All organizations need good, basic UFP's, bar none.** UFP's are the perfect antidote to poisoned work wells. *Employees will gladly tell you what's going on* – the good and the bad – if you just set up a safe, anonymous UFP mechanism.

If your snooty management thinks it doesn't need an UFP, this is a clear signal your organization needs it ten times more urgently than the folks next door.

A WORD ON "MANAGEMENT TRAINING"

Whilst we're busily savaging HR departments in general, we might as well point out another key area where they've miserably failed, "management training".

I've got to tell you . . . in several large corporations I've worked for, I've been stunned to discover that often there is absolutely no "management training" at all. Employees are promoted into management levels and are expected to perform well.

In one corporation I joined, I noticed this phenomenon at the very outset, which was manifestly displayed in some of the crude, unprofessional behaviors of lower level managers I encountered. This went on for four years, as the company lost many good employees who left in disgust. Suddenly, some senior VPs and HR woke up, and one day all employees received this rather incredible e-mail, so desperate and frantic in tone, that I have to share it with you in it's entirety, complete with nauseating corporate buzzwords and all (naturally, corporate names are altered to protect the guilty from embarrassment):

> *Subject: HR NEWS UPDATE: Volume 3 – Issue 2 --- August 1998*
>
> *Required New Supervisor Training*
>
> *The WireTech New Supervisors Workshop (WT501L) covers the leadership skills required to be effective as a supervisor in WireTech's high performance operating environment of the future. The seminar provides exposure to a broad spectrum of topics. It is led by seasoned managers and supplemented by executive interactions. All WireTech supervisors who assume their first supervisory position, regardless of level, will be expected to register to take this workshop within the first six months of taking a new supervisory position. **Existing supervisors who assumed their supervisory position in 1995, 1996, 1997, and 1998 are required to attend this workshop** and should plan to take the workshop by the end of 1998.*
> *For more information, schedules and registration, visit the Learning and Performance Center website at www.lpc.wiretech.com.*[13]

(author's highlights)

TOO LATE

Yep, your eyes do not deceive you: in this company, management and HR were *openly admitting that they had been blowing off management training for the past 5 years*, and now were desperately trying to make up for all the resulting disasters. Smoking guns never cease to amaze me, even though they often merely underline what everybody already knows.

TOO LITTLE

Then, of course, we have to look at the *content* of the actual training once a laggard company finally gets around to finally mandating it. The results here are similarly unimpressive. I once had a rather mediocre lower-level manager describe to me the thrust of his recent management course.

He had a print on the wall of eight people in a meeting, each in a different pose, and each with obviously something different on his/her mind. This manager blathered on about personality differences and a plethora of new age concepts that most cutting edge management consultants discarded 20 years ago.

HOLLOW-SHELL TRAINING

Indeed, the typically useless "management training" ladled out by most corporations mention nothing about devotion to and strengthening the organization, building strong trusting teams, ethics, loyalty cutting both ways, effective personal counseling, installing good reliable upward feedback, the problems of dealing with Jerks in the Workplace. Management Training should wax heavy on indoctrinating managers on important ethical values, but often fail to address any values whatsoever.

In fact, this massive "values deficiency" goes much deeper than corporate management training, as we all discovered in 2002. After the Enron, Worldcom, Arthur Andersen, Aldelphi, and Global Crossing implosions *ad nauseam*, some astute observers have pointed out that even so-called "elite" MBA curriculums have studiously ignored key business values such as ethics, honesty, morality. As Alexander Cockburn recently wrote in *The Nation* magazine,

> "... *nowhere will you find empirical studies on the sociobiological roots of the criminal tendencies of the executive class.*
>
> *Why? The rich bought out the opposition. Back in the mists of antiquity you had communists and socialists and populists who'd read Marx and had a pretty fair notion of what the rich were up to. Even Democrats had a grasp of the true situation. Then came the witch hunts and the buyouts, hand in hand. **Result, an Enron exec could come to maturity without ever once hearing an admonitory word about its being wrong to lie, cheat and steal, sell out your co-workers, defraud your customers.***
>
> ***The finest schools in America produced a criminal elite that stole the store in less than a decade.***"[14]

Righteous, Alex. And deadly accurate to boot.

Getting back to Company Management Training: in short, much of it is counterproductive and doesn't address the core problems of workplace environments today – once again, HR departments have miserably failed to even remotely do their jobs, and the consequences are horrendous.

THE "SKIPPING STONE" MANAGER

A perfect example of the *product* company "management training" grinds out was the lightweight so avidly describing the painting on his wall. This guy was a classic "skipping stone" manager – he wasn't there to build a lasting, vibrant organization that would strengthen the Company. His only goal was to give high-speed viewgraph briefings and impress certain VP's into hiring him as one of their latest hot-shot directors. He took little interest in the vital operations of his own group and keeping the competence level of his employees high – he was far too busy packing his bags, preparing to move up the hierarchical chain . . . a true "skipping stone" manager, vaguely here today, gone tomorrow – long gone before the dire consequences of his selfish negligence could catch up to him.

The corporation this all occurred in, once a mighty member of the Fortune Ten, has since imploded and it's expected will be either broken up into bits or will file for bankruptcy within the next year. It basically shot itself in the foot by ignoring the basics, and becoming obsessed with form, not substance. All the thousands of slick view-graph presentations and PC graphics didn't compensate for too many managers failing to do their fundamental jobs.

There's got to be a lesson to be learned here somewhere . . . to liberally borrow a line from Alexander Cockburn, "You'd think there's at least a *Time* cover in it."[15]

Bonus Section!!

Part IV . . . Reforming "Hopelessly Dead-End" Monopolies: Government Agencies, Academia, and the Military

"There is no credit to being a comedian, when you have the whole Government working for you. All you have to do is report the facts. I don't even have to exaggerate."
Will Rogers

So why are we now going to spend the next three chapters focusing on specific, albeit broad, workplaces: Government, Academia, and the Military?? Simply because highly monopolistic entities like these pose such a huge challenge to decent reform that even I am forced to admit that the mere usage of our favorite book, *Jihad the Work at Work*, while it could help to *temporarily* clean up these cesspools and havens for hard-core jerks, **can not do the job alone**. There are so many *systemic problems* throttling these atrocious, dead-end, fear ridden occupations that only multiple, powerful solutions working in tandem can hope to sanitize the landscape and jump start them into decent, productive entities. I've worked in all these environments as well as in business corporations, and can testify it's much easier to reform competitive businesses than government bureaucracies … much easier. Al Gore should have consulted with me before he tried to "reinvent government" back in the 1990's. Then he wouldn't have wasted so much effort for so little result.

291

It is also instructive and psychologically empowering for us all to be able to clearly look at very difficult work environments and be able to dissect the problems and come up with intelligent ways to solve them. The methodology we employ in *Jihad the Jerk at Work* : ID problems / cite clear examples / isolate root cause(s) / provide workable, safe solutions / measure progress – can be used in almost any difficult field of work. In fact, I ask readers to let me know if I've missed any other real cesspool career area, so we can add it to this section of the book.

Another rationale for this section of the book: if you can actually "clean up" a government agency, a college academic department, or a military unit, you've moved to the *graduate level* of workplace reform. As I've mentioned, these are much more difficult to reform than private businesses and corporations with their built in competitive edges, bias toward efficiency, and tangible bottom lines. So I'm especially interested to hear about your progress in using the multiple-solution approach presented here to reform the "monopolies".

A final incentive for tackling the monopolies: the government and military soak up about 30% of all our incomes in punishing taxes – this is a huge bite. There is convincing evidence indicating that much of this treasure so painfully forked over is wasted – or worse, used in criminally foolish ways to negative effect – due to incompetence, mismanagement, and stupidity. There's no need to belabor the damage to us all when these agencies blunder and fail to perform … just look at the 9/11 fiasco. It is high time all levels of government, law enforcement, and the military are reformed so the waste and dysfunction can be reduced from its present stratospheric level.

Let the reform begin now, and be pursued with evangelical fervor.

Chapter Ten – Government Agencies From Hell: Systemic Folly at Federal, State, and Local Levels

... The fine art of Shooting the Messenger refined

... Most government agencies are incredibly screwed up – it doesn't have to be this way. Why, and a set of workable solutions

... The incredible fax machine story!!

"To make it anywhere in the U.S. government, you have to be absolutely unable to formulate thoughts that have anything to do with logic, common sense, or originality."[1]

> Aukai Collins
> American Islamic Jihad fighter in Chechnya.
> Worked for FBI and CIA to try to curb
> terrorism, but was completely and incompetently
> mishandled by these dysfunctional bureaucracies,
> blowing a chance to place a deep cover operative
> in Bin Laden's Afghan terror camps in 1998.

SYSTEMIC PROBLEMS OF GOVERNMENT AGENCIES

As has been mentioned several times earlier in this book, the absurdities and foolishness that routinely occur in government agencies – federal, state and local – can make the shenanigans of jerks in private business look tame by comparison. It's not an accident that the terms "dysfunctional" and "government agency" are often found lumped together in the lexicon of anglo-saxon phraseology.

In this chapter, we'll identify many of the most common problems plaguing government agencies at all levels, find out what drives all these strange behaviors, look at some incredible examples in 16 different agencies, and, as always, prescribe some real world, workable solutions.

So what's the problem with government agencies?? Is the popular caricature of the bumbling, incompetent bureaucrat true? I've had the opportunity to work in and closely with government agencies, and the problem becomes glaringly apparent in the first 15 minutes of interaction. Most government employees seem to have few career options: they feel trapped in dead end jobs whose main criterion for success has little to do with innovative thinking or more effective performance ... but does revolve closely around keeping the boss happy and, heavens forbid, no boat-rocking. The main objective becomes surviving for 30 years so one can collect one's pension.

HOTHOUSES FOR JERK-BREEDING

Needless to say, this obviously creates the ideal atmosphere that the classic hard core Jerk just thrives in, big time. Truly dynamic, competent young people get out as fast as they can, leaving the deadwood behind.

For those that stay, bailing out after 5 or 10 years becomes more difficult. As opposed to competitive businesses, there's no competitor to go to work for if your boss is a fool, or you can't stand the stifling pettiness of a mediocre workforce. One just has to put up with the idiot until he dies, or the more likely case that he screws up so royally that he's promoted.

Government employees are by far the most unhappy, fear-ridden, hopeless folks I've ever known. There's very little joy of accomplishment and challenge because these are foreign concepts, to be carefully avoided. I estimate that most government agencies are operating at about 50% of their potential, and some a good deal lower than that, due to the stultifying diseases of "pensionitis" and the CYA mentality. In a moment we'll look at 16 federal agencies and their baggage train of horror stories. I just can't think of any government agency that doesn't have a closet full of breathtaking moronities ... mismanagement, scandal, coverup, bullying, waste, fraud, and abuse.

As Will Rogers said, it was no challenge being a comedian – all he had to do was to factually report on the antics of government agencies, without any embellishment whatsoever, to bring the house down, convulsed with laughter. Nothing has changed in the intervening 70 years, Will.

THE VICIOUS CYCLE

Naturally, compounding the problem is the inevitable vicious cycle that kicks into gear. When a competent, decent, ambitious young person sees what's going on, he bails out of government service asap – thus, government agencies have a difficult time retaining good employees. They're left with a stable of time-servers and deadwood that could never make it in a dynamic, private sector company.

The reality is daunting. Just listen to Senator Fred Thompson, R-TN, head of the Senate Committee on Government Affairs:

> *"The fact that the federal government does not adequately hire and **retain** the right people is a root cause"* of many of the problems in government.[2]

and,

> *"If working for the federal government is synonymous with dead end, bureaucratic jobs, then our country will forego the service of some of the most gifted of America's younger generation."* [3]

Yep.

At a medical symposium a few years back, I listened with rapt interest to a distinguished psychiatrist describe the types of life challenges his patients complained about. High on the list were those working in government agencies who had to internalize the daily absurdities encountered on the job – their only relief was to dump it all on to their shrink, to retain what little sanity they had left. The Doc vividly described the unnecessary nonsense that went on – he bluntly stated that of all his patients through the years, government employees were by far the most unhappy and depressed.

"JUST ABOUT ANYWHERE BUT THE FEDERAL GOVERNMENT"

Still not convinced? Then why do the best and brightest from the Ivy Leagues, who are willing to work for low pay at non-profits and universities, completely shun *government* service like the plague?? A recent *Washington Post* article reports:

> *"Princeton, NJ – William Robertson wants Princeton University to give his money back – all $525 million of it.*
> *Robertson's family foundation underwrites the Woo-drow Wilson School of Public and International Affairs, and for years he has lobbied, wheedled, and insisted that school officials channel more students into careers in the US government. And year after year, the school has churned out bright young people who go to work in nonprofit agencies, universities, and private industry –* ***just about anywhere but the federal government.***
> *So Robertson has gone to state court to get his endowment back."*[4]

Well, here's a no-brainer. Obviously the word has gotten out to these bright kids from Princeton: working for the federal government is the kiss of death for any chance of happiness and a satisfying work experience – forget it. This severe dysfunction in federal agencies is so infamous and widely known, the reality is transparent.

It is true, however, that Princeton failed to take the obvious step of at least *requiring* Woodrow Wilson scholarship students *commit* to 3 or 4 years of federal service. (So the family *should* get their $525 million back, now.) But then without serious reform of government agencies, how many would *stay on*??

In the following cook's tour of 16 federal agencies, the grim reality becomes painfully clear. But the solutions are quite obvious, if we but have the intelligence and moral courage to employ them. The well-intentioned Robertson Foundation would do well to put some of the $525 million towards the systemic reform of the federal bureaucracy outlined in the Eleven Point Program found at chapter's end! Only then will any young, competent people desire to work there, and stick around for a meaningful career.

VITAL GOVERNMENT ROLE IN SOCIETY

I hasten to point out that I am not indulging in joyful "government bashing" here. In fact, all this really angers me because it's unnecessary and outrageous. Government agencies perform vital functions, and it's in all our interests that they overcome these present systemic problems and boost their effectiveness. Joseph S. Nye, dean of Harvard University's Kennedy School of Government, says it best:

> *"Private sector disdain for government is shortsighted. Good markets depend on an effective legal and political framework – just look at Russia for a counterexample … if we staff government poorly, we all pay the consequences."*[5]

Do we ever.

A DYNAMIC GOVERNMENT EMPLOYEE

The right person in the right place in a government agency can accomplish wonders far transcending even private sector triumphs. Often they're in a pivotal position that can really influence events positively. The example of J.C.R. Licklider is instructive. Hired by the Pentagon in the early 1960's into ARPA (the Advanced Research

Projects Agency, whose mission was to improve military communications), Licklider basically **inspired the creation of the Internet** by pushing the concepts of "decentralization, connectivity, interactivity, and graphic interfaces ... Licklider was a catalyst, an enzyme that sparked seminal research ...who wrote of the virtues of many subsequent developments including disks and CD's, online libraries, and software floating free of individual machines much like the Java applets now so ubiquitous on the World Wide Web."[6]

He was a broad visionary who persuaded government to pump some much needed cash into university R&D, which enabled the creation of the first computer science departments, which in turn provided the foot soldiers for the computer engineering, PC, and Internet revolutions.

Here is a classic example of a government bureaucrat who hit the mother lode, of what can go *right* when a federal employee gets inspired and performs to his maximum ability, unfazed by hard-core jerks (Licklider *did* have to fight bureaucratic battles with morons, but his innate brilliance, impressive experience, calm demeanor, and determined focus enabled him to decisively prevail.) As John Paulos states in his fascinating book review of *The Dream Machine*, which examines the invention and development of the Internet,

> *"He* (Licklider) *was **a kind of ideal bureaucrat**, whose detailed knowledge and selfless enthusiasm were instrumental in getting America and the world online, and out of that cold basement with the punch cards."*[7]

Every government employee should be made aware of the example of JCR Licklider! And of Leo Pasvolsky.

CAST A GIANT SHADOW

Another classic example of an obscure, lowly Government employee whose heroic work led to seismic human progress, is Leo Pasvolsky. A US State Department employee, Leo almost single-handedly worked behind the scenes for seven long years (1939 – 1946) to set up the framework for the United Nations so that it could avoid the worst pitfalls that destroyed it's predecessor, the defunct & unsuccessful League of Nations (which Leo had personally witnessed). Key concepts such as a powerful Security Council to authorize the use of force gave the new organization some teeth. Naturally, it helped to have visionary, supportive bosses like Secretary of State Cordell Hull and President Franklin D. Roosevelt, but Leo did all the spade work with the evangelical fervor of one who'd seen the appalling consequences (40 million WW II dead) when an international body didn't have focus and proper organization. His genius crafted an organization which battered humanity had desperately needed for a millennium.[8]

In the same breath that I extol the virtues of government bureaucrat Licklider, it's also instructive to explore *why* he behaved so differently from the typical government functionary, and actually accomplished great things. He did not project the typical "take-no-risk" mentality of your normal dead-end bureaucrat – *he'd already had a successful career* as a polymathic psychologist at MIT and in industry (BBN). (Ditto for Pasvolsky, "a Russian –born journalist and economist who covered the failure of the League of Nations first-hand."[9]) So he didn't sport the fear-ridden persona of so many ineffective government employees … he was working for the love and dream of interactive computing, unconcerned about his pathetic pension or petty office politics. If government is *ever* going to rise to it's actual potential, its employees must be freed for all time from the deadwood pension-oriented mindset. We'll explore effective ways to do this later in the chapter. But first, let's revisit the amazing incident that switched on the light and irrefutably revealed the scandal of government employee dysfunction.

THE INCREDIBLE FAX MACHINE STORY
(or, Government Agencies = Lunatic Asylums)

During the past 30 years, I've had several opportunities to work either with or actually in government agencies at local, state, and federal levels. To be blunt, I was not impressed with workplace atmospheres at any of these levels as compared to businesses and corporations I've worked in – in fact, the gap is so great that it begs the question: Why?? Why do government organizations underperform in comparison to private enterprise, in almost any area of measurement?? Salary levels do not explain the dichotomy.

A while back an incident occurred that was so blatant and bizarre that it finally surfaced this governmental non-performance issue to the light of day so it could no longer be diplomatically ignored. I resolved to make a special effort to include it in this book, because it clearly relates to workplace effectiveness and the presence of removable cancer on human society.

At one large corporation I worked in, one of our Departments did a lot of work with a government agency. A good friend of mine, "Craig", worked exclusively on a large government contract and related this story to me.

> *"We had a 2 billion dollar contract with a lot of short deadlines, which necessitated using a fax machine to get hot, urgent items down to our government counterparts (they were way behind the private sector and did not have PC's or use e-mail at all). We noticed it was always extremely difficult to get faxes through, and this got worse as each month passed. I found out that this agency, even though it was dealing with eleven subcontractors worldwide, each with 5 or 6 departments, had a **grand total of only one (1) fax machine to receive the input from 40 fax machines of subcontractors!***
>
> *One day the backup was so absurd I called the agency and suggested to a rather low-level admin person that they increase the number of fax machines. Big mistake!!*
>
> *The next thing I knew, I was called into my **Director's** office (two levels above me), who explained that a high-ranking Government official had called him to complain that I had the gall to suggest ways to improve fax communications between agency and contractor. That role was the*

government's sole prerogative! How dare I.

We both shook our heads and had a good laugh.

Instead of tackling their internal fax problem, incompetent government bureaucrats at three levels decided to just "shoot the messenger".

*Overcome by curiosity at how **anyplace** could really be that dysfunctional, I called the government agency back and finally got an intelligent-sounding admin supervisor on the line. She related that she had just joined this particularly bizarre agency three months ago, and immediately noticed the gross inadequacy of their office equipment, particularly the fact that they had only one machine to receive faxes and that it was hopelessly overloaded and always either running or jammed or out of paper.*

When she brought this up at a weekly staff meeting, she was stunned at the hostile, actually hateful reaction from several government staffers. 'If you don't like the density of fax machines we have here, just go back to your old agency,' one cretin staffer hissed, eyes blazing! She suddenly felt like she was in a lunatic asylum, surrounded by its raving inmates, which, in fact, she was."

Your tax dollar hard at work! "Craig" was one of the most moderate, competent folks I've ever had the pleasure of working with, so I'm sure that this story, as bizarre as it is, is 100% true. It tracked with my observations of poorly performing government agencies, employees, and managers, and got me to really start thinking the **root causes** of this widespread bizarre, petty, absurd, incompetent "governmental disease", and why

"Good Government remains the greatest of human blessings, and no nation has ever enjoyed it."[10]

Dean William R. Inge

GOVERNMENT AGENCIES FROM HELL

Some of you good readers may be musing, "Oh, it can't be *that* bad – government agencies aren't really that screwed up, are they?"

Well, we need only to take the cook's tour of horror stories from 16 Federal Agencies, gleaned from recent reliable, moderate, mainstream media reports. Let's look at the record of the US Agricultural Dept, OSHA (Occupational, Safety, & Health Administration), the Bureau of Indian Affairs (BIA) & Dept of the Interior, the DEA (Drug Enforcement Agency), the FAA, the Coast Guard, the IRS, the INS, State Dept, Food and Drug Administration (FDA), FBI, National Cancer Institute, Nuclear Regulatory Commission (NRC), the CIA, Peace Corps, NSA (National Security Agency), and NASA. **We'll soon discover, to our horror and amazement, that the "Incredible Fax Machine Story" is the operative *norm*, not the exception, in Government Agencies.**

THE US AGRICULTURAL DEPT: "BLAME THE MESSENGER"

From July to September 2002, eight people died from eating listeria-infected turkey, and 54 others were seriously sickened in NY, NJ, Conn, PA and five other states. One of the two suspect food processing plants, Wampler Foods in Franconia, PA had numerous instances of gross sanitation violations in the previous year, which were pointed out by the Agricultural Dept inspector on the site, Vincent Erthal. His incompetent supervisor, Debra Martin, squashed his warnings and nothing was done by the Agricultural Dept until people started dropping dead like flies in the Northeast.

Belatedly, the Agriculture Dept closed the Wampler Plant and samples from the plant's drains tested positive on the strain of deadly listeria monocytogene.[11] As Rep Henry Waxman, D-CA, the ranking minority member on the House Committee on Government Reform said,

> *"I think what we're seeing is a department (the Agriculture*
> *Dept) that has **abdicated its responsibility** to protect the*
> *public in the area of food safety."*

Typically, ass-covering bureaucrats at the Agriculture Department tried to point fingers at the very inspector who tried to correct the problem a year prior, Vincent Erthal – incredibly, they whined that he should have pushed harder to blow the whistle, when *they* were the very morons who had ignored his efforts to begin with. Their own management disregarded Erthal for eight months.[12] And 8 people died horrible deaths. The Agriculture Department's motto is, like so many government agencies, "Blame the Messenger".

MURDEROUS CORPORATIONS UNRESTRAINED: OSHA, THE "TOOTHLESS WATCHDOG" [13]

To get a feel for just how seriously Congress and the government have let down the American people, one need look no farther than the interactions of OSHA, the Occupational Safety and Health Administration, with industrial corporations.

OSHA has completely failed to deal with predatory, criminal corporations like McWane, Inc, a Birmingham, Alabama based cast iron water and sewer pipe manufacturer which has acquired 20 smaller plants in ten states and Canada. On January 8, 9, and 10, 2003, the *New York Times* ran a scathing expose of the ruthless, lawless, amoral activities of McWane, whose horrible flouting of safety laws has killed nine workers since 1995 ("3 caused by deliberate violations of federal safety standards") , and maimed/injured *4600* more (!!) – not *one* of these criminal McWane corporate officials has served a minute of jail time for these gross crimes.[14]

McWane has lied, covered up, bullied workers, grossly polluted the air and water, intimidated and bribed state and local officials, and flouted every OSHA law on the books with impunity. From the *New York Times* exposé, which reads like a passage out of *Fodor's Guide to Hell*:

"Many workers have scars or disfigurations which are noticeable from several feet away.

In plant after plant, year after year, McWane workers have been maimed, burned, sickened, and killed by the same safety and health failures. Flammable materials are mishandled; respirators are not provided; machines are missing safety guards; employees are not trained. The evidence spills forth from hundreds of regulatory files scattered in government offices around the country – more than 400 safety violations and 450 environmental violations since 1995 alone.

Yet regulators and law enforcement officials have never joined forces *to piece this record together, never taken a coordinated approach to end patterns of transgression. Their responses, piecemeal and disjointed, bring into sharp relief weaknesses in government's ability to take on corporations with operations spread far and wide.*

'The current law is inadequate to deal with serious violators, repetitive violators, situations where people are put at risk day after day,' said Charles N. Jeffress, who headed OSHA in the late 1990's.

'The real solution is they need to change the law,' said Mr. Tyson, who ran the agency in the Reagan administration. 'They need to make "killing a worker" a felony.'

Indeed, under federal law, causing the death of a worker by willfully violating safety rules – a misdemeanor with a six month maximum prison term – is a less serious crime than harassing a wild burro on federal lands, which is punishable by a year in prison."[15]   (author's emphasis)

OSHA has levied light fines on McWane, and never any criminal prosecution. The present administrator of OSHA (2003), John L Henshaw, is a weak, ineffective tapdancing politico placed there by President Bush to placate all his fat-cat corporate criminal buddies. Henshaw was a corporate flak for the chemical industry for 26 years. He worked for Monsanto, one of the biggest, most vicious polluters on the planet ... no wonder he's coddled super-polluter McWane so long. Henshaw has gone on the record stating he thinks the current OSHA laws work just fine. With a fox in the henhouse like Henshaw, criminal employee-murdering industry executives need not fear any sleepless nights.

Since 1972, there have been over 200,000 deaths on the job (that's more than WW I, Korea, and Vietnam combined), many due to corporate negligence. **Only 151 of these deaths have been referred to the Justice Dept for criminal investigation, and of those just 8 have resulted in jail time, the longest term imposed just six months.**[16] This is an howling outrage, and shows what you get when your only two political parties, both "business parties", are beholden to corporate bribes 365 days of the year. In the US, it's far safer to be a desert burro than a worker for the scum that run many McWane-style corporations.

BUSINESSES vs. *GULAGS*

Oh, and whilst we're still on the subject, let's just pre-empt the inevitable right-wing TV and radio talk show host (Stalinists like Hannity, O'Reilly, Limbaugh, Scarborough, Cramer, Mathews and the entire Fox News cast, in lock step reading from the same script provided by their corporate masters, tobacco companies, the NRA, and fundamentalist Christian ayatollahs) whining about how tough it is for steel businesses to survive unfair foreign competition. McWane has US competitors that are thriving *without* having to maim and kill their own workers and dump millions of gallons of filth into New Jersey rivers surreptitiously at 2 am. In fact, these companies, like Acipco, "ranked 6th in Fortune magazine's list of the 100 best employers in America"[16], find that treating workers humanely, and God forbid, even well, reduces employee turnover and boosts productivity, sending profits to new highs (McWane worker turn-over, no surprise, is horrific, reaching 100% and 200% annually in some of it's *stalags*).

McWane is just stupidly, brutally, and criminally operated by whorish, lazy thugs, and has been for 100 years. It's founder, J.R. McWane, was a major asshole even by the primitive standards of those barbaric times, and his imbecile descendants have followed daddy's "screw the workers" philosophy enthusiastically to this day. OSHA, Presidents (of both the cravenly subservient business parties), and the Congress simply let them get away with it, in order to collect their hundreds of millions in annual bribes... oops, political "contributions". McWane is not a legitimate business, it's a vast gulag archipelago, basking in the benevolent sun of governmental indifference and corruption.

CORRUPT GOVERNMENT = WEAK OVERSIGHT

To be fair to many dedicated OSHA inspectors, it's hard to do the job right with both hands tied behind your back by Presidents and a Congress who continually suck up to their corporate donors – even if this suits cowardly, sycophant crook bureaucrats like Mr. Henshaw just fine. Remember, this is the same Congress and Executive branch who's stellar regulation of the airline industry and disastrous foreign policy invited the 9/11 catastrophe.

And our "compassionate" President, George W, has just once more demonstrated his sincere concern for all those workers killed and maimed on the job by slashing OSHA's budget again this year (January 2003).[17] This fraud loves to do on a national level what he did with zest as Texas governor: purge any and all government officials who actually are effective in reining in the criminal abuses of robber-baron corporate CEO's.

After you clean up your own workplace, go to Chapter 14 and make plans to get active in the Green Party or progressive Democrats to clean up local, state, and federal governments across the board.

"Every Nation has the Government it deserves."[18]
Joseph De Maistre, letter to X
August, 1811

US DEPT OF INTERIOR CHEATS INDIANS OUT OF $137 BILLION

The saga of the US Government's grossly corrupt "administration" – read theft—of the Indian Trust Fund "is the gold standard for mismanagement by the federal government for more than a century" according to the federal judge ruling on the case, Judge Royce C. Lamberth.[19]

Any BIA (Bureau of Indian Affairs) or Dept of Interior employees that leak the truth about this gross mismanagement are instantly fired, per US Government tradition. One of these, BIA accountant David Henry, "disclosed in the mid-1980's that the BIA had deposited $10 million more in banks than had been dispersed to the IIM (Individual Indian Monies) account holders." After being fired for his honesty, he proceeded to author the 1995 book, *Stealing From the Indians*.[20]

The Dept of the Interior leaders (from both Democrat <Bruce Babbitt> and Republican <Gale Norton> administrations; what can you expect from the two "business parties"?) have consistently lied, obstructed justice, shredded important files "Enron style" in defiance of Court orders, refused to consult with the Indians themselves about any aspect of their own trust funds, and been ruled in contempt of court – and that's just in the last ten years alone. *Over $137 billion has gone missing! They get away with all these crimes, of course, because the Indians have no numerical weight in any Congressional districts enough for anybody in Congress to look out for their interests. So much for democracy in America.*[21]

Corrupt oil, timber, mining, and ranch interests have benefited from this 100 year giveaway, a free ride of fire sale mineral and agricultural rights on Indian lands, aided, of course by their corrupt buddies in the Dept of Interior.

In 1994 the accumulated stench became too great even for the US Congress to tolerate, an entity famed for it's bottomless tolerance of stench! The 1994 Indian Trust and Reform Act (ITRA) appointed distinguished banker Paul Homan, former director of Riggs Bank, to investigate.

After four years of digging, Homan resigned in disgust in 1998. "Homan told the US Senate Committee on Indian Affairs that in his 30 year career as a banker, he'd never seen anything like the accounting mess at the BIA. He also stated he had been sandbagged every step of the way by the Dept of the Interior."[22] My only question is, why aren't dozens of corrupt Dept of Interior bureaucrats rotting in jail??? How do they get away with it???

Every other stone turned over in the federal government reveals a cesspool of corruption, backstreet dealing, and the instant crucifixion of truth tellers. To see where a lot of that $137 billion (plus many other wayward billions) went, one need look no further than the thousands of palatial multimillion dollar, *four* and *five*-**story brick and cathedral glass** *single family* **homes** in gated communities clogged with monster SUV's springing up all over the Virginia and Maryland Washington DC suburbs, built with the public treasures scuttled away by the armies of sleazy lobbyists, parasitic beltway bandits, merchants of death, fat bureaucrats, tobacco & gun advocate whores, hypocritical televalgelists, IMF banker blood-suckers, Rupert Murdock media spin-meisters, third world assassins, election-theft consultants, and industry emissions junk science pimps all sucking off the public tit and greasing the palms of eager legislators and Party Chairmen -- the physical manifestation of this rot is plain to see. Newt Gingrich, the Prince of Hypocrisy, the guru of unapologetic amoral 90's greed, summed it all up tidily when he proclaimed, "Yep, money in politics is a real problem – there's not enough money being poured into politics."

It's no coincidence that of the 10 richest counties in the Untied States, 7 ring Washington DC. Sodom and Gomorrah, relocated to the New World, cashing in on the crass exploitation of weak, the powerless, the disenfranchised. One need not travel all the way to Baghdad or Pyongyang to view grandiose, tawdry palaces of empire built on the bleached bones of innocents.

> *"Every government is run by liars and nothing they say should be believed."*[23]
>
>   I.F. Stone

SETTING THE DYSFUNCTION BAR HIGH – THE DEA

One need only to pick up the local paper to see endless examples of government agency dysfunction close by. A horrendous scandal has just surfaced (Jan 2003) in the New Bedford, Massachusetts, Drug Enforcement Agency branch office, opened with such fanfare and high hopes just three years ago as the answer to that region's huge drug smuggling and violence problem.

But the Agency never even left the launch pad thanks to a bizarre Resident Agent in Charge named John Schaefer, whose gross mismanagement and erratic behavior doomed the operation from the get-go. He had a volatile temper, which is not a desirable personality trait in an Agency whose main mission is to coordinate and focus the efforts of a dozen local, state, and federal agencies toward teamwork in cleaning up a drug-ridden area. Schaefer was unable to get along with any other agencies, engaging in destructive turf battles – **his way of resolving interagency problems was to challenge other law enforcement officers to fistfights!!**[24] Yep, fistfights.

Like Will Rogers, this stuff is so bizarre, I couldn't even make it up – John Grisham himself couldn't have even conjured this one up. Truth is far stranger than fiction, especially in the Byzantine world of the federal government.

Schaefer ruined and micromanaged so many local and regional investigations that other agencies refused to share their drug informants with the DEA – Schaefer had compromised any reputation the DEA once enjoyed. Finally, his best DEA agents complained to the Boston district office about this moron's performance. And how did these highly placed federal DEA Managers handle this problem?? The tried and true way of all federal bureaucracies: "get rid of the complaintants, and sweep the problem under the rug", of course.[25] Shoot the Messengers.

The DEA imbeciles from Boston "began questioning the loyalty of the agents who had criticized Schaefer, and then punished them." They allowed Schaefer to see who they were questioning in their "Investigation", allowing Schaefer to attempt to transfer the 3 agents to duty on the Mexican border, as well as to threaten and browbeat anybody who informed the Boston authorities of this disaster of a field office.[26]

All the nonsense suddenly screeched to a halt when the enraged agents filed suit in court and the whole scandal spilled out into the open. Only when this happens do government bureaucrats scramble to cover up the stench! Schaefer was suddenly "retired" and was hastily packed out of New England before the media could get their hands on the nitwit.[27] (It is truly comforting to note that now, with *Jihad the Jerk at Work* in the hands of thousands of alert employees, imbeciles like Schaefer will be detected and kicked out of government agencies **in the first few years of their employment there**, and most likely end up in jail as well. No more getting away with these criminal behaviors for 30 years via the old fear & intimidation routine, and sliding into a cushy retirement, the tab picked up by the taxpayer. Verily can progress be made in human affairs, if we just put forth the effort.)

The negative impact on the drug-besieged community of New Bedford was not an academic exercise. Whilst federal managers screwed up, it translated into three years of lost opportunity for a crime and drug and violence infested community, which had desperately hoped that the new DEA Office would make a difference – instead, gross mismanagement and stupidity and **that classic hallmark of federal government bureaucracy, *the refusal to take responsibility when things begin to go wrong,*** which is driven by the deadly careerist, ticket-punching, CYA mentality of too many government managers, ruined it all.[28]

Poor management by the DEA destroyed the promise of inter-agency cooperation in New Bedford. It remains to be seen if the DEA can ever restore it's reputation in this drug & murder-wracked community. The *Boston Globe's* investigative report was damning:

> *"Former drug task force members charge that turf battles and personality conflicts caused investigations to be bungled or dropped altogether because investigators refused to trust Schaefer with control of their drug informants.*

> *Shut out of major drug investigations, the hardest-charging local drug investigators – who three years ago jumped at the chance to use federal resources to pursue major traffickers – have either left the DEA office in disgust or were driven out by Schaefer, officials said."*[29]

What is truly amazing is that this disaster dragged on for *three years*, and if the heroic agents hadn't filed a lawsuit, the DEA would *still* be trying to cover up for Schaefer and screwing up the operation. Often, government agencies continue to botch up things interminably – the FBI covered up their corrupt Boston operations for 33 years before the truth finally was revealed, and framed innocent men, the ones who hadn't died in jail, were released from three decades of prison.

However, local social workers are rarely surprised when government law enforcement agencies don't do their jobs. *The Globe* exposé continues,

> *"To Drae Perkins, executive director of 'Treatment on Demand', a grass roots group that works to fight HIV infection and Drug abuse in New Bedford, the DEA's abysmal performance 'was disappointing, but it didn't surprise me ...often you find agencies don't work together – they protect their own fiefdoms instead. Instead of engaging in a collaboration, it appears the DEA had to do everything themselves.' "*[30]

Thus the saga of the DEA in New Bedford, a microcosm of what ails government agencies everywhere: stupidity, failure to take responsibility, careerism, zero concern for the communities they're supposed to serve.

> *"Bureaucracy is a giant mechanism operated by pygmies."* [31]
>
> >   Honore de Balzac
> >   *The Human Comedy*
> >   1842

FAA: THE TOMBSTONE AGENCY

The incredible thing about studying federal agencies is that just when you think you've found the very worst one and none could sink lower, the next one comes along and lowers the bar deeper into the slime. Certainly describes the Federal Aviation Administration (FAA), "the Tombstone Agency" which refuses to act at all until a huge safety problem kills hundred of air passengers[32] ... then it finally enacts measures that the National Transportation Safety Board (NTSB) urgently advised them to do many years before. Why hundreds of FAA slug bureaucrats aren't rotting in maximum security prisons nationwide right now is baffling.

In 1996, after quitting her Inspector General post in the Dept of Transportation in disgust, Mary Schiavo wrote a damning indictment of the FAA, *Flying Blind, Flying Safe.* She cites example after example of the FAA coddling the very industry it's supposed to be regulating, at the cost of hundreds of passenger lives lost in numerous crashes that were easily preventable. In her classic book she states

> *"Time and again, my office uncovered practices that would shock the public: sloppy inspections of planes, perfunctory review of pilots, lax oversight of airline procedures, disregard for bogus airplane parts, sieve-like security at airports, antiquated air-traffic-control systems. Only with a major crash, only with people dead and sobbing survivors filling television screens, does the FAA step up to the plate and make changes."*[32]

The ValuJet disaster is a classic case. In *1988*, the NTSB strongly recommended that fire detection and suppression systems be installed in all commercial aircraft baggage storage areas. The FAA whined about costs and did nothing.[33] On May 11, 1996 a Miami ValuJet was loaded with loosely packed oxygen canisters that started a fire, most probably *on the ground* (!) as the plane taxied to the takeoff runway – smoke detectors could have easily alerted the captain to abort the takeoff. Unaware of the raging inferno in the baggage hold, ValueJet

Flight 592 took off and immediately crashed into the Florida swamp, killing all 110 on board. Another grisly legacy of the FAA, the Tombstone Agency.

The FAA's gross mismanagement of this shoddy ValuJet Airline (now re-named Air Tran, trying to hide it's sordid past) occurred at all levels. Even the FAA's own trench-level inspectors were doing a crappy inspection job. In the three years ValuJet flew, with exponentially surging numbers of emergency landings as the airline grew (15 in 1994, 57 in 1995, and an **astounding** 59 in the first five months of 1996), FAA inspectors conducted 5000 inspections of ValuJet planes without "reporting any significant problems or concerns – shoddy inspections are an FAA plague," according to the Department of Transportation's own Inspector General.[34] This is gross negligence on the part of flaky inspectors, and is reason enough for the FAA to be abolished and replaced by a serious organization. The rot has permeated through and through this hopeless, negligent bureaucracy.

Schiavo relates a stunning chain of events. Her IG office, appalled at the horrendous safety record ValuJet was piling up and deeply worried for the safety of the flying public, sent a powerful delegation down to the Atlanta FAA office. When asked what was the FAA doing about the serious mishaps at ValuJet, the FAA toads in Atlanta were blissfully unaware of any problems at ValuJet (!), and blew the IG off. However, worried about their exposed behinds, they then started taking a serious look at ValuJet, and quickly unearthed a raft of problem areas so severe that in February, 1996 the **Atlanta FAA sent an urgent letter to Washington recommending that this flaky airline be grounded immediately**. FAA HQ responded in typical federal government criminally negligent fashion by burying and hiding the memo.[35] We wouldn't want to upset our fatcat corporate donors, would we??? Rocking the boat and doing your actual job is not the way to get ahead in Washington – it just won't do.

Atlanta FAA official Charles Spillner also asked for more inspectors to police ValuJet's far-flung and extremely flaky subcontractor operations (to include SabreTech, the same criminal clowns who'd ship the loose oxygen containers on Flight 592 three months later) –

his FAA supervisor in Washington responded that if he continued
to make such requests, he'd be fired.[36] This touching little exchange
was made public in a Congressional hearing after the ValuJet crash.
Senior government agency officials have a unique style of "positive
leadership" capable of propelling the levels of incompetence and
criminal negligence to dizzying new heights.

Three months later the Miami ValuJet crashed – with hundreds
of pained, bereaved families on the evening news, the FAA
scrambled to hide their complicity, but courageous people like Mary
Schiavo exposed them for the outraged American public to see.

Immediately after the ValuJet crash, the FAA, led by
Administrator David Hinson, went into it's "cheerleader for the
aviation industry" mode, proclaiming that ValuJet was safe (so what
would one expect from a former Midway Airlines and McDonnell
Douglas exec?? Politicians love to staff the government henhouse
with corporate whore foxes). Hinson tried to hose this smokescreen
around to a national TV audience on ABC's *Nightline*, but Schiavo
was there to blow him out of the water with statistics proving
"ValuJet's safety record was 14 times *worse* than its peers", and
extremely unsafe to fly.[37]

Of course the corruption and criminality in the US Government
runs so deep, one couldn't expect it to end there. Even Mary
Schiavo's *own boss*, Transportation Secretary Fedrico Pena, a
conniving, lying little politico pimp if there ever was one, couldn't
resist proclaiming that "ValuJet is safe", when he was well aware of
its massive safety problems. To these political sleazes, the public
interest is a joke – the only game in town is to keep the big corporate
bucks rolling in. Schiavo's courageous exposé finally shut Pena up,
although he and others tried to browbeat and intimidate her.[38]
President Clinton rewarded Pena's embarrassing and exceptionally
criminal behavior by spiriting him out of Transportation and giving
him the Dept of Energy, so this dunce could now safeguard all the
Nuclear plants in the country from citizen oversight. Naturally, the
most important goal was to keep a token Hispanic as a cabinet officer
… *any* Hispanic would do, incompetent or not.

Their game exposed, the FAA finally grounded ValuJet – and the US Congress, scrambling to try to make up for its pathetic oversight of this criminal bureaucracy, finally mandated that the *only* job the FAA had was to promote airline safety, period. The role as Aviation Industry proponent was eliminated, about fifty years too late. Hinson, a huge embarrassment to all, was quickly retired.

It's instructive to acknowledge that although I regard the Republican Party for the most part as a gang of corporate thieves and criminals, Democrats can often be just as corrupt. *Both* of the high-ranking Cabinet level jiving pimps starring in the last two horror stories, Federico Pena and Bruce Babbitt, were Democrats appointed by a Democrat President. Ralph Nader was right – for all intents and purposes, you can rely on Democrats in power to act like corrupt little Republicans, greased palms trembling and eagerly outstretched for the next Corporate bribe.

Mary Schiavo finally got so nauseated even being in the same *room* as scum like Hinson and Pena, she resigned her Inspector General post in disgust, "dismayed, disillusioned, afraid for the flying public."[39]

BUMBLING FAA LEOPARD DOES NOT CHANGE ITS SPOTS

Five years after she left, the FAA is still as incompetent and deadly as ever. After the Alaska Airways jet crashed off the Los Angeles coast in January 2000 killing 88 people, the NTSB discovered that the horizontal tail flap had catastrophically failed. Alaska Air had neglected for many months to lubricate a part that controlled it, **"the screw and nut had *no* grease on them, causing the thread to wear out ten times faster than expected** … the FAA contributed to the crash by acquiescing with the airline's decision to stretch out maintenance levels 500%". To save a few bucks, it was OK to shift lubrication from every 500 hours to every 2500 hours! Idiots and murderers all.[40]

NO AIRCRAFT TOO SMALL FOR THE FAA TO SCREW UP

The FAA's "oversight" of small aircraft is just as nonexistent. In 1996 a Cessna 206 seaplane ferrying tourists around in Alaska crashed, killing 3 and injuring 1. Not surprisingly, this type of aircraft had a *long history* of FAA abrogation of its responsibilities. The throttle control arm has a record of failing, causing the engine to lose power. "Over the past 10 years, pilots and some of the FAA's own inspectors have urged the agency to issue an order fixing the problem, but the FAA refused."[41] Not enough body bags had piled up ... yet.

Cessna, the aircraft manufacturer, and Teledyne Continental Motors, it's vendor for the throttle control arm, were well aware of the problem *since 1980*, and had been pointing fingers at one another ever since about who should pay for the fix. The FAA failed to step in and resolve the issue – they could have just ordered the two irresponsible companies just to split the cost 50-50, but it was easier just wait for people to die.[42]

The FAA's own maintenance inspector, Ernie Keener, has his own private collection of 25 (!!) of these failed throttle control arms that he's removed from *crashed aircraft*. He tried to get the FAA to act "but I got no support" from FAA brass. Of course not – do you think FAA management actually wants to *serve* the public? They're far too busy schmoozing with their airline industry buddies. Even after the 3 deaths in the Alaska Cessna, the FAA was still stymieing the airworthiness directive which would order a fix of this deadly problem. Ernie Keener pleaded with the *Boston Globe* reporter who interviewed him to find out what happened to the airworthiness directive.[43] Obviously, he couldn't trust his own asshole FAA chain of command to do the job.

BOGUS PARTS, BOGUS AGENCY

Earlier we mentioned Mary Schiavo's role in exposing the huge and dangerous bogus airplane parts business. "Parts industry brokers are totally unregulated, unlicensed, unregistered, untrained, and ungoverned," she discovered, while Inspector General for the US Dept of Transportation.[44]

This total *laissez faire* attitude of the FAA has created a massive, dangerous situation for air travel. Investigations have revealed that 43% of aircraft parts bought from *manufacturers* are bogus (!), and *95% of parts* from brokers are bogus.[45] Many of these bogus parts have cut corners, do not meet specifications, and are extremely dangerous on aircraft. The FAA downplayed the problem until inspections showed that **39% of the parts the FAA purchased for its *own aircraft* were frauds.**[46] And these clowns are supposed to be our aviation *watchdogs*???

The FAA Tombstone Agency has claimed that bad parts haven't caused any deaths … yet. The NTSB strongly disagrees, and has numerous examples of bad parts causing air passenger deaths.[47]

9/11 proved the FAA to be inept beyond belief. This rogue agency should be abolished and it's all it's executives from the past 30 years jailed. We need to completely start over with a new Aviation agency with an entirely different ethos of public service.

THE US COAST GUARD BLUNDERS

In the early morning hours of Sept 15, 2001 "the tugboat Brown Water V was pushing four barges loaded with coiled steel and phosphates, when relief Captain David Fowler lost control."[48]

The barge struck a support column of the Queen Isabella Causeway leading out to Padre Island, Texas, and a huge section of the bridge crashed into the swirling channel. Eight motorists, unaware of the disaster, blithely drove their vehicles into the gaping black chasm, plunged 300 feet, and drowned.[49]

The Coast Guard, which has responsibility for this intercoastal waterway, tried to raise the usual smoke and mirrors, but the nearest big city newspaper, the *San Antonio Express News* did some digging on its own, interviewing many barge captains and owners. They have a different view of the official story. It turns out that a *huge number* of accidents have occurred in the vicinity of this bridge due to the dangerous tides and the bend in the waterway. But few ever get reported to the Coast Guard. Why?

> *"'As a (tugboat) captain, you can't report anything to the Coast Guard, because you're just going to be microscoped,' said Steve Ellis, a local charter captain. The paperwork involved and the embarrassment involved to an operator – you just can't do something like that."*[50]

So the Coast Guard's petty bureaucratic finger pointing process insured that *hundreds of incidents would not be reported* ... therefore they were blinded to the seriousness of conditions on dangerous stretches of the waterway. Eight hapless souls paid the price, screaming in terror until they were smashed into bloody jelly as they hit the ocean 300 feet below. But the real outrage is that bureaucrats take no responsibility for their stupidity, and learn nothing from these tragedies.

ROGUE AGENCY OUT OF CONTROL: BOTTOMLESS CORRUPTION AT THE IRS

In the past several years, testimony of a dozen IRS employees to the Senate Finance Committee has exposed systemic, nationwide Internal Revenue Service corruption, scandal cover-up, retribution against honest employees, and the calculated preying on defenseless taxpayers combined with routine IRS *avoidance* of companies hiring ex-IRS agents as advisors.

In 1998, seven IRS employees paraded in front of the Committee with incredible stories, all true of course. Barbara Latham refused to participate in corrupt IRS activity in Tennessee – as punishment, the 60-year-old administrative clerk was sent out on armed raids, the only one not issued a flak jacket.[51]

Ginger Mary Jarvis worked in the Manhattan IRS office. When she uncovered a multi-million dollar money-laundering fraud, her supervisor pulled her off the case – this same clown was moonlighting as a tax advisor to the very same corrupt corporation.

"Maureen O'Dwyer audits international corporations" in Manhattan – after an audit, a company owed $24 million in taxes, but her manager closed the case with *zero* taxes collected so he could pocket a $2,000 IRS award for closing cases fast. It's just unbelievable. What's even worse is when all these good IRS agents exposed all this criminal activity of their managers to IRS executives, nothing was done to the criminal wrongdoers, but all the whistleblowers were harassed.

> *"In the most devastating testimony at hearings on abuse of taxpayers, seven current and former IRS auditors, criminal investigators and an investigative aide testified in detail about many instances of what they called corrupt conduct, including attempted rape and wiping out hundreds of millions of dollars in taxes without justification.*
>
> ***All seven said that when they reported wrongdoing to management of the Manhattan, Los Angeles and Tennessee tax districts, they were subjected to investigations and other retaliation while the accused were protected and sometimes promoted!!"*[52]

There's no end to this corruption, it's bottomless – we need to conduct massive investigations throughout all federal agencies, bring hundreds of crooks like these to trial, and jail them all for decades, if not longer.

Maureen O'Dwyer had another incredible example:

> *"She also told of two New York men who owed money. One represented himself and cooperated, selling his apartment to pay, while the other retained a representative who was uncooperative, Ms. O'Dwyer said. Her manager gave no leniency to the first taxpayer, she said, but waived fraud penalties for the second because the manager wanted the representative to help the manager get a lucrative job."*[53]

Minh Thi Johnson, an LA based IRS auditor, reinforced the theme that the IRS loves to prey on the weak while cravenly avoiding the strong. Her managers ordered agents to foist bogus tax bills on small, weak, defenseless companies, while totally avoiding large companies who had competent tax advisors. Companies who hired former IRS employees were particularly favored, to include "zeroing out" *all taxes owed* (!!!) because IRS managers tried hard to curry favor with their former buddies to boost their future employment plans.[54] Just mind boggling. This "revolving door" corruption is a huge problem in both civilian and military components of the government and must be stopped cold. More on this at chapter's end.

One of the most bizarre IRS horror stories to come out of the Senate hearings was about rogue IRS manager Tony Deaton, "a senior criminal tax investigator in Tennessee", whose weird behavior mirrored that of the DEA's moronic manager of its New Bedford office, John Schaeffer. And, in both cases, the Government's response was to try to cover up for both of these criminals.

Mr. Deaton "was often drunk on the job, tried to rape a female agent, and talked openly in bars about confidential taxpayer information." He was also "arrested for possessing a large amount of cocaine and drug scales in Government automobile," which indicates his resume included 'major drug dealer'.[55]

No, it gets even *more* bizarre. When Deaton cooked up a scheme in 1989 to try to falsely accuse three prominent political figures of tax evasion, and then try to extort millions from them, his *supervisor*, Tommy A. Henderson, went to his IRS directors, intending to arrest and jail Deaton. Astoundingly, Henderson's supervisors told him to shut up and that he, Agent Henderson, was now the one under investigation![56] Actually, as mind-boggling as this "shoot the messenger" theme is, **it's one you see repeated *over* and *over* and *over* in a broad range of government agencies, common behavior in any time frame you chose.** The only solution seems to be: just shut down the entire government for ten years … apprehend, fire, incarcerate all the crooks and jerks, possibly 10% of the work force. Start completely fresh again ten years later, after the stables have been completely fumigated and a 100% mindset change is ingrained in a new, fresh, invigorated, honest workforce.

To what depth and breadth this gross corruption and incompetence permeates the IRS is anybody's guess, but it is clearly extensive. Years after all this testimony, the IRS acts like it hasn't learned anything. In 1997, IRS employee Jennifer Long testified about IRS abuses and taxpayer harassment in front of the Senate Finance Committee. She sounded a familiar theme:

> *"Long, whose job is to audit tax returns, said at hearings in 1997 that 'many agents are encouraged by management to pursue tax assessments that have no basis in law from individuals who simply can't fight back."*[57]

In true government agency fashion, the IRS has been relentless in trying to punish this truth-teller. In 1999, "IRS officers sent her a termination notice, but never fired her after members of Congress inquired about possible retribution." But the IRS never gives up trying to screw honest employees who don't fit the crassly corrupt mold that's the hallmark of the agency. In 2001 the IRS tried to sabotage Jennifer's application for an accountant's license in Texas, drafting a 3-page cock and bull story listing her deficiencies – it was such a pack of lies that the embarrassed IRS didn't even bother to mail the letter, once they knew Congress had gotten wind of it.[58]

Never underestimate the lengths a whorish government agency will strive for to try to tarnish and backstab and retaliate against honest employees who expose its criminal activities and gross incompetence for all to view. Losses to the nation via tax evasion (as well as outrageous tax loopholes) are now at massive billion dollar levels – much of it's due to IRS corruption and ineptness.

GOVERNMENT CONTRACTORS UNSUPERVISED

Government agencies like to reduce their employee levels and contract out a lot of their work, but this shell game hasn't worked out very well for taxpayers.

Recently (Jan 2003) two managers of JHM Research and Development of Maryland, a company to which the INS contracts out the operation of four huge INS data processing centers nationwide, were indicted by a federal grand jury for illegally **shredding and destroying 90,000 active documents**, "American and foreign passports, applications for asylum, birth certificates, and other documents supporting applications for citizenship, visas, and work permits" secretly, late at night.[59] Sweet Jesus, it just gets weirder and weirder.

And why did these two stellar managers order this criminal, wholesale destruction? To reduce a huge backlog of 90,000 documents that they couldn't handle due to their JHM / INS grossly inefficient operation. Obviously, these two thugs will deservedly go to jail, but the absence of any oversight reflects very poorly on INS contract companies, and the INS itself. What kind of flaky workplace environment was in place that could cause two managers to *remotely conceive* of such a stupid method of reducing backlog??

Why was the INS not aware that its contract company was so swamped that it was dysfunctional?? I'll bet that any honest, in-depth study would find the typical Government Agency mindset: "don't tell me the bad news", "sweep your problems under the rug", "let's not try to solve problems, just hide them", "Got'cha, it's your problem with your firm fixed price contract, not mine."

The "firm fixed price contract" fad, loudly touted by government agencies, both civilian and military, as the answer to streamlining costs is in actuality a huge disaster that has resulted in many lives lost and untold billions of dollars wasted in unnecessary, expensive, endless haggling over contractual gray areas.

EYEWASH DOES NOT A REFORM MAKE

The INS, the negligent agency that granted 15 of the 19 September 11 highjackers rapid visas, has just been abolished and split up into three agencies. This is a typical government response when its abuses become too high profile to ignore ... just shuffle people around and rename agencies and hope the public memory fades. But if the root cause of government agency dysfunction is not addressed as prescribed in this chapter and book, all these successor agencies are doomed to blunder again and again, wallowing in their hopeless inbred miasma.

ENDLESS CONTRACT CATASTROPHE: THE IRS

The exact same scenario unfolded back in 2001 when IRS contractor Mellon Bank lost its contract to run the huge Pittsburgh, PA IRS processing center when it was discovered that "40,000 federal tax returns and payments totaling $810 million were lost or destroyed at the center, which handled documents sent by taxpayers in New England and parts of New York State."[60]

Again, what kind of work ethic and leadership is being projected by the IRS that would lead its contractors to even *dream* of this kind of mindless destruction, much less to actually proceed to torch tax payment checks? It's inconceivable, unless some fundamentally basic absurdity is going on. Was the IRS even watching the ball?? I smell the same rigid "firm fixed price" contract scenario that has wreaked so much havoc in other government agencies.

If these Mellon employees, idiots though they were, "felt they were behind in their work in processing IRS returns", why didn't they and Mellon honestly sit down with the IRS and come up with more effective ways to deal with the problem?? I sense that gross negligence on the part of the IRS played a major role – no surprise from a government agency that tolerates and encourages corruption, incompetence, and criminal activity on the part of its very own employees.

FOGGY BOTTOM AMORALITY

In 1994 a US State Department official, Richard A. Nuccio, testified in good faith to a House Select Committee on Intelligence investigation that the US Government had absolutely no knowledge of any criminal activity on the part of the Guatemalan military. Soon after, whilst double checking his facts, he unearthed numerous CIA cables that proved the opposite, much to Nuccio's horror. The cables clearly revealed that CIA contacts in the Guatemalan military were deeply involved in the murder of innocent Americans in-country, and also in the torture and murder of a captured guerilla.[61]

It was an innocent error easy to correct. Nuccio asked his bosses at the State Department simply to set the record straight, just pass on to the Congress the new information. But like the typical careerist, amoral, cowardly, corrupt government toadies they were, they absolutely refused to do their duty and tell the simple truth to the elected representatives of the American people. Nuccio was shocked and appalled.

So Nuccio did what any decent, patriotic American would. Bumping into then-Representative (later Senator) Robert Torricelli at another hearing, he passed on the new information, and the CIA-Guatemala scandal was blown wide open. Scrambling to cover their bloody crimes, the CIA fired several negligent, corrupt low-level CIA officials – however none of the top-level CIA executives who had orchestrated this sleazy murderous involvement in the destruction of Guatemalan civic life over 40 years were touched.

The scandal also shed more light on the US Government's 40 year criminal record of overthrowing a democratically elected Guatemalan government in 1954 at the behest of the United Fruit Company (now known as "Chiquita") and substituting a bloody right wing dictatorship who murdered 200,000 of it's own people over the next three decades.[62] Incidentally, a witness to this very same 1954 coup, one Doctor Ernesto "Che" Guevara, learned firsthand that the *only* way to prevent the US from destroying a popularly elected government in Latin America was to protect it with ruthless armed force. Such are the innovative ways the US Government **creates endless enemies** for itself worldwide.

And what reward did the CIA, the State Department, and the US Government bestow on Richard Nuccio for courageously bringing these terrible truths to light?? Per formula, the Government "shot the messenger", seizing all his personal papers, investigating him, revoked his security clearance, and effectively destroying his career. Richard's former "friends" in the State Dept, typical government employee weasel swine, refused to even talk to him. The CIA attempted to jail him. And the CIA tried the same smear tactics on Bob Torrecelli, the courageous NJ Congressman who dared to tell the truth to the American public.[63]

Is it any wonder the federal government has a huge attrition rate, as its very best people leave in droves to get away from the stinking corruption, fear, dishonesty, and incompetence embedded everywhere?? Can one be surprised that graduates of the elite Princeton Woodrow Wilson School of Public and International Affairs would rather manufacture Slovakian toilet paper than work in the hellish, sleazy atmosphere of the U.S. federal government?

MASS EXODUS FROM THE FDA

The Food and Drug Administration has the typical predicament of all government agencies: because it's in bed with the very corporations it's supposed to police, it's ethical atmosphere floats in the gutter, it has a huge workload, and its highly trained medical officers and chemists are resigning in mass numbers, to get away from the stench.[64]

A recent *Wall Street Journal* article sums it up this serious attrition problem tidily:

> *"Current and former FDA staffers and an internal personnel survey blame intense industry pressure to speed drug approvals, heavy workloads, **a workplace atmosphere that stifles debate** ...*
>
> *The biotechnology industry contends that the turnover is a major problem. In the division that handles biological drug applications, a fourth or more of the medical-officer and chemist spots are unfilled, FDA records show.*
>
> *The internal FDA report on workforce retention said **workers complained of 'micromanagement of reviews'** and 'tedious review work' and **felt that the agency needed to 'encourage freedom of expression of scientific opinion'**. About 60% of reviewers said they didn't feel they had enough time for professional development, **one-third didn't feel comfortable expressing contrary scientific opinions**, and **a like number felt negative actions against applications were 'stigmatized' within the agency.***

'A number of reviewers added comments stating decisions should be based more on science and less on corporate wishes,' the report said. Asked how long they plan to stay in the FDA drug division, 75% indicated less than five years."[65] (my emphasis)

Well, duh!! What competent individual would want to spend his career in that flaky environment?? **Unless the government makes the radical changes in its ethical and management approach listed at the end of this chapter, it is in danger of just collapsing on its own**, choking on its inbred incompetence and stupidity. The process of collapse is already well advanced, now entering the terminal stage in hundreds of areas.

AND JUST WHEN YOU THOUGHT US GOVERNMENT AGENCIES COULDN'T POSSIBLY GET ANY WORSE …

… we stumble across the FBI, probably "the most arrogant and least cooperative agency in the US Government today". And there's incredibly stiff competition for first place in that category, so we're talking about major league impairment here. This nightmare agency is truly one of the most dysfunctional and incompetent of them all, for fifty years and running.

In-depth studies of the FBI have found it "a sloppy, unresponsive, badly managed, uncooperative, and out of touch agency … poorly trained, poorly motivated, highly political, and having seriously misplaced priorities."[66] Whew. Looks like immediate dissolution, firing the lot, and starting over will be the best approach with this monstrosity.

Over the past ten years, many exposés and events have blown the FBI myth of infallibility to smithereens – and of course 9/11 and the Bureau's pathetic attempted coverup of it's blunders were the final nails in its coffin. I will not enter into great detail here – others have made an airtight case for the dissolution of this disaster of an agency – but I'll now touch on some of the major dysfunctions dominating the FBI that are relevant to our discussion of just what a disaster area most "monopoly" government agencies are, why, and how to reform and **prevent re-emergence of these systemic flaws** engendered by dead-end monopolies.

MAJOR FBI CORRUPTION IN BOSTON

It's difficult to examine anything the FBI has touched for the past 30 years that it hasn't royally screwed up. Up in Boston, the entire population is seething about recent damning revelations that the FBI knowingly sent four innocent men to prison for the 1965 murder of Edward "Teddy" Degan that they did not commit. The FBI also knew of the actual murder plan 2 days before the hit, but did nothing to prevent it.[67] We're not just talking a few rogue agents here – up to a dozen senior FBI executives had full knowledge of this sickening betrayal and crime, and said nothing for 33 years, until federal judges and defense lawyers finally squeezed incriminating documents out of the FBI files. The amorality and sleaziness that pervades the entire agency is a pall and stench that we won't be rid of until the Hoover Building is razed to the ground, and the very earth it stands upon sown with salt (as Rome did with Carthage in 146 BC).

FBI MOTTO: THE END JUSTIFIES THE MEANS

These ethical giants at the FBI rolled in this gutter to "protect" the actual murderer of Teddy Degan, Steven "the Rifleman" Flemmi, who happened to be one of their mob informers. The four innocents who took the rap were framed by another FBI informant, Joseph "the Animal" Barboza, who had murdered 26 people – this qualified him as rock-solid reliable FBI informant material. When Barboza was shipped out to California in the FBI witness protection program, it didn't take him long to revert to old habits. Soon he was in the dock on an air-tight murder charge (which he committed, of course, in cold blood). But who should show up to testify as *character witnesses* for this sleaze to get his sentence reduced? ... several FBI agents.

California law enforcement officers and prosecutors were blind-sided and outraged at this FBI perfidy.[68]

Back in Boston, the KGB, oops I mean FBI, was busy and "pressured parole board members to keep Louis Greco (one of the four framed innocents) and the others behind bars and was involved in a retaliatory investigation of five parole board members."[69] It seems there's no limit as to how far this rogue agency will stoop to screw innocents and to protect bloody murderers. No limit. The two innocents who lived (two others died in prison) spent 33 years behind bars due to a FBI frame up for crimes they didn't commit. To this day the FBI, the archetypal government agency of no sense of decency or shame, has admitted to no wrongdoing and has issued no apologies to the devastated families.

Two of the innocents, Louis Greco and Henry Tameleo, died in prison – Greco's son Louis committed suicide two years after his death in prison. "Here's another family that was destroyed by this FBI complicity with Flemmi and ultimately Bulger."[70]

"Whitey" Bulger, head of the notorious "Winter Hill Gang", was another one of the FBI's murderous informants. In 1995, when local authorities were just about to round him up, the FBI tipped off their favorite son and he escaped. Sentiment has run high in the Boston area just to kick out all FBI personnel from the region since they've done so much criminal damage over the years and cannot be trusted.

FBI CREDO: SCREW UP AND MOVE UP

When the FBI tried to "investigate itself" in Boston in 1997, the investigation was so perfunctory and sloppy that the senior invest-igator, Charles Prouty, came up empty handed. The evidence was so blatant, even Inspector Clouseau could have cracked the case, but Prouty was clueless. As a reward for this stellar performance, he was promoted in 2003 to the #3 post in the FBI, Executive Assistant Director of Law Enforcement, by FBI Director Robert S. Mueller, the same thug who tried to whitewash the FBI 9/11 blunders, and who made a long career before that of sweeping inconvenient truth under the rug.[71]

"Screw up and move up" is the career strategy of choice in the FBI – the sure-fire path to bonuses and promotions. The recent large cash bonus (January 2003) awarded to the mastermind of the FBI 9/11 screwup, Marion "Spike" Bowman, is the final confirmation. Bowman was the same misfit who ran the FBI's National Security Law Unit, whose lawyers were so poorly trained and ignorant of the actual law that they needlessly roadblocked the Minneapolis office from searching Zacarias Moussaoui's laptop hard drive in August 2001, which may have well tipped the US off early to the 9/11 highjacker's plot. As usual, there's no contrition on Bowman's part, no acceptance of responsibility or recognition of fault, no lessons learned.

Screw up, deny it all, cover up, get rewarded … it's the FBI way. It's the U.S. government way.

Even senior Republicans in the US Senate were flabbergasted at the sheer audacity and egregious arrogance of this FBI travesty, the awarding of a large cash bonus to Spike "9/11" Bowman, whose gross incompetence and negligence cleared any roadblocks to the deaths of 3,000 innocents.[72]

TECHNOLOGY LAGGARDS

Despite all the propaganda the FBI has hosed about for 50 years on it's high tech savvy and scientific methods, it's anything but … the last time the FBI had any technology lead was in the early Eisenhower administration – from then on, it's been downhill, a steep, slippery slope of obsolescence.

It's now well known that while the entire world could do sophisticated web searches of complex phrases & concepts on the Internet during the 1990's, in the summer of 2001 the supposedly high tech FBI had no computer system in place with a confidential web search database. It only had a pathetic one word search capability, useless for serious research and investigation. As agents desperately tried to

make sense of the "chatter" and clues to Islamic terror plots brewing, they lacked basic tools that they should have had for six years or
more. The 9/11 disaster caught them flat-footed, in a shroud.

When I reflect back on the decade of the 1990's, I can recall many
peers in corporations that worked with government agencies at all
levels – local, state, and federal. The common joke was consistently
how incredibly backward their government counterparts were: often no
ability to operate via e-mails, horrible office support of such basics as
fax machines, abysmal computer resources. The irony is that many
computer applications sprung from government initiatives during the
50's and 60's, but somehow government entities lacked the foresight to
keep up. Lack of imagination, false economy, and just gross stupidity
has blocked their progress every step of the way. **If government
agencies pull their heads out of the sand and implement the
systemic, invigorating reforms listed in the end of this chapter, they
never need fear this third-class, laggard status again.**

COMEDY CENTRAL: THE FBI'S "JUNK SCIENCE" LABS

It's been recently well documented that the FBI's vaunted Labs,
whose supposedly high tech methods and reputation have allowed
it the final word on hundreds of murder cases nationwide, is in
actuality a shockingly sloppily-run, dishonest clearing house that
falsely renders verdicts it thinks prosecutors want to hear.[73]

The story blew wide open in 1995 (the 1990's were not kind to the
FBI's overblown, inflated image) when FBI Lab Examiner Fred
Whitehurst came forward with testimony citing huge numbers of
problems with the entire FBI Lab operation, to include the stunning
revelation that the Labs had an antique ventilation system that blew
black soot (!!) all over the Lab and its samples mailed in from trusting
law enforcement agencies nationwide (yep, that's not a misprint – Fred
would actually have to wipe the soot off his work area every morning).
The soot contained lead particulate matter, which is a key element in
"bomb explosions, bullet lead, and paint".[74] This meant that all the FBI
Labs verdicts for the last 20 years were now highly suspect, if not

ludicrously compromised. I've seen some incompetent corporate executives in my day, but the gargantuan stupidity of many federal government executives could only be a product of raging hubris and systemic black holes that defy mortal comprehension.

Naturally, the FBI was not concerned about all the false lab verdicts that incarcerated innocent people – it was only concerned with covering up the truth and its sorry butt. For his trouble, Fred Whitehurst was fired from the FBI, even though all his allegations were substantiated. This is how the FBI, and all other government entities, reward its reformers and truth-tellers.

More probing has uncovered just what a can of worms the FBI Labs has degenerated into. Numerous innocent persons were jailed based on FBI Labs "junk science." For decades, FBI "experts" have confidently given testimony that contradicts the methodology used by respected forensic scientists worldwide. FBI Lab "experts" trial testimony about hair, paint, bullets, and explosives have proven to be unreliable and false, over and over again, in courts of law throughout the country. 3,000 past lab cases are now highly suspect!! The FBI's response to this disaster is typical: "no comment" and let's sweep this under the rug pronto and maybe it'll blow over.[75] This pathetic agency should have been decommissioned five years ago.

SEPTEMBER 11

We've already discussed a dozen FBI 9/11 blunders earlier in this book. FBI Director Mueller's attempted coverup of the Phoenix Arab-pilots letter, the gross failure to dig into Zacarias Moussaoui in Minneapolis, and the abject failure to take advantage of deep cover agents that had access to Al Qaeda are all indicative that the FBI will never learn from its many blunders, and should be abolished.

MOLES: THE CLUELESS FBI

There's no boundary to the FBI's incompetence. The FBI's blundering in the Robert Hanssen mole case is mind-boggling. The FBI spent 20 years on a wild goose chase, turning the CIA inside out, to try to find moles that were spying for the Soviet KGB – it turned out that the worst mole of all was a senior FBI *counterintelligence* (!) officer, Robert Hanssen, who sold thousands of secrets to the Russians from 1980 to 1999.

Here's the incredible part: in the mid-1980's, Hanssen's brother-in-law, also an FBI agent, reported to the Bureau that he was sure that Hanssen was a Soviet spy. The most reliable exposure of spies often comes from *relatives* who are in close contact and can fairly easily detect that things are seriously amiss. Typically, the FBI blew off this valuable lead, and our courageous agents inside the Soviet Union and Russia continued to be betrayed and butchered.[76]

When Hanssen was finally caught, Louie Freeh tried to spin it as saavy FBI sleuthing. Nothing could be farther from the truth. The only way these Clouseau's stumbled across this giant 10 foot mole in their midst who gave away the store for 20 years was after a disgruntled Russian agent tipped off the CIA to Hanssen's identity.

ENDLESS BLUNDERS

The 1990's were indeed catastrophic for the FBI, from the blunders at Waco and Ruby Ridge to the smearing without evidence of innocents like Wen Ho Lee and Richard Jewell. The FBI just can't do anything without massive screwup. In each of these cases the striking commonality is the exercise of incredibly bad judgment of FBI supervisors on the scene, and all the way up the hierarchy, an organization in virtual meltdown at all levels.

DISASTER IN PROGRESS

In depth investigations into the FBI have unearthed four (4) other major disaster zones:[77]

1)   The FBI's grossly misplaced priorities

2) It's inadequate investigative work – quite a shock considering it calls itself the Federal Bureau of *Investigation*.
3) Outrageous abuse of power in many areas.
4) A highly political environment, to the exclusion of acceptable performance.

MISPLACED PRIORITIES

The Nation magazine did a brilliant in depth study of the FBI in 1997. To make a long story short, it discovered that the FBI loves to chase bank robbers (good for FBI agents securing those cushy post-retirement jobs as bank security chiefs), conduct drug busts, and chase credit card scams – all tasks which could easily be handled by state and local law enforcement.[78]

What the FBI *avoids* are much more destructive white collar crimes that rob tens of billions from Americans each year. FBI agents hate to dig into the hard work of following the intricate paper trails typically involved in these types of massive crimes – they'd just rather be "breaking down doors", as shown on "COPS" on TV.

The FBI ignores serious civil rights cases, and avoids investigating major local police corruption and malfeasance in other Federal agencies like the INS – this type of crime is perfectly suited for FBI attention, but they avoid it like the plague. It's difficult to get the FBI to focus on their real jobs, and investigate damaging official and political corruption.[79]

It's clear the FBI, or it's successor organization once it's abolished, needs a powerful civilian oversight board to keep it on a strong reform track, and prevent it from sliding into the old bad habits.

ABUSE OF POWER

The FBI study reveals even more damning problems at the Bureau. The FBI abuses its wiretap authority. The "stings" it attempts to try to entrap criminals are often sloppy and counterproductive. Its attempts to enlist rogue informants have often backfired – just look at Boston and Cleveland. The FBI has often abused the information gathered on its background checks of political appointees, a time-honored tactic Herbert Hoover used to blackmail and control Congress and the Executive branch. Its attempts to smear progressives and civil rights leaders is a indelible stain on its honor and reputation.[80]

SLOPPY INVESTIGATIVE WORK

The *Nation* study detailed that the FBI had the worst law enforcement agency record of cases rejected due to sloppy investigative work. The FBI's referrals for prosecution were more likely to be judged "legally insufficient" by US Attorneys. Only 25% of the cases referred to US Attorneys by the FBI resulted in convictions. 33% of cases referred were "legally insufficient". So much for the FBI's reputation as an elite investigative law enforcement agency!![81]

HIGHLY POLITICAL

The study found that the most important task of "successful" FBI officials is protecting the FBI against any kind of criticism. Mueller certainly tried in his attempted 9/11 blunder coverup, just as he did ten years earlier when he stonewalled attempts to investigate Bush 41's role in building up Saddam Hussein in the 1980's, "Iraqgate."[82]

WORLD CLASS CROOKS: THE NATIONAL CANCER INSTITUTE

Seediness and blanket dishonesty seem to seep into and thoroughly permeate and corrupt each and every federal agency. The disease is Washington endemic.

In the 1980's, Robert Gallo was the chief of the laboratory for tumor-cell biology at the National Cancer Institute. He began to try to identify the cause of the AIDS virus then sweeping the country and isolated what he thought was it, the HTLV virus.

However, this was *not* the AIDS virus at all. The French Pasteur Institute found an LAV virus, which indeed was the culprit. Thereupon Gallo asked the trusting French for a sample, then dishonestly labeled it "HTLV-3B" and claimed credit for the discovery. Gallo was over ambitious and arrogant, fitting the Chapter Two definition of a "hard-core jerk" to a tee.[83] (Actually, since his greed and dishonesty killed many people, he has achieved the rarified "Cosmic Jerk" status)

The French were absolutely furious, because Gallo then proceeded to muscle them out of blood test patent rights. Dishonest US officials at the NCI and sleazy politicians (among them, Ronald Reagan) supported Gallo, even though they knew well he was a liar and a thief, as indeed they all were.

Finally after 10 years it was acknowledged that the French were mistreated and robbed, but *only* because reporter John Crewdson of the *Chicago Tribune* had run a huge expose of the scandal. In the interim, Americans were infected by AIDS because Gallo's blood test was far inferior to the French blood test.

> *"The Office of Research Integrity asserted in 1993 that Gallo 'seriously hindered progress in AIDS research' by slighting the French discoveries for so long. His steps to deny the French had the United States patent for the blood test, Crewdson suggests, also had dire consequences. Various studies showed that, at least through 1986,* **Gallo's test was inferior to the Pasteur version; some Americans were infected with AIDS after receiving blood certified as safe by Gallo's test.** *These infections might have been prevented if the French had the United States patent – and the share of the blood-testing market – they deserved."*[84]

So what's the moral of this shocking tale of corruption and greed and dishonesty?? Mainly that US Government agencies are criminally inclined and fundamentally dishonest, caught in the grip of a culture of distain for the truth and integrity, incapable of policing their own, utterly devoid of any concept of shame or decency. The fact that many innocents have died due to these behaviors is of no concern to these contemptible, rotten pirates.

THE NUCLEAR REGULATORY COMMISSION: ONE-QUARTER INCH FROM AN AMERICAN CHERNOBYL

The NRC is another sycophant government agency, in bed with the very industry it's supposed to be regulating. For the NRC, the public safety is a very distant second to pleasing the nuclear power industry.

How much horrendous danger this places the public in became clear in early 2002 when the Davis Besse Nuclear Plant near Toledo Ohio finally shut down for investigative inspection on a compromise date in February. The NRC had cravenly backed off from it's Dec 31, 2001 date to please the First Energy Nuclear Operations Corporation.

> *"When the plant finally closed, on a compromise date in February, 2002, engineers and workers were shocked to find that cracks of the kind that* (Nuclear Regulatory) *commission staff had suspected there had let acidic water leak onto the head, where it had eaten away a 70-pound chunk of steel six inches thick.*
> *Only a layer of stainless steel about a quarter-inch thick had prevented the cooling water from spewing out of the vessel head, in a leak that could have proved catastrophic. The corrosion was the most extensive ever found at an American nuclear plant."*[85]

In other words, 613,000 innocents living in nearby Toledo were a hair breath away from being irradiated, Chernobyl-style, into oblivion.

First Energy is a typical sleazy nuclear power plan operator. When its very own engineers raise any safety concerns, it simply fires them without any fear the gutless NRC will utter whimper one.

"In February (2003) Representative Dennis J. Kucinich of Ohio petitioned the Nuclear Regulatory Commission to revoke First Energy's operating license. Among the charges Mr. Kucinich made was that First Energy fired an engineer, Andy Siemaszko, last September (2002) because he had raised safety issues. Mr. Siemaszko, who is pursuing a complaint with the Department of Labor, had tried to do a thorough inspection of the vessel head during a shutdown for refueling in 2000, but was 'thwarted' by management, according to Mr. Kucinich's petition. He was fired for raising additional safety questions during the current shutdown, Mr. Kucinich says."[85]

(*Author's Note*: Kucinich, by the way, is head & shoulders by far the most experienced, intelligent, decent, and competent of all the Democratic contenders for the 2004 Presidential race. Of course he'll undoubtedly *not* get the nomination, because Americans desire all their candidates look like smooth, preppy movie stars, and shun any candidate who radiates untainted moral courage. Thus the nation has been cursed with utterly mediocre, spineless, ineffective leadership for the past 50 years and has suffered a steady decline, engaging in endless unnecessary wars, enraging large segments of the planet against us, been plagued by a disastrous energy policy, ruinous military-industrial complex, and media monopoly-tyranny – and witnessed the rotting of it's economy, investment climate, educational system, health care, and major infrastructures. Like De Maistre said, people truly get the government they deserve. Wake up, people.)

Whew! Back to the First Energy Corporation …

And which infamous power company was in the thick of the great Blackout of August 14, 2003?? In fact, precipitating the entire fiasco?? Why, First Energy, of course, whose shoddy controls of it's own power system triggered the worst power outage in the nation's history, putting 50 million Americans in the dark, from Ohio to New York, as well as blacking out half of Canada.

FIRST ENERGY – CORPORATE GREED UNCHECKED, AGAIN

On November 19, 2003 the official US Government investigation of the massive August 2003 blackout by the Department of Energy (which corporate right-wingers have tried to abolish for 20 years) released its findings. It concluded that the sleazy First Energy Corporation, the same charlatans overseeing the disastrous Davis-Besse Nuclear power generating plant, also is incompetent on the transmission side of the house. First Energy has neglected its electric grid infrastructure so badly in Ohio that on August 14, 2003, tree limbs shorted out its power lines (let's face it: fire 500 line maintenance men and you can boost the bottom line, right? what difference does a little tree-trimming make, when you're trying to look good for Wall Street analysts … first things first and the public be damned).

Also the Energy Department investigation revealed that *all* the shoddy, cheap alarm systems installed by penny-pinching First Energy on these power transmission lines **FAILED TO WORK AT ALL** …*none* **of them worked**, so First Energy's own Control Center was totally unaware of the emergency until it was too late to take any effective action. Massive amounts of electric power surged un-checked onto adjacent lines, which quickly became dangerously overloaded, which in turn triggered cascading outages that spread all over the region. The regional power controller's (the Midwest Independent Transmission System Operator) alarms and computers also failed to work at all (sounds like some 3rd world country like Botswana!) so the disaster spread all over the Midwestern and Northeastern United States, and Canada.[86]

Of course, the real outrage, not mentioned in the report, is that the *laissez-faire* US Government, bowing as usual to its corporate bribe-masters, has never placed any *enforceable* standards on the Power Industry. The standards are all "voluntary", which means that the power industry can do anything it damn well pleases ... and does. There's also no rigorous inspection system, or any inspection system or oversight at all, which *truly* pleases these corporate management blood-suckers. Professional power engineers have warned about this "disaster-in-waiting" for 20 years, but greedy corporate robber-barons have made sure their compliant, dollar-greased Congressmen and Senators and Presidents perform their appointed role to perfection: namely, doing nothing.

However, with the August 14, 2003 power blackout disaster that caused billions in damages and loss of life, like the 9/11 disaster, the incompetent, corrupt US Congress has finally been forced to act, once again slamming the barn door tight long after the horses, cows, and chickens have bolted.

Now, back to the equally inept NRC ...

The NRC's own inspector general found the NRC grossly negligent in the Davis-Besse affair – but that IG report never would have been released to the public had not its existence been leaked to the press. The only thing that stands between the public and catastrophic disaster is the willingness of a handful of decent government employees to leak damning information to the media. The entire spectrum of US government agencies is a fascist cabal of criminals and self servers bent on keeping the public in the dark. A few brave souls have acted to expose this morass.

The NRC, like the FAA, is a craven cheerleader for the shoddily run industry its supposed to regulate.

YIKES!! THE CIA

The CIA is an obvious example of gross government incompetence and dysfunction. With it's blatant murderous and criminal activity overseas during the past 50 years and its massive blunders leading up to 9/11, it sticks out like a gigantic pulsating sore thumb in a sea of sore thumbs.

Perhaps a summation of its major problem can be found in this prescient letter written by an active-duty case officer in the Agency's clandestine service **three years before 9/11** to *Atlantic Monthly* in response to a long expose run by the magazine on the CIA. The honesty and urgency of the message is striking, and is one of the reasons *this* book had to written, and why it must be acted upon immediately (and also underscores the point that government work-places need more than the individual jerk removal of Chapters 1-6 ... they also need the 100% overhaul detailed at this chapter's end):

> *"As a twenty-year veteran of the CIA, I found Edward G. Shirley's article 'Can't Anybody Here Play This Game?"(February 1998 Atlantic) painfully accurate. Unlike him, however, I am still an active duty case officer with the Agency's clandestine service. I can fault Shirley only for failing to mention the pitiful management that is now running this country's most sensitive intelligence-collection programs. I work with one of those programs. Today's Agency is troubled and is being torn apart from within by the very people who run the place.* **The best people are resigning because of bad management. The best case officers do not chose the management track.** *Those who do are devoured, by a breed of Agency managers who have mastered the art of schmooze. They are the ones who were left standing when all the other case officers with better sense took early outs and retirement incentives and bid the rest of us adieu. By and large, this group of dangerously ambitious people is charged with the day-to-day operations of the Agency. To a man (and woman) they are characterized by incredible egos and raging insecurities that have resulted in inconsistent and incestuous management practices.*[87]
>
> *Name withheld*

The CIA suffers from a numbers game mentality. The *quality* of foreign agents recruited by a case officer is unimportant, it's the *quantity* that earns promotions!! *Ergo*, it's no wonder that CIA operations worldwide are a joke. The CIA blew several chances to infiltrate Al Qaeda Afghan training camps with American Islamic jihad fighters.[88] Once again, a American agency is obsessed with high-tech gizmos but fails to employ human assets. As one CIA official lamented, "We had amazing satellite pictures of them having graduation ceremonies at the camps, but we never had a clue what they planned to do when they left Afghanistan."[89]

The ineptness of the CIA surveillance of two well-known Al Qaeda operatives in Malaysia in 2001 allowed the subjects to just waltz into the US (which the CIA did not bother to inform the FBI of!!) and then pilot American Airlines Flight 77 into the Pentagon on 9/11, unhindered. The CIA's gross lack of coordination with the FBI bequeathed the 9/11 assault a clear running field, a green light to proceed at breakneck speed.

The selection of George Tenet as CIA chief was also a disaster – here's "screw up and move up" in full swing. Tenet is "a sycophant who plunged the CIA covert ops division into one of the most catastrophic debacles of recent years: a bungled coup against Saddam that saw scores of innocent Iraqi cinema-goers blown to bits and hundreds of CIA employees in Baghdad rounded up and shot."[90]

Tenet's latest blunder, blithely allowing the CIA to be browbeaten by Darth Cheney into letting the blatantly bogus Niger uranium hoax be used by Shrub Bush to justify the disastrous Iraq War, should get him fired for good, but in the dysfunctional world of Washington, he'll undoubtedly get a building named after him instead.

The CIA will continue to slide downhill fast – as a CIA insider states, "Congress's decision to drop the 'whistle blower' provision from the 1998 intelligence authorization bill, which would have protected Agency employees who notify Congress of CIA wrongdoing, was a serious mistake. Capitol Hill needs more and sharper eyes inside the DO (Directorate of Operations), not fewer."[91]

ABROGATION OF RESPONSIBILITY: THE PEACE CORPS

The Peace Corps is just another example of a shoddy, sloppily-run government agency. On January 31, 2001, Sheila Poirier of Lowell,

MA got an e-mail from her son, Walter, a 22-year old Peace Corps volunteer in Bolivia.

It was the last communication she ever received. By February 28 she hadn't heard from him in four weeks. In the following days she tried various ways to contact him, without success. Very worried, she contacted the Peace Corps in Bolivia, the folks who were responsible for Walter: these clowns did not even know he was missing, but even worse, didn't even know where he was living and had no clue as to where he was. The Peace Corps HQ in Washington was even more in the dark. The entire apparatus was slow to act, slow in sending out search parties, and laggardly in posting rewards. In other words, it entirely abrogated its responsibility to look out for the innocents under its charge.[92]

Walter Poirier was probably robbed and killed sometime in February, 2001. He died alone and helpless, abandoned by an incompetent, negligent government agency.

Congress's GAO investigated the Poirier case, as well as a broader inquiry into how well the Peace Corps "protects" its 7,000 volunteers overseas. It discovered that the Peace Corps' negligence is shocking. It has consistently failed to properly supervise its volunteers, many naïve young people who clearly are in need of responsible, reasonable oversight. It loses track of them often. From 1995 to 2001, six Peace Corps volunteers have been murdered overseas. Rapes and robberies are common.(What is truly unbelievable is that there is no "buddy system" in the Peace Corps, common in organizations that send folks overseas, *e.g.,* the Mormons, and also in the military, which dramatically reduce dangers. In fact, the absence of it is a negligent outrage.)[93]

Peace Corps management seems to be the poster children of Aukai Collins' take on US government people: no practical common sense, unable to employ logic, incapable of thinking ahead. Typically, the Peace Corps spent a lot of time and effort trying to hide it's gross negligence in the Poirier case, quibbling with aspects of the critical GAO report.

THE PUZZLE PALACE: THE NSA

The NSA is just another dysfunctional government agency – a good friend of mine who has worked at the NSA for 25 years in a highly sensitive position tells me the place is just a disaster area. His management is fundamentally useless. Managers are rotated in to his department to meet racial and gender quotas – just when they learn enough to begin to become productive after a year and a half and start to contribute, they're jerked out and a new, utterly ignorant manager is thrown in. The whole place is driven by ticket-punching and "pensionitis". Since management is so completely useless, the rank and file just totally ignore management, and the organization is rudderless. And people wonder how 9/11 could happen, with sensitive government agencies responsible for national security at the highest levels in such chaos.

NASA: NO SECRET WHY IT'S FALLING APART

Here's an incredibly incompetent, irresponsible, wayward government agency that should have been reformed 15 years ago. The space shuttle program has been a disaster from the getgo, a poorly designed, hugely expensive white elephant that has little to zero practical value. It's been a "prestige project" for politicians and payola for greedy contractors, a useless vestige of the Cold War that's been paid for via exorbitant interest rates with the unnecessary deaths of 14 astronauts.

The program has been screwed up by incompetent government bureaucrats from it's inception in 1980. NASA ignored repeated warnings from engineers on brittle o-rings, but launched the Challenger anyway on that bitter cold January day in 1986. Then the agency tried to cover up their blunder after the disaster. Sixteen years later, in April 2002, when a distinguished blue-ribbon panel warned that safety was being given a back seat in the shuttle program, NASA responded in the time-honored government agency manner: it simply fired most of the panel, and replaced it with more compliant clones. It's the government way: shoot the messenger, hide your mistakes, hope you can retire with a fat pension before the shit hits the fan. *Apres moi, les deluge.*[94]

> *"Dr. Seymour C. Himmel, who was fired from the advisory panel said yesterday that 'we were telling it like it was and were disagreeing with some of the agency's actions.'*
>
> *The eight departed panel members and consultants had long experience with the shuttle's systems and their troubles. In interviews yesterday, some said NASA had developed an institutional myopia about the panel's warnings, advice , and observations, however pointed.*
>
> *'I have never been as worried for space shuttle safety as I am right now,' Dr. Richard D. Blomberg, the panel's chairman told Congress in April (2002, nine months before the Columbia disaster). 'All of my instincts suggest that the current approach is planting the seeds for future danger.'"*[95]

The entire space shuttle boondoggle has merely been a lucrative pork-barrel exercise driven by bonehead senators and congressmen from Texas, Fla, Ohio, Calif, and Ala – and 14 brave astronauts have paid for this corrupt behavior with their lives, needlessly wasted.

COLUMBIA SHUTTLE SCANDAL "SMOKING GUN" REVEALED!!

NEWSFLASH!! You know, as I wrote the words above on NASA and the Columbia tragedy several months ago, I just knew *there just had to be much more to it.* There had to be the *inside story* of what *really happened* in the dysfunctional Columbia engineering / management organization in Houston & Florida after it became obvious that a very large piece of foam broke off from the shuttle during it's January 16, 2003 launch, and smashed into the left wing. The official investigations were just all too hazy and unfocused ... how marvelously convenient for NASA: the Columbia disaster was really nobody's fault, it was just bad luck. There just had to be a massive coverup going on, not reported in any of the "official", "blue ribbon" investigations. 95% of all government "investigations" of itself engage in major coverup, so why not this time?? It usually takes 6 – 12 months for the real truth to come oozing out of the woodwork.

BINGO!! Sure enough, in today's *New York Times* (September 26, 2003) the whole scandal has blown wide open. Turns out that *immediately* after it became known that large foam chunks were torn off the shuttle at launch, 30 engineers demanded that NASA get external photos of the shuttle wings to assess any possible damage.

The *Times'* exposé reveals by name the four (4) mid-level and senior "managers" who were criminally and grossly negligent in flatly denying this reasonable request. **So NASA *deliberately chose to "fly blind"*!!** The photos would have easily shown the significant damage to the left wing, and allowed NASA the opportunity to abort the mission and save the lives of the trusting seven astronauts. In keeping with the venerable *Jihad the Jerk at Work* tradition (borrowed from our favorite Newsletter, Alexander Cockburn's *Counterpunch*) of "naming the names" of criminals and murderers, and actually holding people accountable for their gross crimes, here are the four guilty Cosmic Jerks who murdered the seven astronauts of Columbia. Remember, have no sympathy for these clowns, they all *actively* and *aggressively* and *viciously* and *arrogantly* and *stupidly* sabotaged the external photo request:[96]

Murderer #1: Paul Shack   **– Manager of Shuttle Engineering Office**
Murderer #2: Linda Ham   **– Columbia Shuttle Manager**
Murderer #3: Calvin Schomburg – Senior Thermal Protection Engineer
Murderer #4: Leroy Cain   **– Columbia Flight Director for Landing**

Naturally, as per standard US Government procedure, the official inquiries covered up the criminal roles these four played in the murder of the seven Columbia astronauts. Nobody is ever held accountable for wrongdoing in the US government or military, therefore wrong-doing, crimes, and murder flourish there, and indeed are well re-warded. These four murderers have gotten off scot-free, been given fat taxpayer funded lifetime pensions, been told to shut up, and have been retired with high honors – **THE STINKING DISGRACE OF IT ALL.**

We must demand that *each* of these four criminals be put on trial for murder and *each* be given a 30 year jail sentence without chance of parole.

A PROBLEM WORLDWIDE

The US government is hardly alone in its dysfunction. The United Nations, the European Union, and foreign governments all suffer from the same type of moronic flaws. And all can be reformed.

LOCAL-YOKEL JERKS

Alas, the systemic stranglehold jerks have on government agencies is *not* confined to the federal level. This plague has most local and state and regional governments in its thrall. A good friend moved to the Boston area 15 years ago. She reports she's never seen anything like the high levels of nepotism, corruption, cronyism, and incompetence in government, and the surly attitudes displayed by public employees and their managers toward the public. The regional highway authorities are so incompetent, they've designed numerous high-speed highways that funnel multiple lanes into one another with absolutely no merge zones, creating incredibly dangerous safety conditions.

Large sections of interstate highway have no state patrol presence, so motorists run wild – aggressive driving is unchecked by any police campaigns, unlike in other parts of the country. These same fools have screwed up the highways for the "Big Dig". For ten years, the alternative route through south Boston to Logan airport from I-93 was virtually unmarked, despite numerous complaints from citizens. Even with the multi-billion dollar I-90 extension completed to this huge airport, people trying to drive away from Logan faced a gauntlet of unmarked exits, confusing signs, and unremitting concrete madness.

Of course, the Big Dig itself has been the worst-managed public works project in US history, with a 10 billion dollar cost overrun with no end in sight. Worst of all, it leaks like a sieve! The whole project stinks of corruption and the deliberate misleading of the public. Nothing was spent on mass transit … the two major rail stations in Boston remain mired in the 19th Century, with absolutely no link between them after 20 billion has been spent.

And, naturally, Logan airport itself was the airport of choice for the 9/11 terrorists – who wouldn't select the nation's most lax security quagmire, well known as a hotbed of nepotism and cronyism? In fact, the Director of Security there on 9/11/01 was a completely unqualified bozo who landed the job because he happened to be the chauffeur for Governor Weld in the mid-1990's – yep, the Governor's driver.

Thousands of decent citizens and government employees would just love to clean house in eastern Massachusetts, and everywhere else. Now with *Jihad the Jerk at Work* and the **Eleven-Point Program for Government Reform** listed below, they can romp and stomp.

All the systemic ills that afflict federal agencies truly plague all state and local governments. Whether it's sloppy state oversight of day care centers in Tennessee causing the gruesome deaths of toddlers, or incompetently run homes for the mentally ill in New York State soaking the State for unnecessary and dangerous eye operations, or grossly mismanaged fire departments, police, foster care or schools in New York City, or environmentally criminal negligent airports in Texas that dump oil and contaminants into rivers, or a West Warwick, RI, senior fire marshal's "fire safety" inspection which completely ignored highly flammable illegal "egg crate" polyethylene "sound insulation" plastered all over "the Station" nightclub which 2 months later burned down in 5 minutes killing 100 trusting, young patrons in a horrible, hellish chemical blaze … it all stems from the same root causes, which can be rather easily treated and cured by a set of intelligently applied solutions.

DOUBLE THE PERCENTAGE OF JERKS

Before we plunge in to outlining the proper solution to the monopolistic government workplace morass, it's important to realistically understand what we're up against. The miserable performance of most government agencies is so profound, that I've had to revise my estimated percentage of jerks plaguing these workplaces to *double* the rates infesting private businesses. So one can expect to find up to **10%** hard core jerks and **30%** sycophants/fellow travelers in a typical government entity! That still leaves 60% decent folks, but its easy to see it's *much more of an uphill battle* to clean up a government operation. The reason for this huge percentage increase of jerks is obvious: over time, the consistently disastrous climate at government agencies has good folks clawing for the exit doors, and the jerk population has had zero restraints. We've seen from dozens of examples what catastrophe results from, and how truly bizarre, most government operations are ... just plain weird. And that means, of course, that the **serious systemic approach described below is essential if one really desires to make a significant, long-lasting, positive impact.**

THE QUESTIONABLE ROLE OF UNIONS

It would be irresponsible not to mention one of the big problems in government, the activities of certain unions. Philosophically and historically, I'm sympathetic to the success of unions in bringing better working conditions to working people. I'm not an expert in the role of unions in government but I've witnessed, and also heard from very reliable sources, so many horror stories of abuse of power and just plain abject stupidity by unions, that we can safely say that sadly, too often, "Unions' worst enemy are themselves". I'll leave this parting thought to readers who are faithful union members, whether in Government or in the private sector: don't put up with any stupidity from union officials or members – be as ruthless in *cleaning up your union* as you are with fumigating your workplace, perhaps even more so! Too often "solidarity" is used as a smokescreen to hide flakiness, or even worse.

LET'S CLEAN HOUSE

My advice to decent government managers and employees who really want to clean house is follows:

1) identify a courageous, intelligent, open minded executive in your agency – if you have trustworthy friends at work, form an anonymous reform committee.

2) get him a copy of this book with this chapter annotated and highlighted (*anonymously, of course*) – give him 30 days to come up with a dynamic action plan. Demand he implement the entire 11-Point Program, now.

3) if he wimps out or otherwise fails to produce, keep badgering others all the way to the top of your agency – then start bothering congressional oversight committees and the media until your flaky government agency is truly reformed as detailed below.

4) observe strict security and secrecy, and always keep your group strictly anonymous. Read Chapters 1 – 6 of the book to sharpen your reform tactics.

5) Never give up, until the mission is successfully accomplished. Be ruthless – the American people are depending on you to clean your septic tank agency out. They want you to do them proud. They want a government they can point to with pride, not the shameful mess they're currently saddled with.

TAKE ACTION NOW

Perhaps you may believe, that having unquestioningly made the point that government agencies are 99% dysfunctional, corrupt and incompetent, I desire to gloat and crow over this shambles. Nothing could be further from my mind – I'm appalled, outraged, and even embarrassed as an American that *we citizens have allowed this cancerous rot to spread unimpeded for 50 years.* **We can do much better than this, and we can do it with blistering speed.** It's easy to crab and complain about how screwed up the government is – now we can actually *do something about it,* systemic change that is going to reform it permanently.

THE SOLUTION: *JIHAD THE JERK AT WORK*'S ELEVEN POINT PROGRAM TO REFORM GOVERNMENT WORK-PLACES PERMANENTLY (also applies to any other monopolistic, dead-end workplace such as academia, the military, churches, medical, judicial, law enforcement, *etc.*)

Several of the actions needed to be kicked into gear to reform the mindset of mediocre government agencies are obvious: 1) this book itself, used by the thousand to expose and purge hard core jerks from agencies at federal, state, and local levels. **All** government employees should read and rigorously employ this book when appropriate. 2) good *upward feedback* programs, as detailed in Chapter 9, must be instituted in all government – and military – organizations, mandatory by law, and routinely inspected for substance and quality, by ruthless external inspectors … **no exceptions** for any agencies whether they be FBI, CIA, NSA, homeland security, *etc.* 3) obviously, campaign finance reform needs to kick into high gear to clean up Congress and the Executive Branch, whose bribe-taking and corruption has polluted government and its agencies for the last 100 years. See Chapter 14 for this action plan. If we can't get serious campaign finance reform, citizens should band together and just legally abolish the federal government, convert the Washington DC area into forest, and move to regional governments where voters can keep a closer eye on their representatives, with a whole new set of intelligent ground rules.

However, the problem with this drastic approach is obvious: state and local governments have the same type of "paralysis of monopoly" problems that the federal government has. Therefore the problem isn't really solved by the abolition and shifting of a layer of bureaucracy. The only way the problem will be truly solved is by rigorously implementing the entire "11 Point Program" for fundamental governmental agency reform.

FUNDAMENTAL MINDSET SHIFT

But the thrust of this chapter, Chapter 10, is to move beyond the obvious reforms, and to clearly illustrate that meaningful reform of government must go far deeper than the three listed above.

What is clearly called for is a tectonic mindset change on the part of each and every government employee and manager and executive: and if any of these folks just don't "get it" or exhibit attitude or performance problems on this score, they must be **immediately removed** from any kind of public service. How to achieve this profound mindset shift????

a) *Indoctrination.* Each and every agency must draw up a written credo, a covenant that clearly emphasizes public service over careerism, internal and external frankness and decency over corrupt secrecy, a toleration and even encouragement of honest whistleblowing in a reasonable context, and the need for *everyone to have viable alternate career plans* to free employees from dead-end mentalities. This credo must be drilled into employees – they must want it and gladly adopt it ... ones who can't will be invited to leave the organization post-haste. The credo should be recited en masse semi-annually.

Also, to prepare employees and management to tackle the entire next section on establishing alternate careers, they must be properly educated and motivated to understand the rationale behind the alternate careers program (see below) and, indeed the entire 11 point program outlined here.

b) *Alternate Careers* in place: the centerpiece of the "mindset change" in government agencies is very tangible. Credos aren't enough: in order to really activate government employees to perform to 100% potential, each and every employee and manager must have "backup careers" in place, their individual plan of career change if and when there are layoffs, or the agency betrays them, or they just get fed up and want to leave.

On the face of it this all may seem rather strange, somehow undermining one's dedication to the present job. But when you think about it, and the factors that consistently destroy employee performance, this is **absolutely fundamental to any real mindset change in government service**. The whole problem now (and in the past) in government service is the fear-ridden, dead-end, monopolistic nature of government employment. "Where will I go if I rebel and blow the whistle and leave in disgust??"

Every employee has to have his/her plan in place – it should be *mandatory* that he/she be assisted by a special office in each agency that helps folks work through the options, gets them excited about alternate career plans in business, non-profits, entrepreneurial endeavors, even other government agencies that may be expanding. At a minimum, people can rev up this plan upon retirement.

The plan should be formally spelled out in writing and placed in the employees file – it should be regularly updated and improved upon. It must be a positive exercise that gives each and every employee optimism, hope, and real options. Incentives and rewards should be in place to honor employees with "Grade A" plans as opposed to just "satisfactory" plans. Directors of agencies should push hard to have 100% of their employees with genuine "Grade A" plans. Most important of all goes back to "indoctrination"– employees must *understand* why they're going through this drill, *understand* the historical problems of the monopolistic government agency, *understand* that this is the **only** way to get the place out of the doldrums, and keep it out. Therefore they must all be given an intensive workshop entitled "Successes and Failures of Government" which clearly addresses the root causes of government dysfunction, illustrated with the type of typical horror stories found in this chapter. The basic motivator the workshop will implant in everyone's mind is, "Gee, can't we in government do better than this??" When folks ask this key question, it's the most powerful motivator of all. The vast majority will be thrilled at this progressive move, and will understand immediately the win-win posture this positions their workplace in.

Just listen to James Watson, the co-discoverer of DNA and author of the best seller, *The Double Helix*, when asked why he and Francis Crick discovered DNA before the rest of the world:

> *"Both Francis and I **knew we would have careers even if we failed**, so we weren't desperate. Hence we were willing to trust that an idea that was only 90% certain was worth taking a chance on."*[97]

Part of the education of government employees on alternate career planning needs to include this rationale, and inspirational stories like JCR Licklider and Leo Pasvolsky (see beginning of Chapter) to instill a genuine pride that government workplaces can make a positive difference and do not have to be negative hellholes staffed with hopeless serfs dictated to by mindless autocrats.

c) The government agency that's really sincere about this mindset change will also set up semi-annual jam sessions where all employees get together in groups of 20 or so to share their ideas about alternate career plans and prospects. This will get the whole group into the spirit of alternate careers, to realize that there are exciting possibilities outside of this agency and government, and to breed the optimistic, empowering outlook that "Nobody is trapped here. Nobody." We're only here as long as it's challenging, fun, productive, and satisfying!

Retirees and people who have made successful transitions to other careers should be brought in to inspire the troops.

One caveat, however. Alternate career planning is essential, but the revolving door of government bureaucrats into the very industries they're supposed to be regulating or even associated with, must be slammed shut. Tight. No more FBI agents retiring to become security chiefs for banks. No more IRS agents going to work for companies they've been auditing. Even the *appearance* of these conflicts of interest must be rigorously forbidden, and prosecuted when discovered.

The alternate career program is absolutely essential if we ever hope to pull government agencies out of the institutional hells into which they've descended.

d) Each agency must regularly convene a special *internal* "whistleblower board" whose mission is to fairly resolve all complaints promptly. Shooting the Messenger is absolutely forbidden. The strong impulse of government agencies to betray their own workers is a sick disease that must be stamped out. The board would also determine if management at any level is incompetent and stifling needed reforms – if so, the board would get rid of these kinds of terrible managers. This board could cooperate with internal IG's but would be strictly independent. The board would also have links to the external oversight board (item "g") to request assistance if needed.

e) Government agencies must convene semi-annual internal pan els made up of employees and management to openly tackle the key questions: how is the agency doing?? what's it doing right? what wrong? what are the major problems? what are its major goals and priorities?

f) To back up the alternate career path program with real muscle, the agency should establish generous severance packages, with *portable* pensions and medical plans to ease the transition of those desiring to leave – this category includes those legitimate whistleblowers and others who are screwed by the agency if the protections listed above fail and the messenger is indeed, "shot". This also would include more career transition assistance in the form of information, advice, materials, books, *etc.*

g) Each and every government agency at federal/state/local level, as well as police depts., military branches, the judiciary, *etc.*, must have an independent *external* oversight board that keeps a focused eye on the agency to insure it does not engage in arbitrary, rogue, incompetent behaviors so commonplace now, detailed here in Chapter 10. This oversight board would be comprised of proven, high integrity people from the Congressional GAO, citizens, media reps, and public interest advocates who annually publish a report to the public on how the agency is performing. It would also investigate any whistleblower complaints that escalate to its level, and complaints from the public on any agency malfeasance.

Also, if the board discovers that the agency has not performed to 100% of the Eleven Point Program introduced in this chapter, the agency's management will be quickly removed and replaced with managers who can perform.

ELEVEN POINT PROGRAM FOR GOVERNMENT AGENCY REFORM: (RECAP) FEDERAL, STATE, and LOCAL levels

The 11 points have been sprinkled amongst the previous four pages, so here's a succinct list:

I. Frequent use of *"Jihad the Jerk at Work"* by employees and managers to *clean jerks out of agencies*.

II. Establish excellent, basic *"Upward Feedback Programs"*, as detailed in Chapter 9, in every Agency and organization.

III. Serious *Campaign Finance Reform* must be instituted and enforced for political parties, Congress, and President (see Chapter 14).

IV. Agency *Credos and Covenants* that include and describe the entire Eleven Point Program and motivate employees to enthusiastically embrace same.

V. Establish solid *"Alternate Careers Program"* (ACP) as a positive, optimistic part of all government employment.

VI. Reinforce alternate careers program with intelligent education on the *benefits of the ACP* to employees personally, and the agency as a whole.

VII. *Strengthen the ACP* with several jam sessions a year where employees can share their alternative plans and ideas, and expand their horizons. "Nobody is trapped here!"

**VIII. Convene *Internal Whistleblower and Oversight Board*
to fairly and promptly investigate complaints, and influence direction of agency.**

 **IX. Convene regular *employee/management panels* that
probe the direction and priorities of the agency.**

  **X. *Improve severance packages*, portable medical and
pension plans, and career assistance for those in transition.**

 **XI. Establish *External Oversight Board* that insures
Agency is competently run and has correct priorities.**

CALL FOR COMMENTS

Any serious presidential or congressional candidates must totally
embrace this eleven point reform program now and I invite them to
do so, now. This will allow the public to see who's really interested
in pursuing real governmental reform, and which candidates are just
fluff. I also invite principled citizen action groups like the Green
Party, Public Citizen, Common Cause, *et al.* (and even the two major
parties, Democrat and Republican) to adopt it as a plank in their
reform program, and to use it to challenge all public office-holders
and officials to either "fish or cut bait" on this major reform issue,
and pass it into law at all levels of government: federal, state,
local.

I also invite the public to comment on this eleven point plan. If it
can be improved, I'd like to get your ideas asap so we can finalize it
and act on it posthaste. Combined with the major political reforms in
Chapter 14, we can proactively reform government, society, and
business before it self-destructs and takes the planet with it.

NOW IS THE TIME FOR ACTION

WE MUST END GROSS INCOMPETENCE AND CORRUPTION.

**WE MUST FUNDAMENTALLY REFORM ALL OUR PUB-
LIC INSTITUTIONS TO SERVE THE PUBLIC GOOD, NOT
CORRUPT SPECIAL INTERESTS AND BRIBE-GIVERS.**

*"The government in Washington seldom lacks for a quorum
of cheats and liars; the con games take similar and traditional forms ..."*[98]

Lewis H. Lapham
Editor, *Harpers Magazine*
August, 2003

Chapter Eleven – Cleaning Up Academia, Church, Medical, & Judiciary Quagmires

"Idealists ... foolish enough to throw caution to the winds ... have advanced mankind and have enriched the world." [1]

Emma Goldman
(1869 – 1940)
Russian born American Jewish lecturer, activist, anarchist

In this chapter, we focus on six career areas that have caught our attention over the years as workplaces that seem prone to serious hard-core jerk influence: non-profits, academia, medical, judiciary, law enforcement, and church professions. What we cover here is just the tip of the iceberg, so I encourage readers to write in to give us more insights, if the spirit so moves. As always, personal experiences are particularly instructive in painting the picture of what's actually going on.

My impression is that these career areas are not quite as bad as government agencies – at least there are more options for escape to shift within the profession. However, the volume and intensity of scandal reported in various media over a long period of time indicate "there's a rotten smell in Denmark", that these workplaces must have severe systemic problems, sometimes well over and above private corporations and businesses.

They do tend to be relatively close-ended – they're "small worlds" where it may be more difficult to leave one workplace for another, say, than a more competitive business with ten rivals in the field. Thus jerks tend to have a freer reign, and corruption and idiocy can quickly take hold and be more difficult to eradicate.

THE SIX AREAS

NON-PROFITS:

Non-profits such as political campaigns or charities or activist groups can lull applicants with the siren song of "the cause" and "moral imperatives" (as well as "slave wages"). I admonish those entering these work zones to *be particularly alert*. Don't put up with jerk-like behaviors, no matter how noble the cause. If confronted with it, one must quickly decide whether to bail out or push for low-key reform or launch an EAJ effort, as described in Chapters 1-6.

An example are the half dozen or so classic cases nationwide during the past decade where some errant Directors of regional United Way charities have gotten away with abuse of power and financial theft for far too long. Of course it's especially tragic, since United Way has historically been one of the most effective and trusted charities, supported by the superb work of tens of thousands of civic-minded volunteers.

United Way, to it's credit, has finally caught up with and prosecuted the guilty parties, but the question has continually been raised: Why did employees who knew what was going on keep silent for so long?? Why didn't the alarm bells ring much earlier? United Way and other charities have suffered severe damage to their reputations, and their received donations, as a result. Fortunately, in some cases the damage is only temporary – but some charities have been destroyed by these violations of the public's trust. We'll look at some proactive solutions shortly.

ACADEMIA:

In earlier chapters, we've already seen several examples of glaring problems in schools, colleges, and universities. Even the so-called cream of the crop is not exempt, and in fact may be *more susceptible* to the hubris which often is the midwife of jerk-induced catastrophe.

In Chapter 3 we saw how the corruption and abject stupidity of the staff & faculty of the elite Groton School in Massachusetts destroyed the reputation of this blue-blooded institution overnight.

Reforms that do well in many corporations by helping in the struggle for profitability never even get to first base in many colleges with blinders affixed to their halters. The vague and often ineffective way many colleges measure their effectiveness often obstruct the most rudimentary reforms from even being *discussed*. For instance, organized Upward Feedback is almost unheard of in many universities – out of desperation and self-protection, students have had to set up ad hoc rating systems of professors on the Internet.[2] Some staff and faculty at colleges have expressed outrage at this scrutiny, but if they had instituted the types of decent, confidential upward feedbacks used by some progressive corporations today, they could have preempted the whole issue.

As we'll discuss in Chapter 14, the public school system in this country, for many reasons, is going down the tubes. The rapid "dumbing down" of the entire US population via a weak public education system has created huge problems for us nationally, not the least of which is a population too comatose to stop the election of thousands of crooked right wing politicians who have and are currently sabotaging campaign finance reform, and who support an insanely stupid foreign policy that creates endless disasters, endless enemies, and endless wars for the American people world wide.

In many recent large surveys of players in public education (2003)[3], it's been revealed that one of root problems is that school superintendents and principals and teachers have their hands tied by public school bureaucracies, teachers unions, and a percentage of dullard parents (who are either totally indifferent to their child's education, or refuse to tolerate even minimum standards of student discipline & achievement, or have fascist mindsets that are offended by even the most modest attempts at teaching honest history & current events.)

Contributing to this morass is a monopolistic, government-run school system which has created a fear-ridden, dead-end, incompetently-run workplace that encourages the best teachers to get the hell out as soon as they can. The solution, of course, is the only sensible alternative: substantial vouchers for every child, to be paid to the non-parochial school of his/her choice – voucher schools whose *only* source of income are the vouchers themselves, so "no child is left behind" and a double tier education system is avoided. See Chapter 14 for more details.

It's clear that intelligent, systemic changes must be made throughout academia – primary, secondary, college, & university – if the mess is ever going to get resolved.

MEDICAL:

The medical profession and the greedy businesses that manage it have created an overpriced nightmare where the chances of getting into a deadly auto accident on the road is far less likely than dying of a doctor's gross error in surgery. The public's trust in the medical system is at an all time low, 43 million Americans cannot afford expensive health insurance, and a huge misallocation of resources insure that the largest number of people have no access to medical care. This scandal is well documented in Dr. George Lundberg's new explosive exposé, *Severed Trust: Why American Medicine Hasn't Been Fixed* (2002, Basic Books, NY). As usual, the same culprits raise their ugly heads: greedy, stupid right wing (or even so-called "moderate") politicians – in their standard whorish role for deep pocketed HMO's and multi-millionaires – bent on stopping any medical reforms the country desperately needs. Even the rather modest reform effort of the early Clinton years was met by a huge, corrupt, dishonest, well-funded "Harry and Louise" lobbying effort that throttled it in the cradle.

THE GREAT CANCER COVERUP

Contrary to the American Medical Association's slick PR schmooze that the American people have been brainwashed with, the medical profession in this country is one the most dishonest, whorish, money-grubbing imaginable. A perfect example is the huge cover-up cancer doctors and their puppets at the National Cancer

Institute have perpetrated for the past 20 years with Hydrazine Sulfate, an incredibly cheap drug which has repeatedly demonstrated it can reverse cachexia (the debilitation and weight loss seen in advancing cancer) and induce tumor stabilization in about 50 percent of late-stage patients who have ceased to respond to any other means of treatment. It's in use successfully world-wide, but the US medical profession, and its cowardly media lackeys, have stonewalled it.

Why?? Because cancer doctors make **two-thirds of their annual practice revenue** by buying office-administered cancer drugs at discount prices and reselling them to patients, insurers, and government programs at substantial mark-ups. At 20 cents a Hydrazine Sulfate pill, Oncologists would have to kiss all those BMW's, yachts, Gulfstream Jets, and Florida condos goodbye. Yep, it's all about money, but then everything in the US is. Cancer doctors are among the highest compensated physicians in the US. Cancer Centers and cancer hospitals are **wholly dependent on the plentiful flow of funds from a never-ending procession of cancer patients treated with *expensive* cancer medication and therapy.** If this doesn't constitute penultimate whoredom and even willful mass murder, nothing will, but the mainstream media is terrified to tread onto this sacred turf, and tens of millions continue to die unnecessary, agonizing deaths.

For more information, contact the non-profit Syracuse Cancer Research Institute, (315) 472-6616, (or www.scri.ngen.com) which has heroically and selflessly been fighting the good fight against the evil, dishonest, cowardly medical establishment in the US for two decades. Also, check Hydrazine Sulfate out on World Wide Web-search. You'll be amazed! This whole story was bound to break sooner or later ... so let's make it sooner. It's high time the entire profession of Oncology be prosecuted and thrown in the clink, and be replaced with doctors not blinded by pure stupid cowardly greed, who have some guts, and actually give a damn about their patients.

DEADLY HMO'S

HMO horror stories abound – just ask the person seated next to you! My own wife had terrible allergies for ten years, all through the 1990's – the half dozen times she pleaded with her primary care physicians for a referral to an allergist, they consistently hemmed and hawed and stalled. The HMO system pressures and even rewards doctors **not** to make referrals to specialists … think of the cost savings if we just don't provide any medical care at all, exclaim the bright young HMO MBA's, on the fast track in medical "management".

Finally after 10 years of inflamed, swollen sinuses and when she could stand the pain no longer, she just blew up one day at her worthless physician, who hurriedly wrote out a referral. The allergist she visited was aghast at her condition … bloated, infected sinus passages. He discovered she was allergic to fully 35 different plants and trees, and immediately began vaccinations to work on the condition.

HMO's: PENNY FOOLISH, POUND FOOLISHER

Medical care in the United States is so poorly managed and stupidly run, it's a national scandal. My own elderly mother-in-law needlessly checked herself in to emergency rooms for imaginary illnesses for four years in the late 1990's. Her primary care physician and HMO blindly and stupidly and gladly paid the $150,000 of emergency room bills.

After six trips to visit her, 2,000 miles away, my wife finally discovered the root of the problem: the 15 different medicines she was taking were scattered around her apartment in disarray. She was taking the wrong medicines in the wrong amounts. We then arranged for a nurse to visit her twice a week to properly "lockdown" and organize the pills, which worked beautifully, clearing up the problem immediately. And what was the HMO reaction to the pittance of the nurse's bill? They refused to pay!! They understand expensive emergency rooms, but they can't grasp the concept of inexpensive pill management! No wonder medical costs in this country are out of control – incompetent HMO's don't have the slightest idea of what they're doing. The medical establishment has a profound ignorance of the problems of the elderly, and therefore squanders money wastefully while rejecting proper care.

This coincides with the huge shortage of geriatric doctors in the US today, a problem which will increase tenfold in a few years.[4] Of course, the medical establishment has no plan to address the problem, and will screw this up as it has so many other areas. The present medical system throttling the nation is a curse and a deadly killer, and must be replaced with single payer universal health care immediately. "Harry and Louise" and their puppet masters must be exposed for the frauds they are. The true irony of it all is that countries with universal health systems, *i.e.*, national health insurance, are "better equipped to contain costs and get the most for their health outlays."[5]

This same corrupt Harry and Louise cabal has refined the art of the sabotage of any progress or reform by now engaging endless "Wars of Mass Distraction" (*e.g.*, Iraq) to insure there'll be no money left for any domestic reforms, even one as important as medical reform. It's obvious that a single payer universal health care plan (like Canada's) would go a long way towards resolving many of the ills of our broken health care system.

The Institute of Medicine in Washington, DC just released a study (June 2003) which shows that Universal Health Care would *save* the US economy 50 billion dollars a year by getting health care to critically ill people who desperately need it. Today, when these people get sick and die because they have no access to health care, the loss to the US economy is enormous, approximately 100 billion a year. Universal health care would only cost 50 billion.[6] If the basic morality and common sense of UHC doesn't appeal to one, at least the math will.

A PROFESSION OF GUTLESS CLERKS

The nearly-monopolistic medical profession is riddled with examples of negligence and gross incompetence. A classic example of this just exploded (December 17, 2003) in Pennsylvania and New Jersey – a psychotic nurse, Charles Cullen, moved freely among ten (10!) different hospitals between 1992 and 2003 wantonly murdering over 40 trusting patients via deliberate drug overdoses. Most of these hospitals knew full well there were very serious problems with Cullen's professional behavior, and even suspected him of outright murder. But none bothered to nail this bastard because it was just easier to fire him and pass him on to the next unsuspecting hospital.

These hospitals, all run by gutless clerks, didn't have the integrity to share derogatory information with other hospitals because they stupidly were afraid of being sued ... by a mass murderer, no less.[7] Therefore Cullen was given unfettered opportunity to continue his killing spree, with he did with great delight, thanking God daily he lived in a society totally controlled by unrestrained capitalist greed, zero government oversight, and a total lack of concern for ordinary people.

I predict that thousands of medical employees will have a field day using *Jihad the Jerk at Work* in cleaning up one of the worst cesspools imaginable: the entire medical profession.

JUDICIARY:
The Counterman case discussed in Chapter 3 laid bare the corruption problem plaguing the Judiciary in the US. Frequent use of this book's methodology in exposing hardcore jerks in the legal system, whether they be black robed judges, over-ambitious prosecutors, or corrupt defense attorneys, can help.

LAW ENFORCEMENT:
The problem of embedded hard core jerks plagues police departments everywhere. It's a contributor to the problem of the high rate of police suicides nationwide, discussed in Chapter 3. The Louima case in New York City covered in Chapter 2 is an example of pervasive stupidity and the toleration of Jerks in too many police departments.

THE CHURCH:
The incredible child pedophile priest abuse scandals of 2001-2002 blew the lid off the Catholic Church's deliberate institutional 50 year (or should we say 500 year?) coverup of thousands of these

heinous crimes. Rigidly hierarchical, fear-ridden churches like the Catholic Church are fertile breeding grounds for the worst of hardcore Jerks, and must be reformed via draconian measures. It is very possible that reform will come too little, too late, and that these institutions will collapse under the weight of massive lawsuits. They had plenty of warning in the 1980's from concerned priests within, but the crass stupidity of powerful jerks running the show killed off any reform, and thus will end up destroying the church itself.

This is probably the most classic example of what happens when jerks go unchallenged for long periods of time – the destruction of the host organization is the result!! **This is why anyone who cares about the organization they work for needs to grab *Jihad the Jerk at Work* and start cleansing the place of Jerks NOW. Do it.**

MULTIPLE SOLUTIONS, AGAIN

However, the serious influence of Jerks in these six career areas can only be permanently reduced by a strong, *multi-dimensional* attack. As in the government agencies we analyzed in the previous chapter, use of *Jihad the Jerk at Work* with large numbers of EAJ operations will greatly help, but the *systemic* problems must also be addressed. **The institution of strong Upward Feedback programs, as described in Chapter 9, is absolutely mandatory** for non-profits, academia, medical, judiciary, law enforcement, and church professions – and all those who work in them, from janitor to surgeon to Department Head to Pope.

All six of these career areas should also insure that all employees have solid *alternative or parallel career paths* in place so no one feels "trapped" in any line of work. This is particularly true for rigidly hierarchical organizations like some churches and law enforcement agencies. Also, in highly competitive careers like academia (the US has about a million excess PhD's fighting over a small amount of tenured university professorships) organizations should insure that all employees have realistic alternative career options in related fields to ease the inevitably high percentage of "failed to obtain tenure" cases.

Finally, there are the vital political reforms that must occur if these career areas are ever to recover from the morass most are mired. We've got to get a "no child left behind" (not to be confused with the fraudulent Bush program of the same name), "level playing field" voucher system in place to break the deadly lock of mediocrity the present unworkable public school system has on society – see Chapter 14.

And unless serious campaign finance reform is instituted, a corrupt Congress will insure no progress will ever occur in solving serious problems like the absurd medical system in the US that's earned it the derision of the industrialized world.

Chapter Twelve – Military Disasters: Reforming the Bottomless Pit

"The firing of LTC Albright sent a pretty bad message – basically, any stand-up guy was going to get fired and replaced."[1]

> 1996
> CPT Lane A. Seaholm, USAF,
> on the dismissal of the safety-conscious commander
> of the 76th Airlift Squadron by cretin Group Cdr,
> BG William Stevens – soon after, sloppy pilot
> safety procedures contributed to the crash of a
> squadron T-43 (Boeing 737) in Croatia, carrying
> Commerce Secretary Ron Brown and 34 others,
> killing all on board.

THE MILITARY – AN ALMOST HOPELESS MORASS

As mentioned in Chapter 10, cleaning up jerk-infested corporate workplaces is a breeze compared to tackling the deep-rooted systemic dysfunction of government agencies. We saw it took a full blown **11-Point Program** to surmount this challenge. Now that we've mastered more difficult workplace areas, we're ready to move into the *doctorate* level of workplace reform to tackle one of the most hopelessly screwed up environments of all, the military.

Whether one is progressive, neocon, "moderate", libertarian, conservative, or reactionary is beside the point – any open minded analysis of the track record of the US military will quickly reveal a nightmare of the worst order. It consumes a whopping 52% of federal discretionary spending (for FY 2003 the Pentagon gets a massive 379 *billion* dollars, a 48 *billion* increase over FY 2002, the largest single increase since the height of the Vietnam War), far higher than any other industrialized nation and "26 times as large as the *combined* spending of the seven countries traditionally identified by the Pentagon as our most likely adversaries (Cuba, Iran, Iraq, Libya, North Korea, Sudan, and Syria."[2] Oops, scratch Iraq, but with our insane foreign policies, we won't break a sweat producing endless enemies to fill that vacant slot – and, in fact with a million new recruits for Al Qaeda, it's already filled tenfold.)

Yet for all the hundreds of billions we throw at the military year after year after year, it remains a grossly mismanaged morass of corruption, waste, 24/7 coverup, lies, incompetence, stupidity, and dysfunction. The climate of fear it encases its people in is legendary. Its safety record is abysmal, and its criminal activity in polluting the environment is massive and well documented. Its consistent abuse of its own people with lax toleration of sexual harassment, substandard medical treatment, and terrible housing is a scandal.

After carefully reviewing media reports and studies on the military for the past ten years, one *consistent glaring* problem surfaces *repeatedly*, **in each and every case**: and that's the culture of blatant lying, absence of integrity, and sickening cover-up pervasive throughout all the armed services. In fact, when a high ranking officer actually takes a truly moral stand and tries to justly deal with the scandal *du jour* (*e.g.*, the Rear Admiral IG who objected to the Navy's criminal railroad job in the investigation of the USS Iowa explosion in the late 80's), the event is so rare and unexpected it's the equivalent of a unusual wild albino Panda sighting in the Guangpau hinterland.

The jerk dominated atmosphere of the military is the incubator for this stunning volume and depth of endless corruption and scandal. I've seen hundreds of media reports on military scandals, from fraud on fake anti-ballistic missile data, to gross negligence on dozens of US Air Force Academy rapes, to endemic lying & coverup by generals and admirals about the true causes of deadly preventable accidents which have killed thousands of servicemen, to deadly falsification of Osprey maintenance records, to breathtaking negligence on controlling hundreds of millions of dollars of fraudulent use of military credit cards, to gross negligence in ignoring terrorist threats that led to the preventable deaths of hundred's of marines, sailors, and airmen – to a ticket punching mentality that seriously degrades readiness.

A PENTAGON OF MOONIES

The Pentagon does not hold anyone accountable for corrupt and dishonest behaviors – on the contrary, these behaviors are often rewarded with rapid promotions. And politically, the officer corps gets weirder and weirder as each year passes, shifting from moderate to conservative to far right to nutty far right to Moonie far right. It's downright scary to learn that many of the Pentagon's officers are avid daily readers of the Moonie-controlled *Washington Times*, owned *in toto* by the international crook and mind-control artist, the "Reverend" Sun Myung Moon. The *Washington Times* was founded by Moon's mind-control cult organization, the Unification Church, in 1980 and *has never turned a profit in its 23 years of operation* – the Moonies subsidize the paper to the tune of $15 million annually, with money stolen from its brainwashed followers.

Moon is a convicted criminal who's done jail time, is being sued by thousands worldwide for kidnapping and extortion, and has been kicked out of two dozen countries around the globe. He encourages his followers to be dishonest and steal money – his philosophy encouraged the *Times* to falsify it's circulation count in the 1990's, and dump the unused papers at recycling centers in Alexandria Virginia. Many editors and reporters have quit the *Washington Times* in disgust, citing the Moonie's constant meddling in changing stories and editorials to suit Rev. Moon's nutty far right wing party line. The paper consistently slanders and falsifies, and is a joke in the journalist community – yet it tells naïve, intellectually lazy, moral-coward right wing military officers *exactly* what they want to hear. One can only guess where this scary scenario can lead.

The dominance of corruption in the military explains why it buys trillions of dollars of useless hardware, designed to combat the long-defunct Soviet empire.

Any corporate business behaving in this slipshod, criminal mode would be facing Chapter 11 within two business quarters. Not so the military, untouchable, gouging itself in the public trough eagerly kept full by whorish Congressmen scrambling for every conceivable pork barrel defense project for their home district.

A GLIMPSE OF MILITARY HELL

Major ticket scandal is the military's stock in trade. Any doubts that the military is a terminally sick institution will be banished when the reader peruses *A Glimpse of Hell* by Charles C. Thompson II (WW Norton – NYC – 1999). That a dozen Navy Admirals and Captains colluded in the criminal coverup of the cause of the explosions of shells on the USS Iowa that killed 47 sailors, was a stunning revelation, a damning indictment of the honor and motivations of the entire officer corps. The Reverend Moon would be proud of his boys.

The military is rotten from stem to stern. A megalomaniac Army division commander in Gulf War I ordered his troops to shoot hundreds of Iraqi soldiers (most of whom were scared draftees just trying to get home) in the back as they complied with the 1991 armistice by withdrawing in their vehicles. The Army IG (Inspector General) "investigation" did what IG's are paid to do: cover up the entire affair and above all, protect the blatantly guilty. Seymour Hersh of the *New Yorker* talked to hundreds of soldiers, NCO's, and officers and exposed the real sordid story, just as he did 30 years earlier for the notorious My Lai massacre of 500 unarmed civilians, which the Army also desperately tried to cover up.

The military is often successful in covering up its atrocities, but the truth eventually emerges, even if it takes 36 years. Recently, newspapers in Ohio uncovered the major scandal of the Army's 101st Airborne "Tiger Force". In Vietnam in 1967, this unit slaughtered hundreds of innocent, unarmed civilians in the central highlands. Over a four and a half year "investigation" from 1970 – 1974, the

Army made every effort to cover up these crimes and to make sure no word of them leaked out.[3]

The Pentagon is an institution oblivious to the concept of shame and responsibility. It's consistent lying about the horrific cancers and radioactive effects of tank DU (Depleted Uranium) rounds in Gulf War I, mirrors its incredible incompetence in blowing up chemical weapons sites there without informing its own troops of the hazard, thus contributing to the toxic mix that infected thousands of soldiers with Gulf War Syndrome. Of course, at least the place is consistent ... for the past 30 years it's attempted to sweep the horrible effects of the defoliate Agent Orange under the rug, as it has killed and maimed and deformed thousands of US soldiers and millions of Vietnamese and their newborns. These three mass crimes alone are grounds enough for boarding up and shutting down the entire building, forever. Collateral benefit would be that the loss of 30,000 subscriptions would shut the Moonie's DC propaganda newspaper, the *Washington Times*, down for good.

Foreign military officers working with the US Military are often appalled at the bizarre atmosphere they witness. A distinguished British military officer, LTC D.T. Eccles of the Royal Tank Regiment, who served with US troops in Bosnia, put it this way in 1998. He noted

> "... the reluctance that some officers display to disagree with their superiors, even way in advance of the point of decision. Anecdotal examples of the effective termination of careers for displays of dissent from the opinion of senior officers present are legion. Consequently, independent thought and formal debate is the exception rather than the rule and, in public, a bland and rather unhealthy consensus prevails." [4]

WHY??

So *why* all the hyper-dysfunction?? You'd think with all the emphasis placed at the US military academies on "honor and integrity and discipline and duty", and the bottomless pit of tax dollars poured into the armed forces, that the place would be well run and functional.

Also, *when*?? When did all these systemic problems originate? Any honest analysis would conclude these integrity problems have always been with the military – there's really nothing new here.

Well, then, *who*?? The people the military draws on to fill its officer corps are often highly intelligent, motivated college and service academy graduates. What causes this pervasive corruption of normal, talented people??

A BANAL* CAUSE, A SIMPLE SOLUTION: TALE OF TWO CITIES

The answer to the question of what's driving all this military dysfunction seems to be an enigma to those in the military; as well, it's a puzzle to bemused taxpayers in the civilian world. **But to those of us who have a lot of experience in *both* worlds** (I served ten years in combat infantry battalions in the military, two years in government agencies, and 18 years in large corporations) **the explanation is a no brainer, and obvious to any perceptive gaze.**

In private businesses I've worked in, if I or any of my distinguished colleagues ever got disgusted with the particular company we worked in, it was a rather straightforward matter of jumping ship and hiring on with one of our many competitors, usually with a better job and a higher salary! Happens all the time, and it's generally a win-win, healthy evolution.

In the military as its presently operated, no such option exists. When the typical military officer reaches his 7th and 10th and 15th years of service, it dawns on him that his range of career options is dangerously narrowing, at an exponential rate even. The young, idealistic, open, incorruptible lieutenant has aged, married, saddled with family responsibilities, and promoted to captain and major. He

---

*an appropriate adjective. "Banal" was derived from the French *ban* which developed in French from "compulsory military service" via "something common to all" to "commonplace". (Microsoft Encarta)

realizes that he's stuck. He has no readily marketable skills. This has *a decidedly chilling effect on his willingness to courageously stand up to his boss when the battalion or brigade or division commander starts doing really stupid things* ... which is quite often. Remember, this sordid little scenario is played out over tens of thousands of individual cases, **so the overall effect is truly catastrophic, and easily explains the bizarre aberrations endemic to the military.** And the bad habits stick to the officer all through his career.

In the corporate world, innovative thinking, give-and-take questioning of many of the boss's assumptions, and playing the devil's advocate is *a highly prized skill* that sharp corporations pay handsomely for. I've personally witnessed that the contrast between corporate executive interaction, and military commander/staff interaction, is dramatic. The military runs a distant second in this comparison, and suffers profoundly from it, which truly is the foundation of its systemic dysfunction.

RALPH PETERS RUMINATES

Perhaps you feel I'm offering an isolated observation here – however, I've seen numerous commentary on the identical theme. Just listen to Ralph Peters, a retired LTC and respected "military reformer" who has been described as "one of the best military minds of his generation" (so long as he just focuses on military affairs – like so many former military officers, as soon as he delves into politics, foreign policy, or domestic issues, he's way over his head and a sensational embarrassment to himself every time he opens his mouth):

> *"The worst thing that happened in Vietnam was that it diminished the caliber of the officer corps. Historically, the American elite – our best educated, wealthiest classes – had a tradition of service, but Vietnam resulted in their turning away from the military. The elite nowadays despises the military as a career for their sons and daughters. What we've lost as a result is their moral example.* (oops

... well, excluding Ken Lay, Bernie Ebers, Jeff Skilling, Jack Welch, Andy Fastow, West Point grad Chainsaw Al Dunlap, *etc., etc., ad nauseum* – author note)

The great advantage of having a leavening of officers from the elite was that they were not worried about their jobs or their retirement. They had alternatives in life. So many officers today don't see alternatives. By the time they get to be colonels and generals, they're thinking, 'what's the best retirement job I can get with the defense industry?' It's extremely corrupting – in a moral, if not a legal sense."[5] (my emphasis)

Ralph Peters really hits the nail on the head in the interview quoted above. It's unusual that a career officer would have this kind of insight that I've stated was the province of those who've seen both sides of the career fence, but then Ralph has that keen perception that can spot the glaringly obvious in things military. People who don't feel they have career alternatives become fear-ridden and constricted in their work lives. And hard-core jerks just thrive and feed on these environments. *This is precisely what is always going on in the military, and explains why the military has generally been a screwed-up mess.* Oh sure, it can initially run roughshod over 4th rate militaries with weak popular support, like Iraq and the Taliban (and we hardly need mention the Pentagon's complete lack of planning for and arrogant botching up of the occupation of Iraq, crass & deadly incompetence from day one) – but analyze what 400 billion armament dollars, a whopping 52 % of the discretionary federal budget, buys the country annually, and it's clearly an outrageous sham.

(Note: The only other comment I'd make on Ralph's laser-like commentary above is that the systemic corruption of the officer corps begins long before "the time they get to be colonels and generals". The rot is definitely kicking in at the captains and majors stage.)

A civilian media reporter in the Midwest familiar with things military sums up the problem in very similar language:

*"In the civilian world, our options are somewhat freer. At last resort, if a collision of values cannot be resolved, we may change jobs. Move to another newspaper. Sign on with a different bank. Apply for a position on another faculty. **The career soldier cannot look for another Army to serve.**"*[6] (my emphasis)

A LESSON FROM THE THIRD REICH

The identical theme pops up throughout the histories of militaries worldwide – the absence of a viable alternative civilian career for military professionals doesn't just plague the US. It's as old as medieval times when, at the end of each shoddy little Anglo-French war, the unemployed soldiers of both sides, with no viable civilian trade to resume, turned to highway robbery, brigandage, piracy, and village rape & plunder in order to survive, terrorizing the countryside far and wide until the next sadistic little war of succession or religion got rolling.

Throughout history, military organizations have eventually visited disaster and chaos upon the very societies they were supposed to serve. Examples are endless: the Roman Legions, the 100 years war, the 30 years war, Napoleon's Grand Armee, the German Army in WW I and WW II, the Japanese military in the 30's and 40's, the Soviet military in the 20th Century, and the budget busting US military of the 21st century, complete with twelve (12) nuclear carrier battle groups, each with the power to destroy the planet four times over, many staffed by officers with an unhealthy fondness for the Rev. Sun Myung Moon.

The eminent journalist, historian, and author Gitta Sereny makes just such a telling observation on the dilemma of career soldiers everywhere – in this case, in the German Army of the 1930's and 40's. From her acclaimed 1995 masterpiece, *Albert Speer: his Battle With Truth*:

"When I met the Posers I was already well aware of what army people who served in Russia necessarily had to

have known about the murders there. Not only because the Kommissar Befehl* *and the subsequent verbally transmitted orders told them, but because it was impossible not to either see what was being done or, at the very least (as was the case for many officers on the Chiefs of Staff), hear it described.*

In an ideal world, honorable men such as this would rebel, leave the country, or perhaps opt out, leave the army, put up a moral barricade to separate their private world from such horrors. But realistically, few men will risk all – their wives, their children, life itself – for morality. Realistically, the choices for men such as this are limited.

The Posers were 'army' – in the traditional sense of German army families: solid, with landed but not necessarily titled family backgrounds, conventionally religious, owning perhaps some land but no fortunes, for younger sons little or no money aside from their army pay. In Nazi Germany older army officers, morally reluctant to take the oath for Hitler, could find a pretext to take early retirement and eke out a life on their pensions – General Beck was a good example, and there were others. ***But young army officers, whatever their reservations about political events, could not; their profession, for honorable men entirely linked to their country, was not a readily saleable commodity.***"[7] (my emphasis)

The shortsighted trapping of men in military careers with no alternative options is as bad for nations as it is for the soldiers themselves.

Befehl = order: refers to Hitler's order to German troops invading Russia in 1941 to summarily execute all captured Communist Party Commissars (political officers) attached to Soviet units, on the spot. This blatant violation of the generally accepted rules of warfare was received with unease and alarm by many regular army officers, and was a harbinger of worse to come from the criminals in power.

For Germany, it quickly turned catastrophic. The lesson is clear to us today, and we need to act now to mitigate this catastrophe.

REFLECTIONS OF THE JEDI MASTER

Whenever intelligent observers of the military reflect, the issue of the fear-ridden, "no career alternative" mentality dilemma arises prominent. One of the most stunning and unexpected examples of this was the testimony of the 20th Century's most distinguished and influential military expert, Sir Basil H. Liddell Hart of Great Britain.

Liddell Hart was a combat veteran of World War I, and worked closely with Britain's top commanders – as well, his powers of observation and brilliance quickly propelled him to the forefront as the planet's pre-eminent military thinker and strategist. His outstanding articles and books on mechanized warfare and air power in the inter-war years grabbed the attention of militaries worldwide. The down side to Liddell's brilliance was that all the good guys ignored him, whilst the bad guy totalitarians read him voraciously - ironically, it was the German military that transformed itself into the world's most awesome force by studying Liddell! It took the Allies seven years and 30 million dead to catch up. The entire concept of *Blitzkreig* ("Lightning War"), so successful in overrunning Poland in a short 4 weeks in 1939, and most of the rest of Europe in an astounding 6 weeks in 1940, was based on Liddell Hart's concepts, far ahead of his time. In 6 weeks, the Germans accomplished in WW II what four years of slaughter and six million dead failed to accomplish 22 years earlier.

After WW II, "the entire (surviving) German General Staff, and most of the Allied commanders, paid Liddell Hart the highest tribute"[8], as the godfather of modern war. He enjoyed celebrity status for the remaining 25 years of his life. But one must understand that Liddell hated war and always hoped it could be banished from the human experience. Shortly before he died in 1970, Liddell Hart completed an incisive book of reflections on the military and history, *Why Don't We Learn from History?*, one of the most thoughtful and perceptive insights we'll ever get on the two subjects. His take on the root cause of systemic military dysfunction and **the havoc it wreaks on society** is startling:

> "*I found that moral courage was quite as rare in the top levels of the (military) services as among politicians. It was also a surprise to me to find that those who had shown the highest degree of physical courage tended to be those who were most lacking in moral courage, and the clue to this seemed to be largely in the growing obsession with personal career ambition - particularly in the cases where an unhappy home life resulted in an inordinate concern with career prospects.* **The other main cause in diminishing moral courage, however, was a lack of private means that led commanding officers to wilt before their superiors because of the concern with providing for their children's education. (!!) That factor was very marked in the German generals' submissiveness to Hitler, and this became the more understandable to me because I had seen it operate in Britain in much less difficult circumstances.**"[9] (author's emphasis added)

Here it is again, people ... so long as you have folks in military uniform – officers, NCO's, soldiers – with absolutely no real alternative civilian career options, trapped in their dead-end military careers, **the intelligent moral courage which is the heart and soul of any value-added professional** will evaporate like the morning mist of the Mojave Desert, *circa* 0700 hours. Gonzo, forget it. It's truly scary, but it's real. In human society we therefore have an unending, massive problem on our hands, which has caused us unfathomable catastrophe for untold centuries past. Just in the past 100 years the endless disasters of WW I, WW II, the Holocaust, the IndoChina Wars (including Vietnam), Algeria, Iraq II, *etc., etc., etc.* numb the mind – and you can rest assured, unless we take action now, this sorry DVD will be played over and over and over.

This deadly cycle must be broken, and quickly. I'm sure Liddell Hart would heartily endorse our rather simple solution presented below.

A MILITARY SYSTEM THAT WORKS WELL

A classic example of how an alternate civilian career system works spectacularly well can be found in the Israeli Defense Forces (IDF). Why does the rather small Israeli military have such an excellent track record of combat effectiveness over the past 55 years of its existence, defeating the large armed forces of a half dozen hostile Arab states surrounding it?

(**Author's note**: I hasten to add that I have a lot more sympathy for the Palestinian people than for the state of Israel. The 1948 creation of the latter by Zionists with strong Western support was a monumental historical & moral blunder, opposed by the outstanding American secretary of state at the time, Gen. George C. Marshall, who strongly advised President Truman against it. The best overview of the subject can be found in Edward Said's moderate, incisive *The Question of Palestine* – 1992, Vintage Books, NY – **must** reading for anyone who wants to get the true historical facts. But it's far too late to turn back the clock. At present, only a fair and just peace process that brings disbanded illegal settlements, rapid security, and prosperity to all Israelis and Palestinians can hope to save the region from the raging, endless hell it currently endures. A complete halt to the *annual $3 billion* in weapons of mass destruction the US *gives* to Israel is also mandatory.)

The answer is obvious to even the most casual observer. 80% of the IDF is composed of conscripts and reservists that **have full time civilian careers waiting for them**. They loyally and competently fulfill their military obligations – but they have historically refused to put up with any foolishness. None of the incredible horseshit that routinely occurs in the US military could survive for six minutes in the IDF, because conscript and reservist troops would not stand for it – since they're not fearful about military promotions or careers, and *have stable civilian jobs awaiting them*, they have no compunction about protesting stupid policies or the antics of mediocre commanders. What a contrast to the continual circus in the US military, where scandals are continually allowed to fester unhindered until the roof blows off. Such is the priceless value of a military with soldiers that have solid, viable careers to move to when their active duty ends. It's just a no-brainer.

CUTTING THE GORDIAN KNOT

So you can see where all this is logically heading. **The best, cheapest, quickest, and most effective way to clean up the wreckage the US military has become is to insure that each and every uniformed member of the armed services has a viable, serious "alternate civilian career (ACC)" in place throughout his/her military career.** The officer (also all NCO's) would actually work for 2 weeks annually in his ACC while on regular active duty. Civilian reservists traditionally go on military active duty 2 weeks of every year, so there's no reason this couldn't work in reverse. *Nothing would be more effective in boosting morale and eliminating the fear-ridden environment currently ravaging the US military*.

We'd see the performance of active duty officers and NCO's improve, and it would even benefit 20 and 30 year active duty soldiers when they retire from the military. I've heard of too many sad tales of recent retirees at such a loss when they leave the service that they actually commit suicide.

To be realistic, I can already hear the reactions of some officers to an ACC program. "Oh, Christ, another goddamn special program that diverts us from our combat mission." But if they honestly reflect on what a well-run ACC effort would mean to them personally, as well as to all those around them, they'll understand it will make everyone far more effective during the duration of their military careers. The dread of career transition will be greatly reduced. The presence of real civilian career options will tear down the inhibitions to constructive interactions between seniors and subordinates. Everyone understands, even today, that "a fear-ridden officer is a third-rate officer".

Notice the emphasis on "real civilian career" options – this excludes jobs in the parasitic defense industry, which is historically just an echo of the bad management practices of the military, multiplied. Military people need the ability to make a clean break from the suffocating military-industrial complex vampire.

ONLY A MULTI-FACETED APPROACH CAN REALLY CLEAN HOUSE

In Chapter 10 we discovered the challenge of systemic government agency dysfunction required a complex 11-point program to surmount. It's no different with the Military, except the armed forces are so seriously screwed up it'll take a *18 Point* Program to salvage the wreckage!!!

18 POINT PROGRAM FOR EFFECTIVE MILITARY REFORM

1) Use of *Jihad the Jerk at Work* methodology to purge the military of thousands of hard-core jerks asap. EAJ campaigns (see Chapters 1-6) would defuse the worst of criminal and fraudulent abuses and would bring immediate relief, akin to lancing a putrid, festering sore.

2) Solid basic **Upward Feedback Programs**, as described in Chapter 9, must be instituted in all military units, now. Keep in place for the next 30 years.

3) Establish an **Alternate Civilian Career program** for each and every uniformed service member, from private to general, from sailor to admiral. Annual indoctrination that public service and patriotism, not ticket-punching careerism, is the only acceptable motivation for

all those serving in the military. This includes major changes in indoctrination of service academy cadets, whose present exposure to this concept is pitifully shallow and useless. If these military academies can't get on board, abolish'em all.

4) Annual indoctrination on "**telling the truth** and basic ethics" with example horror stories of the failure so to do – for all uniformed members.

5) Establish powerful **independent civilian Inspector Generals** for all the armed services and major military commands – these would report to Congress and the GAO.

6) **Zero toleration** of any military or DoD civilian **lying, bullying, or cover-ups** – prosecution and conviction of same should bring stiff criminal penalties to include incarceration and fines, loss of pensions and benefits.

7) For the Air Force and other 3 services : the NTSB will establish a civilian-run **NTSB-style body to investigate all accidents**, air and ground, *free of any command influence* and corruption. NTSB recommendations will be implemented immediately.

8) Halt any more manufacturing / development / deployment of Depleted Uranium (DU) munitions, and fully compensate all those sickened by this criminal ordinance. Clean up all DU-contaminated overseas sites asap (*e.g.,* Panama, Iraq, and Kuwait).

9) Establish by law: O-5's and above **can not *ever* work for a defense contractor**. Penalty is 20 years in prison for all parties involved.

10) **Upgrade soldier pay, housing, and medical care** to acceptable standards – this has to take priority over white elephant, extravagant, unnecessary billion dollar weapons systems.

11) **Establish higher severance pay** (15k for every year of service) for those involuntarily separated – also include portable pensions & medical benefits.

12) **Re-establish real civilian control** of the military.

13) **Reduce the Pentagon's budget right now by 15%.** Follow up with another 10% cut annually until the military budget is halved to $200 billion. Abandon high price tag boondoggles like the F-22, Commanche helicopters, new aircraft carriers, any more nuclear subs,

unworkable ballistic missile defense systems. Stop the Air Force's stupid attempt to mothball the A-10 close ground support bomber, the cheapest and most effective ground support aircraft in its inventory (this superb aircraft doesn't look very glamorous, and doesn't cost very much, *ergo* the idiot generals who run the air force desire to scrap it for their favorite white elephant zillion dollar replacement, which flies too fast, too high, and is far too vulnerable to ground fire to offer any effective support to ground troops. Oops, but the cancerous, environmentally unacceptable Depleted Uranium – D.U. –ordinance used by the A-10 will have to be replaced.)

13.5) Fire the top 10 generals in the air force advocating the scrapping of the A-10.

14) **Re-establish the right of anybody** (civilian, military, or even foreigners) **to sue** the military for gross crimes, negligence, etc

15) Reduce the yawning gap between society and the military by:

    a) **re-instating the draft**, with *no* deferrals allowed. That way, future Dick Cheney's can't hide out in seminary schools during wartime.

    b) insure that at least 25% of the **officer corps is drawn from the top 40 ivy-league type colleges** in the country to insert more talent and brains into the equation.

16) Conduct annual seminar for all officers and NCOs called **"issues in society"** so they're not so completely ignorant and cut off from their own countrymen.

17) Expose any military brass who whine and footdrag on the 16 reforms listed above, and **fire them asap**. Voters also need to unelect any congressmen who try to thwart these needed reforms.

18) If the three military academies can't immediately cease the rape and assaults of their female cadets, abolish the academies completely.

> *"Fools say they learn by experience. I prefer to profit by other people's experience."* [10]
> Otto von Bismarck

Part V . . . Moving Beyond the Workplace: Emboldened to Do More

*"Coming in sight of Wades Mill in Hertfordshire, I sat down disconsolate on the turf by the roadside and held my horse. Here a thought came into my mind, that if the contents of the essay were true, **it was time some person should see these calamities to their end.**"* [1]

The Reverend Thomas Clarkson
1785
(After winning the prestigious annual "Morality of Slavery" Latin Essay award at the University of Cambridge, England, he rode towards London to commence his career in the clergy. However, the disturbing facts he had uncovered in the preparation of his essay weighed so heavily on his mind during this journey, he decided to dedicate his life's work to the abolition of the horrendous institution of Slavery. He and his fellow citizens were so effective and well organized, that within 50 years, Slavery was ended throughout the British Empire, and throughout most of the World in the next 50 – this roadside inspiration led to the dissolution of the worst scourge of humankind and the liberation of 300 million souls.)

"Never doubt, that a small group of committed citizens can change the world. Indeed, it is the only thing that ever has." [2]

Margaret Mead

Chapter Thirteen – Jihad the Jerk at Work's Annual "Best and Worst" Contest

"There are thousands hacking at the branches of evil to one who is striking at the root." [1]

Thoreau

In order to encourage the reform of corporations, medium and small companies, government agencies, colleges and universities, the military, and all types of organizations, *Jihad the Jerk at Work* announces its annual "Best and Worst" Awards Contest to reward the best performing groups, and expose the worst.

We invite you to fill in the following forms on our website, and submit them annually (or more frequently!) for as long as you desire. The categories are self-explanatory. We'd love to hear your opinions on who the best and worst organizations, bosses, directors, VP's, fellow employees, HR directors, and upward feedback programs are, as well as hear the funniest "Jerk at Work" story (the truth, no exaggerations necessary) and learn who the best Jedi & EAJ members & allies are. But especially we'd like to know why – some details would be appreciated. Obviously, better descriptions & write ups have a better chance of being selected. The only qualifier is that it's all got to be absolutely true, with no exaggerations ... please. Of course, you know by now that true life is much stranger & more interesting than fiction, so exaggeration is totally unnecessary. Your confidential phone # could be helpful if we need to get more details. We'll keep anonymous your identity (unless you request otherwise) and the personal identities of some of the lower ranking types. However perhaps we won't give higher-ups that protection. After all, that's why they're being paid the big bucks, right?? To take all the well-deserved flak.

Also, you'll have the opportunity to submit the categories of "most successful EAJ campaign", the best "pursuit" operation (see Chapter 5), most successful complaints and suggestions (Chapter 7), most successful "bombshell" campaign (Chapter 8), and the best & worst Upward Feedback programs (Chapter 9).

Naturally we have our "graduate level" and "doctoral level" awards for best reform / turnaround of a government agency and military unit, respectively.

Also to be bestowed is the prestigious "Jerk of the Year" award: the Crown Prince of Jerks and nine runners up. What drama ... what tension ... what fun.

Merely Xerox off copies of the forms below and submit to:

Corporate Jedi
PO Box 438
Lake Hiawatha, NJ 07034 fax: (877) 386-5353
Or E-mail to: rail128@aol.com

Annually, the *Jihad the Jerk at Work* foundation will compile the data, select the top candidates, and send out a national Press Release to an anxious public via AP, UPI, major newspapers, major networks (excluding tabloid, right-wing farces like the Fox network), and magazines such as *Time, Newsweek, the Nation, Counterpunch, Business Week, "Z" Magazine, Forbes, Fortune, etc.* This Press Release will easily draw more interest than, say, the Fortune 500 list, because it'll be much more interesting and relevant to everyone's day to day reality.

Fill in the blanks on the next three pages, and have some fun. As a bonus, all those submitting award winning entries will receive early notifications of award announcements, so you'll be the first to know ... as well you should, since you're on the cutting edge of one of the most significant waves of reform in human history. Also you'll get a free copy of the *next* edition of *Jihad the Jerk at Work*, which well may contain your entry as an illustration. Such a deal.

Note: form below is at www.upublishing.com/forms.htm

Submission for: Jihad the Jerk at Work's Annual "Best and Worst" Competition

(Not restricted to any type of workplace – corporations, small & medium sized businesses, government agencies, colleges & universities, military units … you name it, it's fair game!! Fill in only categories you desire)

date: _____   (the more detail, the better)

CATEGORY: DETAILS: (add as much space as you need)

Best Company / Organization:

Worst Company / Organization:

Best Boss:

Worst Boss:

Best "Director/VP":

Worst "Director/VP:":

Best Fellow Employee:

Worst Fellow Employee:

Funniest Jerk Story:

The Jeffrey Skilling
Jerk of the Year Award:
(& Dave Frasca Runner-Up Award)

Best EAJ Committee Member:

Best EAJ "Jedi" :

Best "Ally":

Best HR Director / employee:

Worst HR Director / employee:

Most Successful EAJ Campaign:

Best "Pursuit" Operation (Chapter 5):

Most successful "complaint / suggestion" (Chapter 7):

Most Successful "Bombshell" Campaign (Chapter 8):

"Bombshell Society" Nominee (see Chapter 8):
Best Organizational Upward Feedback Program (Chapter 9):

Most Successful turnaround of a Government Agency (MRA –
Master of Reform Administration):

Most successful turnaround of a military unit (DRA – Doctorate of
Reform Administration):

Most successful impact on academia:

Category of your choice:

Another category of your choice (& as many more as you desire):

Name & Address: (anonymous submissions are accepted – how-
                  ever, we encourage you to let us know how we
                  can contact you in case we'd like to get more
                  juicy information on your submission – you
                  could well be a winner!! And society wins when
                  it gets the benefit of your experience and wis-
                  dom.)

        Name: _____
        Address: _____
                     _____
        Phone: work _____
               home _____
        E-mail: _____

Chapter Fourteen – On To the Next Crusade:

*** It's High Time for Progressives to Weigh In and Change the World for the Better

*** Why We Need to "Voucher-Revamp" Our Mediocre Public Education System *Pronto*

*** Yep, We Can Do Better Than This!

> *"Human beings yearn to identify with something bigger than themselves."*[1]
>
> David Frum, 2003
> *National Review*
> (and you thought I only read left wing screeds)

THE DOMINO EFFECT KICKS IN

So you've cleaned up your workplace, or perhaps even reformed some arcane, hopeless government agency. *Congratulations*. Having a method that makes it relatively easy to oust a hard core jerk from the midst of your workplace is a priceless insurance policy. Knowing how to pressure lackadaisical management into implementing a solid upward feedback program is also priceless – you can see the results in a more responsive management already. You now know that your workplace can be a happy, productive place to be. You and your co-workers now have the **peace of mind that you can *keep* it that way**, and become more productive and value-added at the same time.

Now that you've achieved this monumental awareness that you indeed can master your immediate environment in a truly constructive way, a new, broader vision may begin to settle in: **"why stop here"??** Why not improve the town we live in, the mediocre educational system our children are mired in – why not clean up this region and improve society?? Why not insist a corrupt federal government in DC get its act together and institute campaign finance reform within 90 days or just be disbanded?? Why not let them know we're not gonna be jacked around any longer?? Why not elect a Green Party government that slashes the bloated Pentagon budget and institutes single payer universal health care and inexpensive medicines like Canada enjoys?? Why tolerate an utterly corrupt, war-driven foreign policy that dances to the tune of criminal corporations and corrupt "religious" zealots??

Why not, indeed??

The value of the *Jihad the Jerk at Work* methodology can far transcend your immediate workplace ... you now have seized the moral high ground and confidence to tackle broader problems and prevail. The disastrous events of the past several years, national and international, although entirely predictable, have now made it clear to even the most indifferent amongst us that unless each citizen takes decisive action now, the future of the human species is in great peril, *sooner rather than later*. If I offend some right wing political sensibilities, that's just tough – we can't afford to continue let fascist morons run humanity over the cliffs of denial into the raging seas of reality far below. Progressives everywhere have undergone a great awakening – it's a new ballgame and the kid gloves have been ripped off.

IT'S A NEW BALLGAME

You know, when you write a book like this, publishers love it since they've done the market research and know that a dynamite topic like this is likely to sell over 2 million 1st Edition copies ... then they always nervously advise, "but for God's sake don't toss any controversial religion or politics in there, it'll hurt sales."

Well, before 9/11 I really planned on following that sage advice (on religion, I still will, the saints be praised) ... just play it safe, focus on workplace jerkbusting, avoid larger issues. But now, as I write this book, I have taped on the wall behind me the 2,819 names (since revised down 70 to 2749 souls) of the "Medical Examiners List of Victims in the World Trade Center Attack" from the August 20, 2002 *New York Times* ... I can hear the innocent victims screaming, smell their burning flesh ... and I know that my own indolence in tolerating my own government's gross corruption and stupidity worldwide helped create this horror show.

So I just can't, I won't, play this suck-ass game any more. Bush and Rove and Ann Coulter and Co think they can hitch a free ride on 9/11, but what they don't realize is that progressives everywhere are outraged at the shenanigans of this lying cabal of right-wing morons, and this rising tide of fury will sweep them out of office, and will turn our society on its head – long overdue. It's time for progressive, principled people everywhere to get serious and start fighting hard to straighten out the utter morass we've allowed our nation and humankind to drift into!!

"WHO DID THIS TO US??"

Oh, about that full 2-page spread of the August 20, 2002 *New York Times* with the alphabetical list of the names and ages of the 2,819 (now 2,749) innocents slaughtered in the World Trade Center attacks ... since I posted it on the wall behind me last year, every time I sit down to work on this book, a sigh of restless souls floats out from the wall, and it's always the same question, one question only: "Who did this to us?? Who??" I try to ignore this intrusion.

"Who did this to us?"

Well, I answer with some Scrooge-like trepidation, obviously the 10 highjackers of the 2 Boston airliners, mostly nationals of our steadfast ally, Saudi Arabia. At the same time they highjacked the noble Islamic concept of *Jihad* and perverted it by callously killing 2,749 innocents, to include small children, women, and the aged – actions all expressly forbidden by the Quran. True Muslims world-wide view the attacks with abhorrence.

And obviously Osama and all his plotting henchmen bear major responsibility.

"Who else?" moan the spirits from the wall. "Who else did this to us?"

Well, I continue, you'd have to include the Bush administration. When it took over after dishonestly seizing power, it immediately and callously and stupidly ceased work on all the efforts Clinton was making to try and solve the Palestinian-Israeli conflict. "Let them just slaughter each other, they'll eventually work it out," was the Bush-Rove mantra. "We need to focus on more important things like tax cuts for the super-rich and corporate welfare for fat cats." This was immediately noted, with great rage, throughout the Arab world – Bush the Simpleton couldn't understand that even though Arabs have darker skins and different customs than ours, they're not stupid, and know a stonewall when they see one.

And, of course, even Clinton didn't do remotely enough, continu-ing to shovel 3 billion dollars in military hardware annually gratis to Israel all through the 90's, who used the Apache gunships and M-16's to slaughter thousands of Palestinians whilst expanding illegal West Bank settlements. This really angered the entire Muslim world. And then Clinton's ambassador to the UN, Madeline Albright, tossed gasoline on the flames when she proclaimed that the deaths of over 500,000 Iraqi children due to US-led economic sanctions "Is worth the price" – boy, that garnered a *lot* of Arab press and recruited thousands for Osama's terror camps. Then Clinton promoted her to Secretary of State!

And, I drone on, other contributors to your horrendous 9/11 deaths were the US Media owned by GE and Disney and Murdock, who continually fawn over and suck up to the US government. They've gotten so unreliable and biased, I have to watch the BBC to find out what's really going on. For sure, the media didn't clue you

2,749 souls into what was really happening – else why would you naively continue to work in the most obvious target on the Planet, on the 90th floor, no less.

Silence from the wall ... and then, "Who else??" These souls have insatiable curiosity. And they've got a lot of time on their hands, a lot more than when they worked 12 hour days for Cantor-Fitzgerald.

Well, I expound, Congress's failure to insist on reasonable airline security, even after being warned by dozens of experts all during the 90's that disaster was just a matter of time, certainly contributed to your horrific deaths. Congress has been bought and paid for by lobbyists, many from the airline industry. With Campaign Finance Reform laughingly being killed off by the two big business parties, what do you expect??

Oh, and the FBI and CIA blundered big time, in myriads of ways, in failing to stop 9/11, and then callously trying to cover up their massive screw ups.

And you'd have to also blame all those "realistic", "moderate" voters who can't be bothered to support the few good politicians trying to push desperately needed reform in Congress and foreign policy. Morality and idealism is for losers, right?? It's just too much effort for "moderate" minds.

"Who else?? " moans the wall. "Who else??" My, we are persistent today.

Now I'm getting more than uncomfortable. Oh, yeah, you could add in so-called "Progressives" like me who knew full well, as early as 1986, the extent of horrendous US foreign policy crimes worldwide, after 2 weeks in the North Carolina mountains reading *The Real Terror Network*, co-authored by Edward S. Herman and Noam Chomsky (South End Press, 1983). God, it was a shocker, really traumatic, to learn the US has conducted itself with deliberate, murderous criminality worldwide for 30 years.

Oh sure, I wrote a half dozen scathing "letters to the editor" protesting our murderous crimes against Nicaragua, and received the usual cowardly threats from "courageous, patriotic" local right wingers, but I really didn't *do* anything effective – in fact, I just eventually went quiet and sold out, like most other folks do ...

Two years later, in 1988, I read that an Arab guy on the New Jersey Turnpike heading to NYC was caught red-handed with a trunkload of high explosives. When confronted by State Troopers, he defiantly retorted, "Well, what about Guatemala??" This exchange was really disturbing. Holy shit, if Arabs are knowledgeable about US crimes in the Western Hemisphere, and then make the connection to all our abuses against them in the Middle East, then it's just a matter of time before they decide to do some serious payback here in the U.S. *Just a matter of time. Just 13 years, to be exact.*

I'm really getting into the swing of *mea culpa's*, but it's not making me feel any better. I also passively accepted the GOP *coup d'etat* of 2000, I continue, and didn't even bother to show up at Bush's January inauguration to protest. I really intended to go, but I'm not a youngster any more ... and, anyway, it was really cold and rainy. By the way, how many of *you* twin towers folks were there, protesting? Probably not a one. You understand – but my 27 year old penniless starving-artist niece who lives near you all in Brooklyn was there, along with Michael Moore, giving Bush the hell he deserved ... after 9/11 her apartment across the river from ground zero reeked of smoke and fumes and death and burned flesh for weeks, until she couldn't stand it any more and fled the City, her own soul smoked and charred ... ... hello ???

The wall has fallen silent ... exhausted ... the long columns of ink-smudged names mutely waver, shimmering up and down the pages. Christ, there were so many of them ...

A ROADMAP FOR ACTION

So, to get you thinking and moving on this crusade this chapter has three sections. The first is a laundry list of some essential actions that need to get rolling to halt our plunging over the cliff. You'll undoubtedly add many other items to the list.

The second section aims at a more deep-rooted and systemic problem that will continue to rot out society unless we fix it fast & thoroughly. Our public educational system has produced a dumb and dumber society of mindless "Fox News", Rush Limbaugh clones. Only a vigorous, "voucher-only" system (insuring that **voucher schools receive** *only voucher funding* **to level the playing field**) that inspires the creation of intelligently-run *progressive* schools in *every* community will produce the kind of intelligent, active citizenry we need to survive as a species. **We've got to fix the problem at the** *source*, **or we'll never get to first base.**

The third section: your "lifeline" section. If you're not already, **you** *must* **get plugged in to intelligent newspapers and magazines that give you the moral high ground** and spine & outrage to fight the good fights. The mass media of TV and print is generally biased toward right wing corporate America, and spews out endless disinformation and utter crap. During the Iraq War, many people could only get an accurate picture of what was going on by watching the BBC. The US media morphed into pathetic Pentagon cheerleaders, that ignored huge parts of the story. If you're not plugged in to honest, progressive media, you're dead meat, effectively useless to the cause. It's easy to get plugged in, just do it … today. And stay plugged in, forever. And take Noam Chomsky's advice, this is not an overnight joy ride.

SECTION ONE: CHICKEN LITTLE WAS RIGHT

Forget about the late-night college BS sessions on "Will mankind be around in 1,000 years?" There's a disturbingly growing feeling that, at the present rate of man-induced catastrophe globally, *mankind won't even make it through the 21st Century*! Some of the best minds of our time "give civilization as we know it only a 50-50 chance of surviving the 21st Century … the choices we make in the next few decades … could decide the fate of life on earth. Humanity has progressed to the point where we are now our own worst enemies."[2] If you continue to vegetate and do nothing and fritter away your time watching mindless TV shows & playing computer solitaire, you will very probably soon have the opportunity of hearing your children and grandchildren curse you and your spineless generation for its sloth and stupidity in letting the planet slide down the tubes to hellish extinction. It's your choice ... get active, or perish.

A) Destruction of the Planet:

1) Despite all the denials from the two whorish "business parties" (Republican & Democrat) the facts are clear that mankind is rapidly destroying the planet. Global Warming is a fact, Antarctica is melting away, the Ozone layer is being destroyed and we're all toast unless we act with blazing speed. Joshua S. Reichert, director of the environment program at the Pew Charitable Trusts maps out a clear course of action, which of course, until we kick the two corrupt business parties out of power in DC, will never get off the ground:

> "What's needed is a serious commitment by the US government, which has done virtually nothing, despite the fact that our nation is the world's largest contributor of greenhouse gases.
>
> Ultimately, we need an economic-wide climate policy that includes mandatory caps on greenhouse gas emissions. Constructing such a system takes time and requires political will.
>
> Meanwhile, there are immediate steps that can be taken:
>
> Specifically, federal policies should be enacted that limit emissions from dirty power plants, increase the fuel efficiency of cars and trucks, provide incentives to businesses to cut emissions and increase the federal investment in developing clean-energy technologies and getting them to market."[3]

Join your local Green Party and raise hell.

2) Mankind is raping and destroying the Planet at breakneck speed. One of hundreds of examples: The shit just hit the fan last week (May 15, 2003) that confirmed what many had suspected for years.

A new respected scientific study confirmed that *just **in the last 50 years***, big commercial fishing fleets, protected by their fat-cat lobbyists & whorish politicians in Washington & other world capitals, have slashed the stocks of big fish by 90% worldwide. **NINETY PERCENT of the earth's large fish have been wiped out!!**[4] Gonzo. **In just 50 years!!** Mankind, driven by sheer greed and stupidity and indifference, is destroying it's own habitat. Christ, at this rate, what's going to happen in the next *five* years? Reduction of the global fish population to tadpoles only?? People everywhere must revolt, destroy the corrupt political systems that are raping the planet, imprison / execute the criminals & politicians that are perpetrating these crimes, and establish safeguards that it can never happen again. Contact your local Green Party and enlist today. Or, as Michael Moore suggests in *Stupid White Men*, just show up with ten friends at your local Democrat party meeting, take it over, and turn it into a truly progressive powerhouse.

GM CROPS – DESTROYING THE PLANET, THE SCANDAL OF THE CENTURY

The latest of hundreds of scandals recently exposed in the "Planet Destruction" category is the incredible damage the growing of controversial "genetically modified" (GM) crops inflicts on the environment. What the big biotech companies like Monsanto and their big media & political allies desperately don't want you to know is that the **super-pesticides** *required* for GM crop cultivation *absolutely destroy a large percentage of every living thing in the area of use*. Our favorite newsletter *CounterPunch* has just broken the story (October, 2003), reporting that the British government recently concluded a three year study that exposes Monsanto's GM crops as a massive threat to the environment:

> *"The Farm-Scale evaluation study, conducted by the Royal Society, is the first large-scale field test of GM crops. It compared the biodiversity in fields planted with three GM crops – corn, beets, and oilseed rape – with the crop of*

> *similar non-GM crops in adjacent fields. The study found*
> *that the super-charged pesticides required to grow GM*
> *crops dealt a severe blow to local farmland wildlife species,*
> *killing bees, butterflies, insects, wildflowers, and birds. The*
> *GM version of Roundup is so potent that it kills almost*
> *every non-GM plant in its path, including non-GM versions*
> *of the crops themselves."*[5]

Of course, even though the study's results were splashed all over the feisty London press, we see not a whisper of this massive scandal in the corporate-slavish US media. Destructive GM crops are a dead item in Britain and Europe, but in the Stalinist US, GM crops are rapidly becoming dominant all over the Mid West. Most Americans naively think they've never eaten any Genetically Modified foods, when in fact you're being stuffed to the gills with them. Monsanto has successfully bribed both the Clinton and Bush administrations to deep-six any move to "label" any foods with GM content, which by now is a huge percentage. This despite the strong desires of 94% of surveyed Americans that GM food be labeled as such.

Monsanto well knows that the labeling of GM foods would be the death knell of same, because nobody would willingly eat this scourge.[6] Therefore, one of the biggest criminal outrages of all time goes untouched in the United States, thanks to the corrupt alliance of Monsanto, the suck up US media, and the two swinish business parties, Republican & Democrat. After reading Chapter 10 and discovering just how incompetent and corrupt the entire US government actually is, we hardly need bother to ask the obvious questions, "Why did the *British* uncover this American-made GM crop scandal first??? Why didn't the *US government* run obvious tests like this during the past 15 years, as GM crops were introduced and took hold all over the country???"

Well, we already know the answer. This government is incapable of taking any action whatsoever which protects its own people. It doesn't give a shit about its own population. It's so controlled by criminal corporate interests, it has become irrelevant to the people of this nation. It needs the total overhaul described in Chapter 10, or the whole rotting edifice will soon be torn down by an outraged citizenry.

3) The population of the planet has *doubled* in the past forty years and is now at an astounding, unsustainable 6 billion people. This disaster has been ignored, and even encouraged by most US political and business and religious "leaders". The current irresponsible Republican administration, kowtowing to the moronic "Christian" Far Right, has aggressively cut back all effective efforts to curb this disastrous population explosion.

The UN says the population will soar to 9.3 billion by 2050, with 4 billion of those living in dire hunger and poverty. To head off this catastrophe the UN desires "universal education, basic health care, and specific actions to empower women to have only the number of children they want".[7] The imbecilic Bush administration and its far right wing supporters have their own brilliant plan: dismantle the UN, and just let the human race reproduce itself into extinction. Even Karl Rove can't spin this puppy.

B) The Total Collapse & Corruption of the American Political System (another endless list):

1) The calculated disenfranchisement of 100,000 black and minority voters in the Florida 2000 presidential election and the subsequent Republican theft of that election resulted in a criminal *coup d'etat* bringing an illegitimate government to power for the first time in the 224 year history of the American Republic. This illegitimate regime has proceeded to ruin the economy, lose three million jobs, slash taxes for the super-rich, drive up the deficit to massive levels, cowardly failed to engage & solve the Palestinian / Israeli problem, destroyed all our close alliances, waged at least one openly criminal war (Iraq) with disastrous consequences, totally botched up both the occupation of Iraq & the reconstruction of Afghanistan, and recruited millions to the banners of the terrorist Al Qaeda movement. We can fantasize that Congress will launch impeachment proceedings before enraged voters kick these criminals out.

2) Endless wars and massive military spending are driving the US deeper into bankruptcy and economic ruin.

3) The medical system in the US is a disaster. The country needs universal health insurance, and it needs it *now*.

4) The 9/11 attacks were a horrendous, criminal terrorist assault, an inexcusable murder of 3,000 innocents. However, we should never forget that our own utterly corrupt political system invited this disaster upon us. A bribed Congress completely failed to boost airline security in the 1990's, even after dozens of airline security experts testified before Congress that disaster was looming. We also can't forgive or forget the inexcusable blunders of the CIA and FBI opened the door wide open to the 9/11 attacks. Our government has been exposed as rotten and corrupt through and through. If it can't get it's act together (and there is absolutely no sign that it ever will), then we, the people, should dissolve it via peaceful, legal means, as is our God-given right. Check out the Declaration of Independence.

5) Campaign Finance Reform is being shredded by corrupt po liticos and sleazy DC lobbyists, even though the vast majority of voters want true reform.. Politics corrupted by bribe money is still the #1 problem in the US today. If the US Government can't get it right, it must be dissolved.

6) The hundreds of recent corporate scandals such as Enron, WorldCom, Aldephi, Arthur Andersen, *ad nauseam* have clearly demonstrated that government is unwilling to apply the most rudimentary brakes on business corruption. The corrupt, greedy Republican Party in particular fought attempts to strengthen the SEC in the 1990's that could have significantly reduced corporate crime.

7) The "media" in the US has spiraled down to "dumber" from "dumb" in the past five years, and sinks lower by the week. The consolidation of the media into huge conglomerates, especially encouraged by right wing puppets like Michael Powell, chair of the FCC, is a disaster for the country, and must be reversed once the Green Party is running the country.

8) The August 2003 massive power blackout in the Northeast US merely illustrates the reality. The US government has well known that the electric power grid in the nation was headed toward disaster, but

incompetently did it's usual nothing, because lobbyists for the power companies desire to keep electric prices sky-high via this antiquated system – Congress, as usual, was easily bribed into doing nothing.

9) The airwaves are clogged with right wing ideologues that strive to outdo each other in juvenile ignorance, hate-mongering, stupidity, lies, slander, distortion, and spreading dishonest poison. Sean Hannity the super lightweight (Fox), Robert Novak the Traitor, John "Bully" McLaughlin, Michael Savage, Joe Scarborough, the has-been congressman from PA (MSNBC), Kudlow & Cramer, both dunces (CNBC), Bill "Goebbels" O'Reilly (Fox), and Rush Limbaugh the draft evader, drug addict, & kingpin supremo of hypocrites worldwide are all poisonous blowhards and hypocritical fascist fools who should be laughed off the air asap. **The way to do this is simply to organize massive boycotts of all their advertisers** – they'll fold posthaste and we can get this poison off the air. So, go now to www.spendingliberally.org, join, and immediately boycott the 20 fatcat Fox News advertisers listed. Do it now! Also, don't forget to write the networks and advertisers so they're well aware of the disaster that is befalling them for subsidizing treasonous right wing jerks.

The books these clowns have written are even more laughable. Although all the networks have spiraled down, the Fox news network of master crook Rupert Murdock is astoundingly corrupt – it's merely a Stalinist mouthpiece of the loony right wing moonie faction of the Republican Party. Again, the way to terminate this monstrosity is to participate in boycotts of all it's advertisers asap. Get cracking.

This list could go on for 200 pages more.

C. Corrupt, Stupid, shortsighted US foreign policies have turned the US into the world's pariah, created endless enemies, and utterly disgraced the Republic:

1) The cowardly and blind support of both corporate parties for the State of Israel is an outrage. Any honest study of the 20th Century

formation of Israel reveals a criminal, deliberate Zionist conspiracy to steal land from it's rightful owners – it's Palestinian occupants. (Read *The Question of Palestine*, by Edward Said, mentioned in Chapter 12 – absolute *must* reading for any American who truly wants to understand the central issue.) Stating this obvious truth is not anti-Semitic: many prominent, principled Jews opposed the formation of a nation-state carved in blood out of other's territory, and have been appalled at the subsequent endless strife and bloodshed. The West, to include the United States, selfishly refused to admit Jewish refugees from fascist Europe in the 30's and 40's – remember the refugee ship "St Louis", which couldn't find a port of debarkation, *ergo* back to the Teutonic Ovens with the lot – so out of a **massive guilt complex** decided to dump the refugee problem "on unwitting, defenseless, dark-skinned Arabs who were prime candidates for colonization anyway".

This craven, blank-check support for Israel has left an indelible stain of shame on the US, not to mention the 3,000 innocents slaughtered on 9/11. The only decent option now is to dismantle *all* the illegal West Bank and Gaza settlements and establish a separate Palestinian state. Eventually the two states will probably merge, leading to a more economically viable, peaceful secular state that treats all it's citizens, Jewish and Muslim and Christian, with equal respect. This can all happen, but won't as long as the US taxpayer blindly writes the $ 3 *billion* (yep, billion!) dollar military hardware check *annually* so Israel can mercilessly blow Palestinians to smithereens, at will.

2) Our dealings with Iraq (as with 50 other countries) has been a 40 year chain of disaster piled upon blunder. We encouraged the Iraqis to attack Iran, fed them sensitive satellite intelligence, and armed them to the teeth. After we kicked them out of Kuwait, wimp Bush I passively stood by whilst Saddam slaughtered the 30,000 Shiites pappy-wimp had encouraged to revolt. Then we imposed cruel sanctions on Iraq which killed 500,000 Iraqi children in the 90's (as well as another 500,000 innocent adults). Madeleine Albright, Clinton's moronic Secretary of State, stated all these

murders were "worth the price" and therefore justified. On 9/11, some of these chickens came home to roost. Madeleine declined to waddle over to ground zero to comment on whether those 3,000 deaths were "worth the price". Then we launched a grossly unjustified War of Mass Distraction on Iraq (Bush's ploy to distract the American electorate away from it's own terrible economy and social disintegration) which resulted in the utter destruction of it's already fragile infrastructure. And the geniuses in the Pentagon and the West Wing and Fox News just couldn't figure out why the ravaged, oft-betrayed Iraqi Shiites didn't welcome us with open arms, scented dates, and rose petals.

3) Our foreign policy continues to blunder wherever one chooses to gaze. Our support of a corrupt Columbian government and its murderous right-wing death squads is just another example.

ACT NOW

I could go on with 200 more examples, but will spare you. I highly suggest you read *Stupid White Men* by Michael Moore and *The Best Democracy Money Can Buy,* by Greg Palast and *Pigs at the Trough* by Arianna Huffington to see just how awful a mess we're in, and for a good road map on how to restore sanity to the US and to the planet. The criminal rightwing Bush administration has stirred up such a stench that there are at least 20 best-sellers in bookstores now that expose this disaster for the entire world to witness. It all points to one inescapable fact: unless we act, and act now, we will have no decent future as a nation or a species. The rodents have seized control and must be ousted. **Link up with your local Green Party and get energized. NOW.** And stay energized for the long haul.

SECTION TWO: THE REAL ROOT OF THE PROBLEM: OUR FLAKY EDUCATIONAL SYSTEM

By now it is apparent to even the slowest of observers that the USA is in the grips of severe dysfunction, and has indeed become the laughingstock of the developed world. The fact that large portions of its citizenry continue to support, year after year, the worst gangs of crooks and thieves (*e.g.,* Bush, Delay, Rove, Cheney, Reagan, Gingrich, Falwell, Robertson, Limbaugh, the Reverend Moon, and the entire Republican Party) that the US has endured in over 200 years is a major clue. We have stolen elections, hopelessly corrupt accounting & CEO's, zero investor confidence in markets, a nose-diving economy, abysmal health care, a dead-end energy policy, criminal unnecessary endless wars, environmental & cultural catastrophe to show for this stupid, misplaced trust.

One obvious explanation presents itself. The public education system in this country is so appalling that it's become the prime instrument for the massive "dumbing down" of large segments of the population. It takes years and years for citizens to recover from the numbing mediocrity imposed upon them by the present monopolistic public school system, **and many never recover at all**, spending their entire lives in a state of narcotic Walmarted indifference to the society around them. They've been so brain-deadened by 12 school years of outright lies, distortion of history, corporate group-think, McDonalds ads in classrooms, and contempt for civic involvement they're lost forever, mindless drones dumbed down into terminal irrelevance.

DUMB AND DUMBER

The #1 problem is that the public school system is held in the grip of fear and stupidity and mediocrity. It's a monopoly where students and parents have no real power because **they have no real choice of schools** competing for their business (unless they're cash rich and can afford to pay for private school in *addition* to paying the one to four thousand dollars real estate tax annually that funds the local public school.) So they're stuck with the crappy government-run public school.

Whenever, say, a high school history teacher, starts teaching the actual truth about some of the more shameful episodes in US history, a few outraged, mindless, right-wing dunce parents can easily shut him up and even get him fired. **So the school quickly sinks to the** *lowest common denominator*. The entire curriculum, textbooks included, is chilled into the Soviet-style mediocrity we see today. But it's really always been this way. I can well remember the absolute lies and drivel poured down our throats in the 1960's in high school history classes in Pennsylvania. 60% was whitewashed tripe. That was before half my class were drafted and shipped out to Viet Nam, many to return in body bags to grieving, uncomprehending parents.

In the 90's in Kansas, the fascist right has even thrown out the teaching of evolution and substituted an absurd creationist ideology, applauded by the Sublime Ayatollahs of the *Wall Street Journal* editorial page. Europeans are openly disdainful of the farce the US educational system has become, with good reason. It's no wonder the public educational system is such an abject failure.

THE "HOME SCHOOLING" EXPLOSION

Another measure of the disgust of parents with the existing, collapsing public school system in the US is the huge surge in the number of students who have been yanked out of failing public schools and schooled "at home" – perfectly legal in all 50 states. The numbers of home schooled children has skyrocketed 130% in the past ten years, from 360,000 to 850,000, with no end in sight.[8]

For the most part, these parents are not religious fundamentalists or extremists – they're regular, moderate folks who see the present monopolistic, no-choice public school system falling on its face, incapable of educating their children properly. They have no choice of public schools, no voucher to present to the public school of their preference, and they cannot afford the annual $ 50,000 for private school for Mary and John – so they conduct home-school.

Naturally, parents are outraged they have to go to these extreme measures, and still have to pay high school-related taxes, taxes from which they do not benefit in any way.

> *"It's a profound irony that the standards movement wound up alienating more parents and fueling the growth of home schooling. The presumption of home schooling is that*

children's distinctive needs come before the managerial needs of the schools."[9]

DOCUMENTED COLLAPSE OF PUBLIC EDUCATION IN PAST DECADE

A new study "drawing together more than 25 surveys done by Public Agenda, a research and policy organization" has just been published (April 23, 2003) and clearly demonstrates that, in fact, *the public school system as we know it has already collapsed in a hopeless heap* – it is no longer remotely functional or value-added. Listen to the study's findings:

> *"Ill mannered pupils, demoralized teachers, uninvolved parents, and bureaucracy in public schools are greater worries for Americans than the standards and accountability that occupy policy makers ...*
>
> *Teachers, parents, and students said they were concerned about the rough-edged atmosphere in many high schools ...*
>
> *Only 9 percent of surveyed Americans said the students they see in public are respectful toward adults.*
>
> *High school students were asked about the frequency of serious fights in schools, and 40 percent said they occurred once a month or more (!!) ...*
>
> *Teachers 'believe in higher standards but often feel they can't count on students to make the effort or parents and administrators to back them up', said Public Agenda president Deborah Wadsworth.*
>
> *Superintendents and principals want more autonomy over their schools, with 81 percent of superintendents and 47 percent of principals saying **talented teachers most likely will leave because of politics and bureaucracy**.*
>
> *Teachers said their views are generally ignored by decision makers, with 70% feeling left out of the loop in their district's decision making process.*

> *According to the report, 73% of employers and 81% of professors said public school graduates have fair or poor writing skills.*
>
> *Teachers said lack of parental involvement is a serious problem, with 78% of teachers saying too many parents don't know what's going on with their child's education. Only 19% said parental involvement is strong in their high school.*
>
> *The study also found that 67% of teachers said their school puts obstacles in the way when they are trying to accomplish goals at work; 83% of teachers said parents who fail to set limits and create structure at home for their kids are a serious problem."[10]*

Please note that all the massive problems cited above, which are a damning indictment of the entire public school system, will be automatically resolved in the voucher-only system introduced below because to **enter or even remain** in the best voucher schools, the owner/administrator will insist that *all* parents, students, teachers, and principals meet basic, *minimal standards of conduct and involvement.* Those that don't are kicked out of the school, immediately, to the applause of decent students and parents delighted to be rid of them.

THE GOLDEN SOLUTION: A VOUCHER SYSTEM THAT'S FAIR – AND WORKS

The surefire cure for the government monopoly public school disaster is easy to envision and implement: it'll just take citizens of good will who are sick of continuing the failed system we're presently saddled with. The current debate on public schools vs vouchers is raging around red herrings. Opponents of vouchers make a important point that vouchers added to privately funded schools will create a two-tiered educational system that leaves poorer children far behind.

But what if every child is assigned a (quite large) voucher amount, that can **only** be used in schools **whose *only* funding source is the**

voucher itself. No additional private funds allowed, unless these private funds are a *gift to the school-at-large*, not tied to any one pupil. *Suddenly, the dynamics of vouchers are dramatically changed.* There is a level playing field. Educational entrepreneurs will immediately start setting up well run competitors to the failing government-run monopoly school, and the most intelligent of these will insist on high levels of attitude and performance from both parents and students, so that the major problems plaguing the old public school don't even have a chance to get a foot in the door of the voucher school (a school which, in actuality, is fully public funded, via vouchers).

And the sharpest of these entrepreneurs will give his/her voucher school a niche appeal, *e.g.* "this school encourages progressive values such as community involvement, rigorous physical fitness, complete honesty in addressing history and contemporary issues – oh, and by the way don't expect to find dangerous or mindless activities like tackle football, push & shove basketball, cheerleading and vapid marching oompah bands at this institution".

Geography would be no limitation. Intelligent parents will want to send their children to the very best (progressive) school in the region. This will immediately blow the whole concept of racially segregated schools to smithereens, since now neither geography nor money stands in the way of the desire of any parent of any color towards getting a top-flight education for their child. The only barrier to this would be flaky attitudes and/or behaviors on the part of the parent or student, which no one has any more sympathy for, at long last. To give desperately poor students a reasonable chance to excel in school, the voucher school may choose to participate in programs like student breakfast so at least these students can come to class with a full stomach.

Naturally, to insure the continued separation of church and state, no voucher school can be affiliated in any way to any religion. So in effect, every "voucher school" is a "secular public school", in the very best sense of the term. Now parents and students will actually have a real choice where they go to school. Many of you are probably aware that some progressive parents in the US have laudably already set up hundreds of alternative schools – now these will be able to receive vouchers, and replace the burden of private finance.

We must admit that those morons whose attitudes and performance bar them from attending the best of the voucher schools will have to take their voucher to a school (possibly the old public school) whose standards are low enough to accept them. And, let's face it, these schools are going to be just as bad as the present-day public schools. That's too bad, but at least we'll have 80% of our students going to excellent schools, as opposed to the meager 5% today (if it's even that high).

However, I predict that intelligent voucher entrepreneurs will solve most of these problems. It's a fact that *regional* vocational schools don't have enough slots for all the young people desiring to learn a vocational trade. *Ergo*, sharp entrepreneurs will set up *local* vocational schools to fill this demand, siphoning off a lot of the students who fall into the academically unmotivated category – and of course, funded by these student's substantial vouchers. All the voucher school has to do is meet the basic accreditation standards of the state to qualify for voucher funding.

The best of the voucher schools will be far more dynamic and effective than the tired old public schools they displace. Let's look at a hypothetical town of 20,000 people to see what unfolds.

The regular mediocre public schools, K-12, continue to run, funded only by the vouchers of students attending. But an intelligent entrepreneur senses that 30% of parents in this town are dynamic and progressive Greens, and would welcome an intelligent, disciplined, progressive school. So he sets up this progressive institution, but perhaps he'll start grades 10-12 first, then a few years later he'll add a middle school grades 7-9, and finally he completes it with an elementary school grades 1-6, and even a kindergarten. All these schools will be relatively small ... no more 5,000 student Bowling for Columbine Highs where administrators completely lose touch with their students.

In addition to the core base of math, English, and sciences, he attracts excellent history, civics, social science, current events, 3rd World Studies, classical string instrument, and problem-solving teachers who can teach intelligent, principled classes without worrying about flak from dimwit right wing parents. Those particular airheads can blissfully keep their flaky spoor in the low tier mediocre public school where they can play in the band at mindless football games. Or better yet, they can set up their own right-wing voucher school (one can imagine the brain-dead Ann Coulter-clone substandard type of teachers they'll attract) where they can be taught how not to think for themselves, to accept whatever corporate lie is shoveled down their throat, to vapidly wave flags, to wear designer clothes, to grovel before mammon, and to flip burgers, since that'll be the only vocation they'll be qualified for.

The point here is whether or not you prefer marching oompha bands, or string symphonies … you and your child will now finally have a **clear choice** where she goes to school, and that will make all the difference.

Our progressive entrepreneur may well decide to fly the flag of the United Nations right next to the US flag – *a sight you'll never see* at today's suck-up, cowed public school. Parasitic military recruiters won't be allowed within a country mile of the place. Instead, you'll see Thomas Paine societies flourish.

Oh, and at the voucher school, there'll be no deadwood teachers hiding behind teachers unions. There will be no need for teachers unions, because the owner / principal will eventually be able to set his teachers salaries and benefits and pensions very high. The principal can hire excellent teachers and get rid of non-performers easily. The teaching profession will enjoy a huge increase in stature and compensation, as it should be. A fantastic, dynamic new career field will be opened up to hundreds of thousands of our best citizens – teaching and administering voucher schools will be an experience a hundred times more satisfying than slaving away in a fear-ridden, bureaucratic, dead-end, ill-disciplined old-style monopoly public school.

Best of all, as has been mentioned, the owner/principal of the voucher school can set the proper standards for both students and teachers. He can insist on civilized discipline at the school, with no toleration for hoodlums and crimes. He can expel asocial students quickly. He can **require** that parents shoulder their proper responsibilities ... and if they fail, the child goes. May sound brutal, but desperate times call for extreme measures. In short, he can finally run a school with high standards, excellent funding (because the best students will be beating a path to his door), superb teachers, principled curriculum, and absolutely no nonsense. It's a high school principal's dream come true. And, most importantly, his product will be high school graduates no longer brainwashed into mindless right wing clones of corporate America and the WWF (World Wrestling Federation).

Very soon, in our hypothetical town of 20,000, the progressive school's superior teachers, enlightened curriculum, and superb college placement track record attract 60%, and then 80% of the town's K-12 students, and makes a nice profit for the owners. There will undoubtedly eventually be room for 2 or 3 progressive school "systems" in town, all competing to outdo the other in providing an excellent education for children.. Everybody wins, but especially the community which suddenly has an infusion of aware, well educated high school graduates, as opposed to the deadwood clones of a few years before. Multiply this by 100,000 towns across the United States, and your entire population just ratcheted up many notches of sharpness and capability. Suddenly, the US citizenry is no longer the craven, corpulent, fear ridden, ignorant mass it once was. In this new environment, the criminal Republican Party as we know it today would become extinct, the Democrats would be shrunk in size, and the Greens would become the dominant Party in power, to the great relief of the entire civilized World. The United States will be well on it's way to true national greatness!! *Mankind would have a chance of actually surviving the 21st century*, and well beyond.

The possibilities are exhilarating and exciting. Let's get this voucher program in motion *now*, nationwide. What are we waiting for?? Contact your local state representative today to get this rolling. Xerox off and send her the previous five pages, or even send him the whole book. Get her energized, or replace her with a better representative who'll take action.

SECTION THREE: YOU'VE GOT TO KEEP *WELL INFORMED*

In the previous two sections of this chapter, we've seen the crying need for your involvement in correcting the disastrous situation the country and the planet is in. We've outlined the way to restructure our lousy educational system. You've been called to arms to support Green Party and progressive Democrat candidates for office at all levels of government.

But I can assure you that if you do not make a conscious effort to keep *continually* **well informed**, you'll be out of the loop before you can say "Martin Bormann" ... oops, I mean, "Karl Rove". You won't find out what's really going on in the world by tuning into CNN. At a minimum, I recommend that all progressives regularly read / watch the following six (6) media. If you can't afford all these yourself, start a progressive club of six folks, and each one can subscribe to one of the publications to be shared all round:

1) *The New York Times*: a lot of good progressives detest the *Times*, but at least you get a good sense of many of the important issues facing the nation and the world. You've got to read the *Times*, seven days a week. Even Noam Chomsky and Edward S. Herman read the *Times* daily.

2) *"Z" Magazine*: I don't necessarily agree with everything in Z, but for superb,unmatched, in depth coverage of the crucial issues of national and international importance, you won't find better coverage anywhere. Nowhere else can you read courageous, ground-breaking articles by Noam Chomsky and Edward S. Hermann that mainstream media is too ignorant or cowardly to publish:

> (508) 548-9063
> *Z Magazine*
> 18 Millfield Street
> Woods Hole, MA 02543-9900
>
> 1 year (12 issues) $30 or low income, $26 gift, $22

3) ***Counterpunch***: is an 8 page newsletter put out by Alexander
   Cockburn that knows absolutely no fear. It's broken ground
   on more dynamite stories than any publication I'm aware
   of. Relentlessly principled, it's the primary source I can
   rely on to cut through the bullshit and get to the crucial
   essence of issues that count. Often hysterically funny,
   always written with a high intelligence that clarifies even
   the most labyrinthine issue. Prepare to have cherished
   illusions shattered, ten years before the public catches on.
   Ruthless, especially toward wolves dressed in psuedo-
   progressive sheepskin (Morris Dees, Jesse Jackson, *et al.*).
   To stay on the cutting edge *one just **must*** subscribe to
   Counterpunch:

>   *CounterPunch*   (800) 840-3683
>   PO Box 228
>   Petrolia, CA 95558
>   published twice monthly, $40 a year
> $30, student/low income
>   worth every penny!!

4) ***The Nation*** magazine: an old standby, more moderate than
   Z or *Counterpunch*. Still, it's reliable and essential to get
   for timely in-depth coverage of a wide range of subjects
   on a weekly basis.

>   The Nation   (800) 333-8536
>   PO Box 55151
>   Boulder, CO 80323-5151
>
> $ 29.97 a year

5) The **BBC** (British Broadcasting Corporation): it took Iraq
   War II to clearly demonstrate how utterly corrupt and
   dishonest all the American TV and cable news coverage
   was. Watching the BBC, which most of the world trusts (it

will never trust CNN again!) was like watching a totally
different conflict than the subservient lap-dog US media
was blathering about. You can find the BBC in most cable
lineups these days, since so many people have stopped
trusting the US media for *anything*.

6) *Harpers Magazine* – monthly. The Lexus of progressive
thought. The monthly editorial by Lewis H. Lapham is the
gold standard on which we all can rely. Lapham's keen
intellect, cool anger, and principled, unflinching courage
inspires the entire progressive movement and keeps us all
sane in a world spiraling in to abject insanity. Also other
excellent essays, commentary, and of course the amazing
and entertaining "Harpers Index", where simple numerical
rankings and statistics expose injustice, evil, and
absurdities of our world. (800) 444-4653

PEELING BACK THE LAYERS OF THE ONION

There it is folks – if you plug in to these six media outlets, you
can stay on top of the issues that count, and as a big bonus (for poor
sods like me who count several right wing ideologues as his own
blood relations) you can easily blow any right winger's screeds to
smithereens in 30 seconds or less, without breaking a sweat. Also, by
now you've probably realized that the "news" you get in your local
paper and cable TV is only 10% of the story, much of it blatant lies
and spin. The criminal right wing in the US control 95% of all media
outlets via boards of directors and heavy-handed advertisers, so the
American people are kept totally in the dark.

If you at least plug into the six media mentioned, you'll be able to
"peel back the layers of the onion" to get at least 80% of the real
story, and you'll be able to blow away any right wing claptrap with
the truth – it's like shooting fish in a barrel, and once you realize that
you're free from the mind control of fascist morons, you'll never
want to go back. You just have to do a little digging to find out

what's really going on in the nation and the world. If you fail to do this, you'll end up with the turnip-like political and intellectual understanding of an Eva Braun, *circa* 1943. No one ever said it was gonna be easy, but it's worth the effort. And *spread the word to people you think highly of*. If you've got a kid sister who's starting to listen to right wing talk shows wax on about "black helicopters", get her a subscription to Z *Magazine* to steer her in a sane direction.

YOU GOTTA GET OFF YOUR BUTT
(my apologies to them's that already are & have been)

But what does it take to make a real impact?? Noam Chomsky, arguably the most brilliant and effective progressive intellectual on the planet today, who's had close contacts worldwide with progressive movements, puts it bluntly in an interview with the respected media critic David Barsamian in the July 2003 Issue of Z *Magazine*:

> **Barsamian***: Often at the talks you give, there is a question that's always asked, and that is, "What should I do?" This is what you hear in American audiences.*

> **Chomsky***: You're right. It's American audiences, you never hear it in the third world.*

> **Barsamian***: Why not?*

> **Chomsky***: Because when you go to Turkey or Columbia or Brazil or somewhere else, they don't ask you, "What should I do?" They tell you what they're doing. It's only in highly privileged cultures that people ask, "What should I do?" We have every option open to us. None of the problems faced by intellectuals in Turkey or campesinos in Brazil or anything like that. We can do anything. But what people here are trained to believe*

is, we have to have something we can do that will be easy, that will work very fast, and then we can go back to our ordinary lives. And it doesn't work that way. You want to do something, you're going to have to be dedicated, committed, at it day after day. You know exactly what it is: it's educational programs, it's organizing, it's activism. That's the way things change. You want something that's going to be a magic key that will enable you to go back to watching television tomorrow? It's not there.[11]

IT'S *YOUR* COUNTRY, TAKE IT BACK!

I swear to you, even if you dwell in Tuscaloosa, Alabama or Platte, Nebraska or even Midland, Texas, you never have to wallow in ignorance again. Plug in, get connected – life is too short to be out of the loop. And don't be afraid to project your new-found knowledge. When a right-wing moron starts pontificating the old lies, blow'em away with the honest, withering truth. Strike a blow for decency – drive the fascists back under the rocks they belong. If you live in the "red colored" heartland & southern states, you're well aware that these areas are the ones that keep dragging the country back into medieval times by swinging elections to right wing morons like Shrub Bush and Delay the exterminator and Jesse Helms the fossil and Trent Lott the racist. That's why it's especially important for you to turn your region into towering progressive strongholds, as many once were. Happy days are here again.

A FINAL WORD

So, in parting, congratulations again on cleaning jerks out of your workplace. I hope you'll take the next step of saving your society and planet by becoming active in local, state, national, and international issues, affairs, and politics. Volunteer to support worthwhile community causes. Lead the battle in shifting public resources towards voucher-only schools where parents & students finally have a school choice, and every community can have wonderful progressive schools free from right wing corporate brainwashing

Support progressive, competent Green Party and Democrat candidates, wherever they can be found. Join the Green Party, but support and vote for a progressive, honest Democrat if he's in a close race with a bird brain Republican! Bring ten progressive friends along with you when you vote, and make sure they're registered to vote long before. Keep well informed by reading the *New York Times* daily, *Z Magazine & Harpers* monthly, *CounterPunch* bi-weekly, *The Nation* weekly, and listen to & watch the *BBC News* daily on internet radio and TV.

Raise hell, join antiwar demonstrations, picket criminal Republican politicos (and any loathsome Democrats) every time they dare to show their miserable faces in public. Write scathing letters to the editor (expect to get anonymous hate mail, hate phone calls, and possibly even death threats – laugh it off, because a lot of right-wingers are ignorant fools and moral cowards – but most importantly, too many are pathetic traitorous hypocrites, who despise freedom of speech and constitutional protections).

Never sell out. Always remain loyal to the cause.

And, most importantly, keep the faith. Decent humankind will overcome its present deadly predicaments if we all row together … **now**. Remember that, just like in typical workplaces I've seen during the past 30 years, over 80% of your fellow humans are decent, honest folk. Together, we'll get through this.

Homily: Empowering & the Domino Effect

If we can overcome Evil at work, if we can oust jerks from there,
Then why not clean up our Town and our environment?
Why not reform our public schools ?
Why not clean up this county and this state ?
Why not improve this fragile society and economy?
Why not reform and clean up our National Government ?
Push it to forge foreign policies we can be proud of …

as opposed to being deeply ashamed of
Maybe we can even help out the planet and its people
Why not?? Let's start now, and never let up.

Chapter Fifteen – Epilogue
(and e-mail us your success stories!)

"To burn always with this hard, gem-like flame, to maintain this ecstasy, is success in life."[1]
> Walter Pater
> The Renaissance, "Conclusion"
> 1839 – 1894
> English essayist, critic

In the 1950's and 60's, from his tortured, dingy jail cell in Nasser's Cairo, the main spiritual guru of the Al Qaeda / radical Islamist movement, Sayyid Qutb ("KUH-Tahb")

"wrote that, all over the world, humans had reached a moment of unbearable crisis. The human race had lost touch with human nature. Man's inspiration, intelligence, and morality were degenerating … Man was miserable, anxious and skeptical, sinking into idiocy, insanity and crime. People were turning, in their unhappiness, to drugs, alcohol and existentialism. Qutb admired economic productivity and scientific knowledge. But he did not think that wealth and science were rescuing the human race. He figured that, on the contrary, the richest countries were the unhappiest of all. And what was the cause of this unhappiness – this wretched split between man's truest nature and modern life?"[2]

Qutb accurately pointed out severe problems in human society, but his solution of fundamentalist Islamic government takeovers is a disaster far worse than the ills he desires to cure – just look at the mess the Ayatollah's have helped create in Iran, Afghanistan, and Saudi Arabia.

The author of the article quoted above, Paul Berman, quickly goes on to say, however, that western and secular and modern societies can not afford to be smug and derisive towards Qutb's philosophy (Qutb was executed by Nasser in 1966), because nobody has even bothered to articulate a real response or solution or competing vision to his analysis – thus a gaping vacuum remains, which we ignore to our peril. 9/11 was a stunning reminder of this reality. (Beware of Berman, however – he's a corrupt classic "cruise missile leftist", who's a shameless apologist for Israel).

It is the major premise of *Jihad the Jerk at Work* that the problems cited by Qutb above are indeed paralyzing society, and forty years later have mushroomed into far more serious and complex disasters than Qutb could even imagine – we looked at a small percentage of these in the last chapter. However, unlike Qutb, we feel that many of the solutions can be implemented via common sense, courage, and decent intelligent action, without the need for medieval religious codes and authoritarian clerics.

Indeed, for 22 years, the Prophet Mohammed, when confronted with the intractable problems of 7th Century Arabia, went into seclusion – and God revealed the scriptures of the Qu'ran to him, which often provided the perfect solution to the *very problem* that weighed most heavily on his mind that day. I have little doubt in my mind, that Mohammed, just as Moses and Jesus before him, was indeed receiving inspiration from God – I can think of no other explanation for the powerful *Sura's* (scriptures) that poured forth, brilliant, just, eloquent, poetic, musical, that would inspire billions of people for the following 1400 years.[3]

So to the root evils that plague modern society, it's merely a matter of deep thought, intelligent focus – and often the solution pops up in a flash of inspiration. In the previous 15 Chapters we've solved some of the worst problems facing modern man: safely & quickly getting rid of hard core jerks in your own workplace, resolving emergency crises requiring extreme measures, creating long term structure for workplace decency via solid upward feedback, systemic effective reform of crippled institutions like government agencies, academia, and the military; restructuring our entire public education system for the infinite better, housecleaning our entire rotten political & media institutions, and saving humanity and the planet from destruction.

Not bad. We've now seen the road map – it's just a matter of acting on it … that means you, dear reader!! If *you* don't act now, then nobody will. We've seen that our economies and institutions are being destroyed by rampant jerkism unrestrained. The fraud level in corporations alone is so high that the FBI has increased it's corporate fraud caseload **tenfold** since the Enron scandal broke. **Tenfold.**[4] And it hasn't even scratched the surface, as investor confidence continues to plummet (and why not – idiot Bush has made sure the SEC remains toothless!) and the rest of the world deinvests from Wall Street and a corporate America that's clearly shot itself in both feet.

The environment of the planet is deteriorating at an astounding rate. Many now doubt humanity can even make it through the 21st Century. In the past 3,000 years, heavenly intervention in the form of Prophets such as Moses, Jesus, and Mohammed stepped in to save the day. But the problems of modern society are so complex and self-induced that a heavenly intervention now is unlikely – no, we're going to have to save ourselves if we're to be saved at all. God has folded his arms, rocked back, and told us, "I'm tired of pulling your irons out of the fire – clean up your own mess for once, you fools." And **after 30 years of observation of many and various work-places, I'm convinced that the #1 problem in society is the unrestrained element of dominant Jerkist tendencies in the hardcore 5%, which, until now, we've had had no handy remedy to combat.**

If, as Alexander Cockburn warns us, "management hasn't been exposed one iota in business schools to the concept that it's wrong to screw employees, cheat customers, bilk clients, and rob investors", then employees obviously need to get cracking, using this book, to expose and root out the very worst of jerks in business and other organizations. It's easy to do – I've done it successfully, and you can too. Get with it.

I'm absolutely convinced, however, that "decent 80%" of society will easily take up the challenge, and restore justice and decency to our daily lives. It's just too easy to not do it. Use *Jihad the Jerk at Work* as your righteous tool to set things straight and to keep it there.

I again invite you to send us any suggestions on ideas you have to improve the EAJ (Eject A Jerk) operation, or other subjects addressed in this book such as upward feedback and systemic reforms of various career areas. Just write, fax, or e-mail your comments.

Finally, be sure to spread the word about *Jihad the Jerk at Work* to friends, relatives, and co-workers. Let's jerk-proof North America. Let's give jerks no safe haven anywhere on the planet.

There are two questionnaires in this epilogue: one, a quick survey on the book's methodology, and the ***other invites you to go into the details of your own successful EAJ operation***. If you feel you have a contribution to this extremely important effort, please fill out (you can just fill in the blanks on our website), print, and send to us:

Regular Mail: Corporate Jedi
              PO Box 438
              Lake Hiawatha, NJ 07034-0438

E-mail: rail128@aol.com

Fax toll-free (877) 386-5353

Jihad the Jerk at Work Questionnaire

_____ I used the methodology in this book for an EAJ operation.

I (did / did not) form a committee to conduct the EAJ operation.

The EAJ package was sent:
      _____ to the Jerk's direct boss.
      _____ directly to the guilty party
      _____ to a VP level
      _____ to CEO level
      _____ to HR level
      _____ other: _____

We (did / did not) have to escalate to a higher level.

_____
_____

The problem was solved satisfactorily within:
      _____ 30 days
      _____ 60 days
      _____ 90 days
      _____ other: _____

Suggestions / Comments on *Jihad the Jerk at Work*'s EAJ methodology: (whether or not you've conducted an EAJ operation)

_____
_____
_____

With the EAJ methodology presented in this book, I am:

_____ Very Satisfied
_____ Satisfied
_____ Not Satisfied

Reason: _____

               _____

               _____

Optional, but helpful in case we need to clarify points you make:

Name:
Phone:
e-mail:

IMPORTANT!

We'd appreciate if you would write up here a detailed account of your EAJ Operation you conducted using this book's methodology (use as much space as you need):

(mail to Corporate Jedi, PO Box 438, Lake Hiawatha, NJ
**   07034-0438**

(or e-mail to rail128@aol.com)
(or fax toll free to (877) 386-5353)

Begin account:

YOUR OWN "BOOK REVIEW" OF *JIHAD THE JERK AT WORK*

We of course would be delighted if you'd e-mail/fax/mail us your own review comments of this book, to be considered for use in the next edition (short & pithy is usually better). Specify the use of your full name, or just initials:

Farewell for now, but look forward to hearing from you.

> **To all those heroic, courageous folks out there**
> **honest, competent, considerate**
> **who daily battle with the jerks, the sycophants,**
>   **the charlatans,**
> **the arrogant fools and criminals of this world ...**
> **May you be ever persistent,**
>   **ever vigilant,**
>   **ever victorious, as is your due**
> **It matters.**

"Greater than the tread of Mighty Armies, is an Idea whose Time has Come."[5]

Victor Hugo

References

Title Pages

1. Princeton Language Institute, editors. *21ˢᵗ Century Dictionary of Quotations* (New York, Dell Publishing, 1993) p. 123
2. Karen Armstrong, *Islam* (Modern Library – Random House – 2002 – New York) p. 6
3. Emily Wax (Washington Post) "In aftermath of genocide, more Rwandans turn to Islam", *Boston Globe*, September 26, 2002 p. A-20
4. Charles N. Douglas, *Forty Thousand Quotations*, (Nelson Doubleday – Oyster Bay, NY – 1917), p. 376

Part I

1. Alan A. Caviaola, PhD and Neil J. Lavender, PhD, *Toxic Coworkers*, (New Harbinger Publications, Inc – 2000 – Oakland, CA), pp 1,2

Introduction

1. Princeton Language Institute, editors. *21ˢᵗ Century Dictionary of Quotations* p. 207, 264 op cit
2. *Maxim* magazine, Sept 1998, pp. 85-88
3. Reed Abelson, "By the Water Cooler in Cyberspace, the Talk Turns Ugly", *New York Times*, April 29, 2001, pp 1, 32
4. Ibid., p. 32
5. Ibid.
6. Harper's Index, *Harper's* magazine, December 3, 2000 . p 13
7. J.F.O. McAllister, "Intelligence: Why the Spooks Screwed Up", *Time* magazine, Sept 24, 2001 p. 44
8. Jim Yardley and Jo Thomas, "For Agent in Phoenix, the Cause of Many Frustrations Extended to His Own Office", *New York Times*, June 19, 2002 p A-18
9. John Miller and Michael Stone, *The Cell* (Hyperion – New York – 2002)
10. Adam Clymer, "Ex-Operative Writes of Decline of CIA", *New York Times*, January 27, 2002 p A-13

11. Princeton Language Institute, op. cit., p 320

12. Ibid.

13. Johnnie L. Roberts and Evan Thomas, "Enron's Dirty Laundry", *Newsweek*, March 11, 2002 p. 27

14. Artyom Borvik, *The Hidden War*, (New York, Grove Press, 1990) p. 19

15. Erica Goode, "The Heavy Cost of Chronic Stress", *The New York Times*, Dec 17, 2002 p. D-1, D-4

16. Princeton Language Institute, op cit p. 228

17. *NY Times* article, March 2002 on testimony of Enron HR executive

18. Norman Solomon, "Dilbert the Defuser" *Boston Globe* op-ed, Dec 7, 1997 p. C-2

19. *New York Times*, Aug. 30, 2001, p A-12

20. Ken Lloyd, Ph D *Jerks at Work* (Franklin Lakes, NJ, The Career Press, 1999) p. 249

21. Michael Duffy, "What Did They Know, and When Did They Know It ?", *Time* Magazine, January 28, 2002, p. 19

22. Charles N. Douglas, op cit p.642

23. Ronald Alsop, "Why They Won – A Close-Up Look at the Top-Rated Schools", *The Wall Street Journal*, April 30, 2001 p. R-6

24. Princeton Language Institute, op. cit., p. 227

Chapter One

1. Chris Dunkerley, "How to Handle a Toxic Boss", *XL Magazine*, London, Jan/Feb 1998, p. 32

2. Ken Lloyd, op. cit. p. 9

3. Diane E. Lewis, "Dealing With Bullies", *Boston Globe*, Dec 31, 2000 p. J-11

4. G.J. Meyer, *Executive Blues,* (New York, Delta Trade Paperbacks, 1998)

5. Diane E. Lewis, op. cit.

6. ibid.

7. Leigh Strope, "Gloomier Economy Makes for Grumpier Workers", Associated Press, *Brockton* (Massachusetts) *Enterprise*, pp A-1, B-6

8. Diane E. Lewis, op. cit.

9. ibid.

10. Letter to Editor, *Army Magazine*, February 1986, p. 12

11. Maggie Mulvihill, "Workplace Violence Can Be Defused", *Boston Herald,* July 17, 2001 p. 25

12. Scott Adams, "The Dilbert Principle", Manager's Journal: Op-Ed for the *Wall Street Journal,* August 10, 1995, p. 28

13. David Sheff, "Interview of Scott Adams", *Playboy* magazine, Dec 1998 p. 51

14. Gretchen Morgenson, "The Enforcers of Wall Street? Then Again, Maybe Not", *New York Times*, June 20, 2002 p. C-1
15. Dow Jones "Fired analyst sues Salomon, cites pressure to alter report", *Boston Globe*, Sept 26, 2002
16. Diane E. Lewis, op. cit. and Gary Namie, *Bullyproof Yourself at Work*, (Benica, Calif., DoubleDoc Press)

Chapter Two

1. Margaret Minor and Hugh Rawson, *The New International Dictionary of Quotations, 2d Edition* (New York, Dutton Penguin, 1993), p. 179
2. ibid. p.146
3. Thomas Jefferson, "The Declaration of Independence" 1776 Philadelphia
4. Marshall McLuhan, quote in *Adam* Magazine, June 2002, p. 30
5. Jim Dwyer, "Concern for Police Witness in Louima Case", *New York Times*, Aug 17, 2001 pp A-1, B-4
6. Dana Canedy, "Louima Rebuilds Private Life, But With Room for a Public Role", *New York Times*, March 2, 2002
7. Robert L. Fitzhenry, *Harpers Book of Quotations* (Harper Perennial / 1993 / New York) p. 235
8. Suzy Platt, *Respectfully Quoted* (Barnes and Noble Books, 1993) p. 223
9. Robert A. Caro, *Master of the Senate – the Years of Lyndon Johnson*, (Vintage Books – New York – May 2003), p. 552
10. Kurt Vonnegut, "Knowing What's Nice", *In These Times* magazine, November 17, 2003 p. 43
11. Edvard Radzinsky, *Stalin* (New York, Doubleday, 1996) p. 261
12. Thomas L. Friedman, op-ed, *NY Times*, July 17, 1999 p. A-23
13. Charles N. Douglas, op cit p. 639
14. Phil Schiliro, aide to Rep Henry Waxman (D-Calif) Bob Herbert column, "No Deal", *New York Times*, April 21, 1997 p. A-15
15. Associated Press, "Ammonia Said to Be Secret to Marlboro", *Boston Globe*, Feb 9, 1998 p. A-4
16. Raymond Bonner, "Shredding of Smoking Data Is Ruled Deliberate", *New York Times*, April 17, 2002 p. A-8
17. Emma Ross, AP "Scientists Say Smoking More Cancerous Than Believed", *Boston Globe*, June 20, 2002 p. A-10
18. Stephen Labaton and Lowell Bergman, "Documents Indicate Ford Knew of Engine Defect But Was Silent" , *New York Times*, Sept 12, 2000 pp. A-1, C-8
19. Ibid.
20. Lynne Terry, "Vichy's Papon on Trial for Deporting Jews", *Boston Globe*, October 6, 1997 p. D-19

21. Erik Eckholm, "Pressed By Media, China Accuses Mine Officials of Cover-Up", *NY Times*, Sept 1, 2001 p. A-3

22. Erik Eckholm, "Frequent Cover-Ups Mask Serious Dangers of Chinese Mines", *NY Times*, July 2, 2002 p. A-3

23. Kevin Cullen, "Priest Cites Cost for Speaking Out" *Boston Globe*, March 23, 2002 pp. A-1, 8

24. Chris Dunkerley, op. cit. p.35

Chapter Three

1. Colleen Rowley, "Colleen Rowley's Memo to FBI Director Robert Mueller" *Time* Magazine Web Site, May 28, 2002

2. Ken Lloyd, op. cit., p 10

3. Erica Goode, op cit

4. Reuters, "Hypertension rates seen rising", *The Boston Globe*, July 9, 2003 p. A-12

5. Diana Jean Schemo, "Suit Says Assaults Are Routine at an Exclusive Prep School", *New York Times*, August 30, 2001 p A-16

6. Andrea Estes, "Suit Alleges Sex Assaults at Groton School", *Boston Globe*, Aug 29, 2001 pp A-1, A-20

7. Ibid.

8. Diana Schemo, op cit

9. Barbara W. Tuchman, *March of Folly* (New York, Ballantine Books, 1984) pp 285, 286, 320, 321, 338

10. Andrea Estes, op cit

11. Raymond Bonner, "Sentence Thrown Out Over Withheld Evidence", *New York Times,* August 30, 2001 p A-12

12. Ibid

13. Seymour M. Hersh, "Overwhelming Force", *The New Yorker* magazine, May 22, 2000 p 48-82

14. Johnnie L. Roberts and Evan Thomas op cit p 26-27

15. Erica Goode op cit

16. ibid

17. Maggie Mulvihill op cit

18. Diane Lewis op cit

19. David Armstrong, "Suicide Epidemic Spreads Through Police Ranks", *Boston Globe,* August 23, 1998 p A-1

20. Robert J Braun, "He Gives Kids a Chance, In Homage to a Childhood That Ended Too Soon", *The Star Ledger* newspaper (New Jersey) Dec 11, 1996 p. 15

21. James Allen Fox, "They Seek to Kill the Company", *Boston Globe,* Dec 31, 2000 p D-1
22. Abraham Verghese, "Wars Are Made, Not Born", *The New York Times Book Review*, Sept 29, 2002 p 21
23. Chris Hedges, *War Is A Force That Gives Us Meaning*, (New York, Public Affairs press, 2002)
24. Edward S. Herman, "Johnstone On the Balkan Wars", *Z Magazine*, Feb 2003 pp 40-44
25 ibid
26. Norman Soloman op cit (*Boston Globe* op-ed)
27. Norman Soloman, *The Trouble With Dilbert,* (Monroe, Maine; Common Courage Press, 1997) p 50
28. ibid p 55
29. ibid p 59
30. ibid p 63
31. ibid p 83
32. ibid p 95
33. ibid p 95-96
34. Mort Rosenblum, *Mission to Civilize—the French Way* (NY, Anchor Press, 1988) p 180-181
35. ibid
36. Bill McKibben, "Heart of Darkness", *Boston Globe* Book Review, Nov 19, 2000 p E-1
37. Patrick Tierney, *Darkness in El Dorado: How Scientists and Journalists Devastated the Amazon* (NY, Norton, 2000)
38. Bill McKibben, op cit
39. Charles N. Douglas, op cit, p.641

Part II

1. Jim Yardley, "Author of Letter to Enron Chief Is Called Tough", *New York Times*, January 16, 2002 p A-1, C-6

Chapter Four

1. Princeton Language Institute, op. cit.
2. Johnnie L. Roberts, op cit p. 27
3. Neil Lewis and Don Van Natta, "Critical FBI Agent Meets Investigators Before Testimony" *NY Times*, June 6, 2002
4. John Westlake, "Pipe Down for the Big Man" (Editorial), *XL Magazine*, London January, 1998 p. 8

5. John Schwartz, "Shuttle Investigation Faults NASA for Complacency Over Safety", *NY Times*, July 17, 2003 p. A-19

6. Lou Kesten, AP, "Company Wanted to Fire Employee", *Boston Globe*, February 18, 2002, p A-5

7. ibid

8. Adriana Huffington, *Pigs At the Trough* (Crown Publishers – New York – 2003) p. 114

9. David Sheff, op cit

10. Mark Maremont, "Abuse of Power: the astonishing tale of sexual harassment at Astra USA" *Business Week*, May 13,1996 p. 88

11. Clifford Krauss, "Dissonance in Montreal After Orchestra Uprising", *NY Times*, April 18, 2002 pp B-1, 5

12. Johnnie L. Roberts, op cit pp 26, 27

Chapter Five

1. Princeton Language Institute, op cit, p 173

2. Margaret Minor, op cit, p 93

Chapter Six

1. Princeton Language Institute, op cit

2. Thomas Paine, quote by Lewis Lapham, *Harpers Magazine*, July 2002, p. 8

Part III

1. Arthur Wohlers, Manuel London, Philip Gallagher, "A Feedback Approach to Management Development" Survey Research Associates. A study appearing in *Journal of Management Development*, 1990

Chapter Seven

1. Princeton Language Institute, op cit p 87

2. Matthew L. Wald, "Regulator's Wariness Kept a Damaged A-Plant Open", *New York Times*, January 4, 2003, p. A-4

3. Princeton Language Institute, op cit, p. 437

Chapter Eight

1. Thomas Oliphant, "Winship's Global Good Works", *Boston Globe Op-Ed*, March 17, 2002 p E-7

2. Matt Carroll, Sacha Pfeiffer, Michael Rezendes, Walter G. Robinson "Church Allowed Abuse By Priests For Years", *Boston Globe*, Jan 6, 2002 p A-1,14,15

Chapter Nine

1. "Upward Feedback Process Turns Skeptics Into Believers", AT&T *Training Today* newsletter, 1995 p 1,3
2. David Downing, *The Devil's Virtuosos*, (1977 & 1993, Dorset Press, NY) p 227
3. ibid p 226-227
4. Christopher Chant, *Warfare and the Third Reich*, (New York, Salamander Books -- Smithmark Publishers, Inc, 1996) p 280
5. Polly Labarre, "Marcus Buckingham Thinks Your Boss Has An Attitude Problem", *Fast Company* magazine, August 2001, p 95
6. Alan G. Walker and James W. Smither, "A Five Year Study of Upward Feedback", *Personnel Psychology*, 1999 Vol 52 pp 393-423
7. Arthur J. Wohlers op cit p 29
8. ibid p 28
9. ibid p 29
10. *Training Today* newsletter (AT&T) op cit p 1,3
11. Arthur Wohlers op cit p 30
12. Mark Jurkowitz, "Two top Times editors resign in aftermath of Blair scandal", *Boston Globe*, June 6, 2003 pp. A-1, A-28
13. "WireTech" HR E-mail August 10, 1998 6:07 pm HR News Update: Volume 3 - Issue 2 August 1998
14. Alexander Cockburn, "An Entire Class of Thieves", *The Nation* magazine, Oct 7, 2002, p. 8
15. ibid

Part IV

1. PJ O'Brien, *Will Rogers, Ambassador of Good Will, Prince of Wit and Wisdom*, Chapter 9, p 157, 1935. (from: Suzy Platt, editor, *Respectfully Quoted: A Dictionary of Quotations*, Barnes and Noble Books, NY 1993)

Chapter Ten

1. Aukai Collins, *My Jihad*, Pocket Books, Simon and Schuster, NY, 2002, p. 215
2. Joseph S. Nye, Jr, "The Quiet Crisis in Public Service", *Cigar Aficianado* magazine, June 2001, p 41.

3. ibid, p. 42

4. Michael Powell (*Washington Post*), "At Princeton, dissatisfied benefactor wants his $525 million back", *Boston Globe*, October 9, 2003, p.A-3

5. Joseph S. Nye, op cit

6. John Allen Paulos, "The Electric Psychologist – How a Perfect Bureaucrat Made People Invent Computing", *NY Times Book Review*, Oct 7, 2001 p. 17 (a book review of *The Dream Machine* by M. Mitchell Waldrop, Viking, NY 2001)

7. ibid

8. Richard Holbrooke, "Last Best Hope", *NY Times Book Review*, Sept 28, 2003 p. 14 (review of *Act of Creation* by Stephen C. Schlesinger)

9. ibid

10. Robert I. Fitzhenry, *The Harper Book of Quotations*, 3rd Edition (Harper Perennial, NYC, 1993) p 182

11. Christopher Drew and Elizabeth Becker, "Plant's Sanitation May Have Link to Deadly Bacteria", *New York Times*, Dec 11, 2002, p A-24

12. ibid

13. David Barstow & Lowell Bergman, "Deaths on the Job, Slaps on the Wrist" *NY Times*, January 8, 9, 10, 2003 p. A-14

14. ibid

15. ibid

16. ibid

17. ibid

18. Margaret Miner and Hugh Rawson, *The New International Dictionary of Quotations* (Penguin Books, NYC, 1993) p. 124

19. Joel Brinkley, "American Indians Say Documents Show Government Has Cheated Them Out of Billions", *NY Times*, Jan 7, 2003 p A-14

20. Brian Brasel-Awehali & Silja J.A. Talvi, "The BIA's Multi-Billion Dollar Shell Game", *Z Magazine*, April, 2002 p. 43

21. ibid, pp 40-46

22. ibid, p 43

23. Robert Fitzhenry, op cit p 184

24. Ralph Ranailli, "DEA Agents feared that boss would go postal" *Boston Globe* Jan 6, 2003 pp B-1, B-3

25. ibid

26. ibid

27. ibid

28. Ralph Ranailli, "DEA office seen as lost opportunity" *Boston Globe*, Jan 12, 2003 pp B-1, B-5

29. ibid

30. ibid

31. Robert Fitzhenry, op cit p.186

32. Mary Schiavo, "Flying Into Trouble", *Time* magazine, March 31, 1997 p. 54
33. Matthew L. Wald, "Document Traces Parts Suspected In Crash", *NY Times* November 19, 1996 p A-16
34. Matthew L. Wald, "Aviation Agency Assailed at Hearing For Role In Valujet Crash" *NY Times*, Nov 22, 1996 p A-16
35. Mary Schiavo, op cit p. 57
36. ibid
37. ibid, p. 62
38. ibid p. 54
39. ibid p. 56
40. Matthew L. Wald "Alaska Airlines Crash That Killed 88 Is Tied to Long Failure to Lubricate Tail Control Part" *NY Times*, Dec 11, 2002 p A-23
41. Matthew Brelis, "Defect Puts Many Small Planes at Risk" *Boston Globe*, Dec 19, 2001 pp A-1, A-16, A-17
42. ibid
43. ibid
44. Mary Schiavo, op cit
45. ibid
46. ibid
47. ibid
48. John Tedesco, "Perilous Currents Swirl Near Causeway" *San Antonio Express News*, Nov 22, 2001 p A-1
49. ibid
50. ibid
51. David Cay Johnston, "Staff Says IRS Concealed Improper Audits and Rogue Agent", *NY Times*, May 1, 1998 p A-20
52. ibid
53. ibid
54. ibid
55. ibid
56. ibid
57. Larry Margasak, "IRS's treatment of whistleblower questioned", *Boston Globe*, April 18, 2001 p. A-9
58. ibid
59. John M. Broder, "INS Workers Accused of Shredding Files" *NY Times*, Jan 31, 2003 p A-22
60. (AP) "Feeling Harried, Workers Hid IRS Returns" *Boston Globe*, Sept 6, 2001 p. C-2
61. David L. Marcus, "Truth and Consequences at the State Dept" *Boston Globe*, Dec 28, 1996 pp A-1, A-4
62. ibid
63. ibid

64. Chris Adams, "FDA Looks to Cure Its High Attrition Rate", *Wall Street Journal*, August 19, 2002 p A-4

65. ibid

66. David Burnham, "The FBI" *The Nation* magazine, August 18, 1997 p 11 – 24

67. Ralph Ranalli, "FBI Reportedly Hid Key Evidence" *Boston Globe*, Dec 21, 2000 p. B-1

68. J.M. Lawrence, "FBI Aided Killer", *Boston Herald*, Aug 29, 2001 pp 1, 12

69. Shelley Murphy, "FBI's role at issue in vain search for freedom" *Boston Globe*, July 16, 2001 pp B-1, B-5.

70. ibid

71. Pete Yost, "Boston Mob-FBI Probe Urged Followup", *Boston Globe*, Dec 9, 2002 p A-4

72. Ted Bridis, "FBI Honors Aide Who Stalled Probe", *Boston Globe*, Jan 10, 2003 p A-2.

73. Mary A. Fischer, "The FBI's Junk Science", *Gentleman's Quarterly* magazine (GQ) Jan 2001, p 113-149.

74. ibid

75. ibid

76. Benjamen Schwartz, "Dirty Little Secrets", *NY Times Book Review*, Feb 24, 2002 p 11.

77. David Burnham, op cit, p 12–20

78. ibid

79. ibid

80. ibid

81. ibid

82. ibid

83. John Horgan, "Autopsy of a Medical Breakthrough", *NY Times Book Review*, March 3, 2002 p. 9.

84. ibid

85. Matthew L. Wald, "Regulator's Wariness Kept a Damaged A-Plant Open", *NY Times*, Jan 4, 2003 p. A-4.

86. Jim Lehrer News Hour, PBS, An Interview With Energy Secretary Abramson, November 19, 2003

87. (name withheld), "The CIA", Letter to *Atlantic Monthly*, May 1998, p 10.

88. Aukai Collins, op cit, p. 243

89. David Johnston, "Lack of Pre 9/11 Sources Is To Be Cited as a Failure of Intelligence Agencies", *NY Times* July 17, 2003 p. A-13

90. Alexander Cockburn, "Terrorist and Brown Noser" *Counterpunch* Magazine, October, 1997

91. Edward G. Shirley (pseudonym), "Can't Anybody Here Play This Game?", *Atlantic Monthly*, Feb 1998

92. Doug Most, "Missing Peace", *Boston* Magazine, July, 2002, p 46-53

93. ibid
94. William J. Broad and Carl Hulse, "NASA Dismissed Advisers Who Warned About Safety", *NY Times*, Feb 3, 2003 pp A-1, A-22.
95. ibid
96. James Glanz & John Schwartz, "Dogged Engineer's Effort to Assess Shuttle Damage", *NY Times*, Sept 26, 2003 pp. A-1, A-16
97. Michael Lemonick, "You Have to Be Obsessive", *Time* magazine interview, Feb 17, 2003 p 52.
98. Lewis H. Lapham, "Notebook: Yankee Doodle Dandy", *Harper's Magazine*, August 2003, p. 9

Chapter Eleven

1. Princeton Language Institute, op cit, p. 228
2. Patrick Healy, "Student Web site for rating faculty drives a rift at Williams", *Boston Globe*, June 3, 2002, p. B-4
3. Siobhan McDonough (AP), "Survey finds many school worries", *Boston Globe,* April 23, 2003 p. A-28
4. Lewis A. Lipsitz, "Where are the geriatricians?", *Boston Globe* Op-Ed, October 13, 2003 p. A-16
5. Robert Kuttner, "Democrats must offer bolder health plans", *Boston Globe* op-ed, May 21, 2003 p. A-23
6. Maggie Fox (Reuters), "Universal coverage is called a savings", *Boston Globe*, June 18, 2003 p. A-9
7. Richard Perez-Pena, "Hospitals Didn't Share Records Of a Nurse Accused in Killings", *New York Times*, December 17, 2003 pp A-1, C-23

Chapter Twelve

1. Philip Shenon & Matthew L. Wald, "Search for Cause of Crash Unearths an Angry Feud", *NY Times*, June 10, 1996 p. B-10
2. from www.nationalhomeless.org website (April 2003)
3. Associated Press, "Vietnam atrocities revealed in report", *Boston Globe* October 20, 2003 p. A-2
4. Lieutenant Colonel D.T. Eccles, Royal Tank Regiment, "Risk Aversion and the Zero Defect Culture", *British Army Review*, #114, 1997
5. Ralph Peters (LTC, US Army, ret.) Interview by Sharon Churcher, *Penthouse*, December 1999, pp 124, 126
6. C.W. Gusewelle, "Remarkable Military Maneuver at Ft Leavenworth", *Kansas City Star & Times,* May 11, 1975

7. Gitta Sereny, *Albert Speer – His Battle With the Truth*, (Vintage Books – 1966 -- New York) p 458, 459
8. Sir Basil H. Liddell Hart, *Why Don't We Learn from History?*, (Hawthorn Books, Inc - New York - 1971), bookjacket quote
9. ibid, pp 29 - 30
10. ibid, p. 15

Part V

1. Adam Hochschild, "Against All Odds", *Mother Jones*, January 2004, p. 68
2. ibid, p. 73

Chapter Thirteen

1. Charles N. Douglas, op cit, p. 640

Chapter Fourteen

1. David Frum, "Unpatriotic Conservatives", *National Review* magazine, April 7, 2003 p. 36
2. Dennis Overbye, "It Was Fun While It Lasted", *NY Times Book Review* of *Our Final Hour, NY Times*, May 18, 2003 p 13
3. Joshua S. Reichert, "Global Warming Is Sinking Us Too, Tuvalu", *Los Angeles Times,* Feb 10, 2002
4. Andrew C. Revkin, "Commercial Fleets Slashed Stocks of Big Fish by 90%, Study Says" *NY Times*, May 15, 2003 pp A-1, A-12
5. Alexander Cockburn, "Virgins, Wise and Foolish: GM Foods Take a Beating", *CounterPunch*, October 15, 2003 pp. 2,3
6. ibid
7. "UN Says Four Billion Will Be Living in Hunger by 2050", *NY Times*, Nov 8, 2001 p A-12
8. Jane Gross, "Unhappy in Class, More Are Learning at Home", *New York Times*, November 10, 2003 p A-1, A-20
9. ibid
10. Siobhan McDonough, op cit
11. David Barsamian, "An Interview With Noam Chomsky", *Z Magazine*, July-August 2003, p. 52

Chapter Fifteen

1. Margaret Minor, op cit, p.179

2. Paul Berman, "The Philosopher of Islamic Terror", *New York Times Magazine*, March 23, 2003 p. 27
3. Karen Armstrong, *Muhammed – A Biography of the Prophet*, (Harper San Francisco – 1993) p. 125
4. Andrew Caffrey, "FBI takes up heavy load of corporate fraud probes" *Boston Globe,* May 6, 2003 pp A-1, C-4
5. Margaret Minor, op cit, p.152

Index

ABOUT THE AUTHOR

Edward M. Fergusson has worked for 30 years in two Fortune 500 Corporations, a mid-sized business, and in government as well as the military. The uncanny similarity of the major problem plaguing all these organizations piqued his interest, and he developed an effective, easy-to-use system to solve it. One of the great attractions of this system is that risk to employees using it properly is greatly minimized, while the reward (swiftly getting rid of a cosmic jerk in one's workplace) is practically a foregone conclusion.

Give the Gift of *Jihad the Jerk at Work*
to Your Friends and Colleagues

Check Your Local Bookstore or Order Here
(or on our Website, www.dunkeldhouse.net

___ **YES**, I want ___ hardcover copies of *Jihad the Jerk at Work* for $24.95 each.

___ **YES**, I am interested in having Edward Fergusson speak or give a seminar to my group, association, organization, company, or school. Please send me information.

> Include $3.95 shipping and handling for one book, and $1.95 for each additional book. New Jersey residents must include the applicable 6% sales tax ($1.50 for each hardcover). Canadian orders must include payment in US funds, with 7% GST added.
>
> Payments must accompany orders. Allow 3 weeks for delivery.
>
> My check or money order for $_____is enclosed.

Please charge my __Visa__Mastercard__American Express__Discover

Name _____
Organization (optional) _____
Address _____
City/State/Zip _____
Phone _____E-mail _____
Card # _____
Exp. Date _____ Signature _____

Call toll free (877) D-U-N-K-E-L-D
(386-5353)

Make your check payable and return to

Dunkeld House
PO Box 438
Lake Hiawatha, NJ 07034-0438

Fax: (877) 386-5353   rail128@aol.com